A Social View of Man

Alan J. C. King

Professor of Education
Faculty of Education
Queen's University
Kingston, Ontario

Walter W. Coulthard

Formerly Head of
    History Department
Thistletown Collegiate
Toronto, Ontario

A Socia

View of Man

Canadian Perspectives

John Wiley & Sons Canada, Limited
Toronto
New York   London   Sydney

Library of Congress Catalog Card No. 75-165507
ISBN 0-471-47795-8

Editorial consultants: Christine Purden Associates

Printed and bound in Canada by
The Bryant Press Limited for
John Wiley & Sons Canada, Limited

Contents

Preface

The primary intention of this book is to help the reader to develop insight into human behaviour, so that he might better understand himself and other people. To this end, the book has been compiled from the perspective of the social sciences.

There are two main sections in the volume. The first, and larger, section includes articles, quotations, extracts, and illustrations from research and publications in the social sciences; the second contains materials which have been designed to expand the classroom experiences available to students. Our materials have been drawn from many different sources, providing a broad range of elements that comprise a unique learning experience.

In the first section, we have adopted a thematic approach to the social sciences, moving from the origin of man through the development of his language and culture, to the establishment of roles and institutions, and finally to the problems faced by man today. Some of the materials are original; some are derived from other sources and have been rewritten; some are extracted from the works of noted authors. While the emphasis has been placed on Canadian materials, to place them in a broader context we have also incorporated materials developed in other parts of the world. In each of the five parts of this section, we present a series of articles clustering around a specific theme. These articles are accompanied and augmented by quotations, longer extracts, tables, charts, diagrams, and drawings. This supportive material clarifies a particular point, deals with a major issue briefly but concisely, presents the issue from a new perspective, and sparks student interest in new areas.

The material has been so arranged as to allow the reader to move quickly according to his own interests, or to read more intensely fully developed themes. It is hoped that, when a student's interest in a specific topic is aroused, he will pursue it beyond the bounds of this book. Indeed, many topics can form the basis of an integrated learning experience, drawing on a wide range of data from history, geography, anthropology, psychology, and sociology.

The second major section of the book deals with the methods and materials of the social sciences. Our intention is to encourage the student to gain experience in the laboratory and in field activities where much growth and understanding can occur. In the sixth and last part, we discuss research methods: the formulation of hypotheses, the testing of them through the use of a questionnaire, and procedures for the analysis and presentation of findings.

We have also included in the second section two simulations to expand the student's learning experience. These simulations have been designed to be accommodated within the typical classroom schedule. Finally, a number of case studies are included to encourage the reader to apply some of the concepts presented in the first section in discussing, understanding, and solving human problems.

The book has been designed to provide opportunities for student discussion, rather than final solutions. Many of the issues that are presented are controversial – for example, the race question, the origins of aggressive behaviour, the role of the female in modern Western society. Other serious questions are raised too, such as pollution and population control. In our view, all these issues are important to the student and to society.

We have attempted to create a book that goes beyond the traditional textbook, a book of high interest to a large number of students. Because we have tried to deal creatively with the issues we have presented, the content of this book is intended to be stimulating rather than exhaustive. If the student is encouraged to pursue some topics in depth, then our purpose will be achieved and our hopes fulfilled.

Acknowledgements

The authors wish to thank the many writers and publishers who kindly granted permission for their publications to be reprinted, summarized, or adapted for inclusion in this book. The following credits are listed in order of appearance of the materials cited.

"The Spindle" by Elias H. Porter. Reprinted, by permission, from Elias H. Porter, "The Spindle", *Harvard Business Review*, Vol. XL, No. 3, May–June 1962, pp. 58–60.

"The Human Animal" by Weston LaBarre. Reprinted and adapted, by permission, from Weston LaBarre, *The Human Animal*, The University of Chicago Press, Chicago, Illinois, 1954. Copyright © The University of Chicago Press 1954.

"Man Before History" by Edwin S. Dethlefson. Reprinted with permission of The Macmillan Company from *History as Cultural Change: An Overview*. Copyright © American Anthropological Association 1968.

"That Old-time Aggression" by J. P. Scott. Reprinted, by permission, from J. P. Scott, "That Old-time Aggression", *The Nation*, January 9, 1967.

"Understanding Human Differences" by C. Loring Brace. Reprinted and adapted with permission of The Macmillan Company from C. Loring Brace, "Understanding Human Diversity" in *The Concept of Race* by Ashley Montagu. Copyright © Ashley Montagu 1964.

"The Concept of Culture" by M. J. Rice and W. C. Bailey. Reprinted, by permission of the authors, from Marion J. Rice and Wilfrid C. Bailey, editors, *Cultural Change: Teacher Background Material* (Athens, Ga.: Anthropology Curriculum Project, University of Georgia, 1969), Publication 36, pp. 4–14.

"Language, the Definition of Reality" by Benjamin Lee Whorf. Reprinted from *Language, Thought and Reality* by Benjamin Lee Whorf by permission of the M.I.T. Press, Cambridge, Massachusetts, 1956. Copyright © The M.I.T. Press 1956.

Illustrations on pp. 50, 51, 54, 56, and 57. Reproduced with permission of Glencoe Press (Beverly Hills, California), a Division of The Macmillan Company from *Communications, The Transfer of Meaning* by Don Fabun. Copyright © 1968 by Kaiser Aluminum and Chemical Corporation.

"The Mechanisms of Communication" by Marshall McLuhan. Reprinted, by permission of the publisher, from Marshall McLuhan, *Understanding Media*, McGraw-Hill Book Company, New York, 1964. Copyright © 1964 by Marshall McLuhan.

"The 'Gatekeeper': A Case Study in the Selection of News" by David Manning White. Reprinted, by permission, from David Manning White, "The Gatekeeper in the selection of the news", *Journalism Quarterly*, Vol. 27, No. 4, Fall 1950, pp. 383–390.

"Deception as a TV Comedy Tool" by Glenn E. Reddick. Copyright 1965 Christian Century Foundation. Reprinted, by permission, from the September 29, 1965 issue of *The Christian Century*.

"The Brainwashing of Prisoners of War" by Edgar H. Schein. Reprinted, by permission, from Edgar H. Schein, "Reaction Patterns to Severe, Chronic Stress in American Army Prisoners of War of the Chinese", *Journal of Social Issues*, Vol. XIII, No. 3, pp. 21–30.

"Our Silent Language" by Edward T. Hall. From Edward T. Hall, "Our Silent Language", *Science Digest*, August 1962. Reprinted with the permission of *Science Digest*. © The Hearst Corporation.

"Advertising Themes and Quiet Revolutions: Dilemmas in French Canada" by Frederick Elkin. Reprinted, by permission, from Frederick Elkin, "Advertising Themes and Quiet Revolutions: Dilemmas in French Canada", *American Journal of Sociology*, Vol. 75, No. 1, July 1969, pp. 112–122. Copyright © The University of Chicago Press 1969.

"Canadian Justice Went North to Untangle Macabre Case" by Chisholm Mac-Donald. From Chisholm MacDonald, "Canadian Justice Went North to Untangle Macabre Case", (CP) August 13, 1970. Reprinted by permission of the Canadian Press.

"Teenagers, Satire, and *Mad*" by Charles Winick. Reprinted, by permission, from Charles Winick, "Teenagers, Satire and *Mad*", *Merrill-Palmer Quarterly*, Vol. 8, 1962, pp. 183–203.

Illustrations on pp. 103–105. Reprinted from *Mad* magazine by permission of E. C. Publications, Inc. © 1970 by E. C. Publications, Inc.

"The Girls' and the Boys' World" by Oswald Hall and Bruce McFarlane. Reprinted, by permission, from Oswald Hall and Bruce McFarlane, "The Girls' and the Boys' World", Research Programme on the Training of Manpower, Report #10, Queen's Printer, Ottawa.

"Dating Patterns Related to Measures of Development in Girls Fourteen and Younger" (two tables) by E. Douvan and J. Adelson. Reprinted, by permission, from E. Douvan and J. Adelson, *The Adolescent Experience*, John Wiley & Sons, Inc., New York, 1966, Table 6.5.

"Some Lethal Aspects of the Male Role" by Sidney M. Jourard. Reprinted by permission of the author. First published in *Journal of Existential Psychiatry*, Vol. 2, 1962 and reprinted in Sidney M. Jourard, *The Transparent Self* (2nd edition), Van Nostrand Reinhold, New York, 1971.

"The Occupational Culture of the Boxer" by S. Kirson Weinberg and Henry Arond. Reprinted and abridged, by permission, from S. Kirson Weinberg and Henry Arond, "The Occupational Culture of the Boxer", *American Journal of Sociology*, Vol. LVII, 1952, pp. 460–469. Copyright © The University of Chicago Press 1952.

"The Truck Driver" by W. E. Mann. Reprinted from "The Social System of a Slum: The Lower Ward, Toronto" by W. E. Mann from *Urbanism and the Changing Canadian Society* edited by S. D. Clark, by permission of the author and of University of Toronto Press, copyright Canada 1961, by University of Toronto Press.

"The Role of the Professional Thief" by Edwin Sutherland. Reprinted and abridged, by permission, from Edwin Sutherland, *The Professional Thief*, The University of Chicago Press, Chicago, Illinois, 1937, pp. 197–228. Copyright © The University of Chicago Press 1937.

"Social Role of the Housewife" by Helena Z. Lopata. Reprinted by permission of the author and publisher, from Helena Z. Lopata, "The Life Cycle of the Social Role of the Housewife", *Journal of Sociology and Social Research*, Vol. 51, No. 1, October 1966, pp. 5–22.

"The Hippies of Yorkville" by Frank Longstaff. Reprinted by permission of the author.

"The Day that Cabbagetown Met Don Mills". Reprinted by permission of the Canadian Broadcasting Corporation, from Robert Rhodes, "The Day that Cabbagetown Met Don Mills", *The Globe & Mail*, Toronto, Saturday, August 29, 1970.

"The Prestige of Occupations in Canada" by John Porter and Peter Pineo. Reprinted, by permission, from John Porter and Peter Pineo, "The Prestige of Occupations in Canada", *Canadian Review of Sociology and Anthropology*.

"Social Classes and Spending Behaviour" by Pierre Martineau. Reprinted from P. Martineau, "Social Class and Spending Behavior", *Journal of Marketing*, Vol. 23, No. 2, October 1958, by permission of the American Marketing Association.

"What We Think of Other People" by O. Klineberg. Reprinted, by permission, from O. Klineberg, "Pictures in Our Heads", UNESCO *Courier* VIII.

"Who Buys What? Projective Techniques in Marketing Research" by Mason Haire. Reprinted from Mason Haire, "Projective Techniques in Marketing Research", *Journal of Marketing*, Vol. 14, 1950, by permission of the American Marketing Association.

The point of view

This book has been designed to provide you, the student, with a basic understanding of the knowledge, skills, and point of view of the social scientist.

What is the perspective or point of view of the social scientist? What is unique about the way in which sociologists, anthropologists, and psychologists look at human behaviour? What advantages does their approach have over a common-sense approach to the understanding of human behaviour? And when you have learned something of the strategies and point of view of the social scientists, what do you really have?

Hopefully, from the materials in this book, the student will learn more about himself and the way he relates to other people. By knowing one's social self, it becomes possible to identify oneself in relation to family, friends, school, church, community, and society at large. Self-knowledge can lead to an understanding and tolerance of others and to an appreciation of the complexities of modern life.

We are concerned with the study of man – not man as a biological animal, although we do devote some space to man's biological development, but man as he relates to other men and to his environment, his physical surroundings. We are concerned with man as a social being. The main approach that is encouraged can be viewed as the response to three simple questions: What? Why? What if?

First, we want an accurate, precise description of the behaviour of man. The in-depth description of man interacting with man is the "What?" of the first question. Second, on the basis of this accurate and reliable information on how man behaves and on how he interacts, we must develop an explanation of how this came about. What were the factors behind man's behaviour? "Why" did he do what he did? "Why" does he feel the way he does? Third, using our knowledge of what does exist and our explanation of the factors that led to this situation, we attempt to predict what would take place if these same factors were again present. The power of prediction of what people will do under certain conditions is the natural outgrowth of the social science perspective; it is the "What if?". The three companion questions – what, why, and what if – are the core of the social science perspective.

Simply stated, we hope that you, the student, will develop a systematic approach to the understanding and prediction of human behaviour.

The Search for Truth

We are looking for sets of truths, but as you will see, truths can vary considerably from situation to situation, depending on circumstances. As a budding social scientist, you must first realize that truth is merely something that is agreed upon, and accepted, by a number of human beings. In reading the materials in this book, you will soon learn that similar behaviours are often viewed quite differently in different parts of the world. A word, a movement, or an act can be given quite different meanings by different people. The social scientist must attempt to understand the circumstances that surround each social situation.

Where do we get our truths? First, we have intuitive feelings about what is right and what is wrong, what is appropriate and what is inappropriate. Although much of how we assess events and situations has been taught to us, a large part comes from our own personal experiences and insights. Some of our feelings and reactions can be tested for truth and some cannot. When we seek our truths intuitively, we often seek them in a way that reflects our own needs and interests. While this is quite natural, it can produce a strong tendency to distort information.

Second, we obtain our truths from authority figures – people we respect and trust, such as our scientists, writers, religious leaders, and politicians. The writings and spoken observations of these people have been true for us in the past, and we expect them to be true for us in the future. However, often we accept the word of our authority figures without thinking critically about what they have said. In some cases, what they have said may have been true in the past, but it is not true at the present time.

Third, much of what we hold dear comes from our past heritage – the traditions of our people. These traditions are reflected in our form of government, in our religion, and in our concept of right and wrong. Our parents, as well as religious and political leaders, pass down the wisdom of the ages. Although a great deal of what is passed down as traditionally right is useful today, many traditions are particularly inappropriate in today's world. In fact, the traditional idea of the role of young people has not proven to be useful in understanding the problems of today's youth.

Fourth, our own common sense has long been a source of truth. Many critics of social scientists, and of sociologists in particular, have suggested that their work is merely an elaboration of what is obvious to everyone. Perhaps there is some truth to this, but at the same time there is considerable evidence that common sense as a source of truth is quite unreliable. The following statements are examples of common sense and traditional truths. What do you think about these statements? Are they true or false?

1) A person's character shows in his face.
2) Children who are unusually bright in school are likely to be below average physically.
3) Men are generally more intelligent than women.
4) A person who cheats in a game of cards will cheat in business dealings.
5) Brunettes are more inclined to be serious and studious than are blondes.
6) Red-haired people are more likely to have a bad temper than are blondes and brunettes.

In their research on the behaviour of people in our society, social scientists have found no evidence to support the above statements. They would say that all six statements are false. However, as sociologist Frank Jones points out in his book, *Introduction to Sociology*:

> The history of science is filled with instances where systematically collected facts invalidated popular beliefs or untested ideas. Actually, these are the more dramatic events. Many findings in any field of science simply confirm common sense. Sociology is no different. It is not surprising, for example, to find that people in industrial societies rank those occupations highest which are highest in income; that people in upper-level occupations are more satisfied than those in lower-level occupations; that liberal ideas are more likely to be expressed by persons of high, rather than low, education.

The scientific method of determining truth is the final one we will discuss here.

The Scientific Method

The scientific method appears to hold out the greatest hope for understanding and predicting the behaviour of man among men. This method has four main features:

1) *Accuracy*. It is important that the information on which judgements are to be made be as accurate as possible. The accuracy of information is not always as easy to determine as it might seem. For example, if we ask a group of teachers why they selected teaching as a profession, they are likely to say, "Because I like to work with children." But if we go into it in greater detail, we find that for many teachers, teaching is not even their first choice of a profession. In many cases, medicine, law, or engineering were their first choices, but these were unattainable because of a lack of funds for tuition fees or other personal reasons. Many others found that when they graduated from university, teaching was the most convenient job opportunity. Therefore, if we explained the choice of teaching as a career on the basis of "liking to work with children", we would be quite incorrect. Although liking children is quite important, particularly for successful teachers, it is usually quite low as a priority when the decision is made.

2) *Precision*. It is important that information be collected in a precise way that takes into account all factors that might have affected the source of the information. For example, if we were to compare the effectiveness of two different methods of teaching, it would be important to select similar children for the groups to be tested; to ensure that each teaching method takes place under approximately the same conditions and uses the same materials; and to make sure that each student is evaluated in the same way.

3) *Systematic approach*. Information should be collected, handled, and presented in a highly organized and systematic manner. We should not pull bits of information together in a haphazard way because we will probably neglect bits that are meaningful or discard bits that do not fit in with our biased viewpoint. We cannot completely escape the influences of our own biases, but if we take a consistent and critical approach, we can reduce their effect.

4) *Straightforward interpretation*. The final step in the scientific method requires that the information that has been collected about some event or events be interpreted as straightforwardly as possible. There are a number of reasons why you might be biased in your interpretation: it might be to your advantage to report something in a certain way, you may be prejudiced against some individual or group and·select only those findings that support your prejudiced view, or you may just be

careless in order to make your task easier. There are many reasons why you might misread information, and you should try to build in strategies for avoiding these pitfalls.

The scientific method is a guide to your understanding of the behaviour of men in society. It is a step toward the development of the ability to think critically, to evaluate the statements of others as well as your own with true understanding, and to observe human behaviour from a broad point of view.

The following selection is fictional, but it does demonstrate how three different subject fields within the social sciences might view a problem in human relations. Although the problem set out in the parable of *The Spindle* is explained in three different ways – by the sociologist, the anthropologist, and the psychologist – their solutions to the problem are the same. There is one consistent feature about their approach to the problem, and that is their use of the scientific method.

The spindle

Elias H. Porter

Once upon a time the president of a large chain of short-order restaurants attended a lecture on "Human Relations in Business and Industry". He attended the lecture in the hope he would learn something useful. His years of experience had led him to believe that if human relations problems ever plagued any business, then they certainly plagued the restaurant business.

The speaker discussed the many pressures which create human relations problems. He spoke of psychological pressures, sociological pressures, conflicts in values, conflicts in power structure, and so on. The president did not understand all that was said, but he did go home with one idea. If there were so many different sources of pressure, maybe it was expecting too much of his managers to think they would see them all, let alone cope with them all. The thought occurred to him that maybe he should bring in a team of consultants from several different academic disciplines and have each contribute to the solution of the human relations problems.

And so it came to pass that the president of the restaurant chain and his top-management staff met one morning with a sociologist, a psychologist, and an anthropologist. The president outlined the problem to the men of science and spoke of his hope that they might come up with an interdisciplinary answer to the human relations problems. The personnel manager presented exit-interview findings which he interpreted as indicating that most people quit their restaurant jobs because of too much sense of pressure caused by the inefficiencies and ill tempers of co-workers.

This was the mission which the scientists were assigned: find out why the waitresses break down in tears; find out why the cooks walk off the job; find out why the managers get so upset that they summarily fire employees on the spot. Find out the cause of the problems, and find out what to do about them.

The Social Sciences: Some Definitions

All of the social sciences take "man in society" as their subject matter. The basic differences lie in the point of view each brings to the study of man in society. History, political science, anthropology, economics, sociology, and psychology are the main fields of study in the social sciences. In this book we have drawn most heavily from the fields of sociology, anthropology, and social psychology.

Sociology. The emphasis in this field is placed on why individuals act the way they do within various groups and societies, and whether their actions are considered normal or problem behaviour by others.

Anthropology. The term anthropology can be directly translated to mean "the study of man". Until quite recently, anthropologists limited their study of man to the study of the physical and cultural remains of ancient man and of primitive tribes who lived in comparatively unknown parts of the world. By studying the remains of tools and other relics of ancient man, including human skeletons, anthropologists have been able to reconstruct cultures. In studying primitive societies, the anthropologist has focused on such factors as family, religion, language, and government.

Social psychology. This field has developed from the overlap between sociology and psychology. Its main emphasis is on understanding man's behaviour in the small-group setting, while a second major concern is how people learn from other people. This field combines knowledge of the physical and biological nature of man with knowledge of how man relates to other men in small groups.

The Effect of Time on the "Truth"

The social scientist learns very quickly that he cannot trust men's memories of their own actions. William J. Lederer, in his book *All the Ships at Sea*, noted that the stories of the survivors of a shipwreck often changed considerably after a period of time. When the ship blew up, it was quite acceptable for the individual to think of saving his own skin. As the survivors of the shipwreck got closer to civilization, many men remembered something new: that they had attempted to save the lives of others at the risk of their own lives.

When Lederer interviewed a signalman immediately after he was rescued, the signalman said:

After I jumped over, I swam as fast as I could, I swam upwind like you always told us. I had no life jacket and got scared. I saw someone floating with his head under water. It was Mr. – . His back was broken; I could tell by the funny way it angled just below the neck. I said to myself if he's dead there's no use in his wasting the life jacket. I took the jacket from him and held on to it. I don't know what happened to Mr. – 's body.

When the man was interviewed a month later, the interview went as follows:

I swam from the ship as fast as I could. I swam upwind just like you always told us. I saw someone floating with his head under water. It was Mr. – . Although his back was broken and his head had been submerged, I figured maybe the doctor could do something for him. I pulled his head out of the water and tied the jacket tie under his chin so that his head'd stay in the air. I trod water for about an hour, just holding onto Mr. – 's life jacket for a rest occasionally. I saw a raft about five hundred yards away. I thought maybe the doctor or a hospital corpsman might be on it. I swam over to it. The doctor wasn't there. We paddled over to where Mr. – had been, but there was no sign of him.

When Lederer met the man five years later, the story had changed even more. Now it was the signalman who had the life jacket. When he saw that the other fellow had a broken back, the signalman removed his life jacket and gave it to him.

I knew he was dead, but figured maybe there was a chance in a thousand he might be saved. It was my duty to try to help him, so I gave him my jacket.

Later, in one of the plush conference rooms, the scientists sat down to plan their attack. It soon became clear that they might just as well be three blind men, and the problem might just as well be the proverbial elephant. Their training and experience had taught them to look at events in different ways. And so they decided that inasmuch as they couldn't speak each others' languages, they might as well pursue their tasks separately. Each went to a different city and began his observations in his own way.

The sociologist. First to return was the sociologist. In his report to top management he said:

I think I have discovered something that is pretty fundamental. In one sense it is so obvious that it has probably been completely overlooked before. It is during the *rush hours* that your human relations problems arise. That is when the waitresses break out in tears. That is when the cooks grow temperamental and walk off the job. That is when your managers lose their tempers and dismiss employees summarily.

After elaborating on this theme and showing several charts with sloping lines and bar graphs to back up his assertions, he came to his diagnosis of the situation. "In brief, gentlemen," he stated, "you have a sociological problem on your hands." He walked to the blackboard and began to write. As he wrote, he spoke:

You have a stress pattern during the rush hours. There is stress between the customer and the waitress. . . . There is stress between the waitress and the cook. . . . And up here is the manager. There is stress between the waitress and the manager. . . . And between the manager and the cook. . . . And the manager is buffeted by complaints from the customer.

We can see one thing which, sociologically speaking, doesn't seem right. The manager has the highest status in the restaurant. The cook has the next highest status. The waitresses, however, are always "local hire" and have the lowest status. Of course, they have higher status than bus boys and dish washers but certainly lower status than the cook, and yet they give orders to the cook.

It doesn't seem right for a lower status person to give orders to a higher status person. We've got to find a way to break up the face-to-face relationship between the waitresses and the cook. We've got to fix it so that they don't have to talk to one another. Now my idea is to put a "spindle" on the order counter. The "spindle", as I choose to call it, is a wheel on a shaft. The wheel has clips on it so the girls can simply put their orders on the wheel rather than calling out orders to the cook.

When the sociologist left the meeting, the president and his staff talked of what had been said. It made some sense. However, they decided to wait to hear from the other scientists before taking action.

The psychologist. Next to return from his studies was the psychologist. He reported to top management:

I think I have discovered something that is pretty fundamental. In one sense it is so obvious that it has probably been completely overlooked before. It is during the *rush hours* that your human relations problems arise. That is when the waitresses break out in tears. That is when the cooks grow temperamental and walk off the job. That is when your managers lose their tempers and dismiss employees summarily.

Then the psychologist sketched on the blackboard the identical pattern of stress between customer, waitress, cook, and management. But his interpretation was somewhat different:

Psychologically speaking (he said), we can see that the manager is the father figure, the cook is the son, and the waitress is the daughter. Now we know that in our culture you can't have daughters giving orders to the sons. It louses up their ego structure.

What we've got to do is to find a way to break up the face-to-face relationship between them. Now one idea I've thought up is to put what I call a "spindle" on the order counter. It's a kind of wheel on a shaft with little clips on it so that the waitresses can put their orders on it rather than calling out orders to the cook.

What the psychologist said made sense, too, in a way. Some of the staff favored the status-conflict interpretation while others thought the sex-conflict interpretation to be the right one; the president kept his own counsel.

The anthropologist. The next scientist to report was the anthropologist. He reported to top management:

I think I have discovered something that is pretty fundamental. In one sense it is so obvious that it has probably been completely overlooked before. It is during the *rush hours* that your human relations problems arise. That is when the waitresses break out in tears. That is when the cooks grow temperamental and walk off the job. That is when your managers lose their tempers and dismiss employees summarily.

After elaborating for a few moments, he came to his diagnosis of the situation. "In brief, gentlemen," he stated, "you have an anthropological problem on your hands." He walked to the blackboard and began to sketch. Once again there appeared the stress pattern between customer, waitress, cook, and management:

We anthropologists know that man behaves according to his value systems. Now, the manager holds as a central value the continued growth and development of the restaurant organization. The cooks tend to share this central value system, for as the organization prospers, so do they. But the waitresses are a different story. The only reason most of them are working is to help supplement the family income. They couldn't care less whether the organization thrives or not as long as it's a decent place to work. Now, you can't have a noncentral value system giving orders to a central value system.

We must recognize, too, that scientific knowledge about man is more difficult to come by than knowledge about the atom. There is a greater investment of money and effort in research in natural science than in social science. If as much money and support were given to the social sciences the results would be impressive. In terms of priority, our society has yet to be persuaded that Alexander Pope is right, that "the proper study of mankind is man".

Meyer F. Nimkoff
Technology and Social Change

One may say that the characteristics of a society are determined by two things: first by the simple fact that the society is composed of human beings; and second, by the internal nature of those human beings. No amount of investigation can explain the characteristics of society by simple reference to the nature of human beings; but by an investigation of human beings arranged in a certain order, yes. The social scientist is studying the structural arrangement of the units and takes the internal structure of the units for granted.

A. R. Radcliffe-Brown
A Natural Science of Society

Sociologist Bernard Phillips points out that the social sciences, and sociology in particular, are considered to be the handmaiden of those anti-human forces that seek to gain total control over the mind of the individual. The sociologist's attempt to make use of scientific methods of investigation is seen as an attempt to force people into a common mold by treating them as punches on an IBM card. The image is the familiar one of the evil scientist who intends to take away man's human characteristics and turn him into some kind of a robot. At a time when the threat of modern technology hangs over everyone, this fear of what the social sciences might do is quite understandable. In his book, *Sociology: Social Structure and Change*, he notes:

But science is a two-edged sword, and it has great capacity for good as well as evil. Whatever dangers are involved in the application of sociology to human affairs are far less than the dangers involved in remaining ignorant. Without the knowledge of how to solve our problems, there is very little chance that they will solve themselves. Rather than blame physical science for having produced its awful weaponry, perhaps we should blame our lack of knowledge as to how to solve human problems by peaceful means.

But although the solution of personal problems may not be found in sociological literature, the study of sociology can give you a better understanding of human behaviour generally, and through this you may be able to work out your own solutions. The literature of sociology sheds light on how people behave, how they may be expected to behave under given conditions, how they came to think, feel, and believe as they do.

David Dressler
Sociology: The Study of Human Interaction

Sociology, and the social sciences generally, operate within the fiery give and take of human values and human conflicts. Like the subject with which they deal, they are, when at their best, controversial in nature.

R. P. Cuzzort
Humanity and Modern Sociological Thought

Behaviour is a difficult subject matter, not because it is inaccessible, but because it is extremely complex. Since it is a process, rather than a thing, it cannot easily be held still for observation. It is changing, fluid, and [lasts only briefly], and for this reason it makes great technical demands upon the ingenuity and energy of the scientist. But there is nothing essentially insoluble about the problems which arise from this fact.

B. F. Skinner
Science and Human Behaviour

What we've got to do is to find some way of breaking up the face-to-face contact between the waitresses and the cook. One way that has occurred to me is to place on the order counter an adaptation of the old-fashioned spindle. By having a wheel at the top of the shaft and putting clips every few inches apart, the waitresses can put their orders on the wheel and not have to call out orders to the cook. Here is a model of what I mean.

Triumph of the spindle. When the anthropologist had left, there was much discussion of which scientist was right. The president finally spoke. "Gentlemen, it's clear that these men don't agree on the reason for conflict, but all have come up with the same basic idea about the spindle. Let's take a chance and try it out."

And it came to pass that the spindle was introduced throughout the chain of restaurants. It did more to reduce the human relations problems in the restaurant industry than any other innovation of which the restaurant people knew. Soon it was copied. Like wildfire the spindle spread from coast to coast and from border to border.

Resources for The Point of View

Jones, F. E. 1963. *An Introduction to Sociology.* Toronto: Canadian Broadcasting Corporation.

McConnell, J. V. (ed.). 1970. *Readings in Social Psychology Today.* Del Mar, California: CRM Books.

Rose, C. B. 1965. *Sociology.* Columbus, Ohio: Charles E. Merrill Books Inc.

Australopithecus

Part 1

The origin and character of man

Until recently it was thought that man had been around for only a few thousand years. The theory of evolution developed by Charles Darwin in the middle of the nineteenth century helped to dispel this idea. Darwin explained the process of evolution by his principle of natural selection. Simply stated, this principle notes that since animals reproduce in numbers greater than are required to maintain their population, there must be a struggle for existence among the members of each species. And since animals in any one species vary and this variation would be inherited, any advantageous variation would increase the chance for the survival of an animal and its offspring. Of course, unfavourable variations in certain animals would lead to their extinction. Nature selected the fittest, and the fittest survived.

Man resembles and belongs to the order of animals called "primates". This order also includes monkeys, lemurs, and apes. Most biologists feel that man did not evolve from now-existing species of monkeys, but emerged through another evolutionary process. Although apes are similar to human beings in many respects, the exact relationship of existing apes to man is still not understood.

For the past forty years, Africa has been the centre for the study of the origin of man. Some fossils have been found of a creature that combined some of the characteristics of both man and ape (Australopithecus). These man-apes walked upright, but their brains were only half the size of that of man today. From their fossils, which date back a million or more years, it was revealed that these man-apes hunted many kinds of animals, and that they lived in bands. They died out about 250,000 years ago. There were other man-like creatures present on earth at the same time as the man-apes, but it appears that Australopithecus represents a once-missing link in the evolutionary chain that resulted in man.

The earliest remains of true man were those of Pithecanthropus and Sinanthropus who lived about half a million years ago. These men were about 5 feet, 7 inches in height, and weighed approximately 150 pounds. In appearance, they had an ape-like head mounted on a human body.

Neanderthal man lived in Europe at the beginning of the Ice Age. He was intelligent enough to survive in a different environment. He hunted, made tools, buried his dead, and lived in a family complex form of group life. He was comparatively short (5 feet, 2 inches) and stocky.

Cro-Magnon man appeared comparatively recently in Europe (about 100,000 years ago). He was somewhat similar to modern man. He fished as well as hunted, made relatively sophisticated tools and implements, used fire to cook food, buried his dead, and created realistic animal drawings on the walls of his caves.

Although some people claim that the modern races of man are descended from various subhuman species, there is no clear basis for this belief. Although there is little agreement as to how the various fossils are related to modern man, it is generally accepted by scientists that all men are variants of one species.

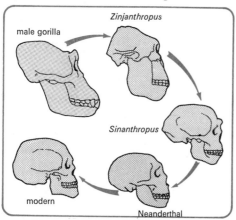

Comparison of skulls

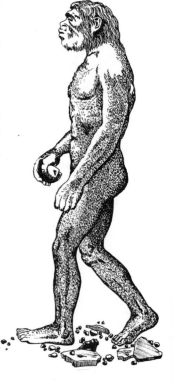

Neanderthal

one

The adaptive animal

Some time ago, there was considerable resistance to the idea that man is an animal, but with the acceptance of the theory of evolution, it is now taken for granted. However, man is a unique animal, who has developed to a stage where he has the power to control and shape a large segment of his environment. The hands, the eyes, and the brain all work together to make possible the magnificent accomplishments of modern man, but it is not clear which of these is the key to his developmental success.

In the following selection, *The Human Animal* by Weston LaBarre, a strong case is made for the significance of man's "grasping hands" in his rapid development. The second selection, *Man Before History* by Edwin Dethlefson, focuses on the life style of early man and the invention of implements that extended his versatility.

*The human animal**

Weston LaBarre

Early man was an earth-bound ape, with empty hands. But it was these same empty hands that changed completely the whole manner of evolution in man and made him unique beyond all comparison with any other living creature. Seen in its separate aspects, the human hand is nothing special. Five-toed paws were part of the original pattern of lungs and legs of even the early amphibians, and they are quite common in later land animals descended from the amphibians. For man to have fingers would be the usual thing to expect: it is the bat's long-fingered wing-hand, the bird's arm-wing, and the whale's handflippers that are the anatomically clever, the spectacular variations on the basic five-fingered theme. Human hands are not unusual, either, as the freed limbs of two-footed animals: there are plenty of instances of this, from dinosaurs to kangaroos. Nor is the hand unique as a grasping organ in man: many of the tree-living monkeys were even four-handed, and thus two up on man – whose specialized foot has lost just about all its skill to hold things.

The uniqueness of man's hand is not in the way that it is shaped but in the way it is used. Of course his ancestors' time in the trees did greatly improve the grasping ability of his hands. It is also true that the fully opposable thumb in man is a further improvement on the monkey-type hand. But in purely physical terms, monkey hands could probably do nearly everything a man's hand could. The main significance of the human hand lies in its being one member of a team composed of hands, brains, and eyes.

When man, heir of four limbs, uses only two of them for walking, his clever hands are then finally freed from use in any kind of walking or running whatever. They can now be used for purely exploratory grasping. The advantages of this are not to be underestimated. Some New World monkeys, it is true, have grasping

Classifying Man

Category	Name	Example
Kingdom	Animalia	
Phylum	Chordata	frogs, snakes, birds, bats, cats, whales, man
Class	Mammalia	bats, cats, whales, opossums, kangaroos, man
Infraclass	Eutheria	bats, cats, whales, man
Cohort	Unguiculata	moles, bats, monkeys, man
Order	Primates	lemurs, monkeys, apes, man
Suborder	Anthropoidea	monkeys, apes. man
Superfamily	Hominoidea	gorillas, orangu-tangs, man
Family	Hominidae	Australopithecine, man
Genus	Homo	Neanderthal man, man
Species	Homo sapiens	man

---

* Condensed and modified.

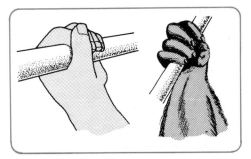

Opposing thumb

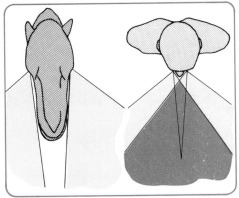

Man has stereoscopic vision

tails, but these are still largely for purposes of holding onto a tree limb; besides, the tail has the grave disadvantage of not being ordinarily in the monkey's field of vision. A better example is the elephant's trunk – perhaps significantly combined, as is man's hand, with great intelligence. But the elephant's trunk is mainly used for feeding; and, besides, there is only one of them. Nor do elephants have stereoscopic vision, to put together a muscular with a visual space-sense. Still, a sensitive grasping trunk is not to be sneezed at as a biological advantage. Elephant-like creatures once made themselves at home in a variety of environments from Siberia to Sumatra, from England to Africa, and from Saskatchewan to South America. But judgment must respect the fact that all of these are extinct except for the elephants of Africa and of Southeast Asia – and these too are dying out.

Grasping hands are not enough: many dinosaurs had them, but they lacked sufficient brains. Intelligence is not enough: elephants have a great deal of intelligence behind their trunks, but they do not have stereoscopic sight; monkeys are intelligent too, and they have stereoscopic vision as well, but they do not ordinarily see their tails. Stereoscopic eyes are not enough either: for the intelligent, tree-living apes have them, with color vision to boot. It is the combination that counts. Man has paired grasping organs, fully in his field of vision and wholly freed from moving the body in a stereoscopic-sighted, big-brained mammal – and these add up to the answer.

The philosopher Anaxagoras claimed that man had brains because he had hands, but Aristotle argued that man had hands because he had brains. When the implications of these statements are better understood and the dust of battle has settled a bit, modern scientists are inclined to give the decision to Anaxagoras rather than to Aristotle. But hands, brains, and eyes are a case, really, of what came first, the chicken or the egg; nor did it all begin, strictly speaking, with man. For in all primate evolution they influence each other mutually and develop progressively together; and the ability to "monkey with things" that man got from his primate ancestors is still one of the keystones of human nature. Certainly such hands and eyes and brains put an animal into closer object-relationship with reality and enlarge the animal ego in the technical sense of increasing awareness and testing of reality. Very literally, such an animal as man has more contacts with reality. But when we remember the conflict of brains and snout for possession of the skull, it is probable that the mouth is also part of the hand-brain-eye complex. Eating is just as much a function of the hand as are tree-acrobatics. Food, as much as safety, both available in the trees, probably took the primates originally into the trees.

It appears that man has paid to have versatile hands at the expense of feet that can do very little but move us from place to place. It is difficult to imagine feet ever being useful for anything but walking. The accidents of evolution rarely give an animal a chance for more than one or perhaps two adaptations of any organ: the more exactly and efficiently an organ is adapted to some special aspect of the environment, the more dependent it is on the accidents of environmental change. The large-scale extinction of certain animals in the past fully illustrates this fact. It is as if that animal goes farthest which holds off its physical specialization as long as possible. The more versatile and flexible a species of animal is, the greater the chance it has to resist extinction. Man can resist extinction because man can adjust to many different climates and conditions.

Nothing like this has ever happened before in evolution. Machines not only can do man's flying, diving, and superhuman seeing and hearing for him, but also *they do his evolving for him*. The critical fact is that the making of machines is done with no narrow commitment whatever of man's body. With human hands, the old-style evolution by body adaptation is obsolete. All previous animals had to make physical changes in order to survive. In a sense they had to experiment with their bodies in a blind gamble for survival. The stakes in this game were high: life or death. Man's evolution, on the other hand, is concerned only with the products of his hands, brains, and eyes – and not with his body itself. True, a flaw in the design of an experimental jet plane may kill a pilot, but that does not make the human race extinct or even wipe out aeronautical engineers.

It is an error to suppose that a spider's web is in this sense a "tool". For, besides being instinctive, the spider web is merely an extension into space of its own non-living substance. No more is a bird's nest a "tool", since neither insight nor teaching and neither memory nor experience plays any part in this instinctual activity.

It is not only the freedom of man's new kind of evolution that is significant; one has to consider the fantastic speed of it as well. It took millions and millions of years from fish to whale to evolve a warm-blooded marine mammal: but man evolved submarines from dream to actuality in a mere few centuries and with no physical change of man himself. It took birds millions of years for their experimentation with flying: but man, in only some sixty years, flies not only as well as birds but actually far better.

Since man's machines change, he has long since gone outside his own individual skin in his relationships with the world. What changes now is not man's mere body; it is "all-mankind's-brains-together-with-all-the-extra-bodily-materials-that-come-under-the-manipulation-of-their-hands". Man's being is expanded to encompass everything within reach of his manipulating hands, within sight of his searching eyes, and within the scope of his restless brain. An airplane is part of a larger self; it is a larger ownership of reality by man. And airplanes are biologically cheap. For, as unconcernedly as a man changes parts in an electric drill, he exchanges the joystick of a plane for the driving wheel of a car.

Man can attach all sorts of devices to his limbs. This process is uniquely human and uniquely freed from the slowness of reproduction and of evolutionary variation into blind alleys from which there is no retreat. Man, with his hands and machines, is not merely a promising animal biologically: he makes every other animal wholly obsolete, except as they serve *his* purposes.

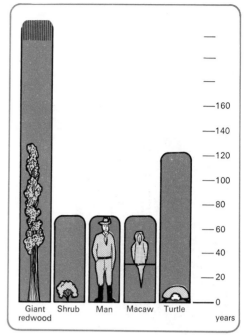

Life span

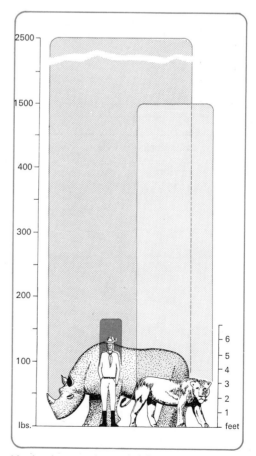

Man's advantage in eye-height

Man before history

Edwin S. Dethlefson

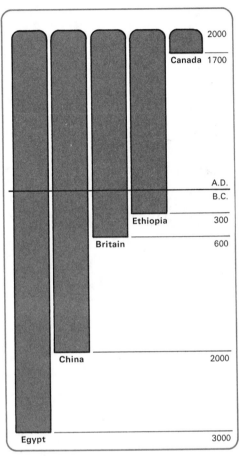

2000

Canada 1700

A.D.

B.C.

Ethiopia 300

Britain 600

China 2000

Egypt 3000

Time spans of selected civilizations

Nearly everyone has read about early men. There are books about cavemen and about ape-men, and every once in a while there are newspaper headlines about someone discovering another "missing link".

But the idea of time is a difficult one for us to work into our mental pictures of bygone life, and most people are content to think of our early ancestors as having lived "a very long time ago". The fact is that the time of our very earliest known ancestors, about two million years ago, is so far back as to be quite beyond our ability to imagine.

Even so, we ought at least to try to picture the lengths of time involved in the changes of our own kind from ape to man. To make it easier, let us start from "now" and work our way back as far as we can.

The first modern men – that is, men who were just like us in almost every physical and psychological way – seem to have evolved by about 40,000 years ago. To the scientist, that amount of time is just nothing at all.

On the other hand, it was at least 38,000 years before Christ, 34,000 years before people began to write things down, and 29,000 years before anyone thought of raising his own plants and animals for food. In other words, people just like us were kicking around *four times as long ago as the beginning of written history* – in other words, "a very long time ago".

We don't need to go back quite so far, though, to learn about these early modern men. We have quite a lot of evidence for man of 15,000 years ago, and, strange as it may seem, the changes between 40,000 and 15,000 years ago were not at all rapid (maybe because there wasn't all that much around to be changed), so we can get a fair picture of the whole scene.

The first modern men lived in shelters they made to suit their habits and the climates they lived in. Some shelters were tents made of skins stretched over bones or wood, while others were probably made of mud and sticks and stones. Modern men lived in caves, too, but if you ever went around counting caves you would know right off that there couldn't have been enough of them to squeeze all the people into, even though there were far fewer people than today. More often people lived in rock shelters formed by the overhang of cliffs.

These modern men had a variety of tools, many different kinds with which to work and hunt – nothing like what we have now, of course, but for those times it was not bad. They had spears and harpoons and a fancy gadget for throwing them. From stone and bone and wood they made almost every sort of useful shape you can imagine – and a few for which nobody has yet figured out any use at all! But then, lots of their problems were different from ours.

For example, these modern men hunted and ate woolly mammoths, elephants, rhinos, and all the smaller animals from deer to mice. And birds, and fish, and maybe even snakes and lizards. And snails, and grasshoppers – but grasshoppers leave no bones, so we can only guess about that.

They ate some plants too, but without farming there wasn't much plant food that people could eat, except berries, and lichens, and certain kinds of roots and leaves and bark, perhaps. Of course it depended on where they were living at the time, but we are talking mostly about western Europe, where archaeologists have studied these people the most.

These European early modern men lived together in groups of families, probably for somewhat the same reasons that we do – a group of men can do a lot more different kinds of things than one man can do. Maybe, too, they enjoyed one another's company....

But maybe each group thought that other groups were to *fight* with. Some people claim that is just human nature, but perhaps it deserves second thought. Anyway, you don't go spear-hunting elephants just for yourself alone, so if you like elephant meat it is nice to have friends.

As a matter of fact the men of 15,000 years ago must have been pretty well organized, because they seem to have done more different kinds of things than earlier folks did. For example, these people were very good artists. They painted most of the famous cave paintings of Europe, and they did excellent carving in stone, ivory, and bone (probably in wood, too, but we have few ways of knowing about that). They decorated many of their bone tools with delicate carvings and carved their spearthrowers into shapes of animals. Most of the art work is so well done that there must have been specialists who spent most of their time doing this sort of thing – which means that other people had to agree to supply them with food, which means people must have had very good reasons for wanting the art work done.

There were probably other special kinds of jobs, too. For example, we know these people had some religious beliefs, and that they had magical beliefs as well. In the first place they buried their dead in carefully made graves. (You can imagine their funerals were in some ways like ours today, and probably happened for the same reasons: rituals, and the beliefs they represent, help people to pass more easily through times of tragedy and to cope with matters they can't rationally explain.) They put clothing and jewelry on their bodies and put food and personal possessions in the graves. They often sprinkled red coloring all over the bodies and covered them over with bones of large animals, perhaps for protection.

Another thing is that most of the cave paintings are of the animals that were hunted ... and most of the paintings are so deep in the caves that daylight never reaches them. Why should anyone put an art gallery in the dark? Perhaps it had some magical or religious purpose that was more important to the people than the art itself. Maybe, in fact, these people didn't think about art at all the way we do. On the other hand we moderns have some types of art that we don't usually think about primarily as art. Many churches contain crucifixes and statues of saints, stained-glass windows and paintings of biblical scenes. These objects are usually aids to worship, rather than objects to be admired simply for their

Probable origins of some of the world's domestic animals

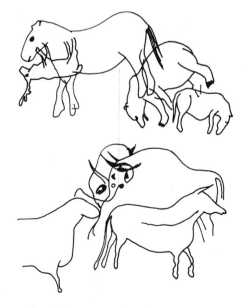

Examples of the cave art of ancient man

A Summary of Charles Darwin's Stages in the "Natural Selection" Process

1) Organisms produce a far greater number of reproductive cells than ever give rise to mature individuals.
2) The numbers of individuals in a species remain more or less constant.
3) Therefore, there must be a high death rate.
4) The individuals in a species are not identical, but are unique in all characters.
5) Therefore, some offspring will succeed better and others less in the competition for survival, and the parents of the next generation will naturally be selected from among those members of the species that have been able to adapt more effectively to the conditions of their environment.
6) Hereditary resemblance between parent and offspring is a fact.
7) Therefore, by gradual change, subsequent generations will maintain and improve on the adaptive qualities attained by their parents.

As a living organism, the human being is an open system and thus is engaged in continual interchanges with his environment. This environment includes not only [things] but other humans as well. . . .

In making these exchanges with his environment the human being, in common with all living organisms, is oriented to adjusting to his environment as well as adjusting the environment to his own uses. These uses are influenced by man's biological structure, for example, his need for air and food. . . .

The direction of evolution is that of the organism's increasing capacity to adjust its behaviour to its environment as well as to control its environment. In the human especially, the individual seems to possess capacities to learn from his experience at a rapid rate.

Bernard Phillips
Sociology: Social Structure and Change

The mammalian line was characterized from its inception by enlargement and specialization of the [front of the brain], with corresponding increase in learning ability and general intelligence. This development went on with extraordinary rapidity, as evolutionary time is measured, and at the transition from ape to man the change was even more accelerated.

C. Judson Herrick
The Evolution of Human Nature

own sake.

Anyway, people with large-scale art-magic projects must have been well organized. In that case, since early modern men were hunters and gatherers of food, we can look at hunters and gatherers of today to get some ideas about how the earlier people were organized.

One thing we notice right off is that it is worthwhile to have *lots of relatives* and for them to be spread out among other groups. This naturally makes it safer to travel around because it extends the area occupied by people who are related to you. If your wife comes from another group, then chances are you can stroll around that group's territory without getting clobbered for trespassing. And if your group has a big job to do, this way they can get another group to help.

In lots of cases extra relatives are added on to your list of "uncles" and "cousins", or even "brothers" or "fathers". That way there are a greater number of people with whom you share emotional ties and experiences and your responsibilities.

Now if everyone in a group has a number of "relatives" in other groups, there is a better chance that these groups will try to get along without fighting. So sometimes two or more groups agree to exchange their sons and daughters in marriage, which tends to make everybody related to everybody else. Which is all very soothing, provided the entire assemblage is brought together and *reminded* every once in a while. So there is also a good likelihood that groups got together to observe special occasions such as magical or religious rites. For example, today we have our national flag, which symbolizes something that we all strive together to uphold. There are even special days, like Dominion Day and Remembrance Day, when people gather together in groups.

If all the people in an ancient group shared a belief in, say, certain kinds of hunting magic, that, too, was something for them to agree on and to work for together.

Let us see now, if we can pull this all together into a picture that makes sense.

Modern Europeans of 15,000 years ago, more or less, lived in small family groups much like our own, with mother cooking and gathering vegetables and small animals (the children helping, of course, and sometimes grandmothers and grandfathers), while the father went hunting with several other fathers. These families lived in tents or rock-shelters that formed communities of many families that probably shared their food and helped one another at various tasks. All the people believed in a religion that included the idea of life after death, and they practiced hunting magic, and probably curing magic, and other kinds of magic too. When youngsters grew up they probably married people from other communities. All the members of a group of communities probably got together occasionally to worship or to make magic, and maybe then they all went on a gigantic mammoth-hunt. There were religious leaders, and hunting leaders, and specialists for all sorts of jobs, from making magical pictures and carvings to building traps and curing the sick.

We have been talking about some of the earliest people who

were built just the same way we are built. Their brains were as big as ours, and probably the main difference from modern people was based on the fact that hardly anything we have today had been invented yet and most of the knowledge we now have wasn't known 15,000 years ago.

Even so, these people don't sound as if they "lived like animals". They surely had language, and we know they already had some serious religious beliefs. And that was all seven times as long ago as the birth of Christ.

How did it happen? Let's look back a little further, to when men didn't quite look like modern men. Let's say 40,000 years ago, fifty times as long ago as the beginning of the Roman Empire. Brains were just about as big as they are today, but faces were much bigger, with heavier jaws and larger teeth. It is as if the teeth were still needed to do some jobs for which tools hadn't yet been invented. The jaws were so much bigger, in fact, there wasn't room for any chin.

If these earlier men had to use their teeth for a lot more things it wasn't necessarily because they were stupid, for they did have a variety of stone tools, not so fancy nor so delicate as later ones, but tools nonetheless. And they had religion, too, for some of them buried their dead with tools and food. And places have been found where they performed magic.

There weren't as many of them as modern men of 15,000 years ago, and with fewer kinds of tools they probably had less reason to be so well organized. They had families, too, but living as they did in the middle of an ice age, food probably wasn't plentiful enough to support really large groups in their travels.

And travel they did, for they hunted woolly mammoths too, when they could get them, and they followed the herds of bison across icy wastes. No doubt the men and women did different kinds of jobs, the men doing heavier hunting and the women foraging and caring for the children, but that is probably all the specialization there was. Still, they believed in magic, and in life after death, so there must have been magicians and medicine men.

Maybe these not-quite-moderns hadn't yet figured out that it was good politics to increase their number of relatives by marrying outside the group, but then maybe there weren't yet so many people that politics was an important thought.

Now if we look back to a half-million years or so ago, we find men with smaller brains than ours, who had only simple kinds of stone tools for cutting and pounding, and who hunted with wooden spears. We can't tell much except that they hunted and traveled in groups. We don't know what sorts of families they had, nor whether they believed in anything much except food. But they were already scattered over most of the Old World (nobody came to the Americas until the time of the modern men), so they must have been doing *something* right. We have evidence of their camps, here and there, and we know that they had discovered fire, which must have been a big thing. They surely wandered around a lot, though, following the game, or even just looking for wild fruits and vegetables, so the women would probably have had to carry and care for the children.

Man Versus Animals

In an attempt to understand the basic differences in learning behaviour between men and animals, an experiment was conducted by the Kellogs. They obtained a very young champanzee of approximately the same age as their own child and they raised the two together. They tried to treat the two infants in as much the same way as possible. The two played together, ate the same food, and even wore the same clothing. For the most part, the chimpanzee learned quite as readily as the child. And in some respects, because she tended to develop faster physically, she more quickly learned those things that required strength and muscular coordination.

Surprisingly, the sounds made by both infants were quite similar when they were hungry, thirsty, and uncomfortable, and even when they wanted toys and other objects. However, as soon as the child began to learn some words, the chimpanzee was soon bypassed. The child became involved in his environment in a way that was not possible for the chimpanzee, and was able to learn ways of behaving and communicating that were beyond the capabilities of the chimpanzee.

The human infant's original helplessness, his lack of scales, fur, or other form of body covering for protection and warmth, and his limited automatic or fixed responses — all of these have long-run advantages. . . . The lack of protective body covering makes it possible for him to live in all zones, provided suitable covering is found and utilized. The lack of original complex patterns of obtaining food, such as lying-in-wait or hunting, is offset by the capacity to perceive relationships and invent highly satisfying ways of obtaining far more than mere biological necessities.

Wayland J. Hayes and Rena Gazaway
Human Relations in Nursing

. . . man has another mental quality which the animal lacks. He is aware of himself, of his past and of his future, which is death ; of his smallness and powerlessness ; he is aware of others as others — as friends, enemies, or as strangers. Man transcends all other life because he is, for the first time, *life aware of itself.*

Erich Fromm
The Art of Loving

Now we could go skipping on back to a million or more years ago, but we are likely to become totally confused by the immensity of the time spans involved. So let's just consider the main points.

In the first place, a fantastically long time ago, some apes discovered they could get along better in the world by using stones and sticks as tools to protect themselves and to get food. As soon as they really got involved with tools it became necessary for them to adjust to hind-legged walking so they could do right by the tools. When their skeletons had evolved to the point where they could walk efficiently, their brains would have to have evolved to the point where they could master the complicated operations of making and using the tools. That meant they had to be born with bigger heads, or born at an earlier and more helpless stage of development.

Since their heads were already as big as could be born without injury, they had to be born more helpless and then spend time learning. That meant their mothers had to carry babies instead of tools. But it also meant that mothers could spend more time teaching the children how to do complicated non-ape things; but it also meant that fathers couldn't just ignore the whole proceeding. The fathers had to feed and protect the mothers *and* the babies, which seems to point to why families got started. A father had to settle for one wife instead of playing the field as most monkeys and apes do. Otherwise unprotected mothers and babies would have starved or been eaten by tigers and we should have become extinct.

It sounds as if the fathers had all the worst of it, but actually, as everyone knows, human families have their rewards, even for dads. After all, a father *did* then have a full-time wife he could depend on, if only because she had to depend on him. Furthermore, children that are taught by the mothers and fed and cared for in a family situation might very well stay around after they grow up, and help their fathers to hunt, instead of simply wandering off as young apes do. And a mother who doesn't have to do her own hunting has time to experiment with foods, and with new kinds of household tools and techniques, to say nothing of just being around to soothe the father's weary brow when he comes home exhausted from the hunt.

Everything had to start slowly, because nobody *knew* what "human" was nor how to be one, to begin with. Our earliest ancestors just muddled along for thousands and thousands of years making little discoveries and blundering into lucky accidents. Our species gradually accumulated knowledge and ways of doing things that made it possible to begin to see ways of doing, and thinking about doing, more and more complicated things.

Perhaps that is why we have such trouble actually picturing lengths of time in the distant past. Time is marked in our minds by things happening, so the slower things happen the more our mind collapses time around the things we remember.

Because it took so long for a few big, basic things to happen – like getting on our hind legs, and starting to use tools, and deciding to live in families, and discovering the unanimity created by common religious beliefs – it is hard for us to realize the period before modern men was as long as it really was.

Of all man's accomplishments it is impossible to single out one as the culmination, but unerringly we know that among the most important was his learning to control fire. Although fire was not used by man until comparatively late in Africa, it was utilized in China about 600,000 years ago. In Europe fire was used by cave dwellers in the Durance River valley of southern France some 750,000 years ago.

Wendell H. Oswalt
Understanding Our Culture: An Anthropological View

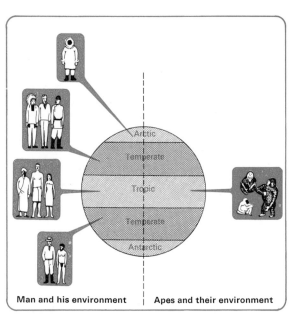

Man and his environment | Apes and their environment

The one species of man lives in many parts of the world and from zero to 16,000 feet above sea level. The many species of ape live in only one climatic zone and from zero to 4,000 feet above sea level

Why didn't things happen faster? And getting back to our modern men of 15,000 years ago, let's keep in mind that even that recently the bow and arrow, and the sled, and the fishhook were not yet known. And it would be nearly 10,000 more years before anyone would discover what a wheel was good for! But it was a mere 5,000 years after that until television. *How about that?*

Out of the dreaming past, with its legends of streaming seas and gleaming glaciers, mountains that moved and suns that glared, emerges this creature, man — the latest phase in a continuing process that stretches back to the beginning of life. His is the heritage of all that has lived; he still carries the vestiges of snout and fangs and claws of species long since vanished; he is the ancestor of all that is yet to come. Do not regard him lightly — he is you.

Don Fabun
The Dynamics of Change

two

Aggressive behaviour: instinct or environment?

The history of man is strewn with evidence of his aggressive behaviour: wars, torture, and cruelty in all their variations. Today every nation, whether rich or poor, channels vast sums of money into weapons for defense – defense against the hostilities of others. At every hockey game, football game, and wrestling match, you can hear the cry "Kill him". Newspaper advertisements seek out "aggressive young men or women" for positions "with a promising future". Is man by his very nature aggressive, or is aggressive behaviour learned?

What is and what is not instinctive behaviour in man is still a controversial issue among scientists. The recent publication of some popular books (*The Naked Ape* by Desmond Morris and *The Territorial Imperative* by Robert Ardrey), as well as the work of a well-known scientist (*On Aggression* by Konrad Lorenz) has only added fuel to the fire. The works of Lorenz and Ardrey in particular have caused a stir among the scientists, because of their theory that man is by instinct an aggressive creature and that much of the violence in contemporary life can be directly traced to this instinctive tendency. However, the majority of present-day scientists feel that the tendency toward aggressive behaviour is something that is learned in a cultural context; something that is either directly or indirectly a product of environmental influence.

The following article presents an evaluation of the work of Lorenz and Ardrey by the noted biologist, J. P. Scott.

An instinct may be defined as a relatively complex activity of an organism that is acting
(1) as a whole rather than by parts
(2) as the representative of a species rather than as an individual
(3) without previous experience or without modification caused by experience, and
(4) with an end or purpose of which the organism has no conscious knowledge.

Encyclopaedia Britannica

A territory is an area of space, whether of water, or earth, or air, which an animal or group of animals defends as an exclusive preserve. The word is also used to describe the inward compulsion in animate beings to possess and defend such space. A territorial species of animals, therefore, is one in which all males, and sometimes females too, bear an inherent drive to gain and to defend an exclusive property.

Robert Ardrey
The Territorial Imperative

That old-time aggression

J. P. Scott

The control of destructive violence between individuals and nations is one of the major practical problems of our times. Its consequences are so great that it deserves a major scientific effort directed toward its solution, and its causes are so many and so various that scientists from almost every discipline, from mathematics through physiology and biological sciences, have something to contribute. *On Aggression* is such a contribution, written by the distinguished European biologist, Konrad Lorenz.

Lorenz apparently began this work as a reaction against the interpretation of aggression as an impulse of destruction directed both toward others and toward oneself. He points out that fighting behaviour in the animal kingdom has evolved in many different ways and usually serves some useful purpose such as the even spreading of animals throughout their living space and the division of land into breeding territories so that adequate food is available for the young. And he describes human aggressive impulses as probably having had some such useful purposes in primitive man. Aggressive behaviour is therefore not necessarily an evil, but is evil because it has been distorted from its original use.

No modern student of the evolution of animal behaviour would quarrel with this viewpoint, and this is a major contribution to the understanding of aggressive behaviour in animals' societies.

Nevertheless, this is a disappointing book, both from a scientific and a practical point of view. Lorenz explains aggressive behaviour on the basis of instinct, an idea which was popular around the turn of the century, and his solution for the problem, a re-channelling of aggression impulses into socially acceptable behaviour, was presented more practically many years ago.

To understand why a modern biologist would publish a book which leaves out of consideration most of the scientific discoveries of the past 50 years requires some knowledge of Lorenz. He is a very intelligent person who picks up ideas quickly and who has a great deal of verbal and written fluency. He also has the ability to make friends quickly and to communicate a sense of excitement, and by these personal qualities he has been able to inspire a great many people to enter the field of animal behaviour, or ethnology, as it is sometimes called. He is also kindly and humanitarian, and this comes through in both his personal contacts and his writings.

At the same time he is a very narrow specialist, who primarily knows the behaviour of birds, and particularly that of ducks and geese, on which his book has an excellent chapter. He evidently reads very little other than material which directly relates to his own specialty. Consequently, when he began observing the behaviour of birds from the viewpoint of native behaviour, or instinct, he went back to the writings of other students of bird life, for much of his theory. Lorenz quotes articles published in 1918, and most of the ideas in them had been worked out years before. These ideas of instinct form a very incomplete and inadequate explanation of behaviour.

One of the major points in Lorenz's theory is that aggression can arise without an outside stimulus. But for a physiologist there must be an indication of changes within the body which would lead to such "spontaneous" aggressive behaviour. A series of these changes are well known in the case of hunger, where the cells use up blood sugar, which in turn stimulates certain centers of the brain which then cause hunger contractions in the stomach, thus making one more ready to eat. The situation with respect to the emotion of anger is quite different. It has been shown that the emotion of anger originates in one portion of the brain, and stimulating this area with electrodes in an animal such as a cat will produce reactions very similar to anger. Without such stimulation the animal is quiet. Evidence obtained from the removal of parts of the brain shows that certain other areas have a stimulating effect on anger, and that these are balanced by other portions which inhibit it. Stimulation from the outside, such as the pain of a blow, will upset the balance and cause the emotion of anger. Thus we have a mechanism which prolongs and even enlarges the effects of stimulation from outside but no means for building up the first stimulation from within. There is no internal change corresponding to the change in blood sugar which results in hunger. In short, the evidence is against Lorenz's notion of aggression occurring from internal stimuli, and indeed, it is difficult to see how this could have evolved. Fighting is an emergency reaction, and it is hard to imagine how natural selection would lead to the development of something that would lead to an accumulation of energy

Unreasoning and unreasonable human nature causes two nations to compete though no economic necessity compels them to do so: it induces two political parties or religions with amazingly similar programmes of salvation to fight each other bitterly and it impels an Alexander or a Napoleon to sacrifice millions of lives in his attempt to unite the world under his sceptre. We have been taught to regard some of the persons who have committed these and similar absurdities with respect, even as "great" men. Most of us fail to realize how abjectly stupid and undesirable the historical mass behaviour of humanity actually is.

Konrad Lorenz
On Aggression

Territory is not the cause of war. It is the cause of war only in the sense that it takes two to make an argument. What territory promises is the high probability that if intrusion takes place, war will follow.

Robert Ardrey
The Territorial Imperative

It is a curious paradox that the greatest gifts of man, the unique faculties of conceptual thought and verbal speech which have raised him to a level high above all other creatures and given him mastery over the globe, are not altogether blessings, or at least are blessings that have to be paid for very dearly indeed. All the great dangers threatening humanity with extinction are direct consequences of conceptual thought and verbal speech.

Konrad Lorenz
On Aggression

Most of the games which children play have an obvious aggressive content. Cops and robbers, cowboys and Indians, are examples of struggles in which the child, identifying itself with one or other side, is attempting to prove that it has some power in the world, some strength with which it can overcome the obstacles which confront it. Some adults, anxious that their children shall not grow into warmongers, proscribe the use of toy weapons, and discourage games in which mock fighting plays a part. It is arguable that by doing so they are more likely to create the very type of personality which they are concerned to avoid.

Anthony Storr
Human Aggression

If society is in danger, it is not because of man's aggressiveness but because of the repression of personal aggressiveness in individuals.

D. W. Winnicott
"Aggression in Relation to
Emotional Development" in
Collected Papers

When you stop to think about it, it is nothing short of extraordinary what trouble people will go to in order to get into more trouble at the bridge table, or on the golf course; and the fascination of the murder story, or thriller and the newspaper accounts of real-life adventure or tragedy, is no less extraordinary. This taste for excitement *must* not be forgotten when we are dealing with human motivation.

D. O. Hebb
Motivation and the Conceptional Nervous System

Conscience might restrain me from killing another human being, robbing him, or subjecting him to oppression *if* the other human being were of my family, my religion, my race, or my nation.

However, conscience might or might not restrain me from killing, robbing, or oppressing another person *if* the context were different, if, for instance, a state of war were declared and killing and its related acts made legal, even mandatory. The most pacific and gentle and humane of individuals are found in what can only be called killer roles in time of war.

Robert A. Nisbet
The Social Bond

Just as the universe needs "love and hate", that is, attractive and repulsive forces, in order to have any form at all, so society, too, in order to attain a determinate shape, needs some quantitative ratio of harmony and disharmony, of association and competition, of favorable and unfavorable tendencies.

Georg Simmel
Conflict and the Web of Group Affiliations
(*quoted in*)
Robert A. Nisbet
The Social Bond

which would unnecessarily put an animal into danger.

This may appear to be a fine technical point, but it has one important consequence. If Lorenz is right, then man can never lead a happy peaceful existence, but must continually be rechannelling "drive" which accumulates within him. He suggests that games are particularly useful for this. If the physiologists are correct, then it is possible for man to lead a happy and peaceful existence provided he is not continually stimulated by violence. Rechannelling will have its uses, because in any real-life situation, there will always be occasions where persons are stimulated toward violence, but it is only one of the many ways provided by modern scientific knowledge for the control of aggression.

As for other major causes of aggression, such as heredity and training, Lorenz simply leaves them out. Heredity has major effects upon the development of aggressiveness, both between different kinds of animals and between individuals of the same kind. Training has equally important effects on the higher animals. We know that through appropriate training methods, an animal like a mouse can be converted into an individual which will attack females and even infant mice, something which mice normally never do. A male mouse, by other methods, can be trained to be completely peaceful. Lorenz has also completely missed (and this may be because of his lack of acquaintance with research done on mammals) one of the major recent findings of research on animal behaviour. Some animals are organized into herds, flocks, tribes, etc., and this is not something which is born into the animal, but is developed, and if disturbed, harmless or even beneficial aggressive behaviour can be transformed into destructive violence. Thus the violent baboons in the London Zoo were a group of individuals strange to each other and hence a disorganized society. The undisturbed societies of baboons on the South African plains represent an entirely different picture. Fighting is present but controlled by dominance order, and is chiefly directed against predators, and one sees the baboons risking their lives for the benefit of a group. Thus a baboon, in common with many other mammals, has the capacity to develop destructive violence under conditions where his social group is disorganized. Whereas under the proper conditions of social organization he has the capacity to develop peaceful and cooperative behaviour, to direct fighting into useful channels, and to act in a manner which might well be described as caring.

One wonders whether the same might not be said of man.

There is an element in human behaviour, however, which goes beyond this simple formulation. Man is a tool user, and one of the tools that men have discovered is that they can organize themselves into groups for the purpose of destruction and violence, and that such trained groups will overcome any individual or untrained group. This is one of the major causes of warfare – its usefulness or apparent usefulness for attaining certain ends – and it presents a problem which can only be solved on the level of human social organization.

In brief, fighting behaviour is a very complex phenomenon, taking many forms, and is stimulated and controlled by many different factors. Any "single factor" explanation, such as that of instinct, is necessarily incomplete.

The Territorial Imperative is a very different kind of book. Briefly stated, Ardrey's main point is that human aggression has an even simpler basis than that stated by Lorenz, namely "man's instinct for territoriality", in which man determines his own area of land and is willing to fight and even die to defend it.

During the Second World War, I published a scientific paper demonstrating that there were inherited differences between the fighting capacities of two pure strains of mice. Males of the gray strain were irritable and quick to start a fight, whereas those of the black strain were slow to start, but once the fighting began they almost always won over the grays. After its publication, I was interviewed by a newspaper reporter who wanted me to say that this situation was "just like ourselves and the Germans". It took some minutes before I was able to persuade him that the resemblance was purely superficial, that mice are not just like people, and that the differences between the behaviour of Germans and ourselves were mostly due to culture, rather than to any profound biological difference.

This amateur level of science reporting has become much rarer than it used to be, but it has survived in full strength in Ardrey's book. To him, a band of monkeys in Madagascar is just like a modern human nation.

Ardrey has read widely in the scientific literature on territoriality, but his ideas, if not as wildly silly as my reporter's, are equally uncritical. He has written these down as they came to him, and the result is a sort of intellectual pizza pie, with tasty tidbits of information embedded in a mass of partially baked ideas.

The facts are that territoriality occurs only in the higher animals and even there in a very spotty fashion.

In primates, our closest biological relatives, there are many cases of species which have no real territories. To take one of the more aggressive primates as an example, rhesus monkeys live in a core area and as a group wander out into a more extended range which overlaps with that of other groups by as much as 80 per cent. There are dominant and subordinate groups, and ordinarily the subordinate groups avoid contact. If they meet unexpectedly, the dominant group will attack, no matter where the contact takes place. There is plenty of fighting, but none of it is related to territory. Baboon groups live in similar overlapping home ranges and two well-known scientists of baboon behaviour never saw a group defend a territorial boundary. Unlike the rhesus monkey, groups tolerate each other, and there are few conflicts even when groups come into close contact around water holes. On the other hand, there are some recently described primate groups that apparently defend rather precise territorial boundaries just as some birds do.

We have no knowledge whatever about the territorial behaviour of pre-cultural man, and even if we did there has been ample opportunity for change to have taken place within the past several hundred thousand years. We will have to make our judgments on territoriality in human beings on the basis of modern man himself,

---

A Study of Aggressive Behaviour in Boys

The experimenters set up a study in which two groups of twelve-year-old boys would develop aggression toward each other. The boys had a similar social background. The study was set in a camp in a large park. Since it was a new situation for the boys, they could easily change old ways and develop new ones appropriate to the new situation.

In the new environment they were given cooperative tasks such as setting up camp and choosing play and work areas. The counsellors were instructed to avoid situations which could have led to competition, frustration, and conflicts within each group. In this way, the members of each group developed strong supportive relationships among themselves in a few days.

The two groups were established separate from each other and contact was avoided except in competition. When each group heard that there was another group similar to theirs, they became suspicious. The experimenters set up a tournament in such a way that, although the sides appeared evenly matched, all prizes were won by the same team. The theory here, of course, was frustration which would then lead to aggression.

After this, the groups began to raid each other's camps and commit increasingly more aggressive acts. When they had a meal together they threw things. When they went to a movie, the boys stuck with their own group and called the other group names.

Then the counsellors stepped in and attempted to get the groups to work together. They did this by creating situations which threatened both groups and required cooperation for a solution. When the counsellors stopped the water supply to both camps, the two groups worked together in this crisis to resolve the situation. Clearly, the threat to the survival of both groups was sufficient to encourage them to work together.

The study shows how aggressive behaviour can be created and, at the same time, how it can be reduced.

From Muzafer Sherif
Reference Groups:
Exploration into Conformity
and Deviation of Adolescents

The invention of weapons which kill at a great distance combined with man's capacity for abstraction, is one great threat to human survival. . . . Is disarmament a practical possibility?

Reluctantly, I am compelled to admit that I see no prospect of it. The need for weapons is rooted in man's biological weakness and vulnerability; and the fact that modern weapons have become absurdly and indiscriminately destructive does not, unfortunately, make it more likely that we can entirely rid ourselves of them.

Anthony Storr
Human Aggression

The clash of values and interests, the tension between what is and what some groups feel ought to be, the conflict between vested interests and new strata and groups demanding their share of power, wealth and status, have been productive of vitality; note for example, the contrast between the "frozen" world of the Middle Ages and the burst of creativity that accompanied the thaw that set in with Renaissance civilization.

Lewis Coser
The Functions of Social Conflict

and here the anthropologists tell us that the importance of territoriality and private property varies enormously between different cultures. To present an extreme example, in none of the Eskimo societies except the Aleut was there any such thing as the defense of "territory", even though the introduction of a strange group into a hunting area might mean starvation and death for the original inhabitants. Other societies have believed that they held rights to certain animals or plants in a territory, but not to others; or they have believed that while the tribe as a whole held rights to a territory, no individual or individual family could claim special rights to any particular piece of ground. In short, there is no evidence that territoriality is or is not a universal condition in modern man, but a great deal of evidence of important cultural differences. There *may* be some biological basis for territorial behaviour in people, but it is equally possible that it is a human cultural invention.

three   *Are there true races?*

Even in what appears to be a clear-cut issue – such as the question of whether true races do or do not exist – there is disagreement among scientists. Those who feel there are separate and unique races claim that races are a natural unit below the species level (modern man is Homo sapiens). They say that races vary from groups of individuals who differ only in the number of occurrences of a few genes, to groups who have been isolated for thousands of years and are nearly a newly evolved species of mankind. The scientists who claim there are no true races state that differences in human beings result from natural selection forces (i.e., the survival of the fittest) that operate in geographical areas, and that these forces do not fit with population boundaries. Since groups have been rarely isolated, populations have always mated and produced children outside their own group and this has tended to scatter genes across the world. And, of course, racial characteristics are inherited individually; they are not passed down as combinations of genes that are inherited as a total unit.

Sociologists feel that scientists' interpretation of the race question is related to their personal values. In order to accept and promote the widely held belief that all men should have equal opportunity, it is necessary to assume that there are no true differences among populations. For, if groupings of people called races are created unequal, the maintenance of world peace and understanding becomes even more difficult. In the selection that follows, C. Loring Brace presents a picture of the distribution of certain characteristics or traits on the basis of geographical conditions. As you can probably guess, Brace would be placed in the school of those who feel that races do not exist.

Understanding human differences

C. Loring Brace

The use of a term such as race, no matter how it is defined, is not sufficient for the understanding of human differences. The most important thing in understanding differences among groups of human beings is the appreciation of the pressures which have operated to influence the expression of each human trait separately. Physical differences in human beings, such as skin color, can best be understood by looking at the location in the world of certain physical features in terms of the history of the forces which influenced mankind. In the section which follows, a few of the most obvious characteristics of mankind will be discussed where the geographical distribution is the same as distribution of the influencing factors involved.

Nowadays, a scientist cannot ignore the uses and misuses of his findings by politicians and special pleaders. He certainly cannot and should not refrain from recording the facts which he discovers, but he had better see to it that the language he uses to describe the facts does not invite misrepresentation. To say that we have discovered that races of man do not exist is such an invitation. It is far better to find out, and to explain to others, the real nature of the observable phenomenon which is, and will continue to be, called "race".

Theodosius Dobzhansky
"Comment", *Current Anthropology*
April 1963

Skin Color

Figure 1 (page 26) shows the probable distribution of skin color throughout the world just before European exploration and colonization changed human distributions on the face of the earth. It can be seen that dark skin is found only among people who live within fifteen to twenty degrees of the equator, although not all

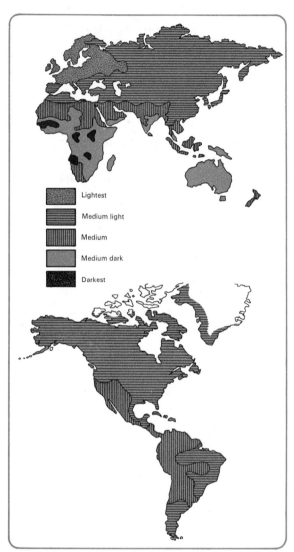

Figure 1   Skin color distribution

	Lightest
	Medium light
	Medium
	Medium dark
	Darkest

It is now generally recognized that intelligence tests do not in themselves enable us to differentiate safely between what is due to innate capacity and what is the result of environmental influences, training and education. Wherever it has been possible to make allowances for differences in environmental opportunities, the tests have shown essential similarity in mental characters among all human groups.

Otto Klineberg
Readings in Anthropology

people who live in the tropics are dark. Furthermore, some people who are generally accounted as being very dark-skinned may be partially exhibiting the effects of heavy sun tanning. The aboriginal inhabitants of Australia – particularly those who did not live in the extreme northern part – frequently bear testimony to the fact that their dark skin color is sometimes due to living out in the sun without any clothing.

In some areas, however, it is clear that people living within twenty degrees of the equator are definitely not noticeably dark-skinned, as is the case with the inhabitants of Indonesia and northern South America. In these cases, the people in question apparently have not been there for a sufficient period of time to have developed skin pigment protection.

Where the ultraviolet component of the sun's rays is strong, as it is in the tropics, the possibility of damage to the living cells in the human skin is always present. Physicians have long noted the much higher frequency of tissue injury and resultant skin cancer in people with relatively light skin as opposed to those with relatively dark skin, where the skin of both has been subjected to excessive amounts of sunshine. Apparently, dark skin has survival value in the tropics as people have suspected for many years.

Against this it has been argued that many dark-skinned tropic dwellers do not in fact have to contend with much strong sunlight. The Congo Negro or the Pygmy of the Ituri forest spend large parts of their lives sheltered by jungle, and yet they are quite well endowed with dark pigment. The answer is that neither of these people has been there for very long. While this at first seems unexpected in view of the widespread certainty that the Negro comes from the jungles of Africa, yet it turns out that this certainty is largely a piece of modern folklore. For one thing, the tropical rainforest is relatively restricted in extent, covering far less area than either dry grassland with scattered scrub trees or full desert. For another thing, survival in the rainforest depends on the possession of iron tools and suitable jungle-adapted crops, both of which are relatively recent in Africa. Apparently, the Congo area has only recently sustained the populations which now live there.

While the equator passes several degrees south of the southernmost regions of India and Ceylon, the whole southern half of the Indian subcontinent from Bombay on down is below the twentieth parallel, and one would expect if our assumptions are correct, that the peoples who have lived in these regions for the longest period of time, and hence who have been longer exposed to the influence of the environment, would show the darkest coloring in their skins. As is expected, the people whom present cultural and language evidence suggest were the most ancient inhabitants of the area are indeed the darkest in color. In general, there is a north-south color variation, with the darkest people in the south. India, then, supports the generalizations which have been made on the basis of skin color distribution in Africa.

In our consideration of the distribution of the various shades of human skin color, no mention has been made of the western hemisphere. In general, it appears that the Indians had not been across the Bering Strait for a long enough time for selection to have had much effect on skin color, even in the most tropic parts of Central and South America. The skin color of our Indians then, like that of the Indonesians, betrays their eastern Asiatic origin.

So far, this presentation has been concerned with light-skinned people moving down into tropic areas where dark-skinned people had prevailed. Of course, in Africa the formidable barrier of the Sahara Desert and the swamps of the upper Nile prevented any such population movements, and in the New World there were no preceding dark-skinned tropic dwellers, but this picture holds true for Arabia, India, and southeast Asia-Indonesia. This southern expansion of light-skinned peoples has been recognized by many generations of geographers, historians, and anthropologists, but very few have grappled with the question of why it happened.

There are two basic problems involved. First, what made these people light-skinned in the first place, and second, why did they press south. The problem of their southerly movement has been treated from time to time, but it will be deferred here until after the discussion of the problem of depigmentation [loss of color]. Some authorities have simply assumed that "white" was the original color for all mankind, although this still evades the question of what adaptive advantage it must have conferred to have originally become established.

To mention clothing brings us to what appears to be the real source of the reduction in skin pigmentation which is so apparent in peoples whose remote origins were in the neighbourhood of 50° north latitude. From the foregoing discussion it seems apparent that a relatively great amount of skin pigment has been of value to a hairless animal living in the sunnier parts of the tropics, and since the fossil record points to just this area as the remote home for all mankind, there is some basis to assume that the remote human ancestors were dark in color. This being the case, our problem is to understand how some eventually became light-skinned.

While there can be no proof for it, this is offered as the most likely means by which it happened. The archeological record shows that relatively successful and extensive human occupation of the north temperate zone as a permanent habitat did not occur until the last ice age. During the previous ice ages, the onset of cold conditions had forced people back south, but by the end of the third ice age, developing human culture had just reached the point where, with some refinement, people were able to adapt to the cold instead of having to flee from it. People stayed in the north, then, taking abundant advantage of the quantities of big game which lived there.

The degree of skin depigmentation, wherever it is found, should indicate the length of time and the extent to which skin pigment has been reduced as an adaptive feature. This is borne out by observation since the people with the palest coloring in the world today are those who can trace their ancestry back to the zone stretching from western through eastern Europe and on into southern Russia where the archeological record gives evidence that human survival depended on the use of clothing for a longer period of time than anywhere else in the world.

Erratic distribution of selected traits associated with Caucasoid (white), Mongoloid (yellow), and Negroid (black) peoples

As far as research and observation have been able to prove, the chromosome number of all the human races is the same and all the five, seven, or ten races (depending on whom we follow) are inter-fertile. . . . The appropriate blood type from one race can be transfused into any of the others without untoward effect. Thus in spite of unquestionable physical differences between people, an imposing substratum of similarity underlies these differences.

Ashley Montagu
Concept of Race

It is a common observation among anthropologists who have worked in many parts of the world in intimate contact with people of different races that racial differences in temperament also exist and can be predicted.

Carleton Coon
The Origin of Races

When considering skin colour, it is important to remember that all skin tends to change colour when exposed to the sun. Since many human beings do not cover themselves as completely as do Canadians and Europeans, many dark-skinned people are in fact considerably lighter than they appear to be. Skin colour is particularly important in societies that have an extensive system of social rankings. Having free time is typically related to upper-class status, because lower-class people often labour outdoors and therefore tend to be darker than upper-class people. Often the protection of upper-class people from the sun becomes a major concern, no matter what skin colour is inherited. In Africa, girls of marriageable age may be kept in a dark hut from the onset of puberty until they marry. In Japan, upper-class women wear large hats along with scarves when they go outside. It is only recently that exposed skin has become — at least to some degree — acceptable. Since in Canada it is often the lower working class that remains inside in factories and offices, paleness of skin sometimes indicates a life of work. And since the upper-class person usually has more time for holidays (particularly in warmer climates), tanned skin is often indicative of upper-class status.

Many of the traits that we use to determine racial classification are not preserved in fossils. Skin color, hair color and form, eye color, basal metabolism, lip form, and nose form all disappear with a corpse's decomposition. We are left with a skeleton, and seldom a complete one. Even today, the best scientist, presented with a skeleton only a decade old, cannot tell for sure whether it is that of a Negro, Mongoloid, or Caucasian.

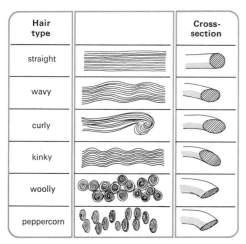

Hair type		Cross-section
straight		
wavy		
curly		
kinky		
woolly		
peppercorn		

Types of hair

Having thus accounted for the forces which produced differences in human skin color, it is now appropriate to make brief mention of the reasons why the recent past has seen such extensive movements on the part of the relatively light-skinned peoples south into India and southeast Asia. The explanation runs like this. The technological and cultural changes which allowed men to survive in the temperate latitudes during the cold of the last ice age, and which led to their eventual skin depigmentation, started trends in cultural adaptation which culminated in the discovery of methods of controlling the food supply by human control of the growth of animals and plants.

The success of this food producing way of life, in contrast to the previous hunting and gathering kind of existence, can be seen in the vast increase in numbers of the peoples whose cultural heritage stems from this source. The food producing revolution occurred earliest in the Middle East starting approximately 10,000 years ago, and before long the area had about as many people as the existing farming techniques could support. The improvement of farming was one result, but another was the actual movement of populations into areas where existing farming techniques could be applied and where the native population was too sparse to provide an obstacle. Climate was a limiting factor to the north, although technological advances eventually effected this, but to the south the opportunities for expansion were somewhat less restricted, and the result was the kind of skin color distributions which we can see in the world today.

Hair

The form and color of the hair of the head is often given an importance second only to skin color by those who feel impelled to make racial discriminations. The geographical distribution of hair follows the distribution of skin color without exception, and in spite of the numerous individuals where the two appear to be unrelated, it is apparent that this is the one instance where what is regarded as two traits vary together for a biological reason. Hair color itself has no particular significance, but hair is a structure derived from the outer skin and will necessarily share elements of the same system for melanin (pigment) production.

Unlike hair color, hair form apparently has had definite adaptive significance. The human head is one of the few parts of the body where the skin is underlain by a rather thinner than usual protective cushion of fat. A good hair covering can serve as protection against injury to bone and that rather vital organ, the brain.

The most striking thing about the distribution of hair form is the tendency for the extremely kinky forms of hair to occur among the same people where the very darkest skin color is to be found. There is no direct relationship between skin color and hair form as is shown by the presence of the most extreme hair form among the only moderately dark-skinned Bushmen of South Africa, so the suspicion is raised that tightly spiral hair may be an adaptive feature, and the reason why its distribution parallels that of dark skin color is that both traits may be responses to related conditions. If dark skin is the adaptive response to high levels of ultraviolet radiation, and the insulation provided by woolly head hair is a response to high levels of heat radiation from the sun, then it is obvious that both adaptations are responses to different challenges evoked by living in an area characterized by an excessive amount of sunlight.

One more thing can be added in considering variations related to the hair. If our argument relating to depigmentation is generally applicable, then among those people who have provided cultural means for the protection of the head for the longest period of time, we should find the greatest amount of reduction in the biological adaptations normally associated with such protection. The same people who were the first to use clothing extensively may be assumed to have provided protection for the head, i.e., hats, and this assumption receives support from the fact that it is among their descendants today that we observe the highest proportion of deficiencies in the normal head protective mechanism – hair. Not surpisingly, it is among people of European derivation that the highest frequencies of gray hair and baldness occur.

Body Build

While the traits discussed above are those most commonly used in making racial distinctions, major differences have also been observed to occur in body build which make sense when considered in adaptive terms. Obviously in a cold climate it is desirable to use the heat generated by activity as efficiently as possible. It is equally apparent that for people to be active in very hot climates, the major concern is for the development of some way of getting rid of the body heat which is created when the food is processed to allow the activity in the first place. Since heat loss occurs at the surface of the body, it is clear that bodies which have different amounts of surface area will differ in the speed with which body heat leaves, as a simple example demonstrates. If one hundred pounds of copper is shaped into a ball and heated, it will hold its heat for a much longer period of time than one hundred pounds of copper stretched out in a wire a half mile long and heated to the same temperature. Not only does shape influence the relationship between surface area and bulk, but differences in gross size can also play a part.

Although there are many individual and group exceptions, it can be said that, on the average, human bulk decreases in the hotter and increases in the colder areas inhabited by man, and the inference has been made that this is related to the greater heat-conserving properties of larger bodies.

But not only are there size differences, there are also differences in shape. Long slender arms and legs are clearly associated with desert-living peoples while short limbs and heavy bodies can be seen in the Arctic. A number of objections have been raised to considering the short limbs of Arctic peoples as adaptive, but it seems quite clear that the danger of frostbite makes long arms and legs considerably less desirable in cold climates.

Against the adaptive value of specific body form in the tropics, it has been pointed out that the tallest as well as the smallest

Harry L. Shapiro has noted in his book, *Heritage of the Bounty*, that the population of Pitcairn Island, where the mutineers of H.M.S. Bounty settled down with a number of the Tahitian inhabitants, demonstrates a consistently high level of physical evidence that has been commented on by several researchers and other travellers. One qualification must be added to the story of Pitcairn Island, however. Apparently one of the British sailors had inherited a tendency toward tooth decay, and that gene or genes has remained in the Pitcairn population, closely inbred for several generations. So, from the point of view of the Tahitians, who apparently had good teeth, the introduction of British genes might be considered a harmful influence, although in general, Pitcairn Islanders are superior physical specimens.

Hence from the genetic point of view, it would appear impossible to regard the world population of today as anything but a hodgepodge. . . .

UNESCO
Race and Culture

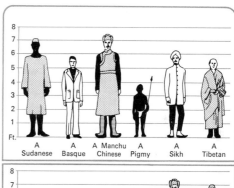

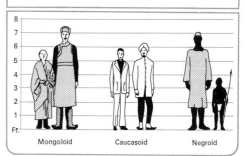

Variations in body build

In short, what we call races are subpopulations of a single overall human population. Unlike the evolutionary course undertaken by most other animals, man has not been divided into increasingly isolated populations which then differentiated into new species. . . . This is not to say that the subpopulations of [man] have been immune to the action of the evolutionary forces, particularly natural selection. But as we have stated previously, man's major adaptation has been to the cultural niche – an environment common to all the subpopulations within our species. Thus every population has an equal capacity for surviving in that niche regardless of the existing genetic differences between these populations.

J. F. Downs and H. K. Bleibtreu
Human Variation

Despite the enormous increase in our knowledge about the nature of the biological mechanisms that operate when populations breed with each other, there has been no noticeable reduction in race prejudice and race bigotry. It is a sad but almost inevitable conclusion that all the information in the world is going to have little if any effect upon emotional attitudes of men toward visible biological differences among and between individual members of Homo sapiens.

John Beuttner-Janusch
Origins of Man

There are many people who attempt to compare races of man with different species of animals, such as dogs and cats, and behaviour based on this analogy is absolutely mistaken. The person who says horses and cows don't mix, so why should Negroes and Caucasians, is talking utter nonsense. Man does not interbreed with other species such as dogs, and neither do other animals; yet, while horses indeed do not mix with cows, they are quite happy to mix with other breeds of horses without regard to colour, size, or shape of head.

Thus in the case of intermarriage, as with intelligence and psychological traits, cultural creativity, and physical characteristics, it is not science but prejudice that finds significant distinctions between the different racial groups within the human species.

J. F. Downs and H. K. Bleibtreu
Human Variation

people in the world live very close to each other right on the equator in east-central Africa. Actually, whether such a view is adequate or not, it can be argued that both extremes of body build are different ways of handling the problem of getting rid of body heat. One way of presenting a maximum amount of surface area to the air is to stretch a given mass into a long, slender shape, and certainly the immensely tall East Africans of the Upper Nile area are about as long and slender as people get. The other way of inducing this effect is to change the body size.

The Pygmy, simply by being small, acquires the same physical situation which is achieved by the African who is normal in bulk but greatly lengthened in shape. Since both are equally efficient ways of getting rid of body heat, the factors influencing which adaptation will occur stem from other sources than a simple concern for heat regulation. The tall East Africans generally are food producers whose subsistence is derived from their cattle. This means that the food supply is relatively assured and that they get regular amounts of protein in their diets. Pygmy subsistence, however, is less assured, and there may be long periods when food is not plentiful and little protein is eaten. This kind of problem would be particularly hard on people who are large enough so that they need a regular and substantial food intake, and of course, would be especially severe for the rapidly growing child. A people who have low nutritional requirements as adults and who grow less rapidly during the critical phases of development will have a better chance of surviving as hunting and gathering populations in the fringes of tropical forests.

With small size being both efficient for getting rid of body heat and the best assurance for survival in an area which often has food shortages, it becomes possible to understand why peoples within the Pygmy stature range exist in such places as the eastern edge of the Congo basin, southern India and Ceylon, the Andaman Islands, Malaya, the Philippines, and the remote parts of New Guinea. With the limited amounts of big game in these areas and before the recent coming of iron tools and weapons in many of them, the survival value of being small is quite evident.

For the reasons discussed under skin color and hair form, the remnants of the ancient inhabitants of southern India and southeast Asia are all very dark-skinned and possess very tightly curled hair. In contrast to this, some of the jungle inhabitants of central Borneo and the Philippines have the reduced coloring and reduced hair curl which is more characteristic of the peoples who have arrived from the north in relatively recent times. At the same time, they are of extremely small size illustrating the selective effect which the problems of survival in such an environment exerts on the human physique regardless of the differences in other traits which may have developed in other geographical areas. In the highlands of New Guinea, as well, there are people of Pygmy stature but, again, with very different faces from those of the short peoples of either Africa, southeast Asia, or Borneo since they come closer to resembling smaller versions of the faces of the aborigines of Australia. Again, the effects of this kind of environment have determined the Pygmy physique despite the differences which have resulted in marked facial differences in the areas considered.

The objective in presenting this explanation has been not only to touch on the major observable variations in man, but also to demonstrate that the various traits in which people differ are distributed according to the environmental conditions responsible for their expression and not because of any association with the racial boundaries designed by man.

People still argue that the backward nations have not progressed as far as we have, and that this is a result of certain racial differences. But for most of the past two hundred years, the peoples of Africa and South America, for example, were prevented by European colonists from receiving education and social advancement. Of course, there is the argument that Europeans and North Americans, who today have a relatively high level of technological development, were always cultural leaders but, in fact, the very opposite is true: civilization came late in Europe and was received very slowly by the barbarian peoples who were the ancestors of our famous contemporaries. Europe, for most of history, has been a backwater that has only developed by adopting advances made in other parts of the world.

. . . How many times will it have to be reiterated that human beings are not "races" or for that matter the simple principle that all men, by virtue of their humanity, have a right . . . to fulfill themselves. None of the findings of physical or cultural anthropology . . . can in any way affect this principle, this is an ethical one — an ethical principle which happens in every way to be supported by the findings of science.

Ashley Montagu
Race, Science and Humanity

Resources for Part 1

Ardrey, R. 1966. *The Territorial Imperative*. New York: Dell Publishing Co.

Leiris, M. 1958. *Race and Culture*. Paris: A UNESCO Publication.

Lorenz, K. 1967. *On Aggression*. Great Britain: University Paperbacks.

Montagu, A. 1970. *Man: His First Two Million Years*. New York: Delta Books.

Ross, H. H. 1966. *Understanding Evolution*. Englewood Cliffs, New Jersey: Prentice-Hall, Inc.

Storr, A. 1970. *Human Aggression*. New York: Bantam Books.

Van den Bergue, P. L. 1967. *Race and Racism*. New York: John Wiley & Sons, Inc.

Relatively little of what most people strive for most of the time is necessary for sheer survival, especially in societies where basic physical needs are amply provided for; and much of what many people want and do seems unrelated or even detrimental to their physical welfare.

Extreme examples are martyrdom, war, and suicide; more generally, there is smoking, drinking alcoholic beverages, dieting for appearance, and so on.

B. Berelson and G. A. Steiner
Human Behavior

Part 2
Man and culture

Culture, as we will use the term, can be defined simply as the way of life of a people. It is that part of human behaviour that we learn through the influence of the environment. Although "culture" is commonly used to refer to the fine arts, in our use of the term it can relate to the activities of a construction worker as well as to the paintings of an artist. And a group of people does not have to be civilized to have a culture, for all societies possess culture, whether modern or primitive, complex or simple.

Of the social sciences, anthropology is most specifically concerned with the study of culture. In the past, the anthropologists have focused their attention on the description and analysis of primitive tribes, but more and more they are applying their research strategies to study the way of life in modern societies.

Culture is sustained through language. Without language our means of learning would be greatly restricted. Like other animals we would have to learn by doing or by observing the behaviour of others. Our history would be lost, almost surely along with our ability to think. A human society without language would be reduced to the level of ape societies. Language makes it possible for man to build on his present culture as well as to maintain those traditions, skills, and items of knowledge that he values.

The materials in this section have been selected to emphasize the interplay between language and culture. The first two selections provide a more thorough development of the concept of culture. The next excerpts move from the development of man's language through the impact of the mass media (newspapers, television, radio) to the use of language in brainwashing techniques. Then we look at the implications of certain cultural differences in various parts of the world, and in particular at French-English differences in Canadian advertising. The last selections present some insights into cultural phenomena that have occurred over the past few years.

one   *The concept of culture*

There is tremendous diversity in the way of life of people throughout the world but, at the same time, there are striking similarities. In order to maintain his existence, man must perform certain functions wherever he is. Man must produce a social system that provides for the continuation of the species. Although men everywhere have the capacity for feeling pleasure, pain, fear, anger, and excitement, these responses can be triggered by quite different situations as a result of cultural influences. Our first selection summarizes elements that are common to all societies.

When we see a group of people together, we have little difficulty in understanding what is transpiring. But, in many instances, much of what is said and done takes place on the basis of interpretations of things that have not been said and actions that have not taken place. We learn to fill in the gaps as a result of exposure to our culture. The second selection demonstrates what happens when we speak and act in ways that are not culturally appropriate.

The concept of culture

M. J. Rice and W. C. Bailey

All animals, including man, have certain biological needs which must be met if the animals are to survive. Food and water are obvious biological requirements for the preservation of life. Protection from extremes of weather and from enemies are others. Furthermore, if a particular species of animal is to continue to exist, individual members of the species must live to produce more of their kind.

In order to satisfy their biological needs, all species of animals have gradually adapted to their environments. Environment includes all external and internal conditions affecting the existence, growth and welfare of the organism: for example, climate, food, and the presence of other animals. The porpoise is a mammal physically adapted for life in the water. The hummingbird's long beak is an adaptation enabling him to obtain food from flowers with deep petals. Nature manifests thousands of such adaptations.

No animal deliberately makes such adaptations to his environment. Such adaptations are the cumulative result of numerous random small changes in a species. All members of a given species vary slightly. Sometimes these slight variations prove to be an advantage to the individual in striving to meet biological needs. Individuals with such advantageous variations are more likely to live to reproduce, and the next generation is more likely to receive these advantageous variations through genetic inheritance. By means of such adaptations to the environment species gradually change. This species change through time is biological evolution.

Man, like other animals living today, is the product of a long series of changes. The fossil record indicates that while other animals were developing in specialized directions through the pressure of their surroundings, man remained relatively unspecialized and therefore not confined to a limited environment or diet. In

In his book *Universals of Culture*, the noted anthropologist, George P. Murdock, has listed the following items which he states have been found in every culture known to history.

separation by age	feasting
athletic sports	law
hospitality	tool making
family	personal names
luck superstitions	joking
taboos	hair styles
funerals	games
etiquette	penalties
courtship	fire making
language	division of labour
dancing	marriage
inheritance rules	decorative art
cooking	trade
housing	medicine
body adornment	mourning
meal times	calendar
folklore	gift giving
modesty concerning	education
natural functions	weather control
visiting	property rights
religion	puberty customs
cleanliness training	surgery
status differences	mythology
residence rules	faith healing
supernatural beings	kinship
cooperative labour	government
music	numbers
ethics	magic
weaning	

If we put together all that we have learned from anthropology and ethnography about primitive men and primitive society, we perceive that the first task of life is to live. . . .

. . . The struggle to maintain existence was carried on, not individually, but in groups. Each profited by the other's experience; hence there was concurrence toward that which proved to be most expedient. All at last adopted the same way for the same purpose; hence the ways turned into customs and became mass phenomena. . . . The young learn from them by tradition, imitation, and authority.

William Graham Sumner
Folkways : A Study of the Sociological Importance of Usages, Manners, Customs, Mores, and Morals

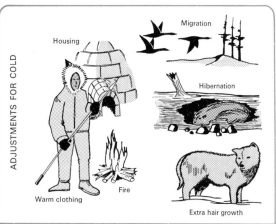

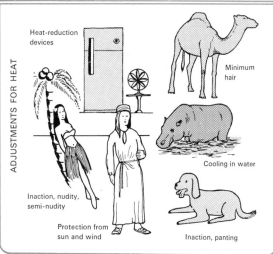

Culture in man replaces the biological adaptations of animals

fact, it has been said that man's only specialization was his unspecialized state which permits many adaptations.

What makes man unique biologically is his complex brain. The change in his brain resulted in a different kind of adaptation to his environment, one that seems more successful than the physical specializations of other animals. Man became a tool-making animal with the ability to communicate about the past and the future. He became the animal that attempts to control his environment rather than physically adapting to it. He could build from one invention to another and pass on knowledge from one generation to another. Man developed patterns of socially learned behavior, called *culture*. Through culture he was able to occupy and subdue many environments that would otherwise have been uninhabitable.

Culture is learned behavior that is passed on from one generation to the next. Animals other than man can individually learn, but can pass on to their offspring only a fraction of their experience, and this only through demonstration or in an immediate situation.

For example, kittens who see their mother kill rats are more likely to become ratters themselves than are kittens who have never seen rats killed. The kittens imitate their parent; but the limitation is limited to specific situations.

Only man, through language, can pass on to his offspring information and knowledge about situations before they are encountered. Boy Scouts study first aid in order to learn how to help injured people if an accident occurs. Man can solve problems in situations that he has not faced before. Man solves problems that are not immediately present in his environment, while animals solve only problems which immediately face them.

Our culture allows us to compress our knowledge in a symbol system. By reading we can follow the history of mankind in five minutes, two hours, or a lifetime of study, but we do not have to relive each crucial step. In the gathering and storage of knowledge, man, unlike the other animals, is not limited to the present. His culture gives him the experience of the past and prepares him for the future.

While there are cultural differences between people in different parts of the world, there are no differences in ability to learn culture. Any normal human child moved at birth to a new culture would learn the new culture as well as any child native to it. The ability of the children of immigrants to Canada to acquire the Canadian culture is one of the best indications that culture is learned.

A child acquires his culture in the process of learning a language. For example, as a Canadian child learns the word "father" or "Dad," he comes to associate this sound with a male member of his household who plays with him, provides for him and punishes him. The Hopi child learns the Hopi word for father and at the same time learns certain behavior which characterizes his father. Yet the Hopi child does not associate his word for father with punishment because in the Hopi culture the child's mother's brother is responsible for his discipline. The language reflects the culture and it is for this reason that it is sometimes difficult to separate the two.

Since language is the means of transmitting culture, both continuity and change in a culture can be seen in the language. All new ideas are verbalized and incorporated into a language, making language a mirror of cultural change.

For example, not all Indian tribes had chiefs or tribal councils. Many tribes had other institutionalized methods of decision-making. After conquest of the Indians, the United States government found it difficult to deal with these varying forms of leadership. As a result the tribes without chiefs or tribal councils were forced to adopt this form of leadership structure in order to deal with the government. In these tribes, new words were invented or borrowed to designate the new leadership positions, or an old word was applied to the new positions, thereby changing the meaning of the word. Thus the change in language accompanied a change in social structure.

Earlier we distinguished between material and attitudinal culture and showed that the two are but parts of a whole. There is a third element within the culture complex.

This third part, intertwined with the other two, is just as evident as visual culture but is often overlooked. It is composed of groups of people within the culture united for a purpose: the institutions. Major institutions center around the family (kinship), work, politics, and religion. Institutions have material and ideal culture to assist them in achieving their aims.

Two points about institutions should be noted. First, institutions in a culture are interlocking. For example, a change in one institution affects the others – an added example of the interdependencies of culture.

Second, language and art are a dimension of all institutions. Language is the vehicle for expressing the attitudes and aims of the institution. It is also the tool employed in the labeling of the social system. Material culture also expresses attitudes and social organization, as for example in artistic creations and in uniforms and insignia.

The learning of a culture is necessarily carried out through social relations between individuals. A child who never sees other humans remains without culture, on an animal level. While a child learns to do things and to speak, he learns at the same time a whole set of social obligations. That is, children behave as they do because their parents and others make demands on them.

Just as the child learns the language of his parents, he gains a knowledge of a set of social expectations. He learns that if he behaves in accord with these expectations, he is rewarded with approval, love, and food. If he does not act in accord with these expectations, he is punished or deprived in some way.

As a child matures, he comes into contact with an increasing number of people. In each case, social relations are established between the child and the new type of individual. The child learns the expected pattern of behavior for each social relationship, and is rewarded or punished in accord with how well he complies with these expectations. In this manner the child learns the structure

Among many preliterate peoples, there is a means of exchange of goods known as "silent trade", whereby trade is facilitated between two communities where each is fearful that its customs could be corrupted through open trade with another group. At a mutually agreeable point, equidistant from both communities, exchange of goods can take place. On a given day, one tribe will deposit its goods and will then return home. On the next day, the other tribe will pick up what it finds and leave its contribution to the exchange. And then on the third day, the first tribe will return and take what has been left there. By this mode of trade, no confrontation between the two communities takes place, and therefore the unique cultural identity of each group is protected.

Competition and Cooperation

Modern culture is economically based on the principle of individual competition. The isolated individual has to fight with other individuals of the same group, has to surpass them and, frequently, thrust them aside. The advantage of the one is frequently the disadvantage of the other . . . competitiveness, and the potential hostility that accompanies it, pervades all human relationships. . . . It pervades the relationships between men and men, between women and women, and whether the point of competition be popularity, competence, attractiveness, or any other social value it greatly impairs the possibilities of reliable friendship. . . .

Karen Horney
The Neurotic Personality of Our Time

Society is everywhere a control organization. Its function is to organize, integrate, and direct the energies resident in the individuals of which it is composed. One might, perhaps, say that the function of society was everywhere to restrict competition and by so doing bring about a more effective cooperation of the organic units of which society is composed.

Robert E. Park
"Human Ecology", *The American Journal of Sociology*, Vol. 42

Nevertheless, no society is exclusively competitive or exclusively cooperative. The very existence of highly competitive groups implies cooperation within the groups. Both competitive and cooperative habits must exist within the society. There is furious competition among the Kwakiutl at the one stratum of society – among the ranking chiefs – but within the household of each chief cooperation is mandatory for the amassing of the wealth that is distributed or destroyed.

Margaret Mead
Cooperation and Conflict Among Primitive Peoples

Many cultures teach children not to be competitive and not to attempt to out-perform their age-
mates but rather to cooperate and stay on a level
with their peers. Confronted with a test, such
children will not perform in the same way as those
taught to value winning. Schoolteachers in
Hawaii are often frustrated because homework is
considered a cooperative endeavor by their students and thus every member of a class may turn
in identical answers. On the mainland this might
be considered cheating. In the islands it is an
accepted way to solve problems.

J. F. Downs and H. K. Bleibtreu
Human Variation

Social scientists have contributed to the understanding of cooperation and competition. Their
observations have led to the following findings:

1) Competition tends to shape the attitudes of
   the competitors. Rivals for something of
   value frequently develop unfriendly and unfavourable attitudes toward one another. On
   the other hand, when individuals or groups
   pursue a common goal, cooperatively, friendly attitudes are likely to develop.

2) Competition often stimulates individuals and
   groups to their greatest achievements. Experiments have demonstrated that when
   employees in a manufacturing plant are
   placed in a situation in which they must
   compete for income and promotion, overall
   productivity is usually increased (although
   the quality of the product suffers at times).
   On the other hand, certain manufacturing
   operations are best handled by cooperation.
   On an assembly line it would not do for an
   employee to work at a faster pace than his
   fellow workers, for this would only upset the
   work rhythm and cut back on productivity.

3) Although the competitive spirit motivates
   much of our behaviour, the stimulus to compete is limited by certain factors:

   Some individuals and groups decline to enter
   a competitive situation, since one person or
   group will lose out to another or others.
   Competition creates anxieties; losing brings
   unhappiness and perhaps feelings of insecurity. For example, a young man who
   enjoys football may not try out for the school
   team lest he suffer frustration and extreme
   disappointment.

   Some people withdraw from competition
   after having lost out a number of times. Thus,
   the slow learner may eventually lose the
   incentive to compete for grades, and may
   even drop out of school rather than pit himself against pupils who achieve more.

of social relationships in his culture.

In all types of social organizations there exist rank or class differences between individuals. Few people of the world assume that all
men are equal. Within each social organization, there are traditional systems of ranking individuals and groups.

These systems of ranking may be based on cultural, language
and educational differences, as well as on economic and occupational position. Sometimes the traditional rank is fairly rigid, such
as the castes of India; or the distinction may be more fluid, such
as that separating the Spanish and Indian sub-cultures in South
America.

All institutions in a society maintain methods of recruiting
members, as well as reasons for membership. The reasons may be
those of age, sex, residence in a particular place, belief in a particular religion, or professional or occupational position.

In addition to birth, age, and residence, sex is used as one of the
bases for membership in groups. . . . An example of change in our
own society (in fact in Western society) is the opening of the professions and businesses to qualified women. Many former male-
only positions are in the hands of women. If the trend continues,
we may have female commercial pilots in this country (provided the dominant attitude towards the "woman driver" can be
changed). Publicized cases of women in unusual occupations, such
as the woman jockeys or female sportscar mechanics, or even
Josephine the plumber in television advertisements, reflect and
direct the change that is taking place.

Kinship groups control reproductive activity. Reproduction,
therefore, establishes certain relationships, as among husband,
wife, child, and in-laws. The aim of the kinship relationship is the
replacement of the population. The replacement of the population includes the education of the new members in the ways of the
culture.

A kinship group, it has been said, is unspecialized in the sense
that man is biologically unspecialized – it can adopt most readily
to a wide number of situations. All manner of social tasks can be
assigned to kinship groups, besides the primary one of replacing
the population. This is one reason why modern Western peoples
tend to underestimate the important of kinship.

Economics is the science of the production and distribution of
wealth. Economic institutions have to do with the relationship of
people to wealth.

There are institutions and social organizations behind the allo-
cation, production, and distribution of wealth. There are groups
having as their purpose the production of goods, and there are
groups concerned with the distribution of goods.

For instance, instead of accumulating material goods, many
hunting and gathering peoples accumulate obligations to share
food. When hunting is poor, one person or family unit will receive
part of the catch of the more successful hunter. Besides being a
form of economic insurance, the general hunter receives prestige
within his group.

Land ownership appears in some form in all cultures, but it is
not always the individual ownership familiar to Canadians. Mi-

gratory hunters and gatherers as well as herding peoples tend to regard the band of people who stay together as a land-holding unit. The band has rights to the land that its individuals occupy in the course of their yearly migrations. Ownership is only one of the possible relations of people to things.

Religion has been defined as a belief in supernatural beings. There is no record of a people who have been without belief in man-like creatures, animals, plants, or even inanimate objects, that are personified with a spirit or soul and which have some power over the destiny of ordinary men.

Religion serves to rationalize the unexplainable, and to give personal tranquility in times of stress. Many events are unpredictable and uncontrollable, and are therefore frightening. Religion, with its rituals and belief system, is one way of attempting some control and understanding of these frightening factors. Cultures differ as to what constitutes the unknown. People without our germ theory of disease will explain illness in other terms – witchcraft, evil spirits or bad air – and try to control it through healing rituals. Without knowledge of meteorology, the Hopi Indians believed that rain was brought by the gods. They used rituals to entreat the gods to bring rain.

The performance of ritual is the main function of most religious institutions. The anthropologist inquires as to the desired ends of the ritual and why those ends are desirable. Most often the answer includes the material of myths or, if the culture possesses writing, their scripture. Every society has such explanations about the unknown. There are, then, two sets of facts to be understood: 1) what the people do; and 2) what the people say about what they do and why they do it.

The important point to remember is that beliefs form a united structure which provides people with an explanation of all their experience. The beliefs are a group of premises upon which to base behavior.

Values are the ideas held by most people in culture. Values derive from the idea systems of all institutions. In some societies, of course, the value system may be identical with the idea system of the religious institution. Examples of individual values might be material achievement in North American culture, cooperation in Hopi culture, and masculinity (*machismo*) in Latin America.

The value system is transmitted to the individual in the growing-up process. It is learned. Behavior conforming with the ideal is rewarded, and non-conformity may be punished by ridicule, ostracism, or imprisonment. Behaviors in this way are invested with emotion. The emotional reactions of different peoples to different situations are determined by their value systems. Of course all human beings have the same physiological basis for common human emotions such as love, hate, joy, and sadness. The attachment of certain emotions to certain behavior patterns is, however, learned.

Although we speak of certain values predominating in certain cultures, not all individuals within these cultures hold the values in the same degree. Variation occurs from individual to individual, both in the degree to which their behavior conforms to the

John W. Bennett and Melvin Tumin make six observations about the competition-versus-cooperation controversy. Briefly, they are as follows. 1) Although society is at bottom a cooperative venture, neither cooperation nor competition can be said to be more natural to man. People can be taught to operate equally well in either a cooperative or a competitive situation. 2) All economies incorporate both cooperation and competition. 3) Most social situations involve both cooperation and competition even though some involve more of one than the other. 4) "Perfect" cooperation or competition never occurs in real life. 5) We know very little about the relative efficiency of these two approaches. 6) It is foolish to favour one of these as superior to the other until we know more about the effects of both cooperation and competition upon individuals and groups. We do know, however, that unrestricted competition is not fair, since people start from unequal beginnings. We know too that such competition produces frustration and other problems. But we need to know more about regulated competition and various forms of cooperation before a final choice can be made.

Differences in culture do not arise because different peoples have different inherited capabilities, but because they are brought up differently. We learn to speak, think, and act the way we do because of our daily associations, and when these change, our habits of speaking, thinking, and acting also change. Children have no culturally based ways of behaving at birth, they only acquire these as they grow up and as a result of a long and complicated process of learning.

Ralph L. Beals and Harry Hoijer
An Introduction to Anthropology

Geographical differences certainly play some part in bringing about cultural contrasts. Human beings adjust to the tropics by using different types of housing, clothing, and foods than those used by people in the Arctic regions. Therefore, we find interesting variations in most aspects of life in these two regions. It is risky, however, to imply that geographical contrasts explain cultural contrasts. Man has the ability to control his physical environment in remarkable ways. This is particularly true of modern man, whose technological know-how makes it possible for him to transform both the tropic and the Arctic regions to suit his needs and support his urban culture patterns. Urban man behaves much the same whether he is living in one climate or in another. Furthermore, it is not uncommon to find people living in the same geographical area who behave quite differently from each other.

While we accept certain cultural values as appropriate, as important for our own course of becoming, it is equally true that we are all rebels, deviants, and individualists. Some elements in our culture we reject altogether; many we adopt as mere opportunistic habits, and even those elements that we genuinely *appropriate* we refashion to fit our own personal style of life. Culture is a condition of becoming but is not itself the full stencil.

Gordon W. Allport
*Becoming: Basic Considerations
for a Psychology of Personality*

Norms

Norms are *ideas* in the minds of members of a group that specify what the members of others *ought to do under specific circumstances*. They are *ideas*, not actual behaviour. About what men *ought* to do, not necessarily actually do. Under *specific* circumstances, not all circumstances.

A. G. Athos and R. E. Coffey
Behavior in Organizations

Norms are the culturally acquired ends or guideposts of social interaction and social order. Probably the greatest single difference between the social organizations of the "lower" orders of life such as ants, bees, and chimpanzees and the social organization of man is that the latter alone is oriented to norms rather than to basal, biologically inherited needs and drives.

Human behaviour is overwhelmingly normative behaviour, normative in the strict sense that it is not primarily directed to, or even actuated by, the physical or biological or "natural" – to use a word here once cherished in philosophical discussions of morality.

Robert A. Nisbet
The Social Bond

A group of workers might have a norm that could be stated, "You shouldn't help the boss any more than necessary." Another group might approach the same situation with a different norm, "You should help the boss as long as it doesn't hurt the group." Clearly, in every situation it is up to the individual to determine if his behaviour is desirable according to the group's norms. In fact, the individual has some margin of choice in his behaviour as it relates to the boss. The decision he makes can be either pleasant or unpleasant, depending on the individual's need for acceptance by the members of the group and on his understanding of the particular situation.

expected behavior pattern, and the degree to which they attach emotions to the behavior.

Values tend to be conservative. Changes in values are more strongly resisted than changes in technology or economics. Because culture consists of interrelated components, changes in technology or economics tend to cause changes in all other aspects of culture. Some of these changes may affect the cultural values – that is, they may result in change in certain behavior patterns to which strong emotional response is connected. Outsiders may regard members of a culture as irrational in resisting certain changes, but to the individuals within the culture, such changes might be in conflict with the central values which they hold most dear.

The preceding sections have concentrated on important aspects of culture: language, technology, economy, social organization, religion and values. It was useful to divide culture in this way for descriptive purposes, but such divisions are only an analytical tool – they rarely exist in the actual operation of a culture.

If a yam farmer (Melanesian) is asked what is necessary to insure a good crop, he will give a description of the techniques of planting plus the rituals necessary to insure the cooperation of the supernatural. We may divide the ritual practices from the technique of planting, saying that one is necessary and the other is not. Such a division may not exist in the farmer's mind. The ritual and the techniques of planting are equally important to him, and both are part of the same process of growing a crop.

The use of such terms as "economy" or "religion" as descriptive tools should not obscure the fact that culture is a unified whole. Each aspect is closely related to all other aspects.

The Kazak people of Central Asia can serve as an illustration. The Kazak herd horses and sheep, their major sources of food. Their technology consists primarily of techniques for caring for their herds. During most of the year grass is sparse, and the Kazak must split into small bands so that their herds will have enough to eat.

This necessity is reflected in their social organization, dealing primarily with the household, which is the smallest unit that can stay together and still accomplish all the tasks necessary for survival. Livestock are not only the basic measure of wealth and social prestige; they are also used to bind groups together as social units. To obtain a wife, sheep and horses are given to the bride's parents. These same sheep and horses may be used by the bride's parents as gifts to secure a wife for their son. In this way, the exchange of livestock is a guarantee of good faith, helping to bind together families which have become related through marriage.

The herding economy also influences the cultural values of the Kazak. Cooperation within the basic living unit, the household, is necessary for the preservation of the herds and the continuation of life on the steppe. The constant migration, necessary to secure food for the herd, makes each household strongly independent in its daily activities. As a result, cooperation with the local group and independence of all outsiders are two important values of the Kazak people. The value of cooperation tends to reinforce the social organization and thereby facilitate the herding economy.

In all cultures there is a tendency for all aspects of the culture to reinforce one another, thereby fulfilling the personal needs of the individual and the maintenance of the social group. As a result, the total culture is more than just the sum of its parts, just as a human being is more than the sum of his body. Each individual part of a culture is linked together into an intricate structure comprising that common interest of the individuals holding the culture.

Culture is the learned behavior that enables the individual man to face the problems of existence – to adapt to and control his total environment.

Culture in daily living

There are many aspects of our culture that we have come to accept without really noticing that we have accepted them. We learn to fill gaps in conversations with the knowledge we have learned about our culture. We learn to expect certain things in certain situations, and when we do not find them, we become quite concerned. In this section we would like to draw on the work of Alfred Schutz and Harold Garfinkel to show how our expectations of what will take place in a situation are in many cases present but unnoticed.

The following is an example of a conversation that might have taken place between a boy and a girl of high-school age. On the left-hand side of the page is the conversation, and on the right-hand side of the page, the hidden meaning is presented.

Bill:
Hi, Sharon! Hey – what did you think of that football game yesterday?

Bill is not particularly interested in football, but there is a dance Friday night, and he would like to take Sharon to it. If possible, he would like to set it up so that he does not have to ask her directly.

Sharon:
Hi! Yeah, the game was great. We bombed them, eh!

Sharon does not know yet what Bill wants. This is the first time that Bill has struck up a personal conversation with her outside their mutual group of friends. Since she regularly attends football games, Bill's introductory remark was well chosen.

Bill:
Those two touchdowns by Garry in the last quarter were out-of-sight. There's a football dance Friday night, eh? That last one was a ball!

Sharon now knows that Bill would like to take her to the football dance. She does not know yet whether Bill is going to ask her directly or not. She likes Bill and would not mind

There are norms that have wider implications. They are part of the broader culture and tend to force people to respond in the same way to certain situations. Yet at the same time, because they apply to all men in a given culture, they are often stated so inexactly that the individual has lots of freedom of decision. For example, a norm common to all cultures is that all men should be honest. Often the norms of a particular group make it difficult to follow this norm. Some factory workers have an understanding, recognized by the group, that it is all right to take home the occasional thing from the factory – that this is in line with their relationship with their superiors and their assessment of their position. In fact, many factory managers assume that this will take place. So we have a group norm taking precedence over the cultural norm of honesty. Another example of the same type is related to cheating in school. In one Asiatic country, cheating is a way of life in college and although students recognize that the behaviour is dishonest, over the years the practice has modified the cultural norm.

The debate between those who urge disarmament and those who recommend military preparedness symbolizes modern man's attempt to create a new set of ideas which can govern his behaviour in the light of contemporary change. As these new ideas emerge and become accepted and formalized on a world-wide basis, we will be witnessing the development of culture as a product of changes in group life.

Ritchie P. Lowry and Robert P. Rankin
Sociology : The Science of Society

A nuclear weapon, a high-rise office building, a pattern of family life, religion, friendship, morality, language, life style generally, as well as each of the prescribed ways we interact with others, is a part of culture. Beliefs, codes of law, systems of philosophy, esthetic, moral, and utilitarian values, all of these as well as the sundry machines, gadgets, and physical structures we find in all human societies are culture. Behind each is a way of thought or behaviour that has been learned.

Robert A. Nisbet
The Social Bond

Beethoven may have had musical talent, but his music built on the technical and artistic accomplishment of Western civilization and particularly on the high value placed upon music in contemporary Germany.

Walter Goldschmidt
Exploring the Ways of Mankind

Reward and Punishment Systems in Our Society

Reward	Punishment
If you expend your energy the way we want you to,	
you'll get . . .	if you don't,
	you'll get . . .

Business

A job	Fired
Advancement	No promotion
Salary increases	No raises
Prestige	Non-recognition
Security	Insecurity

Educational Institutions

Acceptance	Non-acceptance
Advancement	Non-advancement
Graduation	Expelled
Higher degrees	No degrees
Chance for a	Poorer job
better job	

Political Institutions

Participation	Ineligibility
Appointment	Passed over
Elected	Defeated
Honour	Obscurity

Military

Accepted	Not accepted
Promotion	Passed over
Permanent rank	Temporary rank
Medals and honors	Court-martialed
Retirement at rank	Dishon. discharge

Social and Fraternal Clubs
(Rotary, Chamber of Commerce)

Acceptance	Blackballed
Exposure to others	Excluded
Committee work	Not appointed
Officer position	Not elected
Retirement banquet	Expulsion

Don Fabun, *Communications*

A society is people with common ends getting along with one another. A brawl in a barroom is not a society, nor is there yet a society when ten exhausted shipwrecked sailors clamber up on a lonely beach – at least there is none until they begin to work out their common problems of getting a living and of living together. A society has, then, organization. It is people doing things with and to and for each other to the interests of each and all in ways that those people have come to accept.

Robert Redfield
"How Human Society Operates" in
Exploring the Ways of Mankind

Sharon:
Oh, I didn't have too much fun at the last one. I was with Red – he's a bit of a drag, you know. But I guess he's okay. I said I'd go to the dance with him this Friday, but that's *it* for me with him. Are you going?

Bill:
I'm not sure I'll be able to make it – but if I do, maybe I'll see you there, eh? Hey, I've got to get to class. See you later.

Sharon:
'Bye, Bill!

dating him, but she already has a date for this dance. Her mind is now developing a strategy by which she can refuse Bill for this dance and yet still encourage him to ask her for another date.

Sharon has answered Bill's unstated question about going to the dance with him. She has told him that she is going with someone else, but has made it quite clear that she will be available for a date in the future.

Although Bill still does not have a date for Friday night, he does know that Sharon is a future possibility. He has been able to get his answer indirectly, without having to face a direct "No".

It is quite clear from the above conversation that:

1) there were many things that the two students *understood* they were talking about but did not mention – in fact, did not *want* to mention;

2) many of the unspoken messages were understood not only because of what *was* said, but also because of what *was not* said;

3) the reason the two understood each other so well was because they had learned through their culture to expect certain signals to be present in a conversation between a boy and a girl. They were watching for those expected signals;

4) each of the two knew what was taking place, and was quite willing to let it follow its course.

Our culture has provided us with the skills to understand such conversations. But if we were asked how we knew what was taking place, we might have a hard time explaining it.

There are other interesting aspects of the conversation between Sharon and Bill:

1) Both speakers had to figure out the meaning and purpose of each other's words.

2) Both speakers were deliberately vague, because neither wanted to face the question directly: Bill did not *want* "No" for an answer – and Sharon did not want to *give* "No" for an answer.

3) The *order* of the speakers' comments was important, because as the conversation developed, it aided both participants in understanding the *real* meaning of what was being said.

Many of our conversations with other people have this vagueness, this lack of dealing directly with the issues. We soon learn that other people fill in the gaps in our conversations and that we can duck embarrassing issues. After a while, we take this gap-filling process for granted. But what happens when somebody demands that these conversational gaps be filled – that the other person be more specific? The following cases provide a good illustration of what probably would happen.

Case 1

Ed: Hi, George. How are things going?

George: What do you mean, how are things going? Do you mean at school, or with my girlfriend, or what?

Ed: I mean, how are things going? You know, how are things going for you? What's the matter with you anyway?

George: Nothing's the matter with *me*. I just want to know what it is that *you* want to know, and then I'll try to answer your question.

Ed: Forget it! How are you doing with Carol?

George: What do you mean by that question?

Ed: *You* know what I mean.

George: No, I don't.

Ed: Do you feel all right, George?

Case 2

Barbara: Those movie stars are all the same.

Gail: In what way are they all the same?

Barbara: You know – in the way they live.

Gail: What way do they live?

Barbara: Oh, you know – fooling around and everything.

Gail: What do you mean by fooling around?

Barbara: Aw, come on. *You* know what I mean by fooling around.

Gail: No, I *really* don't.

Barbara: What's the matter with you? You do so know what I mean!

Gail: Can't you be more specific?

Barbara: How would you like to get lost?

When a person acts differently from what is expected of him, he can create considerable confusion in the minds of other people. Garfinkel conducted an interesting experiment with his university students, which effectively demonstrated this point. He asked the students to play out the role of a boarder in their own home, for a short period of time. The students were instructed to be particularly polite, to avoid getting personal, to speak formally, and to speak only when spoken to.

In one way or another esthetic pleasure is felt by all members of mankind. No matter how diverse the ideals of beauty may be, the general character of the enjoyment of beauty is of the same order everywhere; the crude song of the Siberians, the dance of the African Negroes, the pantomime of the California Indians, the stone work of the New Zealanders, the carvings of the Melanesians, the sculpture of the Alaskans, appeal to them in a manner not different from that felt by us when we hear a song, when we see an artistic dance, or when we admire ornamental work, painting or sculpture.

Franz Boas
The Esthetic Experience" in
Exploring the Ways of Mankind

The individual does not choose his culture, any more than he chooses his parents. He is born to it. (Of course, a few persons in the modern world renounce their heritage, insofar as they can, and adopt a new country and culture.) Therefore, what the individual is, what he does, what he wears, what he yearns for and cherishes and what he rejects and despises, is set for him by his culture.

Walter Goldschmidt
Exploring the Ways of Mankind

In her book, *Our Inner Conflicts*, the well-known psychiatrist Karen Horney pointed out three contradictions in modern society:

On the one hand everything is done to spur us toward success, which means that we must be not only assertive but aggressive, able to push others out of the way. On the other hand we are deeply imbued with ideals which declare that it is selfish to want anything for ourselves, that we should be humble, turn the other cheek, be yielding....

Secondly, for economic reasons needs are constantly being stimulated in our culture by such means as advertisements, "conspicuous consumption", the ideal of "keeping up with the Joneses". For the great majority, however, the actual fulfillment of these needs is closely restricted. The psychic consequence for the individual is a constant discrepancy between his desires and their fulfillment.

Thirdly, the individual is told by society that he is free, independent, can decide his life according to his own free will; "the great game of life" is open to him, and he can get what he wants if he is efficient and energetic. In actual fact, for the majority of people all these possibilities are limited.... The result for the individual is a wavering between a feeling of boundless power in determining his own fate and a feeling of entire helplessness.

The human animal is a gregarious creature. He very rarely lives alone and if he does he seldom appears to like it. Human populations cluster in groups, and the larger, more stable, and more self-sufficient of these we call societies. Every one of these societies can be described in terms of size, location, man–land adjustments, networks and frequencies of interactions between members, and other such attributes.

Mary Ellen Goodman
The Individual and Culture

Entire systems of behavior made up of hundreds of thousands of details are passed from generation to generation, and nobody can give the rules for what is happening. Only when the rules are broken do we realize they exist. . . . The principal agent is a *model* used for imitation.

Edward T. Hall
The Silent Language

Cultural behaviour ranges from simple acts such as eating with a fork or with chopsticks, or tying a shoelace, to complex mathematical operations and philosophical speculation. A baseball game, an Iroquois game of lacrosse, the wearing of wooden sandals by Japanese, and a prayer meeting are cultural behavior of the participating individuals. The duties of the president and the techniques of safe-cracking, the forms of matrimony and the forms of parliamentary law — all are patterns of behavior learned individually by each person concerned.

Douglas G. Haring
Personal Character and Cultural Milieu

Here we join with those who see culture as one of the several major factors which, taken together, constitute the individual's whole background and context. In this view culture is not *the determinant* of behavior. Culture is, rather, one of the foundations and boundary conditions upon and within which the individual and his potentialities develop. It is an indispensable condition of becoming human, and a powerful force inclining the individual toward humanness of a certain variety and within certain limits.

Mary Ellen Goodman
The Individual and Culture

In eighty per cent of the situations, the families of the students were unable to understand what was happening – they were stupefied; they tried hard to understand, to restore things to normal. Reports from the students about how their families responded to their playing the role of a boarder ranged from astonishment, through shock, to outright anger. The families typically made charges that the students were mean, selfish, inconsiderate, nasty, and impolite. But remember – all that the students were doing was acting politely and impersonally, as a boarder would. Yet members of the families wanted an explanation of why the students were acting so strangely, and asked questions like:

"What's the matter?"
"What's gotten into you?"
"Are you sick?"
"What are you being so superior about?"
"Why are you mad?"
"Are you out of your mind or just stupid?"

One mother got angry because her daughter (as the boarder) asked if she could get a little snack from the refrigerator. The mother replied, "Mind if you have a little snack? You've been eating snacks around here for years without asking me. What's gotten into you?" Another woman, whose daughter spoke only when she was spoken to, angrily accused her daughter of being disrespectful. A father said his daughter was inconsiderate and acted like a spoiled child.

The parents tried to explain why their children were acting in such an odd way, with reasons such as:

"He must be working too hard in school."
"He wasn't feeling well."
"He must have had a fight with his girlfriend."

When this did not result in any change or response on the part of the student (still acting as a boarder), the family members would isolate the student. They would say things like:

"Don't bother with him. He's in one of his moods again."
"Why must you always create trouble in our family?"

When the students explained to their families what they had been doing, it was always accepted – but the family was not amused; they did not find it particularly funny to have been part of an experiment. You can see from this experiment that we learn to expect how a person will act in a given situation – in this case, with his family. When a person does not act in the expected way, we try to find an explanation for the behavior, and become quite anxious and even angry when we cannot understand it.

Other studies have been done which show that your conversational *attitude* toward a person is important. If you give a person the impression that you mistrust him when he says something, or even that you are doubtful about what he is saying, you can make him quite angry. Responses on your part, such as, "You don't really mean that, do you?" or "Are you sure?" could suggest to him either that you wonder whether he is "kidding" you or that you do, in act, doubt what he is saying. In either case, he is unlikely to appreciate the mistrust.

In one study, a group of students were asked to engage someone in conversation and to try to act as though the other person was trying to trick them or mislead them. The students found it quite difficult to play out this role, because they could not "live the part". Only two of the students tried it with strangers and, in both cases, they quickly became embarrassed. In one of these cases, a student kept asking a bus driver to be sure to stop at her street. The bus driver finally said, "Look, I told you once that I would, didn't I; how many times do I have to tell you?"

When the students explained what they were doing, it usually eased the situation that had been created – but this was not true in all cases. One student, playing out her role of implying mistrust, asked her husband if he really *had* worked late the night before, and if he really *had* played poker with the boys the previous week. Although she did not directly accuse him of having lied, she was suggesting that an explanation was required. The husband asked her what she was talking about, and she accused him of avoiding the question. Even after she explained that what she was doing was just part of an experiment, he stalked away quite unhappily. He knew it had been just an experiment, but he could see that it would be quite easy to get into a difficult situation, even though one might not desire the implied mistrust. It left him quite disturbed and also uneasy about his own wife.

It appears quite clear that, in our relations with others, we must give the impression of accepting what they are saying if we are to retain their good will. Mistrust leads to anxiety, followed by anger on the part of the person mistrusted. And so, another thing that our culture has taught us is that unless we are prepared to upset or hurt others, we must accept what others say as truth, when in their presence.

The above are only a few examples of everyday situations that are shaped by what we *expect* to take place in given situations. Much of what we learn in our Canadian way of life is related to what to expect in a given situation. We do not write these things down, nor do we learn them directly. They develop as part of living in Canadian society.

No matter how meager its economic productivity, every sociocultural system has offered a goodly number of opportunities for creativity: supernaturalism, humor, singing, dance, basketry perhaps, and doubtless many others . . . [but] such inventiveness could not be cumulative and survive into modern times until the crucial invention of writing. . . .

Melville Jacobs
Patterns in Cultural Anthropology

The telephone girl who lends her capacities, during the greater part of the living day, to the manipulation of a technical routine that has an eventually high efficiency value but that answers to no spiritual needs of her own is an appalling sacrifice to civilization. As a solution of the problem of culture she is a failure – the more dismal the greater her natural endowment. . . .

The American Indian who solves the economic problem with salmon-spear and rabbit-snare operates on a relatively low level of civilization, but he represents an incomparably higher solution than our telephone girl of the questions that culture has to ask of economics.

Edward Sapir
"Culture, Genuine and Spurious" in
Exploring the Ways of Mankind

The popular notion remains that the temperament of a people is determined by the climate; that the dourness of the Scot and the volatility of the Italian derive from the gloom and fog in one area and the sunshine and warmth in the other. But such a correlation cannot be sustained when we examine the world-wide distribution of human behavior.

Walter Goldschmidt
Exploring the Ways of Mankind

The genuine culture is not of necessity either high or low; it is merely inherently harmonious, balanced, self-satisfactory. It is the expression of a richly varied and yet somehow unified and consistent attitude toward life, an attitude which sees the significance of any one element of civilization in its relation to all others. It is, ideally, a culture in which nothing is spiritually meaningless, in which no important part of the general functioning brings with it a sense of frustration, of misdirected or unsympathetic effort.

Edward Sapir
"Culture, Genuine and Spurious" in
Exploring the Ways of Mankind

two   How man communicates

A few years ago there was one popular song entitled "The Sound of Silence", and another, "The Language of Love". These songs represent attempts to *communicate* with musical sounds and words. Man has a large array of communicating devices, particularly in the modern electronics field. Yet most communication can be defined simply as words or numbers being used to convey a message. Man has refined his ability to communicate, using words and silent language, such as symbols, gestures, and postures. Much of our reality is tied to language: our social values, customs, attitudes, and behaviour are influenced by language. The philosopher uses language to convey an abstract thought. The mathematician puts a problem into symbols. A musician uses musical notes to communicate his composition. A baby, before he learns to speak, conveys only basic messages about his needs, but as his language skills develop, so does his understanding of the reality of life. A child who is deaf or has a speech difficulty works very hard to overcome his disability in order to share in communication through language. Wherever he is on this planet, man uses some kind of language to communicate. A study of language reveals interesting social and cultural implications.

Our first selection shows how language is related to the way in which various groups of men interpret their world and use language to describe their experience and those things which they value highly. The second selection focuses on the symbols and arrangements man has created to communicate and to define basic relationships.

Theories of the Origin of Speech

Speech is an attempt to make our thoughts and feelings understandable to others. There have been many theories of how speech originated, but most of these have been abandoned by serious scholars. The noted anthropologist Ashley Montagu has summarized some of these interesting theories in his book *Man: His First Two Million Years*:

1) The *bow-wow* theory: This theory states that speech is imitative of sounds such as the barking of dogs and other animals.

2) The *pooh-pooh* theory: This theory states that speech comes from instinctive responses caused by pain, heat or cold, happiness, sadness, and other intense feelings or sensations.

3) The *dingdong* theory: This theory states that there is a kind of magical harmony between the sound of something and our sensory impression of it. For every impression we feel something within ourselves and there is an appropriate expression which we can use for it. This might be stated, "Everything that is struck rings. Each substance has its peculiar ring."

Language, the definition of reality

Benjamin Lee Whorf

Each of us interprets the physical world about us and we use language to express what we see and experience. We interpret the world, and our ability to communicate what we experience depends on our ability to use language in a way which others can also understand. Yet language also imposes a structure on what we can explain. To talk at all requires us to participate in an unstated agreement about what words mean when we use them. Our language has a term "double talk", to describe a speech pattern which does not follow the rules. When we speak a language we are in effect bound by that language and the cultural traditions implied in it.

While people may observe the same physical evidence, their interpretation of that evidence is by no means uniform. Only where there is a common language background does a common interpretation develop. Language creates a different interpretation of the world according to the language background an individual has and even when an individual speaks several languages he may not be able to interpret an event as the individuals of each language community would. For example, an Englishman who spoke Chinese, Arabic, and Hindu might still interpret physical evidence as the English language community would do.

The dialects of modern Europe are built upon a common ancient Indo-European language spoken centuries ago by the original inhabitants of the present-day area of Europe and the Black Sea region. The intellectual and scientific thought of Europe was based on Greek and Latin which in turn came originally from this ancient Indo-European language. Thus, when we describe the world we may do so in different dialects of the same basic language group which has developed over thousands of years. Modern scientists describe the world in the same terms but they do so because they are using a common language background of Western Europe. A Chinese or Turkish scientist also describes the world in these terms. He does so because he has accepted the entire system of explanations put forward by Western scientists. The Chinese or Turkish scientist has not begun his study separately from western scientists using a different language base, rather he has accepted the western view for the purpose of scientific explanation.

When Semitic, Chinese, Tibetan, or African languages are contrasted with our own it becomes apparent that these people interpret the world differently according to their language background. For thousands of years the languages of the American native population developed independently of each other and the rest of the world. Some observers have concluded that the interpretations of nature made by these language groups show a limited understanding of nature because they differ in their views and expression from the western European language groups. To limit the evidence offered by these languages in this way would be like expecting a botanist to study nothing but hot house roses and food plants and then to tell us what the plant world is like.

Let us consider a few examples. In English we divide most of our words into two classes, which have different grammatical and logical properties. Class 1 we call nouns, e.g., "house", "man"; Class 2, verbs, e.g., "hit", "run". Many words of one class can be placed in the other class, e.g., "a hit", "a run", or "to man" the boat, but on the lowest level the division between the classes is absolute. Our language thus gives us a division of nature. But nature herself is not thus divided. If it be said that strike, turn, run are verbs because they denote temporary or short-lasting events or actions, why then is fist a noun? It also is a temporary event. Why are lightning, spark, wave, eddy, flame, storm, phase, cycle, spasm, noise, emotion, nouns? They are temporary events. If man and house are nouns because they are long-lasting and stable events or things, what then are keep, extend, project, continue, persist, grow, dwell and so on, doing among the verbs? If it is said that possess and cling are verbs because they are stable relationships rather than stable things, why then should equilibrium, pressure, current, peace, group, nation, society, tribe, sister, be among the nouns? It will be found that an "event" to *us* means "what our language classes as a verb". And it will be found that it is not possible to define an event, thing, object, or relationship from nature, but that to define them always involves a return to the categories of the definer's language.

In the Hopi language, lightning, wave, flame, meteor, puff of smoke, pulsation, are verbs – events of necessarily brief duration cannot be anything but verbs. Cloud and storm are at about the lower limit of duration for nouns. Hopi, you see, actually has a

4) The *yo-he-ho* theory: This theory states that words first came into being as a result of the expressions we make following strong muscular effort such as moving heavy objects and swinging from tree to tree. The body was relieved by letting the air come out strongly, producing sounds such as "heave" and "haul".

5) The *gestural* theory: This theory states that speech came about when men tried to imitate with their voices the gestures they were making with their bodies in order to communicate with people.

6) The *tarara-boom-de-ay* theory: This theory states that speech began when man's early vocal activities tended toward a meaningless humming or singing. When a group of early men succeeded in bringing down an animal, they would have been filled with joy and strike up a chant of success something like "tarara-boom-de-ay". The sounds of this chant could have come to mean, "We have brought the beast down, hurrah. Let's give thanks."

The basic vocabulary of human languages appears to retain about 80 per cent of the total words evolved over a thousand years. Morris Swadesh summarizes this trend as follows.

	% / 1,000 yrs.
Middle Egyptian 2100–1700 B.C. to Coptic A.D. 300–500	76
Classic Latin 50 B.C. to present-day Romanian	77
Old High German A.D. 850 to present-day German	78
Classic Chinese A.D. 950 to modern colloquial North Chinese	79
Latin of Plautus 200 B.C. to French of Molière A.D. 1650	79
Dominica Carib of A.D. 1650 to present day	80
Classic Latin 50 B.C. to present-day Portuguese	82
Koiné to present-day Cypriote	83
Koiné to present-day Athenian	84
Classic Latin 50 B.C. to present-day Italian	85
Old English A.D. 950 to present-day English	85
Latin of Plautus 200 B.C. to Spanish of A.D. 1600	85

Morris Swadesh
"Lexico Statistic Dating of Prehistoric Ethnic Contacts"
Proceedings of the American Philosophic Society, Vol. 96

Considerable variation exists from language to language in terms used for common animals. The following variations on the English word "dog" illustrate this:

English – dog   German   – hund
Greek   – kynos   Apache   – guse
Italian – cane   Hawaiian – ilio
Latin   – canis   Japanese – inu
Russian – cooaka   Samoan   – maile
Chinese – kou   Tahitian – uli
(Peking)

If the difference between human and animal communication had to be summarized in one word, a good choice for that word would be novelty. Every time a bee communicates the location of a supply of nectar, it is repeating a variant of one basic message that has already been transmitted among bees countless times. When an animal gives a call warning others of its kind that danger is imminent, it does not make up a new one; the call is one that these animals have used many times before. There is no novelty here, only a repetition of past communicative events. . . .

[In human language] Almost every sentence which occurs is a novel one and has never occurred before.

Ronald W. Langacker
Language and Its Structure

Contrast between a "temporal" language (English) and a "timeless" language (Hopi)

classification of events by duration type, something strange to our way of thought. On the other hand, in Nootka, a language of Vancouver Island, all words seem to us to be verbs, but really there are no nouns and verbs; we have a view of nature that gives us only one class of word for all kinds of events. "A house occurs" or "it houses" is the way of saying "house", exactly like "a flame occurs" or "it burns". These terms seem to us like verbs because they provide information on how long something has lasted or will last, so that the suffixes of the word for house event make it mean long-lasting house, temporary house, future house, house that used to be, what started out to be a house and so on.

Hopi has a noun that covers everything that flies, with the exception of birds, for which there is another noun. The former noun may be said to describe flying class minus bird. The Hopi actually call insect, airplane, and aviator all by the same word, and feel no difficulty about it. The situation determines the intended meaning. "Flying class minus bird" seems to us too large and inclusive, but so would our class "snow" to an Eskimo. We have the same word for falling snow, snow on the ground, snow packed hard like ice, slushy snow, wind-driven flying snow – whatever the situation may be. To an Eskimo, this all-inclusive word would be almost unthinkable; he would say that falling snow, slushy snow, and so on, are very different things, to be treated in different ways. He uses different words for them and for other kinds of snow. The Aztecs go even farther than we in the opposite direction, with cold, ice, and snow all represented by the same basic word with different terminations: ice is the noun form; cold, the adjective; and for snow, "ice mist".

What is more surprising to find is that various ideas of the Western world, such as time, speed, and matter, are not essential to the construction of a consistent picture of the world. For example, Hopi may be called a timeless language. It recognizes psychological time, which is much like "duration", but this "time" is quite unlike the mathematical time, T, used by our physicists. Three peculiar properties of Hopi time are that it varies with each observer, it does not allow for the idea that another event could be taking place at the same time, and it cannot be given a number greater than one. The Hopi do not say, "I stayed five days", but "I left on the fifth day". A word referring to this kind of time, like the word day, can have no plural. The accompanying picture will give mental exercise to anyone who would like to figure out how the Hopi verb gets along without tenses. Actually, the only practical use of our tenses, in one-verb sentences, is to distinguish among five typical situations, which are shown in the picture. The timeless Hopi verb does not distinguish between the present, past, and future of the event itself but must always indicate what type of validity the *speaker* intends the statement to have: (a) report of an event (situations 1, 2, 3 in the picture); (b) expectation of an event (situation 4); (c) law about events (situation 5). Situation 1, where the speaker and listener both see the same thing, is divided by our language into the two conditions, 1*a* and 1*b*, which is calls present and past, respectively. This division is unnecessary for a language which assures one that the statement is a report.

Hopi grammar, by means of its forms, makes it easy to distinguish between momentary, continued, and repeated events, and to indicate the actual sequence of reported events. Thus the world can be described without reference to the idea of time that we use. How would a physics, constructed along these lines work, with no *T* (time) in its equations? Perfectly, as far as I can see, though of course it would require different ideas and perhaps different mathematics. Of course *V* (velocity) would have to go too. The Hopi language has no word to convey the idea of this word that, in our language, means "speed". What translates these terms is usually a word meaning intense or very, accompanying any verb of motion. Here is a clue to the nature of our new physics. We may have to introduce a new term *I*, intensity. Every thing and event will have an *I*, whether we regard the thing or event as moving or as just enduring or being. Perhaps the *I* of an electric charge will turn out to be its voltage, or potential. We shall use clocks to measure some intensities, or, rather, some *relative* intensities, for the absolute intensity of anything will be meaningless. Our old friend acceleration will still be there but under a new name. We shall perhaps call it *V*, meaning not velocity but variation. Perhaps all growths and accumulations will be regarded as *V*'s. We should not have the idea of rate in the time sense, since, like velocity, rate introduces the idea of a mathematical and language time. Of course we know that all measurements are ratios, but the measurements of intensities made by comparison with the standard intensity of a clock or a planet we do not treat as ratios, any more than we treat a distance made by comparison with a yardstick.

A scientist from another culture that used time and velocity would have great difficulty in getting us to understand these ideas. We would talk about the intensity of a chemical reaction; he would speak of its velocity or its rate, which words we should at first think were simply words for intensity in his language. Likewise, he at first would think that intensity was simply our own word for velocity. At first we should agree, later we should begin to disagree, and it might dawn upon both sides that different systems of understanding were being used. He would find it very hard to make us understand what he really meant by velocity of a chemical reaction. We should have no words that would fit. He would try to explain it by likening it to a running horse, to the difference between a good horse and a lazy horse. We should try to show him, with a superior laugh, that his example also was a matter of different intensities, aside from which there was little similarity between a horse and a chemical reaction in a beaker. We should point out that a running horse is moving relative to the ground, whereas the material in the beaker is at rest.

One significant contribution to science from the point of view of language may be the greater development of our sense of perspective. We shall no longer be able to see a few recent dialects of the Indo-European language family, and the thought patterns of Western Europe and America as the crowning achievement of the human mind. Nor can it be said that present widespread use is due to any superiority on our part or to anything, but a few events of history, that could be called fortunate only from a very narrow

Some scientists working with dolphins have stated that this aquatic mammal does indeed have a language. However, it would appear that dolphin language is based on entirely different principles than human languages. While any person can learn another human language, some scientists who have been working for years with dolphins are uncertain that a language even exists and even less positive that they can really understand anything a dolphin "says".

J. F. Downs and H. K. Bleibtreu
Human Variation

. . . recent experiments with porpoises (which come closest to man in the ratio of brain size to body mass) suggest that we are not quite so unusual in our linguistic ability as we once thought. It is interesting to note that neither man nor the porpoise has any special language organ. The sounds with which we communicate are made by the same set of organs found in one form or another in all mammals : lips, teeth, palate, tongue, nasal passage, vocal cords, and lungs. No mammal is without these or without the ability to make sounds, but only man (and perhaps the porpoise) can communicate with language. . . .

J. F. Downs and H. K. Bleibtreu
Human Variation

If we should withdraw from men their language, sciences, arts, and moral beliefs, they would drop to the level of animals. The characteristic attributes of human nature come from society. But on the other hand, society exists and lives only in and through individuals. If the idea of society were extinguished in the individual mind, and the beliefs, traditions, and aspirations of the group were no longer felt and shared by individuals, society would die.

Emile Durkheim
(quoted in)
Robert A. Nisbet
The Social Bond

The abstract and arbitrary nature of language enables man to communicate with himself — to think and reason and solve problems. He need not learn everything by trial and error, for he can *imagine* the consequences of various alternative acts. He can also imagine things that he has never experienced directly. . . . He can reach beyond his city, his country, and even his own time. Without language he would have little art, and even less science.

John Biesanz and Mavis Biesanz
Introduction to Sociology

Helen Keller did not become a complete social self until one day she perceived that her teacher was communicating with her through symbols. As her teacher, Anne Sullivan, wrote, "We went to the pump, where I had Helen hold her cup under the opening while I pumped. As the cold water poured forth and filled the cup, I spelled out 'water' by tapping on her free hand. The word, which followed so immediately upon the sensation of the cold water running over her hand, seemed to puzzle her. Then she let the cup fall and stood as if she were rooted there. A completely new expression lighted her features. She spelled out the word 'water' again and again. She knelt down and touched the earth and wanted to know its name, and she did the same for the pump and the nearby trellis. Then she turned around and inquired about my name. I spelled out 'teacher' in her hand. . . ."

(*Helen Keller was blind and deaf from birth.*)

A letter from Anne Masefield Sullivan
(quoted in)
Helen Keller
The Story of My Life

Just for fun, read the following description, which is taken from the *Encyclopaedia Britannica*, and then see which of the illustrations it describes.

It is small, with a long nose, ears and tail, the latter being naked and prehensile. The opposable first hind toe is clawless and the tip is expanded into a flat pad. The other digits all bear claws. The best known species is about the size of a cat, gray in color, the fur being woolly.

Three artists were given the description above, and this is what they drew

point of view. We can no longer be thought of as spanning all reason and knowledge. When we think about the incredible degree of diversity in language systems that ranges over the globe, we are left with a feeling that the human spirit is very old, and that the few thousand years of history covered by our written records are no more than the thickness of a pencil mark on the scale that measures our past experience on this planet. The events of a few thousand years mean little in development. The race of man has taken no sudden spurt, achieved no commanding world view but has played only a little with a few of the language formulations and views of nature left from an extremely longer past. Yet neither this feeling nor the sense of dependence of all we know upon the tools of language need be discouraging to science. Rather, it should foster that humility which accompanies the true scientific spirit, and thus forbid that arrogance of the mind which hinders real scientific curiosity and detachment.

On communicating with others *

Man differs from other animals mainly because he has an enlarged forebrain. This makes it possible for him to think and to develop language. It is through language that man can express his experiences in words and symbols that can be understood by other men. Man is able to store his thoughts by using symbols (writing, art, and music), and in this way he is able to pass on his understanding of the world around him from generation to generation. Although it is true that animals also can communicate in a variety of limited ways, they cannot effectively learn from each other nor can they accumulate learning.

   In their natural habitat, animals have ways of warning each other of danger or of trying to attract the opposite sex, or of passing on information. For example, bees give directions to each other by dancing. It has been found that porpoises have a small vocabulary of noises which they babble at each other and seem to understand. Animal trainers have been able to train animals to do very complicated tricks. The young ape can be taught to do many things better than can the young child. It has been demonstrated that an ape can be taught to speak a few words, although of course he does not understand them. Rats, monkeys, and mice have been taught to do things in the laboratory to obtain food or to avoid pain. But in all cases, it has been found that animals cannot plan or communicate in true language. A rat may learn to find its way through a maze by trial and error methods, but the rat cannot prepare for the trip by studying a map.

* The following sources were used in writing this article: Hayakawa, S. I., *Language in Thought and Action*, (New York: Harcourt, Brace & World, Inc., 1964); Condon, J. C. Jr., *Semantics and Communication* (New York: The Macmillan Company, 1966); Henle, Paul (Ed.), *Language, Thought, and Culture* (Ann Arbor: Ann Arbor Paperbacks, 1958); Fabun, D., *Communications* (New York: The Glencoe Press of The Macmillan Company, 1968).

It is easy to think of human language as something that is as natural a process as breathing and, therefore, that it is not necessary to examine very closely. If a person takes his language for granted, he could easily conclude that everyone thinks pretty much as *he* thinks and means what *he* means when he uses a word. If others do not understand, then they must be confused at best and wrong at worst! However, to understand language properly, we must assume very little. Language is acquired through learning, and this learning process can vary considerably from person to person. In this section we deal with language and communication in a manner that points out some important features of human interaction.

In communicating with other people, we learn to expect things. We learn to fill in the gaps. We learn to interpret what is being said from just a few clues. We often see things that are not there, and in some cases, we do not see things that are there. Read the phrase in the triangle below.

OTTAWA
IN THE
THE FALL

Did you find an error in the phrase? Perhaps you noticed that there were two *the*s instead of one. If you didn't notice that there were two *the*s, how would you explain it? Surely it is because we have learned to expect certain combinations of words, and we reject those elements that do not fit in with what we have come to expect.

We tend to select that part of the world that we want to experience at any one time. One possible indication of mental sickness is an extreme tendency of a person to restrict his views to very small parts of reality and to avoid seeing a great deal of what is going on around him. We choose to go into one room of a house instead of another, and by so doing, we limit our experience. The particular place where you are, and the direction in which you choose to look, have important implications as to what experiences you are going to have. Also, of course, what you have learned in the past, together with your emotional condition, contribute to what you will want to see. No two people can be in exactly the same spot at exactly the same time nor can they bring to a situation the same background experiences. It is probably safe to say that many of our problems in communication arise because we are viewing things in different ways than do other people – but we *assume* that we are viewing the same thing in the same way.

Even when you are walking down a city street with a friend, you will even see different things because there are so many different images to view. If you are hungry, you will tend to see restaurant signs. If you are in a hurry, you will be looking for clocks. If

It has been remarked that almost every tragedy represents a failure in communication. In most cases, we may surmise, the failure is due not so much to what has *not* been said, as to what *has* been said ; said, and misunderstood. The truth is that communication is an art, the art of addressing humanity, the art of cooperation in purest form.

Ashley Montagu
Man : His First Two Million Years

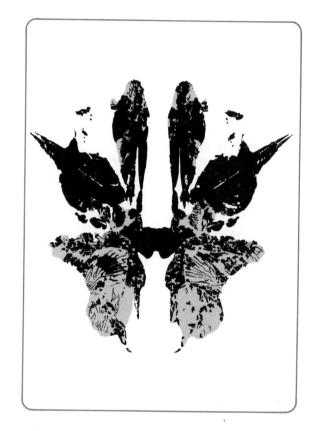

"Two statues"

"Two birds pecking food"

"Butterfly"

"Two pelicans facing each other"

"Flower"

These are some of the things different people have reported seeing in the ink blot. Did you see them ? Do you see them now ? Have you perhaps been taught by other people what to see ? When you are talking to someone, it is well to keep in mind that they may have been "taught" to experience things differently than you have, and perhaps the reason you have difficulty understanding them is that you are not allowing for this.

Parable of the Blind Men and the Elephant

It was six men of Indostan
To learning much inclined,
Who went to see the Elephant,
(Though all of them were blind),
That each by observation
Might satisfy his mind.

The First approached the Elephant,
And happening to fall
Against his broad and sturdy side,
At once began to bawl:
"God bless me! but the Elephant
Is very like a wall!"

The Second, feeling of the tusk
Cried, "Ho, what have we here
So very round and smooth and sharp?
To me 'tis very clear
This wonder of an Elephant
Is very like a spear!"

The Third approached the animal
And, happening to take
The squirming trunk within his hands
Thus boldly up he spake:
"I see," quoth he, "the Elephant
Is very like a snake!"

The Fourth reached out an eager hand,
And felt about the knee:
"What most this wondrous beast is like
Is very plain," quoth he;
"'Tis clear enough the Elephant
Is very like a tree!"

The Fifth, who chanced to touch an ear,
Said: "E'en the blindest man
Can tell what this resembles most;
Deny the fact who can
This marvel of an Elephant
Is very like a fan!"

The Sixth no sooner had begun
About the beast to grope
Than, seizing on the swinging tail
That fell within his scope.
"I see," quoth he, "the Elephant
Is very like a rope!"

And so these men of Indostan
Disputed loud and long,
Each his own opinion
Exceeding stiff and strong.
Though each was partly in the right,
They all were in the wrong!

J. G. Saxe

you are a typical young man, you will be on the lookout for mini-skirted girls – and those are but a few examples.

Psychologists have found that they can understand people to a greater extent by using something called the ink-blot test. In this test you view a series of coloured ink-blots, and you attempt to see recognizable forms. Your interpretation of the ink-blot allows the psychologist to understand to some extent what is going on in your mind. If your suggestion is that the ink-blot looks like people in combat, the psychologist will interpret this very differently from the suggestions of people who see butterflies, birds, or statues.

In the *Parable of the Blind Men and the Elephant*, you can see that the six men describe the elephant in many different ways, depending on their points of view – or in this case, their points of touch. Remember, the more information you have, the greater the possibility that you can make an intelligent judgement about something.

There are approximately 600,000 words in the English language today, and each day the number of words increases as our technology improves and our experiences broaden. The moon-landing experiences have increased our language base, and even new toys contribute. It has been said that in a given day, the average adult in the business world uses about two thousand words. Some of these words have many different meanings. If we look in the Shorter Oxford Dictionary under the word "right", we find three columns of meanings from "a justifiable claim" through "straight, not bent", to a verb meaning "to make straight or to straighten", or to "prove in accordance with truth", and so on, and on, and on. Even the word "meaning" has sixteen different meanings!

The names of people have been used for more than differentiating among individuals; names have long been used to describe people, or in expectation of what someone wants a child to be like. You might have heard people say, "She doesn't look like an Elizabeth, she looks more like a Heather". Protective names used to be given to warriors going into battle, and for a time in Hollywood, actors would be given names like Tab, Rock, Tuesday, and Fabian, although this is not as common now. There are even books that parents can use as a source of names to give to their children. These books usually include the original derivation of the names and the qualities that the names are supposed to represent. For example:

Diana   (Latin) Goodness, divine one. Roman moon goddess, deity of the hunt.

Margaret (Latin) Pearl, honouring Margaret, the patron saint of Scotland.

Kelly   (Irish-Gaelic: Ceallach. Boy's or girl's name) Warrior maid or warrior, brave soldier of the king.

John   (Hebrew) God is gracious.

Wayne   (Old English: Waennan) A wagoner or wagonmaker.

Animals may fight with each other for food, for a mate, or for leadership of a herd or group, but they do not fight each other for things that represent food, or access to a female, or leadership. Because of our ability to cope with symbols that stand for something else, we can communicate symbolically. When we seek social rank, we end up in the right clubs, with the right friends, and these things symbolize status to us. We even use food to symbolize the fact that we believe in certain religions – Catholics, Jews, Mohammedans, and Hindus all have food regulations which state that they cannot eat certain foods at all (even though the foods are not harmful), or they cannot eat certain foods on certain days.

Stripes on the sleeve tell us about military rank. Nurses, policemen, and postmen all wear uniforms that symbolize their occupations. Scholarships and awards are given that indicate success in some field. It appears there are few things that men do or want that do not have some symbolic indication as to their value. Why is it not sufficient to come first in Grade 12 without also receiving some sort of award? There does not have to be any special relationship between the symbol and what it represents. You can say "I am thirsty" without being thirsty. You can dress and talk like a millionaire without being one. Many people in our society attempt to be part of a higher social group by talking like the people in this group, wearing what they wear, and doing what they do. But they usually find out that these are only symbols of what the people do and are, and that the real truth is that the members of this social group have power, influence, and often wealth.

Words have come to take on negative and positive characteristics, because language has two purposes. One of these is to convey emotion and the other is to convey information. Although we tend to think of language as a device that provides us with information, it can also be seen as affecting our feelings. If we look at it this way, language can be seen as having a force. When we are insulted, we tend to insult the person back, just as when we are struck by someone, we tend to strike that person back. The tone of the voice gives us some clues to the emotional content of the words. Loudness or softness, pleasantness or unpleasantness, all contribute to the communication. Sarcasm can be communicated by using a slightly different intonation. For example, "What a great guy!" can be said in such a way that it is a true compliment, but it can also be said sarcastically and be quite critical.

Some words by themselves arouse personal feelings. The word "pig" suggests a foul-smelling animal wallowing in muddy holes. Interestingly, a few years ago in the United States, FBI Chief J. Edgar Hoover stated that policemen would have fewer robbers to chase if people would stop using the word "cop". He felt that the word "cop" was degrading and made the role of policeman more difficult. I wonder how he feels about the term commonly used today to describe policemen.

The word we use to refer to a person indicates something about the way we feel toward that person. For example, we can refer to someone as "that gentleman", or "that guy", or "that fellow", and while the person referred to may be the same, each of the terms reflects a difference in our feelings toward him.

The name of a city or country can have emotional overtones. Since the United Kingdom has been long noted for high quality

There are believed to be about 600,000 words in the English language today. The number is constantly growing, as we add new human experiences to be reported on (through the use of extensions of our natural senses – telescopes, microscopes, spectroscopes) or as we coin new expressions to describe present experiences – hula hoops, me-tooism, high camp, and so on.

The number of words (other than technical ones connected with a business or profession) that an educated adult uses in daily conversation is about 2,000. Of these, the 500 most frequently used have 14,000 dictionary definitions.

This is a pitifully small number of symbols to describe the infinite richness and diversity of individual human experiences.

Some new technologies that add new experiences for us to report:

Cinematography
Cybernetics
Miniaturization
Microbiology
Cryogenics
Biocenology
Electrochemistry

Old technologies we no longer draw experience from, whose words are disappearing from common use:

Alchemy
Chandlery
Heraldry
Blacksmithing
Falconry
Cannonry

Old words once used to describe one experience, that are now used to describe other experiences:

Missile
Compact
Spectacular
Twist
Carpetbagger
Maverick
Gauntlet

woollen goods, clothiers often select English and Scottish brand names for suits and overcoats: "Glen Eaton", "Bond Street", "Regent Park", and "Birkdale". Since France has been fictionalized as a country where "love is in the air", sellers of perfume choose names for their products that are either written in French, or suggest some association with France – "Evening in Paris", "Eau de Love", "Vive le bain", "Si bon", and "Quelque fleur".

The emotional aspect of the language is often so great that people find it difficult to use certain kinds of words. In Canada, this is particularly emphasized in relation to words dealing with bodily excretions. When we stop at a garage, we ask the gas pump attendant where the "rest room" is, although we have no intention of resting. Women tend to use the term "powder room" for this purpose. It tells a lot about our society when we realize that in polite situations we cannot say what a rest room is for without becoming obscene, talking in baby talk, or using medical vocabulary.

In some ways, we do not deal directly with issues relating to money. We mention sums of money in general to people, but it is not polite to enquire into their financial affairs. Even when we receive bills, the bills are worded in an unspecific fashion. For example, "We would appreciate your early consideration of this matter", or "This is just to call your attention to what might have been an oversight on your part".

Words having to do with our bodies and sex bring out great concerns in people. In the nineteenth century, during Queen Victoria's reign, ladies could not bring themselves to say "breast" or "leg" – even when referring to chicken, or duck, or turkey. The terms "white meat" and "dark meat" were substituted, and that is why they are used today. This word problem in dealing with sexual matters can have serious outcomes. Many young people do not understand sexual matters partly because they have no vocabulary in which to talk about them with their parents and teachers. The language used among friends is usually too coarse and the medical language is usually unknown. The recent trend in movies and books toward presenting sex more frankly has in some cases increased the gap between parents and their children because much of what is presented is unacceptable to the parents. While young people are now more easily able to talk about sexual matters, in many cases their parents find it even more difficult. As an aside, it should be noted that the taboos on certain language have some social purposes. When we are extremely angry, instead of expressing our anger in some form of violent behaviour, we can say an obscene word. When we utter a forbidden word, it serves as a useful substitute to smashing furniture or people. It is an extra step we can take to release some of our emotional tension. It is almost comical to look at some of the words that are used to avoid taking "the name of the Lord thy God in vain" (Exodus 21:7), such as "Gee Willikens", "Gosh Almighty", "Gee Whizz", and "Holy Smoke". This is not only true of the Christian and Jewish religions, but is also true in most other religions. Throughout the world, there is a feeling that the names of gods are too holy to be spoken lightly.

There are many words that communicate built-in judgements.

For example, words that describe people in certain jobs – pick-pocket, prostitute, gambler – typically communicate a fact and a judgement on a fact. In the south-western area of the United States, there has been strong prejudice against Mexicans, and the word "Mexican" has come to have a prejudicial overtone. Newspapers and certain individuals have stopped using the word "Mexican", and have replaced it by the term "Spanish-American". There are many issues on which people hold very strong feelings, and we often have to talk in a pretty roundabout fashion if we wish to avoid arousing these feelings. Emotion-laden words can block effective communications. It is just as easy to say "problem-drinker" instead of "drunk", or "government official" instead of "bureaucrat", or "a person who holds different views" instead of "crackpot".

There is a great danger in using words in a way that encourages people to act out the behaviour assumed in the words. We used to call young boys who got into trouble "punks" or "hoods", but then we realized that, by giving such boys a label that indicated we *expected* them to act like punks, we were providing them with an *excuse* to act that way. In an attempt to indicate more positive expectations, we now describe young offenders as "deprived", or "socially-disadvantaged", or we say that they are "having problems of identity". They do not need punishment, they need help in the form of education and rehabilitation. Instead of making them feel entirely at fault, we take a great deal of the guilt onto ourselves.

This tendency for young people to live up to phrases used to describe them has also been found to occur in schools. We call a child a slow learner, and he becomes a slow learner. We start off in elementary school grades with "Bluebirds", "Robins", and "Crows", depending on which reading group a child is in, and the child never escapes being a "Crow". Sociologists call this a "self-fulfilling prophesy". When a teacher says, "You stupid kid, you are never going to pass Grade 11 French", in many cases, the young person accepts that as an evaluation of his ability, and he proceeds to fail French. Although some teachers use this approach to encourage a student to work harder, it can be more discouraging than encouraging.

A good example of how the same behaviour is viewed differently, depending on the point of view, was given by Bertrand Russell on a British Broadcasting Corporation program. Russell was describing how he would view a person holding firm to one particular idea. He said, "If applied to me, it would be stated 'I am firm', if applied to someone I was speaking to, it would be, 'You are obstinate', and if it was applied to someone not present, it would be, 'He is a pig-headed fool'!"

Language is active behaviour. When we make noises, we move muscles. When we get angry, our bodies make many changes in preparation for action, including the making of noises such as growls, snarls, and grunts. Most of us are a little too sophisticated to growl like a dog, but we come pretty close to it when we substitute such words as, "You rotten crud", or "You dirty rat-fink". On the other hand, in response to a more pleasurable sensation, we might say in soft, warm tones, "He is the greatest guy I know".

How many of the following terms do you understand?

Term	Occupation
1 Frogger	Logging
2 Wiggle-tail	Mining
3 Hole in the book	Magazine publishing
4 Pork-chopper	Labor organizing
5 Butcher	Show business
6 Bird dog	Auto sales
7 Technical market	Stock marketing
8 Double truck	Advertising
9 Heeling	Boxing
10 Grass cutting	Aviation

1 A member of a skidding crew who follows the logs in case they become fouled on the way.

2 An excavating drill.

3 A condition produced by the nonarrival or nonacceptance of a story or article that has been scheduled for an issue about to go to press.

4 An official who is considered to be in the union out of self-interest rather than to help workers.

5 Vendor of candy or other items in a theatre.

6 A person who steers a likely customer to a car dealer, for a fee.

7 The condition of a market in which an unnatural level of price is maintained by manipulation or speculation.

8 An advertisement set across two full pages.

9 A manoeuvre in which a fighter, during clinches, runs the laced part of his glove over an opponent's face wound, so as to exacerbate it.

10 Excessive taxiing at takeoff on the flying field.

Adapted from David Dressler
Sociology : The Study of Human Interaction

These kinds of statements are human equivalents of snarling and purring. The trouble with these kinds of words is that they do not supply enough information to enable other people to come to the same conclusion that you have in the use of these terms. Rather than providing us with information on other people and things on which we can base our own judgement, we are left puzzling, "I wonder why he feels so strongly".

There is really not much point in debating with other people such things as who is the greatest hockey player, or which is the best rock group, or which sport is best. In these situations, the answers must depend on the personal interests and preferences of the individuals. However, you gain more information about a person by asking why he likes or dislikes someone or something. When we make a judgement on something, we are actually adding up lots of bits of information. If we communicate a series of judgements without offering the evidence to support what we claim, we make it very difficult for another person to respond intelligently.

How does one discover one's bias? As we have noted before, we tend to see what we want to see. Really to understand one's own bias and those of others, it is necessary to try to determine one's own values and beliefs. With the benefit of this knowledge, we are better able to determine true meanings. For example, if a newspaper tends to support a political party – and some newspapers go so far as to indicate who they would recommend you to vote for – then we will find evidence of support for the party's policies in the reports they print. This is most likely to be reflected in the editorial columns, but also can be seen throughout the newspaper in the articles that have been selected for publication. An interesting exercise is to compare two or three newspapers on the same day to see what events have been emphasized and how the events have been interpreted.

Perhaps one of the most important aspects of communication is developing the ability to be a good listener. The good listener gets more from a conversation or conference. He has learned that he will tie a conversation into knots if he objects over small points. The good listener increases his chances of making effective decisions, because he is able to obtain more information, to understand the person with whom he is communicating, and to fill in the gaps intelligently. J. Samuel Bois, in his book *The Art of Awareness*, outlines what an effective listener does.

1) He listens carefully to understand what is meant, rather than preparing himself to contradict what is being said.

2) He realizes that he must look behind the simple meanings of the words that are used. He must observe the tone of the voice, the facial expression, and the overall behaviour of the speaker.

3) He is careful not to interpret too quickly. He tries to put himself in the shoes of the speaker to try to obtain his perspective. He tries to understand the speaker's feelings.

4) He attempts to put aside his own views and opinions and keep an open mind. This means that he must avoid listening to himself responding to the speaker in his subconscious. He is careful to keep his mind open.

Behaviourists claim it is probably not an exaggeration to say that a specific color situation is accompanied by a specific response pattern of the whole organism. The prevailing color in an environment may have important effects on the kind of communications that take place there. In general, it is felt that the "warm" colors – yellow, orange, red – stimulate creativity and make most people feel more "outgoing" and responsive to others. "Cool" colors – blue, green, gray – have a tendency to encourage meditation and deliberate thought processes, and may have a dampening effect on both the level and the quality of communication. It has even been suggested that people should do creative thinking in a red room and then proceed to a green one to carry out the ideas.

Down the yellow brick road   *or*   From fact to fallacy

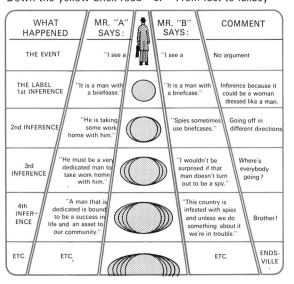

WHAT HAPPENED	MR. "A" SAYS:	MR. "B" SAYS:	COMMENT
THE EVENT	"I see a	"I see a	No argument
THE LABEL 1st INFERENCE	"It is a man with a briefcase."	"It is a man with a briefcase."	Inference because it could be a woman dressed like a man.
2nd INFERENCE	"He is taking some work home with him."	"Spies sometimes use briefcases."	Going off in different directions.
3rd INFERENCE	"He must be a very dedicated man to take work home with him."	"I wouldn't be surprised if that man doesn't turn out to be a spy."	Where's everybody going?
4th INFERENCE	"A man that is dedicated is bound to be a success in life and an asset to our community."	"This country is infested with spies and unless we do something about it we're in trouble."	Brother!
ETC.	ETC.	ETC.	ENDS- VILLE

5) He remains patient because he knows that listening is faster than speaking. He tries not to get ahead of the speaker. While the average person speaks about 125 words a minute, he can listen to about 400 words a minute. It is easy to jump ahead of the speaker and attempt to guess what he is going to say. The effective listener must give the speaker time to tell his story.

6) He does not prepare his answer while he listens. He wants to obtain the whole story before deciding what to say in return. Often the speaker waits until his last sentence to make his most important point, and the good listener must wait.

7) He shows interest in the speaker and what he is saying. This encourages the speaker, increases his confidence, and helps improve his performance.

8) He does not interrupt, except to secure more information or to obtain clarification. He does not try to trap the speaker.

9) He does not quibble about the language the speaker uses, but attempts to understand what is meant.

10) He first looks for areas of agreement with the speaker rather than weak spots.

11) If he is in a conference, he listens to all the speakers and tries to understand all points of view.

12) In a discussion where there is some difficulty in understanding what is being said, he attempts to summarize the speaker's points before responding to them. Not until his interpretation of the points that have been made is acceptable to the other, does he attempt to present his own views.

The above description of the good listener is not always appropriate, of course, because it assumes that the person communicating always has something meaningful to say. It also assumes that some of the premises, or that the premises on which the person bases his discussion, are valid. Often, one or two of the assumptions are invalid, and this makes listening to the remainder of a presentation quite tedious and time-wasting. However, Bois' list is a useful, general guide for the person attempting to be a good listener.

We have noted that some important communications between people are often left unsaid. In some cases, filling in the gaps in our own mind is quite appropriate, but in other cases, we have a responsibility to say something. The following example illustrates this point.

Wife: George, why don't you talk to me?

Husband: (Reading the sports page) What?

Wife: Why don't you ever talk to me?

Husband: But there isn't anything to say. What do you want me to say?

Wife: You don't love me any more.

Husband: (Finally realizing that he has to do something now, but a little annoyed) Oh, don't be foolish, you know I do!

Human communications frequently * seem to have a "loop" or "closed circuit" pattern

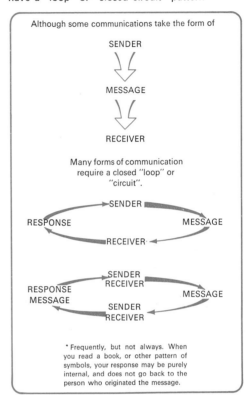

Although some communications take the form of

SENDER

MESSAGE

RECEIVER

Many forms of communication require a closed "loop" or "circuit".

SENDER

RESPONSE   MESSAGE

RECEIVER

SENDER
RECEIVER

RESPONSE   MESSAGE
MESSAGE

SENDER
RECEIVER

* Frequently, but not always. When you read a book, or other pattern of symbols, your response may be purely internal, and does not go back to the person who originated the message.

The following incident was reported by Manning Nash, in his book *The Golden Road to Modernity, Village Life in Contemporary Burma*.

It is very easy to run into communication problems with people who come from different cultures. A good example of this is a situation that developed after the Japanese took over Burma during World War II. At the outset, the native Burmese welcomed the Japanese, but later, as a result of a difference in the interpretation of certain basic terms, they came to dislike them intensely. The Burmese have no word in their language for "Hello" or for "Goodbye". Generally speaking, they say "How are you?" only when a person isn't looking well. Rather than say "Hello" when meeting someone on the street, the Burmese is more likely to say "Have you eaten yet?" or "Where are you going?" or "Where have you been?" Naturally, in their meetings with the Japanese invaders, they called out these greetings as they passed them on the street. The Japanese interpreted these friendly salutations as demands for military information. They responded by abusing the villagers. So, from original feelings of friendship and openness toward the Japanese, the Burmese feeling turned to hatred.

Do I fool around with other women? Don't I give you my whole pay cheque? Don't I work my head off for you and the kids?

Wife: (A bit stuck now because George has made some good points, but still not satisfied) Well, why don't you just *talk* to me sometimes?

Husband: Why?

In a way, the husband is right. His actions alone indicate his love, and really, they speak louder than words. But in another way, the wife is also right. Some things need to be said just to keep the lines of communication open. The husband does not have to say much or say it very often, but it is important at times that he say something.

You might find the following four questions useful in understanding the true meaning of what people say.

1) *Who said it was so?* Learn to reject such statements as "Everybody says that . . . ", or "I heard that . . . ". Find out *who*.

2) *What was said?* Rumour has a way of distorting information. It is important to get back to the original statement and to determine exactly what was said.

3) *What was meant?* Sometimes statements are taken out of context. Sometimes, as we have seen, people use the same words in different ways. You cannot always be sure you will understand what was meant, but it should be a question you ask yourself each time you hear a statement made.

4) *How does he know?* Where did the original information come from? Is this person an authority?

Language is something we have learned, and we must remember that our view of what other people say and do is dependent on our personal experiences. Each of us must share the responsibility for effective communication.

three   The mass media

Marshall McLuhan has coined the phrase "the global village" to describe the world-wide revolution in communication. Today, an individual has access to a wide range of information. One large press wire service claims that any news event in the world can be on the wire in two minutes. Managing information and data is as important as the speed of its collection. Scarcely a day passes when some public figure does not claim he was misquoted, or that some of his activities were presented in an unfavourable manner by a television network. News cameramen have been accused of rigging riot situations to show the police in a bad light. Press agents and advertising and public relations men earn their money by presenting a (usually) favourable view of an event, product, or person to the public. It is significant that one of Marshall McLuhan's books bears the title *Understanding Media*.

The following articles deal with media. The first is a collection of Marshall McLuhan's observations on modern communications. The second is a scientific analysis of how a story for a particular newspaper is selected or rejected. The final article is an analysis of television situation comedy shows that use deception as a social value, and the impact that this has on the young viewer.

The mechanisms of communication

Marshall McLuhan

There is a basic principle that distinguishes a hot medium like radio from a cool one like the telephone, or a hot medium like a movie from a cool one like television. A hot medium is one that extends one single sense in "high definition". High definition is the state of being well filled with data. A photograph is visually, "high definition". A cartoon is "low definition", simply because very little visual information is provided. On the other hand, hot media do not leave so much to be filled in or completed by the audience.

The Telephone

Telephone is a cool medium, or one of low definition, because the ear is given a meager amount of information. And speech is a cool medium of low definition, because so little is given and so much has to be filled in by the listener. Why should the phone create an intense feeling of loneliness? Why should we feel compelled to answer a ringing public phone when we know the call cannot possibly concern us? Why does a phone ringing on the stage create instant tension? Why is that tension so very much less for an unanswered phone on a movie scene? The answer to all of these questions is simply that the phone is a participant form that demands a partner.

Film

In the medieval world, curiosity, the idea of change in organic beings was that of the substitution of one static form for another, in sequence. They imagined the life of a flower as a kind of cine-

It is perhaps the most remarkable aspect of McLuhan's career that so few of his critics (and of course none of his admirers) have ever asked him for proof of his central thesis. Perhaps because they are so readily intimidated? For to hear McLuhan hold forth, you would assume there is some large body of incontrovertible experimental evidence somewhere to support the assertion — and that everybody who is anybody knows all about it. There isn't.

Theodore Roszak
The Radical Vision

A specialist in unnoticed causes, this scholar never delves into a historical situation without emerging with "major factors" nobody quite hit on before.

Benjamin DeMott
"Against McLuhan"
Mass Media and Mass Man

How much can be said for an intellectual vision whose effect is to encourage abdication from all responsibility of mind?

Or, what good is this famous McLuhanacy if it makes men drunk as it makes them bold?

Benjamin DeMott
"Against McLuhan"
Mass Media and Mass Man

Of all the single-factor explanations of human and social behavior I have ever come across, McLuhan's exaltation of "media" is, I fear, the most inane. But to all the objections one can make against him, McLuhan has developed a standard defense. McLuhan's assertions are not, he would have us believe, propositions or hypotheses. They are "probes". But what is a "probe"? It is apparently any outrageous statement for which one has no evidence at all or which, indeed, flies in the face of obvious facts.

Theodore Roszak
The Radical Vision

Taken singly, needless to say, none of the stratagems would rank as original, amazing or troubling; taken in concert they have powerful and obnoxious effect. The complaint isn't that Professor McLuhan puts together a thoroughly fantastic account of the situation of contemporary man; it is that he sets himself up, speaking bluntly, as the constituted pardoner of this age — a purveyor of perfect absolution for every genuine kind of modern guilt.

Benjamin DeMott
"Against McLuhan"
Mass Media and Mass Man

And whether or not the basis of his sunniness is sheer terror, his work does rank as the strongest incitement to optimism yet produced in this age. But the great gift offered is, ultimately, the release from consciousness itself. Those who accept it have clearly won a deliverance, a free way up and out.

Benjamin DeMott
"Against McLuhan"
Mass Media and Mass Man

The Medium is the Message

But in fact McLuhan's thesis is not simply unproven. It is false. There is no independent psychic effect that any mass medium has on an observer other than through its content. Indeed, no one witnesses a mass medium except for its content.

Theodore Roszak
The Radical Vision

matic strip of phases or essences. The movie is the total realization of the medieval idea of change, in the form of an entertaining illusion.

In terms of other media such as the printed page, film has the power to store and to convey a great deal of information. In an instant it presents a scene of landscape with figures that would require several pages of prose to describe. In the next instant it repeats, and can go on repeating, this detailed information. The writer, on the other hand, has no means of holding a mass of detail before his reader.

The movie is not only a supreme expression of mechanism but paradoxically it offers as product the most magical of consumer commodities, namely, dreams. It is, therefore, not accidental that the movie has excelled as a medium that offers poor people roles of riches and power beyond the dreams of avarice.

Radio

Had television occurred on a large scale during Hitler's reign he would have vanished quickly. Had television come first there would have been no Hitler at all. Radio provides a speed-up of information that also causes acceleration in other media. It certainly contracts the world to village size, and creates insatiable village tastes for gossip, rumor, and personal malice.

Since television, radio has turned to the individual needs of people at different times of the day, a fact that goes with the multiplicity of receiving sets in bedrooms, bathrooms, kitchens, cars, and now in pockets. The teenager withdraws from the television group to his private radio.

This natural bias of radio to a close tie-in with diversified community groups is best manifested in the disk-jockey cults, and in radio's use of the telephone in a glorified form of the old trunk-line wire-tapping.

Television

To contrast it with the film shot, many directors refer to the television image as one of "low definition", in the sense that it offers little detail and a low degree of information, much like the cartoon. A television close-up provides only as much information as a small section of a long-shot on the movie screen. For lack of observing so central an aspect of the television image, the critics of program "content" have talked nonsense about "television violence".

Another way of explaining the acceptable, as opposed to the unacceptable, television personality is to say that anybody whose *appearance* strongly declares his role and status in life is wrong for television. Anybody who looks as if he might be a teacher, a doctor, a businessman, or any of a dozen other things all at the same time is right for television.

The "gatekeeper":
a case study in the selection of news

David Manning White

A gatekeeper is a person who decides who will come through a gate. In the news world, the success of a news item in reaching a newspaper depends on it successfully getting through a series of gates. Sometimes the gates are a series of rules which are easily understood but at other times individuals act as gatekeepers. While the gatekeeper has rules he keeps in mind, in many cases, he makes "gatekeeping" decisions about news items that relate to his own personal bias.

The purpose of this study is to examine closely the way one of the "gatekeepers" in the complex channels of news communication operates his "gate".

Our "gatekeeper" is a man in his middle 40s, who after approximately 25 years' experience as a journalist (both as reporter and copy editor) is now the wire editor of a morning newspaper of approximately 30,000 circulation in a highly industrialized city of 100,000. It is his job to select from the avalanche of wire copy daily provided by three news services what 30,000 families will read on the front page of their morning newspapers. He also copy edits and writes the headlines for these stories. His job is similar to that which newspapermen throughout the country hold in hundreds of nonmetropolitan newspapers. And in many respects he is the most important "gatekeeper" of all, for if he rejects a story the work of all those who preceded him in reporting and transmitting the story is negated. It is understood, of course, that the story could have "ended" (insofar as its subsequent transmission is concerned) at any of the previous "gates". But assuming the story has progressed through all the "gates", it is obvious that this wire editor is faced with an extremely complicated set of decisions to make regarding the limited number of stories he can use.

Our purpose in this study was to determine some preliminary ideas as to why this particular wire editor selected or rejected the news stories filed by the three press associations and thereby gain some diagnostic notions about the general role of the "gatekeeper" in the area of mass communications.

To this end we received the full cooperation of "Mr. Gates", the above-mentioned wire editor. The problem of finding out what Mr. Gates selected from the mass of incoming wire copy was not difficult, for it appeared on the front and "jump" pages of his newspaper each morning. Actually, we were far more concerned with the copy that did not get into the paper. So for one week Mr. Gates saved every piece of wire copy that came to his desk. Instead of throwing the dispatch into the waste basket once he had decided not to use it, he put it into a large box next to his desk. Then at one o'clock when his pages were made up and his night's work through, Mr. Gates went through every piece of copy in the "reject" box and wrote on it the reason why he had initially rejected it, assuming that he could recall the reason. In the cases where no ascertainable reason had occurred to him he made no notations on the copy. Although this meant that Mr. Gates had to

Where and when did the first daily newspaper come into existence? One of the earliest publications appeared in Rome around 69 B.C. It was a primitive news sheet called *Acta Diurna* (acts of the day), and described the activities of the Roman Senate. It was posted daily in public spots around the city.

> "Facts About Daily Newspapers"
> Canadian Daily Newspaper Publishers
> Association

The general notion is that the press can form, control or at least strongly influence public opinion. Can it really do any of these things? Hugh Cudlipp, editorial director of *The London Daily Mirror*, and a man who should know something about the effect of newspapers on public opinion, doesn't share this general notion about their power. He thinks newspapers can echo and stimulate a wave of popular feeling but that's all. "A newspaper may successfully accelerate but never reverse the popular attitude that common sense has commended to the public." In short, it can jump aboard the bandwagon, once the bandwagon's under way, and exhort others to jump aboard too; but it can't start the bandwagon rolling, or change its direction after it's started.

> T. S. Matthews
> "The Power of the Press"
> *Saturday Review*

A newspaper can drop the same thought into a thousand minds at the same moment. A newspaper is an advisor, who does not require to be sought, but comes to you briefly every day of the common weal, without distracting your private affairs.

Newspapers, therefore, become more necessary in proportion as men become equal individuals, and more to be feared. To suppose that they only serve to protect freedom would be to diminish their importance. They maintain civilization.

> Alexis de Tocqueville

The press has a negative power — to titillate, alarm, enrage, amuse, humiliate, annoy, even to drive a person out of his community or his job. But of the positive power to which it pretends, and of which the press lords dream — to make and break governments, to swing an election, to stop a war or start a revolution — there is no tangible evidence.

> T. S. Matthews
> "The Power of the Press?"
> *Mass Media and Mass Man*

The good newspaper must walk a tight rope between two abysses — on the one side the false objectivity which takes everything at face value and lets the public be imposed upon by the charlatan with the most brazen front; on the other, the interpretive reporting which fails to draw the line between objective and subjective, between a reasonably well-established fact and what the reporter or the editor wishes were the fact. . . . It is easier to pick out the nearest exit — to fall back on the incontrovertible fact that the Hon. John P. Hoozis said, colon quote, without going into the question of whether he was lying or not.

Elmer Davis
"Must We Mislead the Public?"
The Press in Perspective

Table 1
Amounts of Press Association News
Mr. Gates Received and Used
During Seven-Day Period

Category	Wire copy received Col. In.	% of total	Wire copy used Col. In.	% of total
Crime	527	4.4	41	3.2
Disaster	405	3.4	44	3.4
Political	2,287	19.2	293	22.6
Human interest	4,171	35.0	301	23.2
International Political	1,804	15.1	176	13.6
Economic	405	3.4	59	4.5
War	480	4.0	72	5.6
Labor	650	5.5	71	5.5
National Farm	301	2.5	78	6.0
Economic	294	2.5	43	3.3
Education	381	3.2	56	4.3
Science	205	1.7	63	4.9
Total	11,910	99.9	1,297	100.1

The press — and by delegation, the individual newsman — rightfully has the *institutional license* to gather and make public the news. Society rightfully can expect the press to maintain critical surveillance of the social arena and to provide an independent appraisal of the environment. This requires, it seems to me, the press to remain free from undue influences from other social institutions. And it means that the individual reporter must remain independent from pressures from sources and free as far as possible from such pressures from the news bureaucracy which would interfere with his craft of full and critical reporting.

Walter Gieber
News is What Newspaper Men Make It

spend between an hour-and-a-half and two hours each night at this rather tedious phase of the project, he was perfectly willing to do this throughout the entire week.

When Mr. Gates had turned over the raw material of his choices for the week period, we tried to analyze his performance in terms of certain basic questions which presented themselves. These questions are applicable not only to this particular "gatekeeper", but with modifications to all of the "gatekeepers" in the communications process. Thus, after determining what wire news came in during the week in terms of total column inches and categories, we measured the amount of wire news that appeared in the papers for that period.

Assuming that five lines of wire copy are equivalent to a column inch in a newspaper, Mr. Gates received approximately 12,400 inches of press association news during the week. Of this he used 1,297 column inches of wire news, or about *one-tenth*, in the seven issues we measured. *Table 1* shows a breakdown by categories of the wire news received and used during the week.

It is only when we study the reasons given by Mr. Gates for rejecting almost nine-tenths of the wire copy (in his search for the one-tenth for which he has space) that we begin to understand how highly subjective, how reliant upon value-judgements based on the "gatekeeper's" own set of experiences, attitudes and expectations the communication of "news" really is. In this particular case the reasons given for rejection may be divided into two main categories: (1) rejecting the incident as unworthy of being reported and (2) selecting from many reports of the same event. (See *Table 2*.)

Thus we find him rejecting one piece of wire copy with the notation, "He's too Red". Other stories are categorically marked "Never use this". Eighteen pieces of copy were marked "B.S."; 16 were marked "Propaganda". One interesting notation on a story said "Don't care for suicides". Thus we see that many of the reasons which Mr. Gates gives for the rejection of the stories fall into the category of highly subjective value-judgments.

The second category gives us an important clue as to the difficulty of making choices of one piece of copy over another. No less than 639 times, Mr. Gates makes the notation "Would use but no space". In short, the story (in his eyes) has merit and interest, he has no "personal" objections to it, but space is at a premium. It is significant to observe that the later in the evening the stories came in, the higher was the proportion of the "no space" type of notation. As the evening progresses the wire editor's pages become more and more filled up. A story that has a good chance of getting on the front page at 7:30 or 8 o'clock in the evening may not be worth the precious remaining space at 11 o'clock. Another reason which falls into this mechanical category relates to the use of one press service over another.

As one examines the whole week's performance of Mr. Gates, as manifested in the stories he chose, certain broad patterns become apparent. What do we know, for example, about the kinds of stories that he selected in preference to others from the same category? What tests of subject matter and way of writing did Mr.

Gates seem to apply? In almost every case where he had some choice between competing press association stories Mr. Gates preferred the "conservative". I use this expression not only in terms of its political connotations, but also in terms of style of writing. Sensationalism and insinuation seemed to be avoided consistently.

As to the way of writing that he preferred, Mr. Gates showed an obvious dislike for stories that had too many figures and statistics. In almost every case where one news agency supplied a story filled with figures and statistics and the competing agency's story was an easier going, more interpretative than statistical type of story, the latter appeared in the paper. An indication of his standards for writing is seen in *Table 2*, where 26 stories were rejected as being "too vague", 51 rejected for "dull writing" and 61 for being "not interesting".

Another question that should be considered in this study (and subsequent ones) is: Does the category really enter into the choice? That is, does the wire editor try to choose a certain amount of crime news, human interest news, etc.? Are there some other divisions of subject matter or form which he chooses in this manner, such as a certain number of one-paragraph stories?

Insofar as this "gatekeeper" is representative of wire editors as a whole, it does not appear that there is any conscious choice of news by categories. It would be most interesting and valuable to ascertain how a wire editor determines what one issue or type of story is "the" story of the week. Many times that decision is made by "gatekeepers" above him, or by "gatekeepers" in competing media. Can a wire editor refuse to play a story "up" when his counterpart in the local radio station is playing it to the hilt? Likewise, can a wire editor play down a story when he sees competing papers from nearby metropolitan areas coming into his city and playing up the story? These factors undoubtedly have something to do in determining the wire editor's opinion as to what he should give the reading public the next morning. This brings up the rather obvious conclusion that theoretically all of the wire editor's standards of taste should refer back to an audience who must be served and pleased.

Subsequent to Mr. Gates' participation in the project to determine the "reasons" for selecting or rejecting wire stories during a week, he was asked to consider at length four questions which we submitted. His answers to these questions tell us much about Mr. Gates, particularly if they are collated with the "spot" reasons which came under the pressure of a working night.

Question 1: "Does the category of news affect your choice of news stories?" The category of news definitely enters into my choice of stories. A crime story will carry a warning as will an accident story. Human interest stories provoke sympathy and could set examples of conduct. Economic news is informative for some readers and over the heads of others. I make no attempt to hold a rigid balance in these selections but to strive for variety. The category of news suggests groups that should be interested in a particular story, that is, teachers, laborers, professional people, etc. Wire service reports can't keep a strictly balanced diet and for this

Table 2
Reasons for Rejection of
Press Association News
Given by Mr. Gates During
Seven-Day Period

Reason	Number of times given
Rejecting incident as unworthy of reporting	423
Not interesting (61) ; of no interest to people in this area (43)	104
Dull writing (51) ; too vague (26) ; drags too much (3)	80
No good (31) ; slop (18) ; B.S. (18)	67
Too much already on this subject — interest dying out	62
Trivial	55
Never use this	23
Propaganda (16) ; he's too Red ;* sour grapes	18
Too sensational (11) ; don't care for suicide stories ; too suggestive ; not in good taste	14
Selecting from reports of the same event	910
Would use (whole or part) but no space	639
Waiting for this story to develop further — outcome will be used	172
Too far away to be of interest in this area	40
Too regional	36
Used another press service : better story, shorter, lead more interesting, meatier, or story came in earlier	21
Bannered yesterday	1
I missed this one	1

* In this and other cases where no number follows the reason, that reason was given only once.

News reporters are often defined as being of two main types. There are those who may have a great need for support from people they value and who tend to report the news in a very positive, supportive way. This kind of reporter may regard his act of bringing good news or interpreting news in a positive way as performing a favour that will be rewarded by gratitude and affection. Because he might feel that bringing bad news will result in his being perceived in a more negative light by people, he may distort the news, either to soften it, or because he has become so anxious that he is unable to do a good job with it. On the other hand, a news reporter who sees himself as the butt of criticism might respond by presenting bad news in an unpleasant fashion as an aggressive act against his critics. News is a weapon in his hands; therefore, he may report good news in an inaccurate way because it does not serve his purpose.

The disorder of the newspaper throws the reader into a producer role. The reader has to process the news himself; he has to co-create, to cooperate in the creation of the work. The newspaper format calls for the direct participation of the consumer.

Edmund Carpenter
"The New Languages"
Explorations in Communications

The first Canadian newspaper was the *Halifax Gazette* issued on March 23, 1752, by John Bushell. It was during [the next] 55-year period that all six of Canada's eastern provinces made their press beginnings.

The early newspapers were dependent for their existence on government patronage, therefore were completely subservient to officials of the day. Their content consisted of government announcements and foreign news. The latter was eagerly read even though it was months old. Advertisements were small and unimaginative, ranging from property for sale to general store commodities.

Early news sheets rarely contained more than four pages and publication was usually once a week.

"Facts About Daily Newspapers"
Canadian Daily Newspaper Publishers
Association

It is not possible to assume that a world carried on by division of labor and distribution of authority can be governed by universal opinions in the whole population. . . . Acting upon everybody for thirty minutes in twenty-four hours, the press is asked to create a mystical force called Public Opinion that will take up the slack in public institutions.

Bernard A. Weisberger
The American Newspaperman

reason we could not attempt it. For the most part, the same thinking applies in the selection of shorts, although some are admittedly filler material.

Question 2: "Do you feel that you have any prejudices which may affect your choice of news stories?" I have few prejudices, built-in or otherwise, and there is little I can do about them. I am prejudiced against a publicity-seeking minority with headquarters in Rome, and I don't help them a lot. As far as preferences are concerned, I go for human interest stories in a big way. My other preferences are for stories well-wrapped up and tailored to suit our needs (or ones slanted to conform to our editorial policies).

Question 3: "What is your concept of the audience for whom you select stories and what sort of person do you conceive the average person to be?" Our readers are looked upon as people with average intelligence and with a variety of interests and abilities. I am aware of the fact we have readers with above average intelligence (there are four colleges in our area) and that there are many with far less education. Anyway, I see them as human and with some common interest. I believe they are all entitled to news that pleases them (stories involving their thinking and activity) and news that informs them of what is going on in the world.

Question 4: "Do you have specific tests of subject matter or way of writing that help you determine the selection of any particular news story?" The only tests of subject matter or way of writing I am aware of when making a selection involve clarity, conciseness and angle. I mentioned earlier that certain stories are selected for their warning, moral, or lesson, but I am not inclined to list these reasons as any test of subject matter or way of writing. The clarity trio is almost a constant yardstick in judging a story. Length of a story is another factor (or test) in a selection. The long-winded one is usually discarded unless it can be cut to fill satisfactorily.

It is a well-known fact in individual psychology that people tend to perceive as true only those happenings which fit into their own beliefs concerning what is likely to happen. It begins to appear (if Mr. Gates is a fair representative of his class) that in his position as "gatekeeper" the newspaper editor sees to it (even though he may never be consciously aware of it) that the community shall hear as a fact only those events which the newsman, as the representative of his culture, believes to be true.

This is the case study of one "gatekeeper", but one, who like several hundreds of his fellow "gatekeepers", plays a most important role as the terminal "gate" in the complex process of communication. Through studying his overt reasons for rejecting news stories from the press associations we see how highly subjective, how based on the "gatekeeper's" own set of experiences, attitudes, and expectations the communication of "news" really is.

Deception as a TV comedy tool

Glenn E. Reddick

When television quiz game "fixes" were exposed some years ago, Britisher John Ridley, who had been a big winner on "Dotto" but had received no help in answering questions, was not in the least surprised. What did surprise him was that North Americans should have been so shocked at the revelations. He was quoted as saying:

> Isn't this the land of the fix? Don't you take pride in knowing shortcuts, in getting merchandise at wholesale rates, in bribing your policemen? You sneer at eggheads, you sneer at the starry-eyed people. You ask, "Look, what's in it for me?" You do misuse your television terribly, you know. You lack spontaneity. You lack immediacy. Your people put on programs only to sell merchandise. I'm puzzled that you don't realize that. Why do you expect anything else?

Quiz game fixes are apparently a thing of the past. But that deception is still a handy television tool became apparent to me after I made a study of the "situation comedies". My evaluation was based on personal viewing and on the plots as summarized in the weekly program guide. I set certain limitations: to be considered, a show had to carry a story with comedy intent through an entire half-hour period; no variety programs or programs featuring skits were included; the deception involved had to be deliberate (lying, spying, masquerading), but mistaken identity was ruled out; the deception could constitute either a minor or major part of the plot; only two cartoon series were included.

We find deception in situation comedies appearing in at least four general areas: keeping a person's identity secret, covering mistakes or weaknesses, interesting someone of the opposite sex or keeping romance going, and outwitting an "authority" figure.

The simplest form of deception employed is that whose purpose is to cover mistakes or weaknesses. A woman schemes to make an expensive watch appear inexpensive [so that her husband will not be angry with her for spending so much money]; in order to impress her home economics teacher, a girl who can't cook tries to pass off as her own creation food she has obtained from a restaurant. Under the romantic category we find a boy feigning illness to gain the attention of a girl; a man pretending to be engaged to one girl in order to escape another; a handsome boy substituting for an "ordinary" pen pal when the partner arrives in town; . . . a man donning a general's uniform to gain entrance to an army camp so he can try to patch up a romance.

Fashions in "authority" figures as the central characters in "deception" situations change. Just now the most popular seem to be the employer, the commanding officer and the father – with the deceiver deciding that the victim deserves to be outwitted because he is ignorant, unfair, pompous, inefficient, or hypocritical. Mothers are definitely out, as are physicians, scientists, political figures and clergymen, while policemen, teachers, and school principals are less frequently used in this manner than formerly.

All mass media in the end alienate people from personal experience and, though appearing to offset it, intensify their moral isolation from each other, from reality and from themselves. One may turn to the mass media when lonely or bored. But mass media, once they become a habit, impair the capacity for meaningful experience. Though more diffuse and not so gripping, the habit feeds on itself, establishing a vicious circle as addictions do.

Ernest van den Haag
"Of Happiness and of Despair
We Have No Measure"
Mass Culture : The Popular Arts in America

The child who had TV as a baby-sitter does not turn off all his senses, but walks about the room carrying on a multiplicity of actions and relationships, his attention a special reward for the cleverness of the pitchman, or the skill of the artist. He is king and not captive. As McLuhan would put it, he is not an audience, he gives an audience to the screen.

Anthony Schillaci
"The Now Movie"
Saturday Review

But what about those immediate effects? We now see clearly that violence on a television or movie screen affects viewers by :

1. Reducing their inhibitions against violent, aggressive behavior.
2. Teaching them *forms* of aggression – that is, giving them information about how to attack someone else when the occasion arises.

And third, let us keep in mind that the ethical ending, in which the villain is punished, may keep viewers from reproducing villainy right away, but does not make them forget how to do it. The ethical ending is just a suppressor of violence ; it does not erase.

Albert Bandura
"What TV Violence Can Do to Your Child"
Look Magazine

The media can exert an influence by taking children away from other activities. If the other activities would be harmful to the child (including, for example, activities of a delinquent gang), then the effect of the media would be wholesome. If, however, extensive TV watching or comic book reading were taking the child away from needed physical exercise, or from cultural activities such as practicing on a musical instrument, then we would be more likely to judge the effects to be harmful.

Eleanor E. Maccoby
Effects of the Mass Media

I have been studying the effects of mass media (first comic books, then television) for many years. My definite opinion is that continuous exposure of children's minds to scenes of crime and brutality has had a deeper effect on them than is generally realized – just as the constructive effects of good shows (quite apart from strictly educational programs) are more far-reaching than is generally assumed. Television in the life of the young is either educational or miseducational, but never – in the long-run – neutral. For children, the television screen has become a second reality.

Austin Repath
The Mass Media and You

A couple of years ago a report was made to the American Federal Communications Commission on television-viewing habits of American children. In this report, it stated that the average child between the ages of 5 and 14 witnesses the violent destruction of 13,000 human beings on television. Since Canadian children have the opportunities to watch essentially the same kind of programs, we can assume that the same situation exists. If that figure seems unusually high, consider that children probably spend more time on watching television than on any other activity except sleeping and going to school. Consider also the kinds of programs available when children watch television between 4 and 9 p.m. on week days and on Saturday and Sunday mornings.

How lulling television can be has been widely observed. Most homes soon give in to the temptation of using television to keep the children quiet and out of mischief. It does this, but in a way much different from playing games.

Marriage after marriage is preserved by keeping it drugged on television; television is used quite consistently to prevent quarreling from breaking out by keeping people apart.

Eugene David Glynn
"Television and the American Character –
A Psychiatrist Looks at Television"
Mass Media and Mass Man

One of the basic troubles with radio and television news is that both instruments have grown up as an incompatible combination of show business, advertising, and news.

. . . The top management of the networks, with a few notable exceptions, has been trained in advertising, research, sales, or show business. But by the nature of the corporate structure, they also make the final and crucial decisions having to do with news and public affairs. Frequently they have neither the time nor the competence to do this.

Edward R. Murrow
A Broadcaster Talks to His Colleagues

Deception of or by the employer is a standard formula in shows with business settings. For instance, on one show we find employees agreeing to keep an office mistake secret, but when the boss fires one of the employees she threatens to tell his secretary of the mistake and as a result is rehired at once. In this case we have intimidation by both employee and employer – with everyone happy in the end.

Generally speaking, in situation comedies the father as authority figure is a comic soul whose authority is not acknowledged; mother and children find some way to dupe the poor fellow into thinking he is the one who decides a question, whereas as a matter of fact they had it planned that way in the beginning. Mother is right in there with the kids, speaking their language, but father is so out of touch there is not much reason to take him seriously. When the children have problems it is mother's task to explain to father how they are straightened out.

On the basis of the situation comedies I examined during a five-month period I would estimate that 25 per cent of the situations presented involve deception as a major or minor part of the plot. Here is the lesson those comedies are giving viewers: Deception is a proper device to use when you make a mistake, want to interest or hold the interest of a member of the opposite sex, try to improve your working conditions or your family situation or change the rules of the game, hope to exercise more influence over your employees – or help someone else achieve any of these goals. Furthermore, by employing deception you will have a lot of fun, often achieve your goal even if your deception is discovered, no hard feelings or evil consequences will follow – in fact, the victim is so happy in the end that you can feel free to resort to deception the next time the opportunity arises. If the victim is disturbed, reach for one of his weaknesses (keep them filed for ready use) and use it to intimidate him; he will laugh and the two of you will remain on good terms.

How seriously should such findings be taken? Do they offer implications for religious education?

At the outset it must be acknowledged that there are valid arguments for not taking the matter too seriously. For one thing, deception is not new in comedy; it has been employed by such masters of the art as Shakespeare, Molière, Wilde and Shaw, and it is the stock-in-trade of many musical comedies. Disguise, in particular, offers opportunity and lampooning of stuffed shirts. A major defense offered by the writers and producers of the situation comedies is that no one is shown to be harmed, that the characters remain friends and everything ends happily. True – because deceiver and deceived agree that the goal justified the attempt. It is also true that not all situation comedies rely on deception as a major device.

As to possible effects on child viewers, I have found from questioning a number of bright children aware of standards of honesty that they can easily spot deception and apparently do not associate it with real life. A reporter interviewed children aged eight to twelve at an elementary school and got such comments as these on television's portrayal of fathers: "It's not my family they show; I know the difference." "TV has nothing to do with what really happens." "Television is over-exaggerated. Dads are dads, not nitwits." There is something to the argument, too, that there is in broadcasting considerable antidote in the form of educational and religious programs that, often successfully, promote honesty and respect.

All arguments aside, however, there remain definite reasons for concern about the acceptance of deception as a major tool in television's situation comedies.

Studies indicate that children's viewing habits are coming increasingly to approximate those of their elders, which means that their favorites are the prime-time programs among which situation comedies – always found among any "top ten" listings – are well represented. When sold as daytime reruns, these shows are often placed in viewing periods when many children are watching.

We are told that children identify most readily with characters in life situations similar to their own. Thus it is significant that the majority of the situation comedies have a "home" setting. Alert children may be able to differentiate intellectually between television and real-life situations, but is that recognition also present at the suggestion level? What of the vast audience of children who are not intellectually alert or who have not been exposed to examples of honesty and respect? A fifth-grade teacher reported recently that she has in class pupils who tell of their parents' boast of how they have avoided customs duties by hiding merchandise when they cross the border, of their father's outwitting the boss by padding expense accounts. One can only conclude that such children are quite able to identify with television characters who engage in deception that is apparently fun, that achieves desired goals. Certainly this is an area in which careful studies need to be made.

We know enough about suggestion to recognize that two conditions for high suggestibility are present in situation comedies depicting family life: repetition and passivity. The plots are variations on a basic formula, varying just enough to provide some stimulation. Further, the programs die slowly; some enjoy as many as six reruns. It is probable that for the most part viewers watch the programs not out of active interest but because there is nothing better to do at the moment. They very well may be bored, but the passivity that accompanies their boredom strengthens rather than weakens suggestibility.

A major matter for concern is, of course, the fact that the situation comedies involving deception end happily – even though intimidation may be necessary to ensure that outcome. The incautious viewer may very well conclude that deception has no evil consequences, or at any rate none that cannot easily be overcome. Some writers even laugh off the deception with a wisecrack; thus in one program we have the millionaire and one of his fellow castaways reprimanded for stealing water from the others. "Aren't you sorry?" he is asked. And when he replies, "Sorry that we got caught" the laughter from the soundtrack soars in volume. Again, deception sometime comes close to being rewarded. For instance, when the girl confesses that she has tried to pass off restaurant

The head of the Soviet delegation to the Congress of the United States in one of his first speeches remarked that, on the whole, the very satisfactory delinquency situation in the Soviet Union occasionally has its downs. One of such unfortunate episodes was the permission for some Tarzan films to be shown in the Soviet Union.

In the result, as Mr. Smirnoff puts it – and I am paraphrasing his statement – some of the youngsters in the Soviet Union also started swinging from trees and some of them actually did swing into the upper storey windows. Needless to say, he further commented, after such films were forbidden, this nonsense stopped.

Peter J. Lejins
International Opinions on American Media Violence

Teaching by television has been attempted for a number of years, and in the words of William H. Cartwright, "Ultimately this costly experiment failed." Although it seemed promising for some time, there were a number of factors that led to its downfall. Early improvements came because television teachers were more prepared than most classroom teachers and typically could call on useful support materials. The failure occurred when it was proven impossible to apply the procedures of individualized instruction in a class when all students were required by the television set to move at the same pace. But perhaps a more important factor was the criticism of competent teachers who said that there was no purpose in spending time, energy, and money in preparation for teaching if they were not to be allowed to teach.

The mass of men dislikes and always has disliked learning and art. It wishes to be distracted from life rather than to have it revealed; to be comforted by traditional (possibly happy and sentimental) tropes, rather than be upset by new ones. It is true that it wishes to be thrilled too. But irrational violence or vulgarity provides thrills, as well as release, just as sentimentality provides escape. What is new here is that, apart from the fact that irrelevant thrills and emotions are now prefabricated, the elite is no longer protected from the demands of the mass consumers.

Ernest van den Haag
"A Dissent from the Consensual Society"
Daedalus
The Proceedings of the American Academy of Arts and Sciences, Vol. 89, No. 2
Spring 1970

food as her own creation her teacher tells her: "There is more to homemaking than cooking; it also involves quick thinking and you have shown that, so you get an A".

The highly respectable place in the community the characters in situation comedies occupy would lead one to assume that many of them must be church members and that religion would have some effect on their concepts of right and wrong. But if that is so there is no evidence of it in the interpretations offered; references to religion seldom appear.

Potentially the greatest danger in television's use of deception as a comedy device lies in the portrayal of authority figures. What might be justifiable satire when well motivated and presented occasionally becomes incentive to disrespect when motivation is automatic and portrayals are repetitive. Such examples as the cook's addressing the commander as "Fatso" and the boy's calling his father a "creep" may be extreme, but they reflect the general tone of disrespect permeating many of the situation comedies.

Television, as our British critic reminded us in the opening paragraph above, supplies whatever sells. And today deception as comedy sells. The remedy, obviously, is to stop buying. There is no doubt that the ultimate check on content is audience rejection either through individual or group action – by selective viewing, by boycott of products, by letters to sponsors – or through political measures. Of these means, only selective viewing seems to me to be a long-range answer; the others would be effective only if employed on a scale almost impossible to achieve. Television has such a good thing going that it would take an overwhelming volume of mail and a product boycott of unprecedented proportions to effect more than temporary relief. And there is little hope in legislation. True, initiation of pay TV would undoubtedly result in improved fare – but only for those viewing it; the many who would profit most from higher standards would probably shun the kind of programs it would provide. Competition from pay TV would lead to improvement in commercial fare only if enough viewers switched to it to make that fare unprofitable – an unlikely outcome.

So we return to selective viewing, with its corollary: guidance in such selection. What is needed from schools, churches, and other agencies to which we can expect to turn for help is not guidance of a censorial nature but a program that will explain the role of mass media, particularly television. We do have something of this sort now, but it is confined to higher education. Analytical study of the role played by mass media, particularly in the light of ethical and religious considerations, should have a place at all levels of education, certainly of religious education. In such study I would suggest that high priority be given examination of television's currently successful comedy formula: Deception = Fun. A good text would be Sir Walter Scott's wise words from "Marmion":

> O what a tangled web we weave
> When first we practice to deceive.

Why are people fascinated by detective shows? On one level, they are an intellectual challenge – whodunit? On a deeper level, they appeal to a subconscious desire in most people to resist the law, to do something bad. Another factor is that the life of crime is usually pictured as being exciting in comparison with the day-to-day life of many viewers. For most people, however, the detective story is merely light entertainment.

Austin Repath
The Mass Media and You

I do not advocate that we turn television into a twenty-seven-inch wailing wall, where people constantly moan about the state of our culture and our defense. But I would just like to see it reflect occasionally the hard, unyielding realities of the world in which we live. I would like to see it done inside the existing framework, and I would like to see the doing of it redound to the credit of those who finance and program it. Measure the results by Neilsen, Trendex, or Silex – it doesn't matter, the main thing is to try. The responsibility can be easily placed, in spite of all the mouthings about giving the public what it wants. It rests on big business, and on big television, and it rests at the top. Responsibility is not something that can be assigned or delegated. And it promises its own reward: good business and good television.

Edward R. Murrow
A Broadcaster Talks to His Colleagues

Mass production aims at pleasing an average of tastes and therefore, though catering to all to some extent, it cannot satisfy any taste fully.

Ernest van den Haag
"A Dissent from the Consensual Society"
Daedalus
The Proceedings of the American Academy of Arts and Sciences, Vol. 89, No. 2
Spring 1970

four   *Manipulating human behaviour*

There is a subtle distinction between education and propaganda. While education attempts to inform in a comparatively straightforward way, propaganda is a means of manipulating or distorting the truth to further one particular cause or to damage another. During the Nazi regime in Germany, propaganda as a manipulation of public information was used to create in citizens' minds certain ideas that those in power wished to have accepted – for instance, hatred of the Jewish people and the superiority of the Aryans. Few teachers would be flattered by the implication that the information they are imparting is biased in some way, or that they are propagandizing. The businessman and the advertising executive would not freely admit that their information output to the public is propaganda. Yet the manipulation of attitudinal and behavioural change is crucial to the success of advertising and promotions in a consumer-oriented economy. One man's truth is another man's propaganda. As Leonard W. Doob has written, "The dissemination of a viewpoint considered by a group to be 'bad', 'unjust', 'ugly', or 'unnecessary' is propaganda, in terms of that group's standards" (*Public Opinion and Propaganda*).

In the struggle for man's political commitment, a very serious and potentially dangerous propaganda battle is raging internationally. One of the most dramatic illustrations of this struggle occurred during the Korean War, when young American prisoners of war publicly denounced and renounced the values and beliefs that they had learned at home. After this incident, scientists began to investigate the techniques used by the Chinese Communists to bring about such a complete change in behaviour and attitude. The term "brainwashing" came into the language to explain the method employed. The following selection explains this most effective technique of behavioural and attitudinal change.

Materials on propaganda and advertising have been presented in this section to offer a broad overview of behaviour manipulation.

The brainwashing of prisoners of war

Edgar H. Schein

In this paper I will outline some of the kinds of stress which prisoners of war faced during the Korean conflict, and describe some of the reaction patterns to these stresses. Rather than presenting a complete catalogue of their experiences, I have selected those aspects which seem to me to throw some light on the problem of collaboration with the enemy. I will give particular emphasis to the group factors, because the Chinese approach to treatment of prisoners seemed to emphasize control over groups, rather than individuals.

My material is based on a variety of sources. I was in Korea shortly after the war and had the opportunity to interview extensively 20 former prisoners of war. This basic material was supplemented by the information gathered by three psychiatrists who together had seen some 300 men. On board ship returning to the United States, I also had the opportunity to sit in on bull sessions among the former prisoners in which many of the prison

Chinese Communist Prison Regulations

In dealing with criminals, there shall be regularly adopted measures of corrective study classes, individual interviews, study of assigned documents, and organized discussions, to educate them in the admission of guilt and obedience to the law, political and current events, labour production, and culture, so as to expose the nature of the crime committed, thoroughly wipe out criminal thoughts, and establish a new moral code.

J. A. C. Brown
Techniques of Persuasion

69

Police Strategies

Modern psychology has alerted the police to the potential significance of every detail in the stimulus situation that can be manipulated and controlled, but police do not understand the implications of where such control may lead. In police questioning, an environment is created that minimizes sensory stimulation, maximally exposes the suspect's vulnerability, and provides for complete control and domination by the interrogator.

Philip G. Zimbardo
"The Psychology of Police Confessions"
Readings in Social Psychology Today

On Obtaining Confessions from Criminals

Suggest that there was a good reason for committing the deed, that he has too much intelligence to have done it without rhyme or reason. . . . In case of theft, suggest that the subject may have been hungry, or deprived of the necessities of life; or in homicide, that the victim had done him a great wrong and probably had it coming to him. Be friendly and sympathetic and encourage him to write out or relate the whole story – to clean up and start afresh.

C. D. Lee

The police manuals typically offer strategies for obtaining confessions from suspects. Most commonly it is stated that the suspect should never be questioned in a place that is familiar to him and / or in the presence of someone he knows. The suspect must feel that by going to the police station he has taken the first step in the act of yielding. The place where the questioning takes place should be a bare room with a couple of chairs and perhaps a desk. It is usually recommended that the suspect be given no opportunity to relieve his tensions that might arise from the questioning; bits of paper to ball up, cigarettes to smoke, paper clips to twist, any of these can give the suspect an advantage. If possible, the suspect should not be given the opportunity to become comfortable, and a straight-backed chair is recommended for this purpose. If possible, intensive questioning should be handled by one individual who takes up a position very close to the suspect. The idea here of course is that the suspect will feel psychologically closer to the questioner. The person who conducts the questioning should be dressed conservatively, and have no distracting mannerisms. He should use short, curt gestures to direct the suspect where to sit and what to do.

Ideally, the suspect is placed in a position where he is at a clear disadvantage, and this disadvantage is intensified in every possible way.

experiences were discussed. Additional details were obtained from the Army records on the men.

The typical experience of the prisoner of war must be divided into two broad phases. The first phase lasted anywhere from one to six months, beginning with capture, followed by exhausting marches to the north of Korea and severe conditions in inadequately equipped temporary camps, terminating in assignment to a permanent prisoner of war camp.

The second phase, lasting two or more years, was marked by continuous pressures to collaborate and to give up existing group loyalties in favor of new ones. Thus, while physical stresses had been outstanding in the first six months, psychological stresses were outstanding in this second period.

The reactions of the men toward capture were influenced by their overall attitude toward the Korean situation. Many of them felt inadequately prepared, both physically and psychologically. The physical training, equipment, and rotation system all came in for criticism, though this response might have been merely an excuse for being captured. When the Chinese entered the war they penetrated into rear areas, where they captured many men who were taken completely by surprise. The men felt that when positions were overrun, their leadership was often less than adequate. Thus, many men were disposed to blame the United Nations command for the unfortunate event of being captured.

On the psychological side, the men were not clearly aware of what they were fighting for or what kind of enemy they were opposing. In addition, the reports of the atrocities committed by the North Koreans led most men to expect death, torture, or at least no chance of getting back home if captured.

It was with this background that the soldier found his Chinese captor extending his hand in a friendly gesture and saying "Welcome" or "Congratulations, you've been *liberated*". This Chinese tactic was part of their *"lenient policy"* which was explained to groups of prisoners shortly after capture in these terms: because the UN had entered the war illegally and was an aggressor, all UN military personnel were in fact war criminals, and *could* be shot. But the average soldier was, after all, only carrying out orders for his leaders who were the real criminals. Therefore, the Chinese soldier would consider the POW a "student", and would teach him the "truth" about the war. Anyone who did not cooperate by going to school and by learning voluntarily could be reverted to his "war criminal" status and shot, particularly if a confession of "criminal" deeds could be obtained from him.

In the weeks following capture, the men were collected in large groups and marched north. From a physical point of view, the stresses during these marches were very severe: there was no medicine for the wounded, the food was unpalatable and insufficient, especially by our standards, clothing was scarce in the face of severe winter weather and shelter was inadequate and overcrowded. The Chinese set a severe pace and showed little consideration for weariness that was the product of wounds, diarrhea, and frostbite. Men who were not able to keep up were abandoned unless they were helped by their fellows. The men marched only at night, and were kept under cover during the day, ostensibly as protection against strafing by our own planes.

From a psychological point of view this situation is best described as a recurring cycle of fear, relief, and new fear. The men were afraid that they might die, that they might never get back home again, that they might never again have a chance to communicate with the outside, and that no one even knew they were alive. The Chinese, on the other hand, were reassuring and promised that the men would get back home soon, that conditions would improve, and that they would soon be permitted to communicate with the outside.

One of the chief problems for the men was the disorganization within the group itself. It was difficult to maintain close group ties if one was competing with others for the essentials of life, and if one spent one's resting time in overcrowded huts among others who had severe diarrhea and were occasionally incontinent. Lines of authority often broke down, and with this, group cohesion and morale suffered. A few men attempted to escape, but they were usually recaptured in a short time and returned to the group. The Chinese also fostered low morale and the feeling of being abandoned by systematically reporting false news about United Nations defeats and losses.

In this situation goals became increasingly short-run. As long as the men were marching, they had something to do and could look forward to relief from the harsh conditions of the march. However, arrival at a temporary camp was usually a severe disappointment. Not only were physical conditions as bad as ever, but the sedentary life in overcrowded quarters produced more disease and still lower morale.

What happened to the men under these conditions? During the one- to two-week marches they became increasingly apathetic. They developed a slow, plodding gait, called by one man a "prisoners' shuffle". Uppermost in their minds were fantasies of food: men remembered all the good meals they had ever had, or planned detailed menus for years into the future. To a lesser extent they thought of loved ones at home, and about cars which seemed to them to symbolize freedom and the return home.

In the temporary camps disease and exposure took a heavy toll in lives. But it was the feeling of many men, including some of the doctors who survived the experience, that some of these deaths were not warranted by a man's physical condition. Instead, what appeared to happen was that some men became so apathetic that they ceased to care about their bodily needs. They retreated further into themselves, refused to eat even what little food was available, refused to get any exercise, and eventually lay down as if waiting to die. The reports were emphatic concerning the lucidity and sanity of these men. They seemed willing to accept the prospect of death rather than to continue fighting a severely frustrating and depriving environment.

Two things seemed to save a man who was close to such an "apathy" death: getting him on his feet and doing something, no matter how trivial, or getting him angry or concerned about some present or future problem. Usually it was the effort of a friend who

Propaganda

People have been using propaganda for thousands of years. In our day-to-day activities we use it. Experts have refined these techniques to such a state that they have become powerful weapons in swaying the beliefs of large groups of people. You will notice, however, that if you can apply to propaganda statements the scientific method of seeking truth, you can determine their validity and accuracy.

The most common strategies used by expert propagandists are summarized below, accompanied by the symbols for them.

Name calling – giving an idea a bad label – is used to make us reject and condemn the idea without examining the evidence.

Glittering generality – associating something with a "virtue word" – is used to make us accept and approve the thing without examining the evidence.

Transfer carries the authority, sanction, and prestige of something respected and revered over to something else in order to make the latter acceptable; or it carries authority, sanction, and disapproval to cause us to reject and disapprove something the propagandist would have us reject and disapprove.

Testimonial consists in having some respected or hated person say that a given idea or program or person is good or bad.

Plain folks is the method by which a speaker attempts to convince his audience that he and his ideas are good because they are "of the people", the "plain folks".

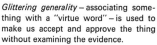

Card stacking involves the selection and use of facts or falsehoods, illustrations or distractions, and logical or illogical statements in order to give the best or the worst possible case for an idea, program, person, or product.

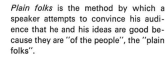

Band wagon has as its theme "Everybody – at least all of *us* – is doing it"; with it, the propagandist attempts to convince us that all members of a group to which we belong are accepting his program and that we *must therefore follow* our crowd and "jump on the band wagon".

Once we know that a speaker or writer is using one of these techniques in an attempt to convince us of an idea, we can separate the technique from the idea and see what the idea amounts to on its own merits.

Adapted from
Alfred McLung Lee and Elizabeth Bryant Lee
The Fine Art of Propaganda

The Turkish Prisoners of War: A Different Story

I told the Chinese commander of the camp that while we were a unit, I was in charge of the group. If he wanted anything done, he was to come to me, and I would see that it was done. When he removed me the responsibility would not fall on him, but on the man next below me, and after that the man below him. And so on down the ranks until there were only two privates left, then the senior private would be in charge. They could kill us, I told him, but they couldn't make us do what we didn't want to do. Discipline was our salvation and we knew it. If a Turk had responded to an order from his superiors to share his food or lift a litter the way some of your [American] men did, he would literally have had his teeth knocked in. Not by his superior either, but by the Turk nearest him.

A Turkish Officer

During World War II, an attempt was made to encourage German troops to surrender, by dropping leaflets describing conditions in Allied prisoner of war camps. Such leaflets showed actual pictures of conditions in a Canadian prisoner of war camp where the prisoners were photographed playing darts, ping-pong, and cards. A typical breakfast of bacon, eggs, toast, and coffee was mentioned. The whole pamphlet was truthful propaganda. When it was tried out on German prisoners in Italy, who knew of the treatment given prisoners in Allied camps, they refused to believe it: even the truth was too far removed from the opinions held by the prisoners. This outcome justifies the observation that, when a fact is presented that is completely different from the judgement held by a group, the fact will be rejected by that group.

In his purges, Stalin succeeded in turning proud and brave men into cringing cowards by depriving them of any possibility of identification with the party they had served all their lives and with the Russian masses. These old Bolsheviks had long cut themselves off from humanity outside Russia. They had renounced God. There was for them neither past nor future, neither memory nor glory outside the confines of Holy Russia and the Communist party — and both these were now wholly and irrevocably in Stalin's hands. They felt themselves isolated from everything that constitutes the essence of life. So they confessed. . . .

Eric Hoffer
The True Believer

maternally and insistently motivated the individual toward realistic goals which snapped him out of such a state of resignation. In one case such "therapy" consisted of kicking the man until he was mad enough to get up and fight.

Throughout this time, the Chinese played the role of the benevolent but handicapped captor. Prisoners were always reminded that it was their *own* Air Force bombing which was responsible for the inadequate supplies. Furthermore, they were reminded that they were getting treatment which was just as good as that which the average Chinese was getting. One important effect of this was that a man could never give *full* vent to his hostility toward the Chinese, even in fantasy. In their *manner*, their *words* they were usually solicitous and sympathetic. The Chinese also implied that conditions could be better for a prisoner if he would take a more "cooperative" attitude, if he would support their propaganda for peace. Thus a man was made to feel that he was himself responsible for his circumstances.

Arrival at a permanent camp usually brought relief from many of these physical hardships. Food, shelter, and medicine, while not plentiful, appeared to be sufficient for the maintenance of life and some degree of health. However, the Chinese now increased sharply their efforts to involve prisoners in their own propaganda program, and to undermine loyalties to their country. This marked the beginning of the second phase of the imprisonment experience.

The Chinese program of subversion and indoctrination was thoroughly integrated into the entire camp routine and involved the manipulation of the entire social life of the prison camp. Its aims appeared to be to manage a large group of prisoners with a minimum staff of guards, to indoctrinate them with Communist political beliefs, to interrogate them to obtain intelligence information and confessions for propaganda purposes, and to develop a corps of collaborators within the prisoner group. What success the Chinese had stemmed from their *total* control of the environment, not from the application of any one technique.

The most significant feature of Chinese prisoner camp control was the systematic destruction of the prisoners' formal and informal group structure. Soon after arrival at a camp, the men were segregated by race, nationality, and rank. The Chinese put their own men in charge of the platoons and companies, and made arbitrary selections of POW squad leaders to remind the prisoners that their old rank system no longer had any validity. In addition the Chinese attempted to undermine *informal* group structure by prohibiting any kind of group meeting, and by systematically encouraging mutual distrust by playing men off against one another. The most effective device to this end was the practice of obtaining from informers or Chinese spies detailed information about someone's activities, no matter how trivial, then calling him in to interrogate him about it. Such detailed surveillance of the men's activities made them feel that their own ranks were so infiltrated by spies and informers that it was not safe to trust anyone.

A similar device was used to obtain information during interrogation. After a man had resisted giving information for hours or days, he would be shown a signed statement by one of his fellow prisoners giving that same information. Still another device was to make prisoners who had not collaborated look like collaborators, by bestowing special favors upon them.

A particularly successful Chinese technique was their use of testimonials from other prisoners, such as the false germ-warfare confessions, and appeals based on familiar ideas, such as peace appeals. Confessions by prisoners or propaganda lectures given by collaborators had a particularly demoralizing effect, because only if *all* of the prisoners supported resistance could a man solidly believe that his values were correct, even if he could not defend them logically.

If the men, in spite of their state of social disorganization, did manage to organize any kind of group activity, the Chinese would quickly break up the group by removing its leaders or key members and assigning them to another camp.

Loyalties to home and country were undermined by the systematic manipulation of mail. Usually only mail which carried bad news was delivered. If a man received no mail at all, the Chinese suggested that his loved ones had abandoned him.

Feelings of social isolation were increased by the complete information control maintained in the camps. Only the Communist press, radio, magazines, and movies were allowed.

The weakening of the prisoner group's social structure is particularly significant because we depend to such an extent on the reactions of our associates in judging ourselves and others. The prisoners lost their most important sources of information and support concerning standards of behavior and beliefs. Often men who attempted to resist the Chinese by means other than *outright* obstruction or aggression failed to obtain the active support of others, often earning their suspicion instead.

At the same time the Chinese did create a situation in which meaningful social relationships could be had through common political activity, such as the "peace" committees which served as propaganda organs. The Chinese interrogators or instructors sometimes lived with prisoners for long periods of time in order to establish close personal relationships with them.

The Communist doctrines were presented through compulsory lectures followed by compulsory group discussions, for the purpose of justifying the conclusions given at the end of the lectures. On the whole, this phase of indoctrination was ineffective because of the crudeness of the propaganda material used in the lectures. However, its constant repetition seemed eventually to influence those men who did not have well-informed political opinions to start with, particularly because no counter arguments could be heard. The group discussions were effective only if their leader was someone who could keep control over the group and keep it on the topic of discussion. Attempts by the Chinese to use "progressive" POW's in the role of leaders were seldom successful because they aroused too much hostility in the men.

The Chinese also attempted to get prisoners to use mutual criticism and self-criticism in the fashion in which it is used within China. Whenever a POW was caught breaking one of the many camp rules, he was required to give an elaborate confession and

In one study, first-year high school students were exposed to one of three types of propaganda regarding care of their teeth. One group received a very forceful approach. They were shown pictures of diseased gums and the dangers that could result from poor tooth care were emphasized. A second group received a more moderate appeal which described the advantages of teeth care in an impersonal way, making use of pictures of lesser impact than the first group. A third group received a minimal appeal through the use of X-Ray photographs and pictures of healthy teeth. Even though students were more interested in and more worried by the forceful approach, the minimal appeal group got the best results in terms of the behaviour of the students.

Irving L. Janis and Seymour Feshbach
Effects of Fear-Arousing Communications

The following factors are usually considered in the development of effective propaganda:

1) *Use of slogans:* Slogans are catchy terms and tend to simplify and polarize ideas. The following are examples:
"If you don't do it, it won't get done."
"The right man for the right job."

2) *Simple language:* The ideas must be presented in simple words so that they can be grasped without consideration of subtleties.

3) *Stereotypes:* Treat categories of people as one, with the use of such terms as the French Canadians, the lower class, the administration.

4) *Colour words:* To have more impact, use words that produce sensations: "sweat" has greater impact than "perspiration", "grimy" than "soiled".

5) *Distortion:* Use some factors that might affect the acceptance of the message. When selling cigarettes, focus on taste and smoothness and avoid reference to excessive use and its dangers.

6) *Repetition:* The more times you repeat the name of a product or idea, the greater the chance of the person's recalling it when he has to make a decision. When someone asks you what kind of detergent you want, a name comes to mind because you have heard it so often on television. The same is true of toothpaste and many other products.

7) *Falsification:* Propaganda often contains out-and-out lies. Hitler believed that the great lie would be more likely to be accepted than would a little one.

Anti-smoking propaganda may stress the almost inevitable horror of lung cancer, and safe driving propaganda may make use of traffic accident figures during the holidays to remind drivers to slow down and be careful. We have no evidence that such programs have any effect, because no adequately controlled studies have been made of them, but they are continued because of the firm belief people have in the [value] of fear aroused as a means of persuasion.

Henry C. Lindgren
An Introduction to Social Psychology

At a city health fair, visitors were exposed to a film showing the effects of lung cancer. Those under "high arousal" conditions saw a film portraying the story of a young smoker whose diseased left lung was removed because of a cancerous growth. Those under "mild arousal" saw only the first part of the film where the patient was only taken as far as the operating room. The visitors were given a questionnaire to fill out and were urged to take a free X-Ray. Apparently the high fear appeal was most effective, for in that group they were not only more likely to have taken advantage of the free X-Ray but they also indicated that they were more concerned.

Howard Leventhal and Patricia Niles
A Field Experiment on Fear-Arousal
(with data on the validity of
questionnaire measures)

In another study using three levels of arousal and two categories of smokers, light and heavy, different results were obtained. The "mild arousal" was more successful in getting the light smokers to have chest X-Rays taken. The "medium arousal" was more successful in getting the heavy smokers to have chest X-Rays taken.

Howard Leventhal and Jean C. Watts
*Sources of Resistance to Fear-Arousing
Communications on Smoking and Lung Cancer*

... propaganda does not emanate from all conditions of conflict. Such unscrupulous tactics are resorted to only when one or the other of the competing groups realizes that an emotion-laden half-truth is a far more effective manipulator of men than is the unadulterated truth. If a group supporting an ideology is able by employing such tactics to galvanize a man's emotions to an intensity which obliterates his rationale, then the propagandist has at his discretion the support not of men but of puppets who will dance when the string is pulled.

Timothy C. Jeffery
"Propaganda: Enemy of Democracy?" in
Social Problems in a Changing World

self-criticism, no matter how trivial the offense. In general, the POW's were able to use this opportunity to ridicule the Chinese by taking advantage of their lack of understanding of American slang. They would emphasize the wrong parts of sentences or insert words and phrases which made it apparent to other prisoners that the joke was on the Chinese. Often men were required to make these confessions in front of large groups of other prisoners. If the man could successfully communicate his lack of sincerity, this ritual could backfire on the Chinese by giving the men an opportunity to express their solidarity (by sharing a communication which could not be understood by the Chinese). However, in other instances, prisoners who viewed such public confessions felt contempt for the confessor and felt their own group was being undermined still further by such public humiliation.

Various tales of how prisoners resisted the pressures put on them have been widely circulated in the press. For example, a number of prisoners ridiculed the Chinese by playing baseball with a basketball, yet telling the Chinese this was the correct way to play the game. Such stories suggest that morale and group solidarity was actually quite high in the camps. Our interviews with the men suggest that morale climbed sharply during the *last six to nine months* of imprisonment when the armistice talks were under way, when the compulsory indoctrination program had been put on a voluntary basis, and when the Chinese were improving camp conditions in anticipation of the soldiers' release. However, we heard practically no stories of successful group resistance or high morale from the first year or so in the camps when the indoctrination program was seriously pursued by the Chinese. (At that time the men had neither the time nor the opportunity to play any kinds of games, because all their time was spent on indoctrination activities or exhausting labor.)

Throughout, the Chinese created an environment in which rewards such as extra food, medicine, special privileges, and status were given for cooperation and collaboration, while threats of death, non-release, reprisal against family, torture, decreases in food and medicine, and imprisonment served to keep men from offering much resistance. Only imprisonment was consistently used as an actual punishment. Continued resistance was usually handled by transferring the prisoner to a so-called "reactionary" camp.

Whatever behavior the Chinese attempted to produce, they always *paced* their demands very carefully, they always required some level of *participation* from the prisoner, no matter how little, and they *repeated* endlessly.

To what extent did these pressures produce either changes in beliefs and attitudes, or collaboration? Close observation of those who returned home and the reports of the men themselves suggest that the Chinese did not have much success in changing beliefs and attitudes. Doubt and confusion were created in many prisoners as a result of having to examine so closely their own way of thinking, but very few changes, if any, occurred that resembled actual *conversion* to communism. The type of prisoner who was most likely to become *sympathetic* toward Communism was the

ne who had occupied a low status position in this society, and
or whom the democratic principles were not very meaningful.

In producing collaboration, however, the Chinese were far more
effective. By collaboration I mean such activities as giving lectures
for the Communists, writing and broadcasting propaganda, giving
false confessions, writing and signing petitions, informing on fellow POW's and so on; none of these activities required a personal
change of belief. Some 10 to 15 per cent of the men collaborated
on a regular basis but the reasons for this response are very complex. By far the most important factor was the amount of pressure
the Chinese put on a particular prisoner. Beyond this, the re-
ponses of the men permit one to distinguish several sets of motives
that operated, though it is impossible to tell how many cases of
each type there may have been.

) Some men collaborated to obtain better living conditions and
more food; these men were without any kind of stable group
identification, and exploited the situation for its material benefits without any regard for the consequences to themselves, their
fellow prisoners, or their country.

) Some men collaborated because their egos were too weak to
withstand the physical and psychological rigors; these men were
primarily motivated by fear, though they often offered other
reasons for their behavior; they were unable to resist any kind
of authority figure, and could be blackmailed by the Chinese
once they had begun to collaborate.

) Some men collaborated with the firm conviction that they were
infiltrating the Chinese ranks and obtaining intelligence information which would be useful to the UN forces. This was a
convenient excuse for anyone who could not withstand the
pressures. Many of these men were initially tricked into collaboration or were motivated by a desire to communicate with
the outside world. None of these men became confused about
their beliefs; what Communist beliefs they might have pro-
fessed were for the benefit of the Chinese only.

) The prisoner who was vulnerable to the Communist appeal
because of his low status in this society often collaborated with
the conviction that he was doing the right thing in supporting
the Communist peace movement. This group included the
younger and less intelligent men from backward or rural areas,
the malcontents, and members of various minority groups.
These men often viewed themselves as failures in our society,
and felt that society had never given them a chance. They were
positively attracted by the immediate status and privileges
which went with being a "progressive", and by the promise of
important roles which they could presumably play in the peace
movement of the future.

Perhaps the most important thing to note about collaboration
is the manner in which the social disorganization contributed to
it. A man might make a slanted radio broadcast in order to communicate with the outside, he might start reading Communist
literature out of sheer boredom, he might give information which

Propaganda and Advertising

Advertising as used today is primarily a type of
propaganda. The essence of propaganda is that
it conditions people to act in a way favorable to
or desired by the propagandist. It deliberately
attempts to influence, persuade, and convince
people to act in a way that they would not
otherwise act.

Edmund D. McGarry

Advertising is not a plot. Nor are most advertising
people wily plotters. They are salesmen, in print
and over the air. And just as most good salesmen-
in-person seek to know all they can about their
prospective customers, so do most manufacturers
and their salesmen-in-advertising undertake to
learn all *they* can about their prospective customers. Motivational research is done primarily
for two reasons: first, to find out what people
know about products (and services), and second,
to find out what people want in products (and
services) that may not currently be there.

Fairfax M. Cone
Advertising Is Not a Plot

How much is spent on advertising in Canada?

Out of every dollar's worth of goods and services
produced in Canada, less than 2c. goes for
advertising. Or, if you look at it another way, the
total amount spent in Canada on every kind of
advertising – including your local stores and
theatres, national advertisers, and the federal
and provincial governments – is less than 15c.
per person each day. The cost of all food advertising is about 3c. per day per Canadian.

Canadian Advertising Advisory Board
Advertising Today

In business [propaganda] is used primarily by
sellers to obtain a market by conditioning people
in the market to accept the particular products
offered. The growth of new techniques of communication has greatly extended the range of
propaganda penetration, has expanded the number of products advertised, and has increased
the total amount of propaganda disseminated;
but the aim of the messages carried is essentially
unchanged since the beginning of civilization.

In fact, the use of force of argument instead of
physical force marked the change from savagery
to civilized living. "The creation of the world,"
said Plato, "is the victory of persuasion over
force."

Edmund D. McGarry

... it has been estimated that to build a single modern car by hand could cost between $50,000 and $70,000; printing a single copy of a book might run up to $5,000 or $10,000, depending upon the author's fees, the artwork costs, type of paper, binding, etc. Advertising, however, like other forms of promotion, helps to sell thousands of cars and books so that the manufacturer can make use of high-volume, low-cost production methods.

So money spent on advertising frequently *saves* money for the customer.

Canadian Advertising Advisory Board
Advertising Today

When you see a woman who has found herself, you know it. There's a quiet excitement about her that says, "I like being me." Have you found the real you? Some women never do. In fact many women never make the most exciting discovery of all: they should have been a blonde.

(An advertisement for a hair-colouring product.)

People don't want to be told that a car is safe. It gives an image of the humdrum and ordinary. So it makes them feel that they're ordinary people. They want a car to lift them out of their ordinary lives. They want to feel power at their command. A good advertisement is one that creates excitement about the car.

(The opinion of a car manufacturer.)

Grandmother cherished her furniture for its sensible, practical value, but today people know that it is hardly the practical considerations which determine their choices between Post's and Kellogg's, Oldsmobiles and Buicks, or Arpege and Chanel No. 5. They know that package color, television commercials, and newspaper and magazine advertisements incline them toward one preference or another.

Sidney J. Levy
Symbols for Sale

There is a brand of margarine which, while good and wholesome, is available for housewives who like it inexpensive, another for those who want one that is soft when taken straight out of the refrigerator, another for those who desire, or are advised to use spreads with a high content of essential fatty acids, another for those who want the butteriest of buttery tastes. Whatever consumers want, we try to let them have. The only limitation is that enough customers must want it for us to be able to supply it at a price they are prepared to pay.

Lord Cole
Chairman of Unilever Ltd.

he knew the Chinese already had, and so on. Once this happened however, the Chinese rewarded him, increased pressure on him to collaborate, and blackmailed him by threatening exposure. At the same time in most cases, his fellow prisoners forced him into further collaboration by mistrusting him and excluding him. Thus a man had to stand entirely on his own judgment and strength, and both of these often failed. One of the most common failures was a man's lack of awareness concerning the effects of his own actions on the other prisoners, and the value of these actions for the Chinese propaganda effort. The man who confessed to germ warfare, thinking he could repudiate such a confession later, did not realize its immediate propaganda value to the Communists.

A certain percentage of men, though the exact number is difficult to estimate, exhibited continued resistance and obstructionism toward Chinese indoctrination efforts. Many of these men were well integrated with secure, stable group identifications who could withstand the social isolation and still exercise good judgment. Others were obstructionists whose histories showed recurring resistance to any form of authority. Still others were idealists or martyrs to religious and ethical principles, and still others were anxious, guilt-ridden individuals who could only cope with their own strong impulses to collaborate by denying them and over reacting in the other direction.

By far the largest group of prisoners, however, established a complex compromise between the demands of the Chinese and their own value system. This adjustment, called by the men "playing it cool", consisted primarily of a physical and emotional withdrawal from the whole environment. These men learned to suspend their feelings and to adopt an attitude of watching and waiting, rather than hoping and planning. This reaction, though passive, was not as severe as the apathy described earlier. It was a difficult adjustment to maintain because some concessions had to be made to the Chinese in the form of trivial or well-timed collaborative acts, and in the form of a pretended interest in the indoctrination program. At the same time, each man had to be prepared to deal with the hostility of his buddies if he made an error in judgment.

Discussion

This paper has placed particular emphasis on the psychological factors involved in "brainwashing" because it is my opinion that the process is primarily concerned with social forces, not with the strengths and weaknesses of individual minds. It has often been asserted that drugs, hypnotic techniques, refined "mental tortures" and more recently, implanted electrodes can make the task of the "brainwasher" much easier by rendering the human mind submissive with a minimum of effort. There is little question that such techniques can be used to force confessions or signatures on documents prepared by the captor; but so can withdrawal of food, water, or air produce the same results. The point is that the Chinese Communists do not appear to be interested in obtaining merely a confession or short-term submission. Instead, they appear to be interested in producing changes in men which will be lasting and self-sustaining. A germ-warfare confession alone was not nough – the POW had to "testify" before an international commission, explaining in detail how the bombs had been dropped, nd had to tell his story in other prison camps to his fellow POW's.

There is little evidence that drugs, posthypnotic suggestion, or mplanted electrodes can now or ever will be able to produce the ind of behavior exhibited by many prisoners who collaborated nd made false confessions. On the other hand, there is increasing vidence that Russian and Chinese interrogation and indoctrination techniques involve the destruction of the person's ties to riends, family, country, and personal identity. When the partial lestruction of his idea of himself is successfully accomplished, the erson is offered a new identity for himself and given the opporunity to identify with new groups. What physical torture and leprivation are involved in this process may be either a calculated ttempt to degrade and humiliate a man to destroy his image of imself as a dignified human being, or the product of circumtances, i.e., failure of supply lines to the prison, loss of temper on he part of the interrogator, an attempt to inspire fear in other risoners by torturing one of them, and so on. We do not have ufficient evidence to determine which of these alternatives represents Communist intentions; possibly all of them are involved in he actual prison situation.

Ultimately that which keeps human beings going is their personality integration born out of secure and stable associations with mportant individuals and groups. It may be possible to produce emporary submission by direct intervention in brain processes, ut only by destroying a man's self-image and his group supports an one produce any lasting changes in his beliefs and attitudes. By concerning ourselves with the problem of artificially creating ubmission in man, we run the real risk of overlooking the fact hat we are in a genuine struggle of ideas with other portions of he world and that man often submits himself directly to ideas nd principles.

To understand and combat "brainwashing" we must look at hose social conditions which make people ready to accept new deas from anyone who states them clearly and forcefully, and hose social conditions which give people the sense of integrity vhich will sustain them when their immediate social and emoional supports are stripped away.

What almost guarantees the honesty of advertising and advertising people is advertising itself. Punishment for sinning is swift and sure. It comes from a public that deeply resents being fooled and that will not buy any product again that has failed to live up to its original advertising promise.

Fairfax M. Cone
Advertising Is Not a Plot

Code of Canadian Advertising

The Code, summarized below, has been prepared by the Canadian Advertising Advisory Board. These standards apply with equal force to both print and broadcast advertising.

1) False or Misleading Advertising – An advertisement has to be substantiated by fact.

2) Public Decency – No advertisement which is vulgar or suggestive in any way will be accepted.

3) Superstitions and Fears – An advertisement which is designed to exploit superstition or fear will be rejected.

4) Exploitation of Human Misery – An advertisement which offers false hope for the mentally or physically ill will not be accepted.

5) Price Claims – An advertisement will not be accepted if it makes false price claims or comparisons with other products.

6) Testimonials – Any advertisement which offers testimonial evidence of benefits must be substantiated.

7) Disparaging Claims – Disparagement of other companies' products cannot be accepted unless definite substantiation can be called upon.

8) Professional or Scientific Claims – Statements made by professionals or scientific authorities must not be distorted for the convenience of advertising.

9) Guarantees – All guarantees or warranties presented in an advertisement must be fully explained therein or the public must be advised where they can find such information.

10) Advertising to Children – An advertisement presentation which might lead to the moral, physical, or mental damage of a child will not be accepted.

11) Imitation – An advertisement which is so closely related to another advertisement claim that it deliberately confuses the consumer will be rejected.

12) Bait Advertising – Products or services must be available to the public at the prices or terms stated in advertisements.

The world is made up of many kinds of people living in many conditions in many different cul tures. During the last century, when Europeans came into contact with other cultures – usually through conquest – they made judgements about the inferior nature of the cultures they en countered. From Cairo to Canton, the European imposed his culture wherever he could. Often his life style was a transplant of the situation at home. The broad cultural significance of the sub ject peoples' life styles was neglected or misunderstood by the colonial administrator, missionary, and businessman.

In more recent times, anthropologists and sociologists have begun to make comparative studies of other cultures. When another society is studied, a new frame of reference is established within which to view all cultures and, more particularly, one's own. While each society has unique solu tions to a similar problem, the success of the solution varies greatly. It is possible to learn a great deal, both positively and negatively, from cross-cultural comparisons through the exploration of the ways in which other societies have met a particular problem or challenge.

In every society, the common element is man, who has common needs, desires, and feelings. While learning about other men and other cultures, we learn about ourselves and our own culture. The following selections give us a view of other people and their view of the world. The first selec tion deals with a comparative view of the use of space and time in North and South America. The second selection describes the problems that beset advertisers in Quebec when they tried to sell their products through a sales promotion that was in cultural collision with some aspects of Que bec society.

Among the eastern highlanders of New Guinea, character ideals are such that

The child most liked and admired by adults . . . is the one who commands attention by tantrums, by a dominating approach to his fellows, by bullying and swaggering, by carrying tales to his elders. These actions epitomize the character- istics so desirable in the "strong" man and woman. . . . They are the mark . . . of the fighter and warrior. . . .

Ronald M. Berndt
Excess and Restraint: Social Control among a New Guinea Mountain People

Our silent language

Edward T. Hall

There are deep and subtle differences between the people of North America and their South American neighbours. Surface differences can be seen and dealt with. What defeats all of us are the hidden elements in man's psychological make-up whose presence are all too often not even suspected.

Like germs that can't been seen, there are many unseen factors that cause psychological difficulty. All one sees is the outward be- haviour by people of basic cultural differences – surface display.

I will examine three topics to demonstrate a point. These are time, space, and friendship. Unseen differences between the North American and his neighbours differ in all three.

I first became aware of space as I learned aspects of human be- haviour when I noted that people raised in other cultures handled it differently. In the Middle East I felt crowded and was often made to feel anxious.

Fellow North Americans also found it hard to adapt themselves to houses and offices arranged so differently, and often commented on how there was too little or too much space, and how much space was wasted. These spatial differences are not limited to offices and homes: towns, subway systems, and road networks usually follow patterns that appear curious to one not accustomed to the culture.

The "natural" way to describe space may be different in two cultures. For instance, I discovered in Japan that intersections of streets were named and the streets were not.

These differing ideas of space contain traps for the uninformed. A person raised in North America is often likely to give an unintentional snub to a Latin American because of the way he handles space relationships, particularly the physical distance between individuals during conversations.

A conversation I once observed between a Latin and a North American began at one end of a 40-foot hall. I watched the two conversationalists until they had finally reached the other end of the hall.

This maneuver had been effected by a continual series of small backward steps on the part of the North American as he unconsciously retreated searching for a comfortable talking distance. Each time, there was an accompanying closing of the gap, as his Latin friend attempted to reestablish his own accustomed conversation distance.

In formal business conversations in North America, the "proper" distance to stand when talking to another adult male who is simply a business acquaintance, is about two feet. This distance diminishes, of course, at social functions like a cocktail party, but anything under eight to ten inches is likely to irritate.

To the Latin, with his own unique culture, a distance of two feet seems remote and cold, sometimes even unfriendly. One of the things that gives the South or Central American the feeling that the North American is *simpatico* is when he is no longer made uncomfortable by closeness or by being touched.

North Americans, working in offices in Latin America, may keep their local acquaintances at a distance – not the Latin American distance – by remaining behind a desk or typewriter. Even North Americans who have lived in Latin America for years have been known to use the "barricade approach" to communication, and to remain completely unaware of its cultural significance.

They are aware only that they "feel comfortable" when not crowded, without realizing that the distance and the desk often create a situation that distorts or gives a cold tone to virtually everything that takes place. The hold of the cultural pattern is so strong, however, that the Latin is sometimes observed trying to "climb over" the interviewing obstacles – leaning across the desk for instance – in order to achieve a distance at which he can communicate comfortably.

Latin Time Lag

As with space, there are many cultural differences associated with time which characterize each people. The North American has developed a language of time that involves much more than being prompt. He can usually tell you when his own cultural patterns have been violated, but not how they work. His blood pressure

---

In Bali, on occasions . . . when the strictest etiquette must be observed the children are not much in evidence, so quiet are they. . . . The hierarchy of age recognized in any family group . . . [is such that] every child knows that he is allowed to "speak down to", scold, and order about his younger brothers and cousins, just as he himself is spoken down to and ordered about by brothers and all relatives older than he.

Jane Belo
"The Balinese Temper, Character and Personality"
in Mary Ellen Goodman
The Individual and Culture

Along about half a millennium ago, say the 14th century, in Canton, China, some inspired artisan introduced the carving of concentric spheres from a single piece of ivory. Today, when a Westerner first sees one of these, he is most likely to ask, "How did they get the little spheres inside each other?"

And the answer that anyone of Eastern persuasion would give is, "The little spheres were always inside the larger ones, but it took the skill and vision of a master artist to set them free."

Don Fabun
The Dynamics of Change

Among the Andaman Islanders there is such a strong emphasis upon generosity that no man would fail to give away the large and better part of the pig or dugong he has killed. Among the Arunta of Australia there is no value placed upon generosity but, by customary law, a man is simply expected to give certain parts of the animal to particular relatives. On the other hand, societies with large populations do not need such institutions – they can afford to let people starve to death if it is within their ethical system to do so.

Walter Goldschmidt
Exploring the Ways of Mankind

To the [North American] woman a system of plural wives seems "instinctively" abhorrent. She cannot understand how any woman can fail to be jealous and uncomfortable if she must share her husband with other women. She feels it "unnatural" to accept such a situation. On the other hand a Koryak woman in Siberia . . . would find it hard to understand how a woman could be so selfish and so undesirous of feminine companionship in the home as to wish to restrict her husband to one mate.

Clyde Kluckhohn
Mirror for Man

Some Comparisons Between our Culture and Another More Primitive Culture

Trobriand Islanders	Canadians
Settlement pattern	
Live in villages with a few houses set in two concentric rings	Live on farms, in villages, towns, cities, and metropolitan areas
Social and settlement pattern	
One arc of houses shelters the king, his wives, and their children	House location bears no relationship to kinship or friendship, but is based on economic status with people of similar income living close to each other
Kin and location	
Each village is owned by a sub-clan and the head man is usually the eldest	No kinship groups own a village, town, or city. In some isolated areas, because of intermarriage, a tendency toward kin relationship occurs
Household groups	
Family lives together, sometimes with other relatives; the head man may have several wives	Family lives together until children mature. Other relatives may live there, but this is not preferred
Adolescent housing before marriage	
Boys live together after maturity; girls live with relatives	Boys and girls usually live at home until marriage. The sexes are segregated
Property ownership	
Houses and livestock are owned by the men and not by the women or families	Houses may be owned, rented, or purchased over a long period by carrying a debt
Dwelling design	
Dwellings are small and built of local materials; usually have one room	Variety of dwellings made of many materials, both natural and synthetic. Tremendous differences in size of dwellings

rises, and he loses his temper when he is kept waiting; this is because time and the ego have been linked.

As a rule, the longer a North American is kept waiting in his own setting, the greater the discrepancy between the status of the two parties. Because of their high status, important people can keep less important people waiting. Also, very important business takes precedence over less important business. The North American has developed a pattern for seeing one person at a time, but individual appointments aren't usually scheduled by the Latin American to the exclusion of other appointments. The Latin often enjoys seeing several people at once even if he has to talk on different matters at the same time.

In this setting, the North American may feel he is not being properly treated, that his dignity is under attack, even though this simply is not true. The Latin American clock on the wall may look the same, but it tells a different sort of time.

By the North American clock, a consistently late man is considered undependable. To judge a Latin American by the same time values is to risk a major error.

This cultural error may be compounded by a further miscalculation. Suppose the North American has waited 45 minutes or an hour and finally gets to see the Latin American with whom he has an appointment, only to be told, with many apologies, that "there is only five minutes – maybe a meeting can be arranged for tomorrow or next week?"

At this point, the North American's schedule has been "shot". If it is important, he will have to make the time. What he may not understand is the cultural pattern common in Mexico, for example, and that is that one is very likely to take one's time before doing business, in order to provide time for "getting acquainted".

First meetings leave the North American with the feeling he isn't getting anywhere. If not forewarned he keeps trying to get down to business and stop "wasting time". This turns out to be a mistake.

In Canada and the United States, discussion is used as a means to an end; the deal. One tries to make his point with neatness and dispatch – quickly and efficiently. The North American begins by taking up major issues, leaving details for later, perhaps for others to work out.

Discussion, however, is to the Latin American an important part of life. It serves a different purpose and operates according to rules of form; it has to be done right. For the Latin American, the emphasis is on courtesy, not speed. Close friends who see each other frequently shake hands when they meet and when they part.

For the Latin American it is the invisible social distance that is maintained, not the physical distance. Forming a new friendship or a business acquaintance must be done properly. The Latin first wants to know the human values of a new acquaintance – his cultural interests, his philosophy of life – not his efficiency. This is all accompanied by elaborate and graceful formal verbal expressions, which people in North America have long felt too busy to take time for. They tend to assume familiarity very quickly, to invite new acquaintances to their homes after one or two meetings.

But the Latin American entertains only friends of very long standing in his home – and never for business reasons.

Of course, times are changing, because there are an increasing number of Latin businessmen who now demand punctuality even more strictly than in the North. However, there are still a great many times when the old patterns prevail and are not understood. The hidden differences seem to center around the fact that in the North, the ego of the man is more on the surface, whereas in the South preserving institutional forms is important.

It has been observed that in North America, friendships may not be long lasting. People are apt to take up friends quickly and drop them just as quickly.

A feature influencing North American friendship patterns is that people move constantly. The North American, as a rule, looks for and find his friends next door and among those with whom he works.

There are for him well-defined, hard-and-fast rules governing the obligations of friendship. At just what point our friendships give way to business opportunism or pressure from above is difficult to say.

In Latin America, on the other hand, while friendships are not formed as quickly or as easily as in North America, they often go much deeper and last longer. They almost always involve real obligations. It is important to stress that in Latin America your "friends" will not let you down. The fact that they, personally, are having difficulties is never an excuse for failing friends. You, in turn, are obligated to look out for their interests.

The weight of tradition presses the Latin American to do business within a circle of friends and relatives. If a product or service he needs is not available within his circle, he hesitates to go outside; if he does so, he looks for a new friend who can supply the want.

Apart from the cultural need to "feel right" about a new relationship, there is the logic of the business system. One of the realities of life is that it is dangerous to enter into business with someone over whom you have no "control". The difference between the two systems lies in the controls. One is formal, personal, and depends upon family and friends. The other is technical–legal, impersonal, and depends upon courts and contracts.

Europeans often comment on how candid the North American is. Being candid, he seeks this in others. What fools him is that the Latin American does not readily respond to others. One has to be known and trusted – admitted into the circle of friendship – before this happens. Even then, what is not said may be just as important, and just as much noticed, as what is said.

Until we face up to the reality of the unseen cultural differences, and make them quite clear, difficulties in communication are going to continue. These unseen cultural differences drain the great reservoir of goodwill that the people of the Americas feel in their hearts for each other.

Occupation	
Occupation depends on the jobs that need to be done	Highly specialized jobs requiring training

Housework	
Many tasks, gathering and preparing food. Helpers are available usually from among the relatives. Men and women frequently work together on some tasks. Men look after children	Household tasks performed by the wife, who cooks, shops, cares for the children. These tasks are occasionally shared by other family members

Marriage and divorce	
Marriage and divorce are a matter of personal will and approval of the girl's family	Elaborate ceremony for weddings, both legal and religious overtones. Divorce requires prolonged legal activity

Navaho Shame and Eskimo Guilt

In every society, when someone breaks a law, there must be a reaction to this by the society. Among Navahos, the wrongdoer usually explains that he was possessed by a witch and he (Navaho witches are men) caused the evil to be done. The society accepts this excuse because the tribe believes that evil is done by a witch. Navaho males avoid being accused of witchcraft, since witches are beaten and even killed by the outraged tribe. Navahos consequently avoid any behaviour that might attract community attention and a subsequent charge of witchcraft. But wrongdoing is less serious than witchcraft.

The Eskimo society has many opportunities for transgression. If an individual transgresses a spirit's authority or if he does not wear an amulet, he feels guilt and shame. After the repentent sinner has admitted his sin, he is then accepted back into the community and is treated like a disobedient child who needs help and sympathy.

There was an old English custom, called "beating the bounds", in which a villager would take the boys once a year around the bounds of the village territory and at each point marker give the boys a thrashing so that the boundaries would be impressed on their memories enabling them later on to recall the limits of the territory. Also when a boy's father introduced him to someone important, he would knock him down at the important man's feet, saying, "Now you'll remember this."

Ralph Linton
The Cultural Background of Personality

An American researcher, E. Paul Torrance, has conducted a number of studies on stress-seeking behaviour in young people. He collected thousands of imaginative stories by children aged 12 and younger. These stories were written about animals and people displaying behaviour associated with trying conditions that involve stress; for example, "The lion that won't roar", "The monkey that flew", "The cat that won't scratch". The study described below involves four groups of children, one from the public schools of Toronto, one from the public schools of San Juan, Puerto Rico, and two from schools in the United States. Of course, it is assumed that when children are asked to write stories about flying monkeys, roarless lions and timid cats, they will indicate in those stories something about the values of their cultures. In this study, the two American and the Puerto Rican groups tended to emphasize the self-acting nature of man, with the individual responding to his own needs rather than to outside pressures or personal challenges. However, the Canadian group differed markedly. The Canadian stories reflected greater responsiveness to social and other pressures.

The Canadian and Puerto Rican groups were similar to each other and differed from the American groups in that they showed higher proportions of non-stress-seeking behaviours. The Puerto Rican stories emphasized a rather active pleasure-seeking direction not leading to stressful situations, while the Canadian stories described a more emotionless kind of avoidance of stress situations. The Canadian heroes tended to encounter opposition more frequently than the heroes of the other stories. The Toronto group emerged as only moderately stress-seeking and largely in response to social and other external pressures. It suggests a more conservative approach to stress behaviour.

The American is shocked by the Chinaman's lack of chivalry toward his wife; the Chinaman is shocked by the American's lack of reverence toward his parents. The American jokes about the absence of toilet soap in his chamber in a French hotel; while the hotel keeper shrugs his shoulders at the American's willingness to use a cake of soap after previous guests instead of carrying his own soap.

Edward A. Ross
New-Age Sociology

The French, the English, and the Germans have entirely different ways of using their material possessions. What stands for the height of dependability and respectability with the English would be old-fashioned and backward to us. The Japanese take pride in often inexpensive but tasteful arrangements that are used to produce the proper emotional setting.

Edward T. Hall
The Silent Language

Advertising themes and quiet revolutions: dilemmas in French Canada

Frederick Elkin

Canada has recently experienced what has popularly been called a "Quiet Revolution". The French Canadians who make up some 80 per cent of the population of the province of Quebec, and most of whom have been economically and educationally far behind their English-Canadian compatriots, rebelled in two respects. First they challenged their tradition-oriented way of life and sought to modernize the province. Second, they fought, not for the first time, against their lower status and demanded their rights of equality with the English Canadians. The movement had been smoldering with occasional outbursts for many years, but its intensity and rapidity, beginning in 1960, was so great that the term *revolution* is not inappropriate. A new government, supported by mass media, youth, intellectuals, labor, and significant segments of the church and business community, led the movement to update French Canada economically and socially and to become "maîtres chez nous".

No aspect of French-Canadian life remained untouched by the Quiet Revolution. Modernization was one central theme, evidenced in the increase of highway construction, the reform of the police structure, the letting of government contracts by tender, new direction in education, and legislation awarding more rights to women. A rebirth of the French language and culture was another theme. Expo, the international fair in 1967, was still another indication of the energy and confidence generated. Underlying and giving a push to the entire movement was a strong spirit of modern French-Canadian nationalism.

As part of a larger study of advertising and social change in French Canada, we have analyzed French-language national advertising before and during the Quiet Revolution. The problems associated with advertising, because their rays extend so widely into the society, strikingly point up issues and dilemmas occasioned by the rapid social change.

Advertising Themes Before the Quiet Revolution

National advertising, like other industry in Quebec, was introduced primarily by English-speaking Canadians and Americans. The general policy was to take a very carefully prepared English advertisement and turn it over to a French-Canadian translator for a quick, routine, more or less literal translation. Translation was not considered difficult; presumably anyone who knew both languages could do the job.

Over the years, French-Canadian translators and clerks, through working in advertising agencies, underwent an informal apprenticeship and learned the advertising business. At the same time, doors formerly closed were opened and many French Canadians attained positions of moderate responsibility. In the 1950s, the French Canadians who were moving ahead in advertising began to argue that French Canadians had a distinctive culture and that French-language ads were often badly translated, inappropriate, and ineffective. Minor adaptations *were* sometimes made: A girl at a typewriter, called Betty in an English advertisement, became Blanche in the French; a coffee ad in the French translation added "Préparé à Québec". But few changes touched on basic themes, styles or personality differences. French Canadians argued that the advertisements were Anglo-Saxon in spirit and were passing the French Canadians by. The ads, they said, should be directed to the values, interests, and dispositions of French Canadians. In a few instances, the French Canadians were permitted to develop distinctive campaigns, the most notable occurring during the Korean War in 1951. A series of ads was developed in which the themes turned back to the heroes of the past, to the heroic explorers, settlers, and pioneers of early Canada. The recruiting ads for the navy, for a life at sea, referred to the courageous fishermen of Brittany and Normandy who founded Canada and such famous sailors of French-Canadian history as Champlain, Cartier, and d'Iberville.

To the French Canadians in advertising, the campaign was a major event. For the first time, tens of thousands of dollars were turned over to French Canadians to create ads to be directed solely to French Canadians. The armed forces campaign had sought to recruit soldiers. Why, argued the French Canadians, could not the same principle be carried over to commercial products?

Some companies were willing to try. Labatt's Brewery developed a new campaign for its anniversary "50 Ale" known in French as "Bière 50". The English campaign stressed the "modern" touch with scenes of golf and various social activities. The campaign in French, however, featured a short, stocky lumberjack, known as Monsieur Cinquante, wearing a checkered shirt on which appeared a number 50. The lumberjack, strong and fearless, was a well-known symbol in French-Canadian history and lore. A Monsieur Cinquante walked the street giving out fifty-cent pieces to passersby and appeared on television commercials discussing hunting and fishing in Quebec. In magazine cartoon-type advertisements, he scored a spectacular hockey goal and rescued a skater in distress while holding on to a cliff with one bare hand. The advertising copy spoke of the beer as "brassé dans le Québec au goût du Québec" – brewed in Quebec to the taste of Quebec.

At the same time, Labatt developed still another campaign with a distinctively French-Canadian flavor. This campaign, focusing on the company name, centered on tracing names back in time, a subject of popular and fascinating interest in Quebec. The approximately five million French Canadians in Canada today may be traced back to only ten thousand or so French settlers who arrived on this continent in the sixteenth century. Thus, a relatively small group of men passed down their names to modern French Canadians and many similar names are held by thousands of families.

The interest in the past among French Canadians has always been linked with the glory of French Canada's early history. The popular historians portrayed the settlers as courageous, valiant, and hardy pioneers who, under great hardship, cleared the forest, hunted wild animals, fought the Indians, and tilled the land.

Competition is present to some degree in every society, but can take many forms. The fiercely competitive Kwakiutl and the non-competitive Zuni offer an interesting contrast. The Kwakiutl work very hard and accumulate wealth that is used as a basis for personal status, rather than to provide living comforts. Although they compete for status in their everyday lives, this competition reaches its peak at the famous "potlatch". Here the chiefs and the members of the leading families compete with each other to see how much they can give away or destroy. It is conceivable for a family to spend the best part of their lives accumulating wealth, then give it all away or destroy it in a single potlatch. However, by doing this they establish the social status of their children. Those who keep their goods receive considerable criticism from members of the tribe.

By contrast, the Zuni do not concern themselves with the accumulation of goods, nor do they compete in individual skill areas. Most of their goods are owned by the entire community, and it is considered in very bad taste to demonstrate individual superiority. It is difficult for the Zuni child to exist in the North American culture because he does not believe he should make a lot of money, get the highest grades, run the fastest races, or jump the highest.

Arapesh men and women both display a personality that might be described as feminine. In her book, *Sex and Temperament in Three Primitive Societies*, Margaret Mead found that men as well as women were trained to be unaggressive, responsive to the needs and demands of others. But among the Mundugumor, both men and women developed as ruthless, aggressive individuals, with a minimum of maternal and feminine aspects. Both men and women of the Mundugumor behave in a manner that we in Canada would expect only of undisciplined and very aggressive males. The Arapesh ideal is a mild, responsive man married to a mild, responsive woman, while the Mundugumor ideal is just the opposite – a violent, aggressive man married to a violent, aggressive woman.

Although shocking to us, there are tribes in the world who practice infanticide, that is, the killing of new-born children. The Eskimo, the Bushmen of the Kalahari, the aborigines of Northern Australia, and many other peoples who live in difficult environments where they must be constantly on the move seeking food, find it necessary to remove anything that might be detrimental to the livelihood of the entire tribe. Yet, although it is clear that, for the continuation of the existence of these tribes, infanticide is a necessity, the experience is extremely painful for those mothers who become pregnant while still carrying babies in their arms.

All head-hunting is tied up with supernaturalism and the belief that dead men's power can be taken with their heads. Polynesian wars were frequently undertaken to obtain sacrificial victims. Ashantis and other West Africans kept prisoners for sacrifice. The bloody religion of the Aztecs called for thousands of war prisoners for human sacrifice to the gods – a fact that proved their undoing when they came to grips with stout Cortez. The Aztecs fought to take prisoners; the Spaniards fought to kill. They baptized only survivors.

E. Adamson Hoebel
"Man in the Primitive World"
in Mary Ellen Goodman
The Individual and Culture

There are many differences in the values of primitive societies – differences that result in interaction that is far outside our narrow range of experience. An example of these pronounced differences can be seen in the mountain Arapesh of New Guinea and the Eskimos of Greenland. For the most part, the Arapesh are a peaceful, friendly, genuine, and cooperative people. However, they do tend to have poor anticipation of future problems, and they lack individual ambition. They have no clear hierarchy of leaders, and the most admired person is the all-round man. On the other hand, the Eskimos are definitely individualists. They value initiative, self-reliance, and aggressive behaviour. Although these cultural traits were recently developed to sustain the existence of these primitive groups, they have been encouraged by the way each tribe treats its young.

The whole way of life of the Hopi is cooperative and peaceful; this, indeed, is the spirit of their religion. A boastful, aggressive Hopi is unknown. In the first place, his culture provides him with little or no opportunity to learn such characteristics and, should such learning occur, members of his society put considerable pressure on him to "unlearn" them.

Blaine E. Mercer and Jules J. Wanderer
The Study of Society

It is no exaggeration to say that while the Chinese glorify their ancestors and the Hindus glorify their gods, the Americans glorify their children.

The American family (by its glorification of the children) . . . fosters an overwhelming sense of self-importance in the growing child, and it correspondingly minimizes the importance of the older people who are responsible for bringing them up.

F. L. K. Hsu
"Clan, Caste, and Club"
in Mary Ellen Goodman
The Individual and Culture

Labatt, taking advantage of its French-sounding name and the fact that one settler was a namesake, launched a campaign entitled "Vieux noms du Québec" – old names of Quebec. In all these advertisements, the copy, like the campaign of the armed forces, appealed to the traditional and heroic glory of the French-Canadian past. The sketches were idealized and the biographies written in flowery and embellished style. To cite one example, the family name *Caron*: "It is thus that our gallant ancestors toiled under the yoke of harsh labor and suffering to establish and make prosperous the new colony which has so long and proudly borne the name of New France."

Thus, French Canadians in advertising even before the Quiet Revolution were not without influence and were sometimes given budgets to develop their own campaigns. What is striking in these campaigns, however, is that the themes almost always harked back to the French-Canadian past. Heroes were sometimes pioneers of two centuries ago; the lumberjack was a traditional folk figure; the songs stemmed from childhood or rural life. The appeals were to a heritage, patriotism, and loyalties learned long ago in the schools and around the fireplace. None, in the slightest way, suggested any threats to the powers that be. The military advertisements, for example, did not mention the fate of the French language or culture once recruits joined the forces, and the lumberjack advertisement did not observe that he was an unskilled worker in the employ of the English.

Advertising During the Quiet Revolution

Like other middle-class French Canadians, those in advertising were deeply emotionally involved and eager to participate in the Quiet Revolution. In part, this meant upholding the values of the Quiet Revolution; in part, it meant fighting within the English-controlled advertising world for more French-language advertising, more attention to its quality, and more original campaigns. But herein lay a dilemma. To contribute to the Quiet Revolution and receive recognition from French Canadians, they had to be aggressive toward the English; but if they fought too vigorously they jeopardized their chances for successful careers. In the final analysis, the French Canadians in advertising resolved this dilemma by fighting for French-language advertising while simultaneously stressing their knowledge of advertising and their faith in its purpose. Specifically regarding the themes of advertising, they promoted ideas which were appropriate to the spirit of the Quiet Revolution, yet effective presumably, in increasing sales.

Such themes were found, above all, in references to national and ethnic identity. To French Canadians, such advertisements demonstrated a concern with and respect for French Canada; to English Canadians they were appropriate appeals to the emotions of the target group. The French-Canadian ethnic identification was represented in several ways:

1) *Testimonial-type references*. This is a common device. The person represented may or may not be a public figure, but he is,

by name or otherwise, identified as French Canadian. For example, in newspaper or magazine advertisements, an insurance broker, Monsieur Pellerin, is shown using a Pitney-Bowes Automatic Stamping Machine; a Monsieur Lalonde is being interviewed by a Mutual Life Insurance Company agent about a combination life insurance–mortgage policy; and a French-Canadian teacher is borrowing $1,800 in thirty-five minutes from the Bank of Nova Scotia.

2) *Geographical references.* Gage Envelopes headlines an ad in French "Fabriqué au Québec"; Dow Breweries, in an ad for Black Horse Ale, says, "Brassé à Montréal et à Québec"; and Kodak displays a picture of the Citadel in Quebec City instead of, as in the English original, the Parliament Building in Ottawa.

3) *Language and symbols.* Labatt Breweries introduced a series of ads with "Dans la Belle Province"; and Molson Breweries, for one of its beers, used a traditional rooster symbol; dozens of companies sought identification through the expressions, "chez nous", and "les Québecois"; and such idioms as "ça bouge au Québec", "d'ac", or "le magasin à l'accent français" abound.

4) *Current activities indicating progress.* A few companies associate themselves with progressive economic developments. Moore Business Forms, for example, cites its factory in Quebec and displays photographs of French-Canadian company managers who use Moore products; and General Motors of Canada, when opening a new plant, headlines an ad "Ils ont construit les premières Québecoises".

5) *Popular culture of Quebec.* Quaker Oats Company, with appropriate advertising copy, introduces Capitaine Crouche as a French counterpart for Cap'n Crunch and a cereal, Tintin, modeled after a famed French language cartoon character. Other companies refer to such popular leisure and sports activities as fishing, hockey, skiing, and snowmobiling.

All told, such advertisements with an ethnic identification make up but a minor proportion of French-language advertisements by national English companies.

But even such a low proportion means thousands of repetitions in the course of a year and, compared with the situation before the Quiet Revolution, represents an enormous increase.

The Case of Kébec

The hazards faced by English advertisers in attempting to adapt are strikingly shown in the incidents surrounding the launching of a new beer, called Kébec, by Dow Breweries. The basic device of the campaign was tried and true – associate the product with a sentiment deeply felt and approved by the potential buyers, in this case the ethnic identity and nationalism of French Canadians. Citing ads in the newspaper *Le Devoir*, the campaign began with a teaser-type advertisement reporting an announcement to follow

... The New Zealander's attitude towards work generates less drive and eagerness to get ahead and advance in his job than is typical of Americans. ... [The New Zealander is] less disposed to continue striving in the face of adversity and to practice self-denial for the sake of attaining long-term occupational goals. ... Self-denial, of course, is by no means foreign to the New Zealand character structure, but it manifests itself principally in areas unconnected with vocational matters.

David P. Ausubel
"The Fern and the Tiki"
in Mary Ellen Goodman
The Individual and Culture

Most individuals are so influenced by the norms with which they are familiar that any other mode of behavior is unthinkable. When informed that certain Tibetan tribesmen exist all winter without a bath, that the Caribs relish the eating of certain tree worms, that the Polar Eskimo eats decayed birds, feathers, flesh, and all, the average American is inclined to be disgusted or incredulous. Yet one of the writers has seen aboriginal peoples in the jungles of South America who were nauseated by the taste of Grade A canned peaches, who laughed in derision at his practice of tooth-brushing, and considered the white man's firm refusal to pluck out his eyebrows an example of rank exhibitionism.

John L. Gillin and John P. Gillin
Cultural Society

A factor implicit in a variety of diverse phenomena may be generalized as an underlying cultural principle (theme). For example, the Navaho Indians always leave part of the design in a pot, a basket, or a blanket unfinished. When a medicine man instructs an apprentice he always leaves a little bit of the story untold. This "fear of closure" is a recurrent theme in Navaho culture. Its influence may be detected in many contexts that have no explicit connection.

Clyde Kluckhohn
Mirror for Man

... emotions felt by one people may not occur in that same form elsewhere. When a Kwakiutl child dies, the father's emotional experience is a peculiar combination of grief and shame – grief at the loss of his child, and shame because he has been "insulted" by his universe, and because his prestige and security have been threatened. It may be that the Kwakiutl father never feels grief without its accompaniment or overtone of shame. ...

A. Irving Hallowell
"Psychological Leads for Ethnological Field Workers, Personal Character and Cultural Milieu"
in Mary Ellen Goodman
The Individual and Culture

Anthropologist Victor Uchendu tells us that the Igbo children of south-east Nigeria share two worlds. Unlike Canadian children who are typically confined to their own world and to their own unique experiences, the Igbo children participate in the world of the children *and* in the world of their parents. They take active part in their parents' social and economic activities. One could find them almost anywhere: at the market, at the village or family tribunal, at funerals, at feasts, working on the farm, and at religious ceremonies. They share with their parents the responsibilities of entertaining their parents' guests. There are no children's parties from which the parents are excluded, nor are there any parents' parties from which the children are excluded. The children do not even have separate sleeping quarters. Igbo children take an active and important part in the work of their village.

Canadian Justice Went North to Untangle Macabre Case

Chisholm MacDonald

(CP) — Children dying naked in the snow . . . the man who said he was God . . . the girl clubbed mercilessly by her brother. . . .

It was all testimony in a 20th century courtroom, a canvas tent on wind-whipped Belcher Island, N.W.T., 29 years ago.

The judge was from Toronto and accustomed to court decorum, but he listened with sober patience to the Eskimos' tales of terror. Outside, the howling huskies echoed a dismal refrain.

The trial lasted three days, and its judgment wrote a final chapter in the weirdest and most bizarre case of superstition and human slaughter ever to bring white man's justice to the Canadian North.

The next day, August 22, 1941, a boat left the barren furtrading islands in Hudson Bay with three Eskimo men, taking them away to prison terms for manslaughter.

But it all started many months before that, with a setting like a story book thriller: wintry winds whining through the lonely Arctic night and the Eskimos, with little else to do, huddling in their igloos and telling stories of religion and the supernatural.

Before it ended, nine persons were to die — from vicious beatings, gunshot wounds and harpooning, or from exposure when driven naked into the frigid outdoors to perish in the snow.

One of the story-tellers that winter was swarthy, 27-year-old Charlie Ouyerack. In the nocturnal atmosphere of northern lights and

and showing a bit of a symbol. In the following four days, advertisements continued to report the forthcoming announcement, with each succeeding advertisement presenting a bit more of the symbol. On the next day came the grand launching. On the top left side of a large advertisement was a portrait of Jean Talon, a hero of French-Canadian history. On the top right side were pictures and names of nine French-Canadian executives of Dow Breweries, including a vice-president who was also a member of the Board of Governors of the University of Montreal. In the lower right side was the new trademark, a design of a large bottle of beer on which was the complete symbol, a stylized "K" and the name Kébec and, just to the left, a figure in the costume of the old French regime holding a flag which resembled that of the Province of Quebec. The cross and fleur-de-lis of the Quebec flag were replaced by a part of the "K" and a crown, the symbol of Dow Breweries. The copy of the advertisement reads as follows: "The Management of Dow Breweries of Quebec presents to you La KEBEC. A true beer expressing the taste of modern Quebec. Reflecting the image of the State of Quebec today. La Kébec is perpetuating in French Canada a centuries-old tradition of quality. The French Canadians who direct Dow Breweries of Quebec are to a degree the successors of the great Jean Talon, the illustrious governor of New France who was also the first director of a brewery in Canada. The vaults of the old brewery of the King form part of the inheritance of Dow Breweries of Quebec and the name we have chosen signifies the blending between the Quebec of today and the Quebec of our French origins. In Quebec . . . La Kébec".

The nationalistic overtones of the advertisement are evident. Kébec was the original Indian name given to the site chosen by Champlain for the capital of New France and an old spelling of Quebec. Jean Talon was an honored historical figure after whom streets and hospitals were named. The advertisement mentions Quebec eight times and Kébec four times. The copy also speaks of "l'Etat du Québec", the term adopted by strong nationalists and separatists to suggest that Quebec deserved to be called a state in its own right. It was explicitly announced that the directors of Dow Breweries in Quebec were French Canadians, with no mention that the majority of shares were held by an English-Canadian company. And a final nationalistic touch was the trademark with its flag resembling that of Quebec.

Two days later another advertisement for Kébec appeared with a copy of a painting representing a dancing party at the governor's palace at the time of Jean Talon. The copy spoke of "Kébec" as a descendant of the beers brewed in New France by the great Jean Talon, of the French-Canadian directors of the company, and again displayed the trademark of the bottle and figure holding the flag. But the very same day a storm broke. On page 3 of *Le Devoir* appeared a story in which the RIN, the Rassemblement pour l'Indépendence Nationale, the largest and best known of the separatist groups, accused Dow Breweries of scandalously exploiting the Quebec flag and insulting the Quebec population for commercial reasons. The company was referred to as the "Toronto Dow

Breweries" and "Toronto capitalists", and was accused of replacing the fleur-de-lis by the crown, the very symbol of Quebec colonialism. RIN asked all "indépendantistes" and all self-respecting French Canadians to boycott not only Kébec beer but all the products of the "Toronto Dow Breweries", and invited the provincial government to take all necessary measures to prevent the exploitation of national symbols for commercial ends.

The argument was taken up in the student newspaper at the French-language Université de Montréal. An open letter by two students addressed to the vice-president, who was a member of the University Board of Governors, spoke of their "stupification and profound disgust" at the treatment given the official flag of "l'Etat du Québec". Another student writer bitterly condemned the brewery for exploiting nationalism for commercial ends and for its "burlesque transformation" of the national flag.

Just two weeks and a day after the appearance of the first complete advertisement, the director of Dow's Public Relations Department announced that this campaign for Kébec beer was being withdrawn. But the company admitted no offense. The management, according to the release, had never intended to take advantage of sacred symbols; they were in fact, through the name Kébec, doing their part to help give the province its "visage français". They had sought a name and a presentation that was indisputably French Canadian.

This incident has several implications. First, this advertising campaign was not very different in tone or quality from many other contemporary campaigns in Quebec, but it did go further than others in adapting the flag and thus linking a sacred symbol with the "profane" aim of selling beer. Even more important, because Dow was controlled by an English-Canadian corporation, critics could claim that the whole compaign smacked of blatant and deliberate deception. Further, looking at the French-Canadian groups themselves, the lines of action were relatively easy to choose for separatists or others whose position was extreme. What better incident to draw attention to themselves and show that their interests lay on the side of the French-Canadian public versus the unscrupulous English-Canadian corporation! For those, however, who sought to tread a balance, acting on behalf of the Quiet Revolution presented complications. We have no reason to doubt that those French Canadians who launched Kébec beer, among their varied attitudes, did feel that they were contributing to the "visage français" of the province and the Quiet Revolution.

French-Canadian advisers approached their audience – as advertisers generally do – as a group of individuals responding to particular themes. The audience was diagnosed as French Canadian, potential beer purchasers or beer-purchase influencers, having strong feeling toward their province. The campaign was appropriately developed. But, as was have seen, the diagnosis was inadequate and the campaign boomeranged. Wherein lies the blunder? The error, we suggest, was not in the interpretation of the ideology but rather in the image of the social system of the province.

The advertiser, wittingly or otherwise, has some image of the falling meteors, he became imbued with the biblical accounts of creation, told in the Kittoktangmuit language of his people.

Thus gripped by religious fervor and confusion, Ouyerack finally stood up, proclaimed that the end of the world was at hand and that he was Jesus Christ.

At about the same time, a neighbor, Peter Sala, decided that he was God.

Their zeal caught favor with some, disfavor with others among the islands' 150 residents.

Ouyerack and Sala told their people that material things were of no further use. Some then shot their dogs, and one man even destroyed his most valuable possession – his rifle – in the belief that he would not need it again.

But 13-year-old Sarah Apawkok said she did not believe that Christ had come, and let it be known that she didn't. Infuriated, her elder brother, Alex, yanked her by the hair and beat her mercilessly.

Then Mina, Sala's sister, and Akeenik, a young widow, dragged the unconscious girl into a nearby igloo where Akeenik killed her by crushing her skull with a rifle.

Sensing that further carnage might develop, a man called Alec Keytowieack protested and attempted to leave. But he was tortured by Sala with a sealing harpoon, and shot and killed by another fanatic, a man known as Ablaykok. Like Sarah, the body of Keytowieack was left in an igloo without burial.

About two weeks later, Alec Epuk openly denounced the new-found theology. Ouyerack persuaded Epuk's father-in-law, Peter Quarack, to shoot Epuk because he was an unbeliever and therefore a devil. Epuk was killed and his people, instead of performing the customary obsequies, threw stones from a distance until his body was covered.

Then Mina, further gripped by religious frenzy, ordered a group to disrobe and "go out on the sea ice to meet Jesus". With threats of evil that would befall those not obeying, she frightened some into discarding their parkas and boots.

Six adults and seven children followed her out on to the ice. Four of the adults and three children managed to get back safely, but the others perished. The two adults were Mina's own mother and sister, while two of the four children were the son and adopted son of her brother – the self-deified Peter Sala.

Justice came finally. Sure, if not swift.

In the spring, fragmentary reports of the incidents filtered out to northern-based RCMP from a radio set up by a Hudson's Bay Co. trader on the islands' rocky wastes. An RCMP plane was sent in from Ottawa, about 750 miles away and, bit by bit, the story was pieced together.

As a preliminary move, Mina was charged with the death of the four adults and three children; Wuarack with killing Epuk; and Ablaykok with the death of Keytowieack, whose body could not be found.

On April 17, the three prisoners were flown to Moose Factory, Ontario, about 300 miles south at the foot of James Bay, pending further investigation. By then, the Hudson Bay ice began to crumble and the ski-equipped plane had to leave the islands.

In July, Inspector D. J. Martin made the flight again and the investigation continued.

This time, Ouyerack and Quarack were charged jointly with the murder of Epuk; Ablayok and Sala with the murder of Keytowieack; Apawkok and Akeenik with the murder of Sarah.

Then came the judicial party, headed by Mr. Justice C. P. Plaxton of the Ontario Supreme Court. The group reached the islands August 19 after a journey by schooner from Moose Factory. The trip, because of bad weather, took 13 days compared with the usual four or five. At Great Whale River alone, a week of travelling time was lost because of fog and storms.

The trial began the following day, with Mr. Justice Plaxton seated at a plain table, in a moss-floored tent. A Union Jack and a picture of the Royal Family adorned the judicial bench while miners, reporters, and a schooner crew were the jury.

One by one, Eskimo witnesses recounted the happenings of the winter. Sixteen said they believed Sala and Ouyerack were God and Christ at the time of the slayings. They also believed that Satan had inhabited the bodies of the victims.

At the end, Sala and Ouyerack were sentenced to two years and Ablaykok to one year at hard labor at Chesterfield Inlet, far to the north, on reduced charges of manslaughter. Apawkok was acquitted and Quarack given a two-year suspended sentence. Mina, who had been brought into the courtroom screaming and strapped to a stretcher, was adjudged insane and Akeenik was acquitted on grounds of temporary insanity.

Apawkok and Quarack remained on the islands. The others never returned.

In later years, the Hudson's Bay post on the Belchers was abandoned and the Eskimos all evacuated. But long after, piles of crudely assembled gravestones still stood against the Arctic winds — monuments to nine persons who died because of a strange faith.

Among Eskimos, it is considered a gesture of hospitality for a man to "lend" his wife to a visitor:

"Refusing isn't fitting for a man!" Ernenek said indignantly. "Anybody would much rather lend out his wife than something else. Lend out your sled and you'll get it back cracked, lend out your saw and some teeth will be missing, lend out your dogs and they'll come home crawling, tired — but no matter how often you lend out your wife she'll always stay like new."

Hans Ruesch
Top of the World

social structure to which he directs his message. In the past, the English advertisers and their French-Canadian advisers took for granted the traditional image of the French-Canadian social structure, recognizing the superior position of the English and the power within the French-Canadian community of such groups as the church, political parties, and liberal professions. No ad would ever have threatened these significant groups. With the Quiet Revolution the social structure had obviously changed, but the significance of the change was not taken into account by the English- and French-Canadian communicators. They continued to take the social structure for granted and continued to view the effective audience as a group of isolated individuals responding to particular themes. For advertising of everyday products and services, this image was sufficiently relevant to be successful. However for this particular advertising campaign, in the changing emotional context of the Quiet Revolution, the image served badly. It ignored completely such new power groups as separatists, student activists, and liberal journalists who, in their desire to gain attention in the mass media and mobilize forces, had assumed an importance probably superior to any other groups in the province.

The opportunity offered to the separatists and strong nationalists in this particular instance fitted nicely, as we have seen, into their own power and political struggle. It gave them an issue which enhanced their position and a target, the English companies, which could only, since they had to avoid controversy, retreat as quickly and gracefully as possible.

To what degree are the advertisers who wish to take advantage of French-Canadian symbols placed in a dilemma that cannot be solved? Might any such symbol be considered commercial exploitation? The answer, as some of the earlier examples indicate, is not necessarily "yes" – testimonials and numerous other devices have been successfully adopted. But these messages and devices have had precedents, have been tempered in style, and have not so obviously given newly emergent power groups the opportunity for exploitation.

Looking at this material from a broader viewpoint we find support for four points.

1) When the lower status group does not threaten the dominant group, it is free, and in fact even encouraged, to express traditional aspects of its culture which, while serving important psychological and social functions, simultaneously reflect the group's position of lower status. Thus the French-Canadian advertising personnel before the Quiet Revolution met no opposition when they introduced folk symbols into their advertisements. Thus, too, the nonthreatening Indians and Eskimos are encouraged to develop their native arts, the southern Negroes to sing spirituals and folk songs, and immigrant groups to initiate language and folk-dance classes.

2) When the lower status group gains sufficient power and will to pose a threat, the dominant group seeks to turn the lower status group sentiments to its own benefit. In our study, the advertisers adapted French-Canadian nationalism. In other

contexts, national American advertisers in Negro-oriented magazines cite testimonials from Negroes; corporations invite lower status group members to take figurehead positions and some companies organize company unions with profit-sharing plans.

3) Members of the lower status group who seek conflict will try to turn the arguments of the dominant group to their own advantage. Thus French-Canadian separatists argue that the English companies defile their sacred symbols. They say likewise that French-Canadian directorships in English-controlled companies more likely represent "window dressing" than a recognition of French-Canadian talent and influence. Similarly, militant students and labor leaders argue that invitations by officials and management to join committees are merely "tokenism" and attempts to turn aside legitimate grievances.

4) Those members of the lower status group who simultaneously advise the dominant group and identify with their own group's hopes, seek to resolve resulting personal dilemmas by presenting different images to the two groups. The French-Canadian advisers in our case study argued to the English that they had a good campaign and to the French that they were contributing to the "visage français". The Negro, student, or labor liaison representative in other conflict situations may stress his militancy before one group and his statesmanship or spokesmanship role before the other.

Every Balinese sleeps with his head either to the North (in North Bali, South . . .) or to the East. He may not even lie down for a moment in the opposite direction, for the feet are dirty and may not be put in the place of the head. To lie in the reversed position is said to be "lying like a dead man". . . . The implication is that only a dead man, who could not help himself, would lie in this dangerously wrong way.

Jane Belo
"The Balinese Temper, Character
and Personality"
in Mary Ellen Goodman
The Individual and Culture

When a public-health movie of a baby being bathed in a bathinette was shown in India recently, the Indian women who saw it were visibly offended. They wondered how people could be so inhuman as to bathe a child in stagnant (not running) water.

Edward T. Hall, Jr.
in Alan Dundes
Every Man His Way

The lack of privacy . . . finds its extreme expression in many well-to-do families in North China. Here the rooms are arranged in rows like the cars of a train. But instead of each room having a separate entrance, all the rooms are arranged in sequence, one leading into another.

F. L. K. Hsu
"Americans and Chinese : Two Ways of Life"
in Mary Ellen Goodman
The Individual and Culture

The Ontong Javanese call a person poor not when he is lacking in material goods, but when he lacks the resources of shared living. When he lacks family, working partners, intimate friends, he is then considered poor.

C. George Benello
in Gerald F. McGuigan
Student Protest

One must look to an underdeveloped society for an example of out-and-out uncontrolled capitalism. We find it among the Kapauku Papuans of West New Guinea. Until they were "pacified", these people were head-hunters and cannibals. They are strict "rugged individualists" in economic enterprise. They not only have a true money (the relatively scarce cowrie shell) and savings, but also a system of speculation and a market regulated by supply and demand. There is a system of sales and lease contracts, of the use of paid labor, and of absolute and unrestricted private ownership.

six

Cultural phenomena: fads and fashions

There are many aspects of our culture that represent a response to a continuing need for personal identity. Because we live in a fast-changing period of time as a result of vast technological and social changes, we seem to require a constant redefinition of ourselves. This redefinition is accomplished in part through changes in clothing, music, entertainment, and life style. We do not seek these changes in a straightforward way because we do not know exactly what we are seeking. Our feelings about this search for change are vague and almost unconscious; they represent a kind of groping for a personal answer to a dissatisfaction with larger social concerns. The development of fashion trends and faddish behaviour is indicative of our response to this need. It is difficult to determine whether the manufacturers and advertising industries cater to this need, or take advantage of it to increase sales. Probably it is a combination of both.

In the area of women's fashions, we are currently passing through another major controversy centred on skirt length – the mini-skirt versus the midi-skirt. If in fact fashion merely represents the meeting of a need for change in an area where individuals have some direct influence, we can expect the change to take place. Children's toys have tended to be faddish – from hula hoops, to skateboards, to frisbies. College students have gone from flagpole sitting, through eating live goldfish, to "panty-raids", to crowding students into phone booths and Volkswagens. Music tastes can be seen as faddish, and they have corresponded with the rise and fall of various musical artists.

Beatlemania as a fad is discussed in the first selection that follows. The Beatles collectively and individually have had tremendous impact on young people over the past few years. Not only have they initiated trends in music, hair style, and dress, but also they have taken strong stands on social issues in their music and in their activities. In the second selection, Charles Winick explains the continuing success of *Mad* magazine on the basis of its ability to meet the needs and interests of adolescents.

Beatlemania *

Are you a Beatle lady? Got a crush on the Beatles? Heart go bingo for Ringo? Then you're swinging! For a ring-ding smile to match, try X toothpaste . . . gives your teeth a gleam, tints your gums a "yeah, yeah" pink.

(A toothpaste advertisement in a London subway.)

As most people know, the Beatles are a group of four young musicians who have experienced considerable success throughout the world. Their names are George Harrison, John Lennon, Paul McCartney, and Ringo Starr. They had played together in Liverpool, England, for a number of years before they produced the reaction in audiences that came to be known as Beatlemania. Their strongest response came, perhaps, from adolescent girls, whose behaviour consisted of screaming, hysterical moaning, and fainting. Similar reactions have been produced by other singers and rock groups in the past few years, but probably never to the extent of the mania induced by the Beatles. In the following pages we have summarized the study conducted by A. J. W. Taylor on the impact of the Beatles as they passed through Wellington, New Zealand, on a world-wide concert tour.

* Adapted from a study conducted by A. J. W. Taylor.

At press conferences and interviews, the four long-haired Beatles were found to be friendly and quick-witted, speaking with pronounced Liverpool accents. They dressed in sharp clothes and appeared to be relatively unaffected by the success they had achieved. They did not appear to be concerned by the fact that their audiences could not hear their music because of the high audience noise level, but rather gave the appearance of some concern if people *did not* respond to them excessively (and therefore noisily). They felt that they had had more impact throughout the world than any other group before their time.

Interestingly, they indicated that young people needed opportunities to be aroused, and they felt that they were making a social contribution by providing this outlet for them. They felt that they had become successful as a group because they played a particular throbbing kind of beat that tended to bring their audiences to a screaming, roaring point. They estimated that their audiences were made up of 80 per cent teenaged girls and 20 per cent young men.

Because the Beatles were of working-class background, many young people felt they had contributed to the breaking down of the social class barriers. Young people admired them for the ease with which they were able to communicate with all kinds of people. It has been stated that the Beatles have contributed to increased solidarity among young people throughout the world – but at the expense of a widening of the gap between the young and their parents. The high-voltage atmosphere created by the Beatle concerts provided young people with an opportunity to react in a number of ways that were not completely acceptable to their parents; naturally, many parents were quite concerned.

For this particular concert, it was necessary to take elaborate precautions to control the crowds that surrounded the Beatles wherever they went. Publication of the traffic routes the Beatles would take, and television, radio, and newspaper coverage had prepared the country well in advance for their arrival. An air of expectancy had settled over Wellington.

The two-and-a-quarter hour, continuous program was so well designed that the audience participation increased as the concert proceeded. In the early part of the show, two minor rock bands and their leaders encouraged the audience to stamp their feet, clap their hands, and to move around. It is well known that this technique has the effect of lowering the individual's resistance and of establishing a feeling of group solidarity among the audience. Naturally, the climax of the show was reached when the Beatles appeared for the final half-hour of the concert. The whole audience had reached a point of restlessness, and the noise that was generated at their final appearance was so great, that when the Beatles sang, they could not be heard; they seemed to be merely opening and closing their mouths as they rocked backward and forward. In this instance, as in other Beatle performances, members of the audience attempted to reach the stage, and some young people broke through the cordon of policemen at the front of the stage, resulting in mass confusion. After the Beatles were safely led from the stage and the house lights were turned on, a dishevelled,

Fashion is custom in the guise of departure from custom. Most normal individuals consciously or unconsciously have the itch to break away in some measure from a too literal loyalty to accepted custom. They are not fundamentally in revolt from custom but they wish somehow to legitimize their personal deviation without laying themselves open to the charge of insensitiveness to good taste and good manners. Fashion is the discreet solution of the subtle conflict.

Edward Sapir
"Fashion"
Encyclopedia of the Social Sciences

There is in fashion a demand for attention too strong to be explained as desire for approval. It might be called ego-screaming ("Look at me!"); it has "shock value".

Orrin E. Klapp
Collective Search for Identity

The fashion trends of the 1960s and 1970s show an increased concern in the following areas:

1) *Style as a form of rebellion*. Protest and rebellion against many aspects of our contemporary life has naturally contributed to a similar trend in fashions. In fact, it is quite possible that this trend is a useful outlet for anxiety associated with rebellion.

2) *The need for personal identity*. With increased automation and computerization of numerous clerical tasks, life for many people can be a faceless existence. Fashions that feature the "Look at me!" approach are useful in developing a personal identity.

3) *A shift away from the traditional success model*. In Canada and the Western world we have emphasized hard work as a route to success. But there is a trend toward valuing a life of pleasure and style and minimizing the importance of hard work. This produces a completely different set of values for the fashion world to encourage.

4) *Escapism*. The emergence of beatniks, hippies, yippies, groupies, teenyboppers, and the language associated with these deviant groups have made it possible to use their extremes in clothing and language as extensions of fashion.

Fashion also needs to be related to social change. While fashion changes often appear irrelevant or trivial, they are generally related to more significant behaviour. Both fashions and fads serve as weathervanes indicating changes in the social structure and in the style of life.

Kurt Lang and Gladys Engel Lang
Collective Dynamics

There is in fashion a tendency to extremes that cannot be explained by the desire to identify oneself with an "in" set or even to achieve an interesting look. Indeed, about the time one concludes that fashion is conservative, governed by good taste, it contradicts that by breaking out in extremes that we call "high fashion" or "faddism".

Orrin E. Klapp
Collective Search for Identity

Some fashions are attractive for no other reason than their great expense. The dresses custom-made in the great fashion houses command exorbitant prices not only because they are in great demand and thus scarce; their fantastic price itself contributes to the demand. The style itself is less important than the need to consume what is dear and therefore a mark of prestige.

Kurt Lang and Gladys Engel Lang
Collective Dynamics

When Eton schoolboys were given the choice of keeping or abandoning their traditional formal school uniforms with the long tails, stiff collars, and top hats, they chose to keep them. The easy explanation of a decision like this is that they were "conservative". I do not think this is the true reason, as anyone who has felt the currents stirring in Britain would probably agree. A better explanation is that they wanted to preserve a distinctive identity, rather than be blended with other English schoolboys, and were willing to put up with the discomforts of an archaic uniform for this sake. They saw a threat in keeping up with fashion.

Orrin E. Klapp
Collective Search for Identity

distraught, still noisy and exuberant crowd of young people could be seen.

It was clear that the throbbing rhythm of the beat had played a major part in arousing the audience. Even though the audience had a difficult time in hearing what was being played on the stage, it was estimated that the noise level produced by the electric equipment was nearly as great as that of a jet taking off. Although music experts have commented on the relatively high quality of the Beatles' music, the Beatles themselves said that their purpose was to write simple tunes for young people who are constantly falling in and out of love.

Two procedures were used to obtain subjects for the study.

Observers were placed at points where young people would have a chance to demonstrate their feelings about the Beatles. The observers were instructed to invite two categories of young people to join discussions about the Beatles. The first group was identified by jerking body movements and persistent screaming and roaring (Enthusiasts), but the second group (Resisters) remained apparently calm in spite of the excitement around them. However, this approach was not particularly effective as many of the young people did not turn up at the discussion sessions. A second procedure involved the selection of subjects who fell into the same age brackets as those who attended the concert. These young people were classified as Enthusiasts and Resisters depending on 1) their response to music played by the Beatles on a tape recorder; 2) their participation in a discussion about the Beatles; 3) the scores they obtained on a test of Beatlemania (an instrument designed by the researchers); and 4) the eagerness or lack of eagerness with which they responded to copies of the Beatles' autographs as a reward for completing the test program.

A group of young people selected by the second procedure were set up in similar ratio to the audience at the main concert. The 40 females and the 10 males with the highest scores on the Beatlemania scale were classified as Enthusiasts and the 50 females and 10 males with the lowest scores made up the Resisters group. The remaining group of 122 young people who obtained median scores were called the Middle group.

The following is an indication of the kinds of responses that were given on the test of Beatlemania.

Beatle Enthusiasts

Question 4 If you could have got up on the stage, what would you have done?

Answers "Touched their hair or clothes."
"Screamed, because it is not often you can scream and get away with it."
"I would have tried to touch or hold them until the police dragged me away."

Question 5 How did you *feel* about the Beatles?

Answers "I can't describe the feeling very well, except to say that the beat and their personalities moved me so that I had to scream my appreciation. I was very excited."

"Teenagers wanted something like this to happen, and here it is."

"They made me feel as if I wanted to laugh and cry at the same time."

"After singing and clapping with them I felt I knew them."

Question 6   How different are they from other groups that you have known?

Answers   "They are original and not carbon copies of other groups."

"They have a real pounding beat."

"Their form of music has its own piquant quality that is almost brilliant in its simplicity. The lyrics of the songs have their own style."

"The singing has a wild, uninhibited sound that no other music has got."

"They made me feel wonderful."

Question 9   Did you mind standing up to dance or scream in the Town Hall?

Answers   "I screamed only between songs and did not approve of people standing up and twisting."

"I enjoyed screaming with the rest – I would have minded by myself."

"You can forget your troubles and let off steam."

"I was stirred up."

"I didn't mind screaming – it seemed automatic – I wasn't conscious."

Beatle Resisters

Question 4   If you could have got up on the stage, what would you have done?

Answers   "Cut their hair."

"Called for a decent singer."

"Couldn't be bothered getting up on the stage."

Question 5   How did you *feel* about the Beatles?

Answers   "Good luck to them."

"Anyone who screamed wanted their heads looked at."

"Their singing – if it can be called that – was lousy."

"Only interested to see them because such a fuss was made of them."

Question 6   How different are they from other groups that you have known?

Answers   "They rely on sheer volume of sound – not a fancy effect."

"They are followed by girls screaming."

Two social tendencies are essential to the establishment of fashion, namely the need for union on the one hand, the need for isolation on the other. Should one of these be absent, fashion will not be formed – its sway will abruptly end.

Georg Simmel
"Fashion"
The American Journal of Sociology

A "snob" effect works against universal adoption of a fashion and thus counteracts the bandwagon effect which induces women to follow along. Among some groups, demand for a fashion decreases precisely because others share in it. The first to accept a new fashion are therefore also the first to abandon it as soon as too many others have accepted it. An extreme example of this is the deliberate effort on the part of some to be indifferent to fashion.

Kurt Lang and Gladys Engel Lang
Collective Dynamics

There can be no doubt that men are ready and eager for change in clothes, readier even than their better halves. . . . There have been far more changes in men's clothing in the last two and a half years than in women's. . . . What suits a woman today will suit a man tomorrow?

Ernestine Carter
The New York Times

A fashion movement does not develop a social structure, leadership, division of labor or morale, but it belongs under the category of social movements by virtue of the fact that it removes dissatisfaction with an existing social situation. It "changes" the situation, but only symbolically. People express their unrest in something new which seems objectively to have little to do with the cause of the unrest. But the mere creation of something new serves subjectively to change the old situation.

Arnold M. Rose
Sociology: The Study of Human Relations

The Craze

Smelser defines a *craze* as "mobilization for action based on a positive wish-fulfillment belief". If panic tends to be a headlong rush away from something, a craze is the opposite, "a rush with sound and fury toward something (they) believe to be gratifying, as in manias, booms, bandwagons, 'fashion races' and fads".

Ritchie P. Lowry and Robert P. Rankin
Sociology: The Science of Society

The Fad

Faddish behaviour involves fewer people [than crazes], is more personal, shorter in duration, and tends to be socially disapproved. There is "something unexpected, irresponsible or bizarre" about many fads [or crazes]. Among the more widely publicized have been the swallowing of goldfish, sitting on flagpoles, wearing one earring at a time, shaving the top of one's head, crowding into telephone booths, etc. The persons who engage in wild fads are not necessarily under great personal stress or abnormally isolated from the main current of society.

Ralph Turner and Lewis Killian
Collective Behaviour

Fashion

What identifies fashion is its novelty value, its seeming departure from custom. Fashion, Sapir tells us, is "the legitimate caprice of custom"; it is custom in the guise of departure from custom. In going along with fashion, we deny the old-fashioned; what counts against the latter is its age. But custom completely lacks novelty value. It is age that legitimates custom. Custom is time-honored rather than fashionable and is passed from generation to generation.

Kurt Lang and Gladys Engel Lang
Collective Dynamics

"They are a lot worse than any group I have known."
"They are so different that it makes them ridiculous."

Question 9   Did you mind standing up to dance or scream in the Town Hall?

Answers   "I'm not easily carried away by mob hysteria."
"I couldn't hear them because of the screaming."

People can be stirred to great heights of enthusiasm if they are emotionally involved in group kinds of activities. Their involvement can be encouraged if they are persuaded to support some cause and it can be induced on an emotional level. Their resistance can be reduced by leaders who create a feeling of oneness, of group solidarity. But it is clear that the rate of involvement by any one individual in a group can vary substantially in terms of his personal characteristics and the strength of the manipulative techniques to which he may be subjected.

From this study it appears that the young females who responded positively to the subtle and direct group pressures set up by the Beatles were not particularly different from "normal" girls. However, the enthusiastic girls did tend to be younger, more gregarious, assertive, active, worrying, excitable, and more inclined toward emotional instability than either the Middle group or the Resisters.

There were no major differences between the male groups, except that the Middle group of males was more inclined to emotional instability than either the Enthusiasts or the Resisters.

Perhaps the girls were attracted by the male image of the Beatles, and conceivably a group of female musicians might have changed the response of the boys. However, the fact that older adolescent girls were relatively unresponsive to the Beatles' influence suggests that the Enthusiasts themselves would probably grow out of their stage of youthful exuberance and responsiveness to group pressures. From other research we know that girls tend to show more emotional instability than boys, and that this instability is most pronounced through the period of adolescence.

Each generation seems to need its own unique musical stimulus for group identity and emotional release. Recently we have shifted from the relative smoothness of the Tijuana Brass to the hard rock of the Woodstock generation. It is change that produces a feeling of unique identity for young people. It would seem that we can expect perpetual change in the music of the young.

Teenagers, satire, and Mad

Charles Winick

Advertising and other media are among the major targets of *Mad*. It has a masthead on which "Fumigator", "Bouncer", and "Law Suits" are among the staff titles listed. It sells special identifying materials. It has a character called "Alfred E. Neuman", who is a foolish-looking boy often shown in the magazine. He usually appears with the caption, "What – Me Worry?" He is always grinning, has tousled hair and a missing tooth. The face was originally used in an advertising slide at the turn of the century and adopted by *Mad* several years ago. His name was given him by a member of the magazine staff. Neuman has become a symbol of the magazine.

The name "Melvin" appears occasionally, as does an avocado plant called "Arthur", and a child in a cart. The nonsense word "potrzebie" appears from time to time in the magazine. On one recent cover, Alfred E. Neuman's girl friend, "Moxie", who looks much like him, is dressed as a drum majorette. She is beating a drum on which there is a picture of Neuman with a black eye. The drum belongs to Potrzebie High School, the Latin motto of which is "Quid, me vexari?" (i.e., "What – me worry?").

Mad started in 1952 as a comic book which lampooned other comics (e.g., *Superman*) and sold at the regular comic price of ten cents.

Its format of the extended comic magazine story differs from the text emphasis of earlier satire magazines, although its vocabulary level is fairly high. An average story has perhaps ten panels covering three pages, and an average issue of 17 stories. Some authors are well-known comedians like Steve Allen and Orson Bean. Surveys have indicated that the bulk of the readership is probably concentrated among high school students, although there is some readership in colleges and among adults. Fifteen *Mad* anthologies have been published successfully. There are few areas of the country in which it does not enjoy some popularity, although it is most popular in cities. *Mad*'s stemming from comic books was probably responsible for its initially having more boy than girl readers, but both sexes are now equally represented among its readers. *Mad*'s ability to deal with satire and to develop an audience seemed to provide a clear-cut opportunity to study some aspects of satire's appeal to teen-agers.

An analysis of the magazine was conducted in order to determine how often various kinds of subject matter appeared. All eight issues published during one year were examined and each story was placed into one of eleven subject categories, which had been established on the basis of preliminary analysis of previous issues. *Table 1* gives the incidence of each theme.

Each of the categories shown in *Table 1* represents a satirical treatment of a subject; laughing at it by using its established vocabulary or trappings. Although satire includes both the understatement of *irony* and the exaggeration of *parody*, there is less irony than parody in *Mad*. However, much of *Mad* is in the form of parody, since it treats the same subject as the original but burlesques its style. Thus, the category "Advertising" would include

It may be that the nineteenth-century fashions of large complicated "Victorian" houses, with their ornate "dust-catching" furniture and large, ruffled hoop- and petticoat-supported dresses were expressions of the "need" of Victorian women to find new "functions" in house and dress care when their eighteenth-century functions declined as a result of the Industrial Revolution and its concomitants.

Arnold M. Rose
Sociology: The Study of Human Relations

A dress buyer says of the clothes designer Balenciaga:

He's the master of understatement. Any woman who walks into a room in his clothes – however simply cold they look – must be noticed. She doesn't need added drama. She doesn't need a collar or cuffs. It's all there in the cut. His dresses have the simple secret that will make everyone notice a girl like this.

Table 1

Incidence of Eleven Subject Categories Appearing in *Mad* Magazine over Period of One Year

Theme	Percentage of total
Leisure time activity, other than media	21
Advertising	19
Magazines, newspapers, and radios	18
Television	10
Biographies of noted persons	10
Movies	6
Transportation	5
Politics and international relations	4
Business customs	3
Special groups in the population	2
Education	2
Total	100

When we call something a fashion, the judgement usually involves a bit of debunking. Pinning the fashion label on a cultural commodity is an effective, if roundabout, way of demoting it. The label suggests, first, that the commodity is *transitory*, not lasting or permanent. Second, its *novelty* – not any intrinsic rationality – governs its acceptance; the value of what is fashionable is independent of its rational utility. Third, the label suggests the *trivial*.

Kurt Lang and Gladys Engel Lang
Collective Dynamics

No satisfactory theory has been advanced to explain why fads and crazes "catch on". However, they usually must have at least one characteristic in order to capture popular imagination. A fad must be appropriate to its time. People would not be receptive if it completely violated their sense of propriety. The frug and certain other recent dance forms, which would have been shocking a few years ago, have become fads. But in the same period, attempts to popularize "mate swapping" have made little headway.

David Dressler
Sociology: The Study of Human Interaction

There are additional features of modern life which tend to encourage fashion races. The anonymity of urban life encourages individuals to express their individuality in fashion which often borders upon the daring. The cut of the dress frequently pushes modesty to the limits and is a form of expression and an assertion of freedom from the demands of society. Fashion can be a kind of victory for the individual as he tries to escape the boredom and regularized existence of modern society.

Ritchie P. Lowry and Robert P. Rankin
Sociology: The Science of Society

what appear to be real advertisements. Readers who know the original can easily recognize that the manner of presentation of the advertisement is satirical.

For example, one story classified as advertising was called "The Hip Persuaders", and presented "hip" versions of ten, very familiar, advertising campaigns, each one treated in one panel. One such advertisement showed a man wearing earphones with antennae coming out of his spectacles and about to put a wicked-looking pizza pie into his shining teeth. The headline read, "He lays on only GLEEM, the choppergrease for cats who can't sand after every scoff." The reader can respond to this on three levels. He can recognize the well-known advertisement which recommends a toothpaste for people who can't brush after every meal. He can also identify "hip" people who are in touch with the secret language of a group of people. He can also understand the translation of the advertising slogan into "hip" language.

Another popular format for a *Mad* story is like Fielding's approach to *Jonathan Wild*, in which the actions of a highway man are described in fake admiration, in the language usually bestowed on great leaders and the satire consists in the linking of things which are not normally linked together.

An example of such high satire is "The National Safety Council's Holiday Weekend Telethon", in which a telethon is the theme. An announcer urges people to go out and get themselves killed in a highway accident, so that the Safety Council's quota for the holiday weekend will be met. Drivers are told that the program will pay their toll if they crash into another car while on a toll bridge. Children are told that they can contribute to the total even if they have no automobile by going out and playing on a highway after dark, when it will be easier for them to be hit. Similar appeals are used throughout the rest of the story (i.e., "The family that drives together – dies together.") As in *Jonathan Wild*, the mood is sustained; viewers of the telethon are urged not to tie up the lines by telephoning in nonfatal accidents, because only fatal accidents can be used. As the story progresses, the number of deaths listed on the scoreboard mounts.

Over half of *Mad*'s contents are concerned with leisure and adult mass media (newspapers, television, etc.). The central purpose of media in preparing adolescents for life in our society makes this major theme of *Mad* of special interest. The leisure and media activities and problems of adolescents, however, receive little coverage. Other adolescent problems are either not treated or treated without much gusto. Thus, the teen-age reader can enjoy the role of a spectator as he reads about how sick and silly is the rest of society. One possible reason for the relative absence of satirical material of direct interest to adolescents is that adolescents may have difficulties in seeing comic elements in situations in which they are involved.

The teen-ager can laugh at those younger than himself, as well as those who are older. One article on magazines for younger children, for example, featured a magazine called "Petal Trend, The Tricycle Owner's Magazine", with articles on customizing tricycles, the *Grand Prix de Disneyland*, and similar subjects. Much of the satirical material on younger people is not separate but is worked into the details of the panels of stories on other subjects. Thus, one panel in a 14-panel story on "halls of fame" dealt with a copywriter who wrote advertisements for babies, with slogans like "Ask the kid who wets one". The artist who regularly draws a child in a cart in his stories never offers an explanation of why the child is there.

Personal Interviews with Readers

Although readers of *Mad* range from eight-year-olds to college students and adults, the most typical *Mad* reader is a high school student. Personal interviews were conducted with 411 regular readers of *Mad* with an average age of 16.2, in order to determine the readers' attitudes toward the magazine, pattern of reading, and participation in other typical activities of teen-agers. The respondents were asked questions on stories they would have published in *Mad* "if editor", what they liked most about it, how they read an issue, with whom they discussed it, how often they read magazines for teen-agers and comic books, and how they liked rock-and-roll music.

Stories in Mad *if editor*. The average age respondent gave eight stories which he would run "if editor", with a range from four to 22. The responses were coded into the categories developed in the content analysis. Most respondents cited stories which had already appeared in *Mad*. *Table 2* gives their specific choices.

There was a high degree of agreement between what actually appeared in *Mad* and what the readers would put in the magazine. The only major category which *Mad* readers said they would like to see in the magazine and which had not been previously coded was Alfred E. Neuman. In the analysis, there was no category for Neuman because he has not been the subject of stories, although often figuring in them.

Readers would, however, like more of some subjects and less of others. They want more satire on business customs, education and movies and less attention to other mass media. Respondents expressed no interest in seeing problems of adolescence like parents, vocational choice or sex, treated by the magazine. Its readers seem to prefer that matters close to them not be satirized with the exception of movies and education. The magazine occasionally carries articles on parents, in which parents and the family are presented as being relatively unattractive.

More boys than girls selected the business customs area. Their interest in business customs may reflect adolescents' special fascination with adult business behavior; much of which *Mad* has helped them to perceive as foolish and immoral. The readers may regard such stories as clues and "how to" guides to the world of business which they may soon be entering. Some readers may want stories on business because of the inadequacies of high school instruction on business and their feeling that this is an important and mysterious area of life that they do not understand. Others may want more on business, because the work done by their fathers is increasingly removed from the children's knowledge and

Men are worse than women now – they drive us mad. They come in every week. "What have you got that's new?" Even the ones who haven't got money try to be original. They'll sew black patch pockets on a white jacket or something like that.

The opinion of the manager of a men's boutique (quoted in) Orrin E. Klapp *Collective Search for Identity*

In the past few years the male cosmetics industry has burgeoned into a business which grosses annually some 350 million dollars and is still expanding.

A. Strauss in Orrin E. Klapp *Collective Search for Identity*

Table 2

What Readers Would Put in Issue of *Mad* if They Were Editor

Theme	Percentage of total
Advertising	17
Business customs	14
Leisure time activity, other than media	14
Movies	12
Alfred E. Neuman	11
Education	7
Biographies of noted persons	6
Television	5
Transportation	4
International relations	4
Special groups	3
Magazines, newspapers, and radio	2
Miscellaneous	1
Total	100

At last week's collections the shaven model was greeted with cries of dismay. "The Bold Body" looked stunned, was possibly pretty (although it was hard to tell) and remained to all questions, silent. "She's dumb," explained a guest. "She must be. Only a dumb chick would let them do that to her."

A comment in a fashion magazine (quoted in) Orrin E. Klapp *Collective Search for Identity*

Table 3

What Readers Like About *Mad*

Reason	Percentage of readers who cited reason
Makes fun of and satirizes things	44
It's funny, comedy	37
Stories on famous people	25
Like everything in it	24
Makes me laugh	22
Makes fun of itself	22
The ads	21
Tells how things work	19
Not afraid to attack things	19
It's crazy	19
The jokes	19
Alfred E. Neuman	18
Has current events	18
Well done, well written	17
Not like other magazines	17
The stories	16
It's fun	12
It's relaxing	8
It's silly	7
Cheers me up	2
Miscellaneous	2
Total	388

less product-orientated, so that the children have a dim impression of just what their fathers do in the business world.

The interest in movies reflects teen-agers' extreme "movie-going" activity. Movies are important for teen-agers as the traditional "safe" date. It is also possible that the procedures whereby the movie stars of today are made into stars have been so widely publicized that teen-agers are cynical about the techniques of making stars, and would like to see them satirized. There is often so little to say about the artistic qualities of some movie stars that their publicity stresses how they were "discovered", and teen-agers may wish to see more satire on this aspect of the movies.

The interest in education perhaps reflects readers' feelings that the subject should get more treatment in *Mad*, so that they might have a better vocabulary for laughing at it. Another possibility is that some teen-agers feel that their school and teachers are quite inadequate and that the sensationalist criticism of education in popular media is wide of the mark. *Mad*'s integrity might seem to these teen-agers to make it an ideal means for candid and informed criticism of the schools.

Since the respondents are regular readers, their general acceptance of *Mad* content is not surprising. It is curious that readers did not mention major social issues of our time, like "atomic war", as subjects for satire. There seems to be a tacit understanding that there are some subjects which are best left alone, even satirically. Teen-agers may be so fatalistic about nuclear war that they could not face even a satirical treatment of the subject.

What liked about Mad*?* The reasons given by the respondents for liking *Mad* were coded into several categories. The average respondent gave approximately four reasons. The proportion citing each reason is shown in *Table 3*.

The respondents described the appeal of the magazine mainly in generalities and the third person. Relatively few responses refer to the reader's response in the first person ("relaxing, makes me laugh, fun, cheers me up"). In view of the complex and perhaps threatening nature of satire and of humor, it is hardly surprising that the readers did not verbalize many details of the magazine's appeal. Over half of the reasons cited clearly refer to the magazine's satirical and witty content.

One reason for liking *Mad* ("famous people, how things work") is its role as socializing agent. Some teen-agers may be learning skills for functioning in our society by acquiring the procedures for survival which are spelled out in witty detail by *Mad*. They may, thus, be learning rules for antisocial behavior, while laughing at those engaged in such behavior. *Mad* has carried seventeen different articles with titles beginning "how to" and many other articles with similar themes.

Reading *Mad* may thus be a kind of problem-solving activity. The teen-ager may feel that he is learning to emulate "gamesmanship" while laughing at it. He can be an inside "dopester" while laughing at inside dopesters. It would be analogous to, for example, a reader of Ovid's *Art of Love* or Castiglione's *Book of the Courtier* studying them for the apparent purpose of ridiculing love-making and the courtier's life, respectively, but actually sopping up much "how to" information on these subjects. Thus, a recent *Mad* article on the "Practical Scout Handbook" is a parody of the *Boy Scouts' Handbook* in terms of various social situations. A discussion of scout teamwork urges the reader to keep on the alert for accidents, so that he can call an ambulance and then a lawyer. The reader is advised to act surprised if the lawyer offers him part of his fee, but to turn him in to the police for "ambulance chasing" if he doesn't. The reader can thus smile at the advice; which is typical of the literalist content of much of *Mad*. He can also experience dislike of people who behave in this way, while at the same time absorbing the advice. The same appeal can be seen, for example, in recent books which deplore sex and consist largely of examples of sex to which the reader can feel superior while enjoying them.

Few respondents said that they discuss the details of their enjoyment of the magazine with their friends. They said that they did often discuss it in general terms (i.e., "did you see the last issue, did you see the story on – ?"). There appears to be no specific social context of teen-agers within which the magazine is unusually likely to be discussed.

A number of respondents (22 percent) praised the consistency of the magazine, which manifests itself in *Mad*'s making fun of or attacking itself in "house" advertisements. Such advertisements seem to say, "We can't criticize others without criticizing ourselves." A typical advertisement urges readers to buy a picture of Alfred E. Neuman, so that street cleaners may be kept busy gathering up the pictures when they are thrown out. An anthology from the magazine is called "The Worst from *Mad*" and refers to "sickening past issues" from which it is culled. The editors run their own pictures and laugh at them. These are examples of what many readers see as the infectious high spirits and enthusiasm with which the magazine is edited. Such enthusiasm seems to have a special appeal for young people, who are likely to respect competence in any form and apparently interpret the self-mocking advertisements as expressions of consistency and competence. The respondents commenting on how well written *Mad* was (17 percent) also are praising the competence of the editors. The implication may be that the authors of *Mad* are professional enough to have absorbed all the skills of the people they are satirizing, but have chosen to use their skills in making fun of society and even of themselves. Inasmuch as there is considerable agreement that a distinctive feature of juvenile delinquency is its celebration of prowess, it is possible that the teen-age reader perceives *Mad* as a kind of delinquent activity which has somehow become successful; and, thus, one way of demonstrating prowess by antisocial activity.

Relatively few readers (3 percent) volunteered any features of the magazine which they did not like. These features were relatively independent of their enthusiasm for the magazine. Thus a reader liking a great many features might still mention some which he did not like. Alfred E. Neuman heads the list of least-liked features; one half of those who expressed some dissatisfaction did so because Neuman "runs too often", "looks too dopey", and similar reasons.

Fads and Youth

It's all part of the cult of the young. If you want to sell to the young, then it follows that you need bright young designers with fresh, lively ideas, and the place to look for them is the art schools.

Carl Bode
in Orrin E. Klapp
Collective Search for Identity

You can't not dance in a discotheque. First, the dances are too easy not to be tried. Second, they're too sexy not to dance. Third, that pack of people on the floor is having too much fun for you to resist joining them.

Walter Winchell
in Orrin E. Klapp
Collective Search for Identity

Teenagers hold a jealous possession of their folkways. When adults took over the twist, young people dropped it like a hot pizza and moved on to dances that were exclusively their own – at least for a while. There is a dedicated effort to create dance steps so exhausting that no adult in his right mind would try them.

Paul C. Harper, Jr.
Who Am I?

Life magazine describes the spirit of youth at night on the Sunset Strip in Los Angeles:

What you do on the Strip is simply go there and dig: each other, the sights and sounds, mostly yourself. Just go there – and feel it, man, freak out a little and see how beautiful it all can be. It's all so simple, so non-competitive, so free from traumas of success or failure.

Fashion is allowed free sway because it is assumed to move only within the limits of what is culturally approved. Traditional ways of doing things, institutionally accepted attitudes, ideas that matter are not affected, and thus individuals are free to indulge themselves in the marginal, and sometimes bizarre, vagaries that the world of fashion opens to them.

Kurt Lang and Gladys Engel Lang
Collective Dynamics

Paula Stern has studied the role of magazines in shaping the behaviour of people and says that magazines such as *Ingenue* push teenagers into adult posturing. "The format is peppered with advertisements for engagement rings, pictures of desirable adolescent boys, and occasionally a plan of attack such as dinners for two." The ads for cosmetics and clothes are nearly the same as those in magazines designed for their mothers. Typical of women's magazines, *Ingenue* includes at least one article concerned with a problem. Recently, it explained in "The Hardest Thing About Growing Up" that "inevitably, relationships with boys affect relationships with girls". It supported the statement, "I don't trust other girls in the same way any more. They become rivals." This is one way girls learn sayings such as "women can't work with other women when men are around", and "never work for a woman".

If a girl manages to survive *Ingenue* without getting married, *Glamour* picks her up ("How Five Groovy Men Would Make You Over Into Their Dream Girls"). Where the boys are is where it's at for the reader who is shunted from high school to college to career to marriage to motherhood – "Find Your New Look, College into Career Make-over. Job into Mother Make-over".

Of the 74 respondents who cited Alfred E. Neuman as a reason for liking the magazine, 56 percent were in the group which was not doing well at school. It can be speculated that the less successful students are more likely to identify with Neuman because he conveys a feeling of failure, defeat, defensiveness, and uninvolvement. His non-worry slogan has a "let the world collapse, I don't care" quality, and his appearance suggests stupidity. One fan admiringly said that "If Alfred E. Neuman jumped off the Empire State building, he would be laughing." A few readers thought that Neuman was a staff member of the magazine, although he does not appear on the masthead. It is possible that his silliness and appearance of being someone who doesn't know any better helps to make the magazine more acceptable, by making its attack less committed.

An adolescent who is doing well at school might enjoy the magazine because of its "joshing" of the very symbols of status and achievement to which he is attracted. The less effective adolescent may like *Mad* because of Neuman, who represents an "I don't care" attitude and non-achievement. The magazine may thus appeal to teen-agers at opposite ends of the scale of achievement for quite different reasons, while giving each one a chance to feel superior.

Most of the respondents (71 percent) who commented on the magazine's basing its stories on current events were in the group which was doing relatively well at school. The more alert readers, thus, seem to derive pleasure from their ability to recognize the relationship between an actual happening and its being satirized by *Mad*. A few called the agreement between *Mad* stories and current events to their parents' attention, perhaps as one way of making their parents feel that the magazine has some educational value. Perhaps the identification of such current events material may help to remove the guilt feelings which the magazine's satirical content may produce.

Even though doing well at school does have some status among teen-agers, it is more important for them to achieve good grades by appearing to do little work *without* making any special efforts to get good grades. Adolescents' group norms operate to keep effort down. Therefore, if a *Mad* reader can scoff at his elders and society, by seeming to learn something about current events, he is obtaining increased satisfaction.

Perhaps one way in which the group can act differently from adults is by regular readership of a magazine which largely mocks the adult world. This is a world which the magazine's readers have not yet engaged directly, but which they are approaching during a period when they are trying to learn who they are and what their feelings are. By enjoying satire on this adult world, they can approach it while mocking it. They can also mock the world of younger children.

This ability of adolescents to take a socially acceptable medium, the format of which involves conformity to group norms – like a comic magazine or rock-and-roll – while using the medium to express hostility and aggressiveness, is in line with what is known about adolescents' needs. They want both to belong and not belong, to have and have not, to enjoy but also to attack.

The very name of *Mad* implies not only aggression ("mad at") but also the foolishness ("mad as a hatter") of much of civilization. This kind of approach – enjoying media which imply conformity while at the same time using them to rebel against it – is a special kind of escape, which is strongly developed in adolescents.

Adolescence has long been known to be a period of contradiction, and of growing awareness of contradictions. A major problem of adolescents is how to express their hostility while seeming not to do so.

This ability to *express* aggressiveness seems to have found some relatively recent outlets, but the *presence* of the aggressiveness has often been noted by other investigators. The most intensive study ever made of adolescent fantasy – using cartoon-like pictures as a stimulus – found that its major theme was aggression. Even "mild" boys and girls told extremely aggressive stories, with considerable destructive violence. There were over three times as many themes of "aggression" expressed by the adolescents studied, as sex, the next most popular theme. Anxiety, Oedipal conflict, moral issues, success striving, and turning stories into jokes, were other common themes; all of these elements can be found in *Mad*.

A study conducted before the "hey-day" of comic books suggested that high school students are less likely to respond to pictorial humor than to verbal and intellectual humor. *Mad* would seem to represent a combination of these elements. The use of the comic format may help to remove some sting from the aggressive content for some readers because of the association of comics with "kid stuff". Another reason for special appeal of the comic format is suggested by previous studies of adolescent humor, which report that visual presentation of humorous material makes it easier for adolescents to respond to it. Many adolescents have had much experience with the comics in their younger years. The great majority (89 percent) of the respondents had read comic books before *Mad*. A convincing case could probably be made for the comic book's having replaced the fairy tale as a major carrier of our culture's value to young people. *Mad*, along with some other comic books, is not permitted in schools by many teachers and even by some parents in their homes, thus adding the lure of the forbidden to the magazine.

During the interviewing, a number of respondents referred to *Mad* as "our magazine". They meant that *Mad* expressed their point of view so effectively that they had almost a feeling of ownership about it. *Mad* reinforces membership in the teen-agers' peer group – it's the "thing to do". As one respondent said, "All the kids read *Mad*." This suggests that the less, as well as the more, conservative teeners enjoy it. There is so much interest in *Mad* that one fan has published a complete cross-index to the magazine. It is likely that this in-group feeling is strengthened by the several personalities in the magazine who are never explained: Neuman, Arthur the plant, the child, and potrzebie. A number of the respondents mentioned that they had "discovered" these features by themselves. Their having done so seemed to contribute to their feeling of being a member of an in-group.

Certainly the writers of "fashion copy", ever sensitive to the sentiments of their readers, take the class-symbolic functions of women's dress for granted :

If at first you don't succeed, change the way you dress. (*Ladies' Home Journal*)

Clothes for climbing, or what to wear on your way up the ladder; to build that graciousness which leads first to charm and eventually to financial advancement, proper, attractive clothes are a sound investment. (*Mademoiselle*)

> Bernard Barber and Lyle S. Lobel
> in Robert R. Evans (ed.)
> *Readings in Collective Behavior*

Historically, clothing has been one of the most convenient, and visible, vehicles known for drawing class distinctions. In early New England, a woman was permitted to wear a silk scarf only if her husband was worth a thousand dollars. Medieval London had detailed specifications on the amount of affluence that was necessary before a person could wear ermine, cloth of gold, or silk. Rothenburg, Germany, still exhibits the heavy wooden collar that was locked, during the Renaissance, around the neck of any woman who tried to dress beyond her class.

> Vance Packard
> in Robert R. Evans (ed.)
> *Readings in Collective Behavior*

. . . we parted with approximately four weeks' salary for a little sheaf of fine wool with crepe. It was distinctive, expensive, original. We were distinguished, elegant, proud. Two weeks later we saw the sheaf — cheapened but very recognizable, on Sixth Avenue (at a price!), and in subsequent weeks we followed it on its downward path all the way to Fourteenth Street and a raging popularity at six-ninety-five. Result: discard. . . . (*Mademoiselle*)

Bernard Barber and Lyle S. Lobel
in Robert R. Evans (ed.)
Readings in Collective Behavior

The shape of our clothing varies in another interesting way by class. As you go up the class scale, you find an increasing number of fat men. Among women the opposite is true. You rarely see a really plump woman on the streets of the well-to-do suburbs surrounding New York. The slim figure is more of a preoccupation with women of the two upper classes. As you go down the scale, the married women take plumpness more calmly.

Vance Packard
in Robert R. Evans (ed.)
Readings in Collective Behavior

Practically no respondent referred to the magazine's money-making success, which did not seem to have made much of an impression on readers. Many commented on how widespread the readership among their friends was. "Most of the other kids read *Mad*" and "we swap old copies back and forth" were typical comments. The wide readership of the magazine by other teen-agers helps to maintain its appeal; especially in the face of the considerable opposition to it by parents and other figures of authority. Readership of *Mad*, thus, reinforces membership in a kind of teen-age conspiracy.

It is perhaps this sensitivity and response to the near-intolerable which has helped to make what is now called "sick" humor an established part of adolescent humor. Stories like, "I stepped on my mother because I wanted a stepmother", have been told by teen-agers for decades.

A special appeal of a magazine of satire like *Mad* is that *the satirist can say things which even a reformer or critic cannot easily say. It may be easier to laugh at something than to discuss it straightforwardly.* The adolescent both wants to make contact with the symbols of success in the outside world, as some do by autograph collecting and fan clubs, and, at the same time, wants to believe ill of them. *Mad* provides its readers with an opportunity to "go away a little closer" from some important institutions.

This hostility seems to have a special need to find expression in high school and college students. They enjoy the absurd and satirical, as well as the opportunity to release pent-up emotional energy, and feelings of superiority. Satire may have a special appeal to relatively young people, because it can be viewed as a reflection of the inner dependence of childhood, which is projected onto noted individuals and institutions, in order to attack them. Satire can be regarded as a weapon of the weak; and adolescents may regard themselves as being relatively weak. *Mad* offers an opportunity for a kind of defensive reaction to social institutions. The adolescent readers of the magazine face the prospect of going out into the adult world, not with anxiety but with an opportunity for obtaining satisfaction through laughter, as they achieve mastery over the adult world by continually assuring themselves that its institutions and personalities cannot be taken seriously.

Politicians, celebrities, teachers, parents, businessmen . . . they're all making important statements these days. The trouble is, they usually say one thing, but mean another! And there's nobody around to translate for you ordinary clods! Except maybe us, the fearless men of MAD! (Who's around to translate the statements we make that say one thing and mean something else is another problem!) Anyway, back in issue #97, we ran an article which translated some of these statements. Now, here are more examples of the difference between —

WHAT THEY SAY ... AND WHAT IT REALLY MEANS

ARTIST: BOB CLARKE
WRITER: GEORGE HART

Resources for Part 2

Brown, J. A. C. 1963. *Techniques of Persuasion*. England: Penguin Books.

Deer, I. and H. (eds.). 1965. *Languages of the Mass Media*. Toronto; Englewood Cliffs, New Jersey: D. C. Heath Co.

Fraser, L. 1957. *Propaganda*. London, England: Oxford University Press. Don Mills, Ontario: Oxford University Press.

Gordon, D. R. 1966. *Language, Logic, and the Mass Media*. Toronto: Holt, Rinehart & Winston (Canada) Ltd.

Graham, G., and Rolland, S. 1963. *Dear Enemies: A Dialogue on French and English Canada*. Toronto: The Macmillan Co. of Canada Ltd.

Henry, J. 1963. *Culture Against Man*. New York: Random House.

Indian-Eskimo Association of Canada. *Cultural Encounter*. Toronto.

Irving, J. A. 1962. *Mass Media in Canada*. Toronto: Ryerson Press.

Kennaway, J. 1963. *The Mind Benders*. Toronto: McClelland & Stewart Ltd.

Larsen, O. N. (ed.). 1968. *Violence and the Mass Media*. New York: Harper and Row.

Lee, A. M. *How to Understand Propaganda*. New York: Holt, Rinehart & Winston.

Oswalt, W. H. 1970. *Understanding Our Culture*. New York: Holt, Rinehart & Winston Ltd.

Part 3

The roles of man

All the world's a stage
And all the men and women merely players
They have their exits and their entrances
And one man in his time plays many parts
William Shakespeare

William Shakespeare was a careful observer of human behaviour and his plays provide insight into why people behave as they do. Some sociologists feel that roles can be better understood if the individual is compared to an actor playing many parts. A play has a script to be followed, a director, an audience, and players: kings, clowns, lovers, villains, and heroes. Similarly, each of us plays different parts in life such as father, mother, son, daughter, employee, friend, and neighbour. Some roles are played one at a time, others are played all at the same time. For example, a person can be a father, husband, and host all at the same time, while other people play other roles. To be a host requires that someone be a guest; to be a husband requires that someone be in the role of wife; to be a father requires that someone be a son or a daughter. A whole pattern of relationships is established in a situation where people interact. Imagine the situation if the man playing the host were to play that role at the gas station or the supermarket. Such behaviour would be inappropriate. A role is appropriate to the social situation, and is played in relation to the demands and expectations of others.

The acting out of a role could be said to occur according to the script or situation, with perhaps a few more options open in real life than in a play. The director could be a boss, a supervisor, a teacher, a parent, or a policeman. The role of employee is played in relation to the role of supervisor played by someone else. The audience is all those people who observe a person in a role. An employee can play his role to the audience of other employees, customers, the public, and the boss. This audience will judge how well a role is played. The performance will depend on the individual's personality and personal background, as well as his society. Thus, being a man in Canadian society requires slightly different role performance than being a man in China, Russia, or New Guinea.

The idea of a role is a useful concept with which to make an analysis of individual and group behaviour in order to explain what is happening in situations where individuals and groups are interacting. The focus may be on an individual or on a grouping of individuals who display certain behaviours. As you would expect, a specialized vocabulary has evolved to give precision to role description. The idea of role remains based on the individual actor behaving toward other people according to expectations. Other people react and control behaviour through approval or disapproval. Most people engage in behaviour that is approved by others whose opinions are valued. Thus, a hippie wishes approval from other hippies, a student seeks approval from other students, a banker seeks approval from other bankers. If a role performance is not accepted by others, they indicate this in their behaviour. The hippie may have to leave his commune, the student may be shunned by fellow students, the banker may be asked to resign from his professional association. These reactions are obvious, but there are others more subtle: a frown, a raised eyebrow, a body posture.

The whole idea of role is as complex as is human behaviour. It is subtle but helpful in understanding ourselves in relation to our society. It provides a perspective with which to observe individuals and groups responding to immediate and past external influences.

one   *Male and female*

Although there are obvious physical differences between males and females, most of the social behaviour of the sexes is learned. The family into which a child is born gradually creates a series of situations for him to learn his appropriate sex role. Family relationships become fixed around the boy as a son and the girl as a daughter. Children learn to relate to each other as brothers and sisters. Boys and girls are given different toys with which to play, they wear their hair and clothes differently, and they are encouraged to perform different kinds of tasks. Girls are encouraged to identify with their mothers and help with her tasks, and boys with their fathers.

Outside the home, the process of sex role socialization is continued, through the church and school, through Girl Guides and Boy Scouts, and even through clique and gang activities. As far as the work world is concerned, boys tend to select professions such as engineering, medicine, and law, and girls have traditionally selected nursing, secretarial work, and elementary school teaching.

In the past few years, socially active women's groups have been highly critical of the role of women in modern society and have demanded changes. Contemporary styles of hair and dress often make it difficult to distinguish between males and females – with embarrassing consequences for the person who makes such a mistake.

The following selections explore the implications of differing male and female roles in society. The relationship between school and the work world is examined from the point of view of boys and girls in a small Canadian city. Some of the arguments of the Women's Liberation Movement are presented in a series of excerpts from noted leaders in the field. Sidney Jourard explains why men die earlier than women, and makes suggestions for improving the lot of man. The last selection deals with the changes in the concept of male and female roles that occur with marriage.

The girls' and the boys' world

Oswald Hall and Bruce McFarlane

This study began as an exploration of the transition from the life of a student to the life of a gainfully employed person. Initially, we had viewed the work world as one organized by men for men, with women invading it at various points. We looked on the school world as a fundamentally co-educational world, offering roughly identical services to boys and girls. In the course of the study we modified these notions appreciably.

To begin with, the school world of Paulend and Croydon turns out to be, fundamentally, a feminine world. It provides an academic atmosphere in which girls thrive and boys fail. The girls manage it with marked success at a relatively early age. The boys linger in it, showing conspicuously higher failure rates. It is a world to which girls adapt with relative ease. Boys appear to reject it, and eventually it rejects them.

Moreover, the school is a feminine world in a vocational sense. It prepares girls admirably for their careers in the work world. The skills they learn are immediately transferable to the job world. Especially is this true for those who continue to university,

Most parents hear wedding bells the minute a girl is born, most parents see an executive office when a boy is born, and the relentless conditioning starts on its merry way. Educate a girl for the marriage market, educate a boy for success. That you, as a human being, as a separate identity, may not want or fit in with either of these goals is considered not a sign of independence but of deviation – pointing to the couch – or in social terms – failure.

Marya Mannes
Who Am I?

Every time the point of sex-conformity is made, every time the child's sex is invoked as the reason why it should prefer trousers to petticoats, baseball-bats to dolls, fisticuffs to tears, there is planted in the child's mind a fear that indeed, in spite of anatomical evidence to the contrary, it may not really belong to its own sex at all. . . .

Margaret Mead
Male and Female

If you have seen children at play, you know that they do assume the roles of others, both in their minds and in actual behavior. A three-year-old, "playing house", becomes Mama and treats her doll the way she believes she herself is treated by her mother. She praises it for keeping its dress clean, scolds it for not coming when Mama calls, spanks it for wetting the bed. In assuming attitudes toward the doll that duplicate those her mother adopts toward her, the child shows she has internalized the attitudes of a particular other person, her mother.

David Dressler
Sociology : The Study of Human Interaction

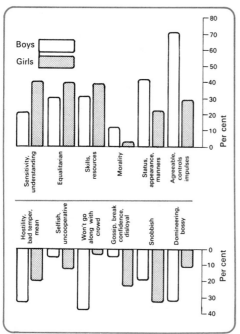

Factors related to popularity in dating and friendship patterns, as seen by fourteen to sixteen-year-old boys and girls (from E. Douvan and J. Adelson, *The Adolescent Experience*)

Sources of popularity with boys

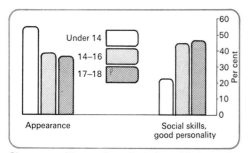

Changes with age in popularity with boys for girls (from E. Douvan and J. Adelson, *The Adolescent Experience*)

those who prepare for school teaching and nursing, and those who enter clerical occupations. The skills learned in school seem ideally adapted for transfer to the job with little time delay.

For the boys, it is otherwise. Those who drag along to senior matriculation are in many cases unfitted for university work. If they choose school teaching, they find themselves in a girls' world. If they head for a strictly masculine type of work, the skilled trades in industry, they find that their jobs have little connection with their prior schooling. There seem to be few places where skills learned by boys in school, even in vocational school, can be applied to a specific job. The contrast between boys and girls is indeed startling. The graduate of a stenography course can start work immediately as a full-fledged stenographer. The graduate of a four-year course in mechanics starts as an apprentice.

Moreover, the girl who fails to adapt to the requirements of a commercial course can drop out and register for a brief period in a business school from which she can step into a real job. The business school cushions her fall from the academic world. There are no comparable institutions which can help the boy step from his half-completed schooling into the enjoyment of a well-established job.

In this context, it is worthy of note that our society provides much more in the way of specialized training facilities for girls than for boys. The two outstanding examples are our nursing schools and our teacher-training colleges. Both nursing and teaching represent short-term careers for girls. The short working-career of most girls means that we train, in any one generation, several recruits for each available position. Indeed, school teachers themselves recognize this state of affairs by referring to the emergence of a "trousseau" teacher, implying that a teaching certificate is the modern equivalent of a dowry. Our society provides a costly scheme for training nurses and teachers. Perhaps we should say that the ostensible function of our nursing schools and teacher-training colleges is to produce teachers and nurses for the society; however, their major function for the girl is to provide an effective and extensive marriage market. On the other hand, one is hard put to discover comparable outlays for boys embarking on long-term work careers of a comparable level of complexity.

To a significant degree, the work world shows signs of feminine growth. Its growing edge seems to be on the clerical side, and here girls have traditional advantages. Automation, in the community studied, seems to have slowed the flow into skilled jobs and speeded up the flow into clerical operations. This differential in girls' opportunities and boys' opportunities is most obvious in the larger industries of our community. They have recently employed substantial numbers of girls, but very few boys.

Furthermore, the employer of white-collar workers seems to take girls with very limited formal schooling. Even those with no high school training are found in such work. And, insofar as girls outpace boys in the school system, they enter the world of clerical jobs at a much earlier age. The boys in our sample who entered white-collar jobs were substantially older than the girls.

Even when the girls enter the world of apprenticeship they

enjoy an advantage. They require less schooling, and a shorter training period. Our only apprenticeship trade for girls in this report is hairdressing; since it is associated with a booming service industry, the girls entering it appear to have assured income and secure future. As theirs is largely a *local* service institution they can move along to become proprietors.

Two other measures of comparison may be employed. The ease of finding jobs is roughly similar for girls and boys. However, far more girls manage to make their initial job their permanent job. Moreover, not only are the number of jobs per person higher for boys than girls, the periods of unemployment for the boys last longer. Even the hazards of pregnancy do not seem to overbalance these advantages of the married girl in the job market.

The differential advantages of girls over boys, in school and in the invasion of the work world, may be attributed to innate superiority of one over the other. On the other hand, it may be essential that we should scrutinize, much more rigorously than we have in the past, our institutions for educating and training boys and girls, and for projecting them into the job world. On the face of it, these institutions appear to serve the girl much more satisfactorily than they do the boy.

Who on earth, their parents moan, will marry this stringy girl with her false eyelashes and shuffling gait? Who will employ this bearded boy with his grunts and records, his pop and pot? On the other end, how gratified are parents when their clean-cut athletic sons get high marks and their clean and pretty daughters marry the clean-cut boys who get good jobs?

Marya Mannes
Who Am I?

The threat of failing to behave like a member of one's own sex is used to enforce a thousand details of nursery routine and cleanliness, ways of sitting or relaxing, ideas of sportsmanship and fair play, patterns of expressing emotions, and a multitude of other points in which we recognize socially defined sex-differences, such as limits of personal vanity, interest in clothes, or interest in current events. . . .

Margaret Mead
Male and Female

The case for a change in the role of women

Perhaps you do not remember, but it was only a few years ago that women got the vote. Now many women want full equality with men in all aspects of day-to-day living. Women have organized themselves into groups such as the Women's Liberation Movement (popularly called Women's Lib) and have begun actively pressuring big business and government for a new deal. The following series of excerpts presents some of the arguments currently advanced by women.

We are damaged — we women, we oppressed, we disinherited. There are very few who are not damaged, and they rule. . . . The oppressed trust those who rule more than they trust themselves, because self-contempt emerges from power-lessness.

. . . Nothing will compensate for the irreparable harm it has done to my sisters. . . . How could we possibly settle for anything remotely less, even take a crumb in the meantime less, than total annihilation of a system which systematically destroys half its people. . . .

Roxanne Dunbar
No More Fun and Games

Forgotten by history, loaded down from generation to generation by informal sanctions which she herself helped to impose, required by society to follow custom which easily became tradition, told she was and should be, passive, interested only in things, warned to avoid thinking, woman in general has tried to conform. The early iconoclasts were lost sight of, yet the number of women who challenged the theory that woman's whole being was passive grew steadily and ruggedly.

Lillian O'Connor
For a Better World Today

Study after study has shown that children are not harmed by the fact that their mothers work (that, on the contrary, they frequently benefit), but employed mothers are still made to feel that they are shirking their maternal responsibilities.

Jo Freeman
"The New Feminists"
The Nation

A woman is first defined by the man to whom she is attached, but more particularly by the man she marries, and secondly, by the children she bears and rears — hence the anxiety over sexual attractiveness, the frantic scramble for boyfriends and husbands. Having obtained and married a man the race is then to have children, in order that their attractiveness and accomplishments may add more social worth. In a woman, not having children is seen as an incapacity somewhat akin to impotence in a man.

Marlene Dixon
"Why Woman's Liberation?"
Ramparts

In sheer quantity, household labour, including child care, constitutes a huge amount of socially necessary production. Nevertheless, in a society based on commodity production, it is not usually considered even as "real work" since it is outside of trade and the marketplace. This assignment of household work as the function of a special category "women" means that this group *does* stand in a different relationship to production. . . . The material basis for the inferior status of women is to be found in just this definition of women.

Margaret Benston
"Political Economy of Woman's Lib"
The Monthly Review

In a society in which money determines value, women are a group who work outside the money economy. Their work is not worth money, is therefore valueless, is therefore not even real work. And women themselves, who do this valueless work, can hardly be expected to be worth as much as men, who work for money.

Margaret Benston
"Political Economy of Woman's Lib"
The Monthly Review

Looking at marriage from a detached point of view one may well ask why anyone gets married, much less women. One answer lies in the economics of women's position, for women are so occupationally limited that drudgery in the home is considered to be infinitely superior to drudgery in the factory. Secondly, women themselves have no independent social status. Indeed, there is no clearer index of the social worth of a woman in this society than the fact that she has none in her own right.

Marlene Dixon
"Why Women's Liberation?"
Ramparts

Chemical and Engineering News made a study of chemists' salaries last fall which showed that, with seniority held constant, women with Ph.D.'s made less than men with only B.A.'s. James J. White recently compared all the women who graduated from law school in the last ten years with a similar group of male law graduates. With every variable he could think of controlled, the figures still showed that a year after graduation the average man earned 20 per cent more than the average woman and that ten years later he earned 200 per cent more.

Jo Freeman
"The New Feminists"
The Nation

We really don't have many fatuous hopes of taking over. We would like, very much, a fair shake. We are each half of a person, we are each less than we could be. If we did not have these rigid sex roles, we would all have so much more room for spontaneous behavior — for doing things that we feel like doing, for following our own instincts, for being imaginative, for being creative. The great thing about it all is that we could not only change this, but in the process, really improve everything else as well.

Kate Millett
Sexual Politics

In the last fifteen years I've experienced several generations of change — from real drudgery to push-button living. Right after the war, during the housing shortage, we moved into a log cabin built to be a summer cottage. The only plumbing was a drain in the kitchen sink. On dark winter nights we wrote Christmas cards by oil lamp, the kids did homework by flashlight in bed. *That* was drudgery.

Now we have additional rooms, new appliances, everything. I *know* how much time appliances save, especially when the kids are grown up and gone. I don't know how other women spend the time their appliances save, but I spend mine in reading and politics.

Katherine Holmberg
in Bernard Asbell
The New Improved American

The major thrust of the new movement is not to prove that women are as good as men — almost. Neither is it to say that women are "different but equal", if only they'd be recognized as such. Its challenge, is much more fundamental: the women's liberation movement has begun to question whether what we define as feminine and masculine has anything to do with being female and male. And it is objecting outright to the traditional dominance of male values and of men as their agents.

Jo Freeman
"The New Feminists"
The Nation

The vast bulk of recorded history will give us very little encouragement, for there have been splendidly endowed women in every nation who thought great thoughts. We must develop scholars who will delve into original arguments and winnow out the essential; the great, warm, humanitarian ideas so that girls tomorrow will not be lured aside by the trivia of personal idiosyncrasy. We must reject totally and at once the thought that the brain that comes with a little girl-baby is somehow inferior.

Lillian O'Connor
For a Better World Today

According to the WLF, liberation goes far beyond gaining more rights. It is dedicated to a total restructuring of society, much as is the New Left, and is not content simply to integrate women into male-defined goals and values. And it is adamant that any new society must destroy the social definition of women as sex objects whose major function is the care and maintenance of men and their children.

Jo Freeman
"The New Feminists"
The Nation

The very stereotypes that express the society's belief in the biological inferiority of women recall the images used to justify the oppression of the blacks. The nature of women, like that of slaves, is depicted as dependent, incapable of reasoned thought, childlike in its simplicity and warmth, martyred in the role of mother, and mystical in the role of sexual partner.

Marlene Dixon
"Why Women's Liberation?"
Ramparts

We must teach our children, all of them, boys and girls alike, that insecurity is the fate of *man* and is not the peculiar prerogative of women.

Lillian O'Connor
For a Better World Today

After experimenting with sex equality for many years, the Soviet government modified its principles of equality by preventing women from doing work that might harm them or prevent them from bearing healthy children. Though women undoubtedly played a more important role in the military forces of the U.S.S.R. than in any other nation, they engaged in little actual combat. It was realized that there were many men's tasks that women could not and should not do.

S. Stanfield Sargent and Robert C. Williamson
in Faud Baali and Clifton D. Bryant (eds.)
*Introductory Sociology : Selected Readings
for the College Scene*

L. M. Terman and C. C. Miles, after their extensive research into "sex and personality", summarized as follows : Males are interested in adventure and strenuous occupations, in machinery and tools, science, invention, and business. Females turn toward domestic affairs and the arts ; the occupations they prefer are more sedentary, ministrative, and charitable or humanitarian.

Terman and Miles also described differences in male and female emotional behaviour. Males are more self-assertive, aggressive, hardy, and fearless, also rougher in manners, language, and sentiments. Females are more sympathetic, timid, and sensitive ; they are more moralistic and emotional and admit more weakness in emotional control. Another study found that boys are more aggressive, "naughty", and unruly ; girls are more nervous, shy, anxious, and jealous. Personality test studies of adolescents and adults show women to be more submissive and neurotic and less self-confident than men. However, these differences between men and women are often very small.

L. M. Terman and C. C. Miles
*Sex and Personality : Studies in
Masculinity and Femininity*

Some lethal aspects of the male role

Sidney M. Jourard

Men die sooner than women, and so health scientists and public health officials have become justly concerned about the sex difference in death age. Biology provides no convincing evidence to prove that females are intrinsically more durable than males, or that tissues or cells taken from males are weaker or less durable than those taken from females. A promising place to look for an explanation of the perplexing sex-differential in death rate is in the transactions between men and their environments, especially their relations with other people. In principle, there must be ways of behaving among people which prolong a man's life and ensure his fuller functioning, and ways of behaving which speed a man's progress toward death. The present paper is devoted to an overview of some aspects of being a man in North American society which may be related to man's faster rate of dying.

The male role requires man to appear tough, objective, striving, achieving, unsentimental, and emotionally unexpressive. But seeming is not being. If a man *is* tender, if he weeps, if he shows weakness, he will likely be viewed as unmanly by others, and he will probably regard himself as inferior to other men.

Now, from all that we can fathom about the *subjective* side of man, as this has been revealed in autobiographies, novels, plays, and psychotherapists' case histories, it seems true that men are as capable as women at responding to the play of life's events with a broad range of feelings. Man's thoughts, feelings, wishes, and fantasies know no bounds, save those set by his biological structure and his personal history. But the male role and the male's self-structure will not allow man to acknowledge or express the entire breadth and depth of his inner experience, to himself or to others. Man seems obliged, rather, to hide much of his real self from himself and from others.

Research into what people tell about themselves has shown that men typically reveal less personal information about themselves to others than women. Since men, doubtless, have as much "self", i.e., inner experience as women, then it follows that men have more personal "secrets" from the world than women. It follows further that men, seeming to fear being known by others, must be more continually tense than women. It is as if "being manly" implies the necessity to wear a kind of "armor". Moreover, if a man has "secrets", "something to hide", it must follow that other people will be a threat to him ; they might pry into his secrets, or he may, in an unguarded moment, reveal his true self in its nakedness, thereby exposing his areas of weakness and vulnerability. Naturally, when a person is in hostile territory, he must be continually alert, closed, impassive, and restless. All this implies is that trying to seem manly is a kind of "work", and work imposes stress and consumes energy. Manliness, then, seems to carry with it a chronic burden of stress and energy-expenditure which could be a factor related to man's relatively shorter life-span.

If telling about oneself is an indicator of "openness", and if openness is a factor in health and well-being, then the research in self-disclosure seems to point to one of the potentially lethal aspects of the male role. Men keep their selves to themselves, and impose thereby an added burden of stress beyond that imposed by the activities of everyday life. The experience of doctors who undertake psychotherapy with male patients suffering peptic ulcers and similar disorders seems to support this contention. Psychotherapy is the art of encouraging people to talk about themselves and their real feelings, and research has shown that when treatment is effective the patient has to show his feelings. This is usually accompanied by an improvement in physical health.

There is another implication of the fact that men are less inclined to talk about themselves than women. Men tend to relate to other people on an I–it basis more than women. They are more adept than women at relating impersonally to others. Women (often to the despair of businesslike men) seem to find it difficult to keep their relationships *im*personal; they sense and respond to the feelings of the *other* person even in a business situation, and they respond to their *own* feelings toward the other person, seeming to forget the original purpose of the impersonal relationship.

Studies of leadership show that the leaders of the most effective groups maintain maximum "distance" from their followers, avoiding the distraction thereby of intimate personal knowledge of the followers' immediate feelings and needs. But not all of a man's everyday life involves impersonal leadership role. For example, a man may "lead" his family, but he is not a father twenty-four hours a day. Personal life calls both for insight and for real concern for others. Women, trained toward motherhood and a conformity, both engage in and receive more openness from others than do men.

If men are trained, as it were, to ignore their own feelings, in order more adequately to pursue the impersonal aspects of manliness, it follows that they will be less sensitive to what one might call "all is not well signals" as these arise in themselves. It is probably a fact that in every case of outright physical or mental illness, earlier signs occurred which, if noted and acted upon, would have averted the eventual breakdown. Vague discomfort, boredom, anxiety, depression probably arose as consequences of the afflicted person's way of life, but because these signals were "weak", or else deliberately or automatically ignored, the destructive way of life persisted until breakdown finally forced a withdrawal from the illness-producing role. Women are probably more aware of physical concerns and will notice their "all is not well signals" sooner, and more often than men, consult a doctor sooner, or seek bed-rest more often than men. Men, by contrast, fail to notice these weak "all is not well signals" and do not stop work, nor take to their beds until the destructive consequences of their manly way of life have progressed to the point of a "stroke", or a total collapse. It is as if women enlarge such inner distress signals even when they are dim, while men, as it were, "tune them out" until they become so strong they can no longer be ignored.

It is a fact that suicide, mental illness, and death occur sooner and more often among "men whom nobody knows" (that is, among unmarried men, among "lone wolves") than among men

These technological advances have abruptly replaced muscle power, indeed improved on it. Who needs a male muscle to run a machine? And, cars aside, the female can control automation as skilfully as any male.

Prowess in athletics or competitive sports is beside the point, pertaining to male vanity, and nothing will replace that. I am concerned with how technology affects the male sense of identity for these are factors which underlie all serious, social unrest. And inasmuch as the female no longer depends on the hunt for food or masculine muscle for strength, she can, in these respects, stand beside the male as his equal. But all of this remains, nonetheless, disconcerting for the male.

He asks himself: "What am I if I am not hunter, breadwinner, provider?" This question causes in him deep anxiety and agony of soul. He begins to experience physical and sexual insecurity. Indeed he doubts his very existence. This is why so many of our males today are embracing one or other of the popular existentialist philosophies – including Playboyism.

And for the same reason the male worries about his disappearing role as warrior. The male has always been the warrior.

The case of Joan of Arc is an unusual exception, not to mention the fact that Saint Joan had more going for her than technology. But in terms of our principle – female power increases directly as technology advances – we see again that muscular strength and fleet-footedness have nothing whatever to do with mechanized all-out war. To serve in defense of our country, in the age of ICBMs and ABMs, MIRVs and CURVEs, we need only master skills of pulling levers and pushing buttons. Surely women can perform these more elegantly than their counterparts. All of which explains why the government is in a quandary over the armed forces. So much for the Canadian male warrior.

John McDonough
Toronto *Globe and Mail*
April 1970

They [the heroines of the Old West, such as Calamity Jane, Cattle Kate and Annie Oakley] possessed a cold courage whether they were using their sex to steal military secrets or holding up a stage coach. Their appetite for life, action, and excitement was insatiable. They committed espionage as coolly as they sipped their tea, seduced men in high places for their country and their causes; held their liquor, rode like Comanches, dealt stud poker, packed guns, rustled cattle, and played road agent with great efficiency and picturesqueness.

James D. Horan
Desperate Women

Nevertheless, though the man's individual emotional security largely depends on his roles as husband and father, these must necessarily become secondary to his primary role of bread-winner. And the occupational role differs widely from the roles of husband and father, in terms of ends, obligations, involvement, and emotional content.

Many men try to solve this conflict by carrying over into family life the standards and attitudes useful in building the career. Needless to say, these are in direct opposition to the woman's values, and therefore a potent source of strain within the family.

D. F. Aberle and K. D. Naegele
"Middle-Class Fathers' Occupational Role
and Attitudes Toward Children"
American Journal of Orthopsychiatry
Vol. 22, 1952

Robert Winch has compared the preparation for marriage in our culture with that of the Arapesh of New Guinea. He says that the degree to which our culture creates a clear separation between the recreation, glamour, and romance of dating and the responsibility of marriage can best be seen when we contrast premarital activities in our society with those among the Arapesh. Among these mountain people, the betrothed girl goes to live in the house of the family of her husband-to-be while she is still very young (six to eight years old). During the years of her betrothal she is treated as a member of the family into which she will marry, is integrated into the family's activities, and engages in a variety of domestic duties. In contrast with our culture, that of the Arapesh creates expectations concerning premarital behaviour that are consistent and continuous with those regarding marital behaviour.

But in North America, Winch says, marriage brings a fairly sharp break from the previous way of life, especially for women. Our culture does not prepare people very well for marriage, which it presents as the drably monotonous anti-climax to romance. The chase is the source of fascination when boy-meets-girl, and by implication, married life is too dull to warrant continuing the story *after* boy-meets-girl. Our culture creates the stereotype of the young, nubile girl as the "love goddess" and of the wife as the fork-tongued, hatchet-faced battle-ax of the cartoonist's caricature. In the face of these conflicting images, it is not astonishing that problems arise in marriage.

who are loved as individuals, known persons, by other individuals, known persons. Perhaps loving and being loved enables a man to take his life seriously; it makes his life take on value, not only to himself, but also to his loved ones, thereby adding to its value for him. Moreover, if a man is open to his loved one, it permits two people – he and his loved one – to examine, react to, diagnose, evaluate, and do something constructive about *his* inner experience and his present condition when these fall into the undesirable range. When a man's self is hidden from everybody else, even from a physician, it seems also to become much hidden even from himself. Men who are unknown and/or inadequately loved often fall ill, or even die as if suddenly and without warning, and it is a shock and a surprise to everyone who hears about it. One wonders why people express surprise when they themselves fall ill, or when someone else falls ill or dies, apparently suddenly. If one had direct access to the person's real self, one would have had many earlier signals that the present way of life was generating illness.

It is a well-documented observation that men in our society, following retirement, will frequently disintegrate and die not long after they assume their new life of leisure. It would appear that masculine identity and self-esteem are rooted in a man's work. If men can see themselves as manly, and life as worthwhile, only so long as they are engaged in regular work or have enviable social status, then clearly these are weak factors upon which to base one's existence. It would seem that women can continue to find meaning in life long after men feel useless and unneeded.

If health, a productive life, happiness, and creativity are valued goals for mankind, then we must all seek new ways of redefining the male role, to help it become less physically and emotionally harmful, more expressive of the "complete" man and more conducive to life.

Marriage as role change

The move from childhood to adulthood involves many stages in a complex industrial society. A young person is not a child one day and an adult the next, as is the case in some tribal societies. Under the age of twelve, a child pays half-fare on public transportation vehicles. If he is a Roman Catholic, he may have made his first communion and have accepted full responsibility in his religious life. A Jewish boy at thirteen years of age may have celebrated his bar mitzvah and said, "Today, I am a man." Yet he cannot drive a car until he is sixteen years old; he must wait until age eighteen to see a restricted movie, and until age twenty-one before he can hold property or vote. Such a long period of adjusting to the changing role creates many strains for the individual and his family. There are often many conflicting ideas about how and when the young person should be treated as an adult. A young man may be his mother's little boy, but if he joins the army, he is a man to the sergeant and is expected to behave as one. Often the youth so treated responds to the expectation by adjusting his behaviour.

Perhaps the single most obvious sign of adulthood is marriage – the ceremony that marks the end of one role and the beginning of another. The median age for marriage in 1964 was 23.1 years for men and 20.5 years for women. Fully 75 per cent of marriages occur within a four- or five-year period on either side of age 21, which coincides with another great role-changing ceremony – graduation from university or college. Brides are 2¼ years younger than the grooms on the average, and in 10 per cent of cases, the same age. There are marriages among both younger and older people, but the number is considerably fewer.

The wedding ceremony can have both legal and religious meaning, as well as emphasize the changing roles of the bride and groom. A couple may marry at City Hall after a brief period of notice, or they may marry in a large ceremony. Many non-church-goers may feel it important to marry in front of family and friends in a church. Some couples who have married in a brief civil ceremony have said that they felt nothing had happened. For couples who plan a large wedding, great preparation is necessary. The bride is the centre of attention. She goes to showers given by her friends, at which she receives gifts. She makes choices as to how the ceremony will be carried out, the flowers, colour and style of bridal costumes, and place and nature of the reception. The bride is the centre of attention through this period, as family and friends prepare for her role change. A large wedding may be felt necessary in view of the bride's family's social position. She may have a large circle of friends who need to be made aware of her role change. The prestige of her father and family may depend on certain ostentation. A middle-class family may require only a small wedding, since their family and circle of friends may be small and the number of people who will be affected by the role change would be correspondingly small. In fact, the couple may plan to move away to a different city or country and thus see very few of their old friends and family again. Compare this situation to a royal wedding which has significant social and political overtones. Notables from around the world may attend to give recognition to the status of the bride as a royal leader of the nation. Questions of inheritance, royal lineage, and the national policy are connected to the role. The people of the country watch and, to a degree through news media, participate in the role change while affirming their own role as citizens of the nation. Different classes in the society take differing amounts of interest in such weddings, however.

For most marriages, the formal ceremony takes place in front of the family and friends of both participants. The ritual and ceremony require the seating of the families in the church in a certain way. There is a special place for the bride's mother and father as well as for the groom's. Frequently, the bride's father "gives her away", signifying the changing nature of his daughter's relationship and role. When the bride signs the marriage certificate, she gives up her maiden name. Rice (the symbol of fertility) or the modern equivalent, confetti, is thrown. The car is decorated with signs that proclaim "just married". The bridal couple attend a reception as man and wife, where speeches, ceremonial cake-cutting and formal introductions of the new bride and groom take

Many simple societies have institutionalized ways of putting marriageable girls in touch with prospective husbands. The Ekoi of Nigeria, who admire fat women, send girls away to be especially fattened for marriage. The Yao of central Africa and the aborigines of the Canary Islands send their daughters to "convents" where old women teach them the special skills and mysteries that a young wife needs to know. But parents in all societies have more in mind than just getting their daughters married. They want them married to the *right* man of their own class or higher.

David Dressler
Sociology: The Study of Human Interaction

Role Conflict for Girls

Many girls experience a great deal of role conflict in today's world. Komarovsky discovered much evidence of this conflict among college girls, particularly among the brighter and more serious students. The chief conflict she finds is between the "feminine" role and that of the career or professional woman. One student's father, for example, wants her to get an *A* in every subject and to prepare for a profession. But her mother says, "That *A* in Philosophy is very nice, dear. But please don't become so deep that no man will be good enough for you." The student wonders how she is to pursue any course single-mindedly, when those she loves and respects have such differing plans and expectations for her. Another closely related conflict faced by college women centres around whether to be oneself in relations with men or to play the expected feminine role, i.e., being dependent and inferior. Komarovsky found that nearly half of her informants had occasionally "played dumb" on dates — concealed academic honors, pretended ignorance, or allowed the man the last word in discussion. But they felt unhappy at such hypocrisy, being only too aware of the counterpressure on the college girl to excel and to develop her skills to the utmost.

M. Komarovsky
"Cultural Conditions and Sex Roles"
American Journal of Sociology
Vol. 62, November 1946

Generally speaking, it would seem that it is the girl with a "middle-of-the-road personality" who is most happily adjusted to the present historical moment. She is a girl who is intelligent enough to do well in school but not so brilliant as to "get all *A*s"; informed and alert but not consumed by an intellectual passion; capable but not talented in areas relatively new to women; able to stand on her own feet and to earn a living, but not so good a living as to compete with men.

S. Stanfield Sargent and Robert C. Williamson
in Faud Baali and Clifton D. Bryant (eds.)
*Introductory Sociology: Selected Readings
for the College Scene*

place. Then the couple leave the reception early for a honeymoon at an undisclosed location.

During the honeymoon, the couple can practise their new roles as man and wife. When they return to their old society, they are more secure in their new roles. For the bride, a new name and new legal relationships result from her becoming a wife. The new husband has also experienced a role change in becoming a husband, but to a much smaller degree than his bride. For the husband, activities related to career and making a living will go on much as before. The job will continue to absorb much of his interest and provide a sense of identity in terms of role, status, and class in society. The husband's identity will tend to be defined in terms of career. However, for the bride a whole new set of conditions will influence her role. Being a housewife, a homemaker, a part-time worker, a mother, will require the girl to conserve a greater sense of role inside the home and family. Career considerations that might have been significant before marriage will likely diminish after marriage, as role changing takes place. Some preparation for this new role has been going on long before the wedding ceremony. The girl has probably played with dolls and at housekeeping, and worked with and observed her mother as a homemaker, so that the expectations of the role of wife are not completely unknown. The wedding ceremony is the obvious external sign of a role change for which a girl has been preparing since childhood.

two   Some roles people play

We have names for the behaviour we expect of persons in different situations. For example, the client of a doctor plays out the role of a patient while a doctor is playing out his role. Teachers act in the way that students would expect them to act. If a teacher acted in an unexpected manner in front of his students, the students would not know how to respond. In fact, one of the main reasons for the slowness of social change in our society is that we experience considerable difficulty in accepting new roles for ourselves and others.

Not everyone playing a certain role plays it in the same way. We know generally where a quarterback will stand and what kinds of things he *can* do in a given situation, such as make a hand-off or a pass, but we do not know what he *will* do. There is usually quite a bit of scope for an individual when he plays out a role, but there are general expectations associated with that role to which he conforms. Not all students are alike, but they behave in a variety of ways that we have come to expect as fitting the role of a student.

In the following section we explore the role played by individuals in a wide variety of occupations (if the roles of a hippie and a professional thief can be called occupations). The main articles are "The Occupational Culture of the Boxer", "Social Role of the Housewife", and "The Hippies of Yorkville". A series of descriptions of roles of the nurse, the policeman, the advertising man, the teacher, the truck driver, and the professional thief also are included.

The occupational culture of the boxer

S. Kirson Weinberg and Henry Arond

Herein is described the culture of the professional boxer as discovered by personal experience, by reading of firsthand literature, and by interview with sixty-eight boxers and former boxers, seven trainers, and five managers. The aspects covered are recruitment, practices and beliefs, and the social structure of the boxing world.

The juvenile and adolescent culture of the lower socio-economic levels provides a base for the boxing culture. Individual and gang fights are encouraged. The best fighter is often the most admired, as well as the most feared, member of a gang. A boy who lacks status tries to get it and to restore his self-esteem by fighting. Successful amateur and professional boxers furnish highly visible role-models to the boys of the slum; this is especially so among urban Negroes at present. Since he has otherwise little hope of anything but unskilled, disagreeable work, the boxing way to money and prestige may appear very attractive. As an old-time manager put it, "Where else can a poor kid get a stake as fast as he can in boxing?"

As the ability to fight is a matter of status among one's peers, is learned in play, and is the accepted means of expressing hostility and settling disputes, boys learn to fight early.

One fighter thought of becoming a boxer at the age of ten, because he could not participate in team games as a child; his mother insisted that he had a "bad heart". He stated, "I tried to fight as

The Policeman

The role of the police officer is often quite stressful. In training, policemen are told that their job is a 24-hour-a-day one: many policemen are expected to respond to problem situations even when they are off duty, and they are always on call for major events such as rock festivals, student activisim, and criminal chases. Even their relationship with the opposite sex can be affected by their image. One police recruit was surprised to find that his girlfriend's father would not even let him into the house. Many police departments have rules about an officer's style of life and conduct. Recently in one city a young policeman sued the police commission for reinstatement after he had been suspended because he was commuting from a suburban area. The rules stated that he was required to live in the city.

When a young man applies to join the police force, many authorities insist that his private life be investigated. Once on the force he must be very careful about how he spends his money, since he is always open to suspicion of taking money from gamblers and other criminals in exchange for preferred treatment. Any signs of unusual wealth will be interpreted by neighbours as evidence of illegal or bribe-taking activities.

Most police departments are set up along semi-military lines, and it is very difficult for the police recruit to develop personal relationships with people above him in the hierarchy. When on the job, the police officer is closely supervised by his superiors. In some cases he is required to call the station at specified intervals.

Although the policeman is defined as an enforcer of the law, he is also supposed to help those in trouble. There is considerable conflict in the enforcing of police regulations. The policeman must maintain control of the public and at the same time must skillfully handle people and not allow himself to be provoked into unlawful action. Often when he is apprehending a suspect, he is impeded in his work by bystanders; this is particularly true in his work with university students, hippy activists, political demonstrators, and industrial strikers. He is required to have considerable knowledge of the law because, if he makes a false arrest, unfavourable criticism could result for himself, his department, and his city. He is forced to make split-second decisions on legal issues, and is allowed very little room for error.

Although the policeman is not always active when he is on duty, he must always be at the ready to respond to a wide array of events that require his involvement.

The Nursing Profession

When girls enter nursing, they are likely to be faced with a number of identity stresses. Although when asked their purpose for entering nursing, girls typically state that the reason is their desire to help people, many girls see nursing as an opportunity to work with high-status people (doctors) on a professional level, and with any luck, to marry into this eligible group. However, the student nurse soon realizes that this goal is not likely to be attained. While some doctors do marry nurses, most in fact do not. Medical students and doctors tend to associate with each other, not only in the hospital but in social life as well. There is little interaction between doctors and nurses in the cafeteria, lounges, or any other place. Doctors and medical students tend to think of nurses as an occupational group that has lower status than their own. This relationship between nurses and other medical professionals requires quite a difficult adjustment for the nurses. Most girls are used to a co-educational environment where they have equal status with boys, and it is difficult for them to accept a lower-status occupation.

Nursing is essentially an all-female occupation category, and for many girls this induces some stress. Most nurses in training, when given the opportunity to indicate what their most important role in life would be, say "wives and mothers".

soon as I got old enough, to be the roughest, toughest kid on the block." He fought so frequently and was arrested so often for fighting that one policeman told him that he might as well get paid for it. At the age of fourteen he participated in fights in vacant lots in the neighbourhood. Because of his prowess as a fighter, the other boys in the neighbourhood began to respect him more, and he began to associate status with fighting. When he was about seventeen, an amateur fighter told him about a gymnasium where he could learn to become a "ring fighter" instead of a "street fighter". He claimed, "I love fighting. I would rather fight than eat."

Most boxers seem to have been influenced to become "ring fighters" by a boxer in the neighbourhood or by a member of the family. One middleweight champion claimed that he "took after" his brother, followed him to the gymnasium, imitated him, and thus decided to be a boxer before he was fifteen years old. Another fighter was inspired by a neighbour and became his protégé. He continually followed his hero to the gymnasium and learned to fight himself. Eventually, the neighbour induced his manager to take his protégé into the stable. A third fighter has stated:

> I was twelve when I went to the gym first. If there's a fighter in the neighbourhood, the kids always look up to him because they think he's tough. There was an amateur in my neighbourhood and he was a kind of hero to all us kids. It was him that took me to the gym the first time.

A former welterweight and middleweight champion who has been boxing since he was eleven years old has written in a similar vein:

> I didn't do any boxing before I left Detroit. I was too little. But I was already interested in it, partly because I idolized a big Golden Gloves heavyweight who lived on the same block with us. I used to hang around the Brewster Center Gym all the time watching him train. His name was Joe Louis. Whenever Joe was in the gym so was I. He was my idol then just like he is today. I've always wanted to be like him. (Sugar Ray Robinson, "Fighting is my business", *Sport*, June 1951.)

Some managers and trainers of local gymnasiums directly seek out boys who like to fight and who take fighters as their models. One such manager says that he sought boys who were considered the "toughest boys in the block" or "natural fighters". He would get them to come to the gym and to become amateur boxers. He entered some in tournaments, from which he received some "cut", then sifted out the most promising for professional work.

It is believed by many in boxing circles that those in the lower socio-economic levels make the "best fighters":

> They say that too much education softens a man and that is why the college graduates are not good fighters. They fight emotionally on the gridiron and they fight bravely and well in our wars, but their contributions in our rings have been insignificant. The ring has been described as the refuge of the under-privileged. Out of the downtrodden have come our

greatest fighters. . . . An education is an escape, and that is what they are saying when they shake their heads – those who know the fight game – as you mention the name of a college fighter. Once the bell rings, they want their fighters to have no retreat, and a fighter with an education is a fighter who does not have to fight to live and he knows it. . . . Only for the hungry fighter is it a decent gamble.

It can be inferred tentatively that the social processes among juveniles and adolescents in the lower socio-economic levels, such as individual and gang fights, the fantasies of "easy money", the lack of accessible vocational opportunities, and the general isolation from the middle-class culture, are similar for those who become professional boxers as for those who become delinquents. The difference resides in the role-model the boy picks, whether criminal or boxer. The presence of one or several successful boxers in an area stimulates boys of the same ethnic groups to follow in their footsteps. Boxing, as well as other sports and certain kinds of entertainment, offers slum boys the hope of quick success without deviant behaviour (although, of course, some boxers have been juvenile delinquents).

Within the neighbourhood the professional boxer orients his behaviour and routine around the role of boxer. Usually acquiring some measure of prestige in the neighbourhood, he is no longer a factory hand or an unskilled labourer. He is admired, often has a small coterie of followers, and begins to dress smartly and loudly and to conceive of himself as a neighbourhood celebrity, whether or not he has money at the time. Nurtured by the praise of the trainer or manager, he has hopes that eventually he will ascend to "big-time fights" and to "big money". The money that he does make in his amateur and early professional fights by comparison with his former earnings seems a lot to him.

At the outset of his career the boxer becomes impressed with the need for training to improve his physical condition and to acquire the skills necessary to win fights and to avoid needless injury. When he has such status as to be sought out by promoters, he assigns a specified interval for training before the bout. But in the preliminary ranks he must keep himself in excellent physical shape most of the time, because he does not know when he will be summoned to fight. He may be booked as a substitute and cannot easily refuse the match. If he does, he may find it difficult to get another bout. The particular bout may be the chance he has been hoping for. The fighter is warned persistently by tales of the ritualistic necessity of "getting in shape" and of the dire consequences if he does not. "There is no more pitiable sight," stated one boxer, "than to see a fighter get into the ring out of condition."

The boxer comes to regard his body, especially his hands, as his stock-in-trade. Boxers have varied formulas for preventing their hands from excess swelling, from excessive pain, or from being broken. This does not mean a hypochondriacal interest, because they emphasize virility and learn to slough off and disdain punishment. But fighters continually seek nostrums and exercises for improving their bodies. One practised Yoga, another became a physical cultist, a third went on periodic fasts, others seek out lotions,

When asked what they think the female role should be in our society, they reply "home and family" first, and then "work and career", "glamour", "community service", "religious calling" or "inspiration", in various combinations. Conflict is set up between the nursing ideas of home and family and the life of training in an all-female environment. Social contacts are made difficult because of unusual hours of work, special pressures, and the strict rules that usually govern nurses. Uncertainty about the nurse's role as a female can develop out of this social ambiguity.

The job situation for nurses is different from that of many professions. While doctors and dentists do not deal with patients until they have had appropriate training, nursing students are given responsibility immediately to play out aspects of the nursing role. The nurse is expected to deal competently with patients in the very early stages of her training. As a nurse she must act in a third-party role between the doctor and the patient. Conflict sometimes arises between the patients' needs and the doctors' recommendations. She must act to aid and comfort the patients without providing information about their condition that might be detrimental to their health.

Frequently, the student nurse encounters situations that are extremely demanding and that few girls in her age group ever experience. The acceptance of the rigours of training, the relatively low status of the occupation of nursing, the expectation of an early demonstration of ability, and the segregation of men from women can make the nursing training period a very stressful time. However, the successful nurse who enjoys the occupation she has chosen has the tremendous satisfaction of being intimately involved with the public and of providing an essential and integral service for the welfare of others.

The Truck Driver

Many factors urge this choice on the younger men. In the first place, since the area is dotted with truck depots, this work is convenient, an important factor in the lower Ward; also, word of openings travels quickly along the grapevine, for instance, in the pubs. Although among the bigger companies the trend is towards careful screening of applicants and an emphasis upon stable, young married men, such hiring is still casual or somewhat haphazard. Secondly, for various reasons this occupation has more prestige than factory employment: it is more masculine, is outside rather than inside, gives the individual more freedom and sense of independence, involves more variety and excitement. Thirdly, it has advantages over comparable jobs in providing opportunities, for instance, for regular short stop-offs, commonly made at grills or beer parlours, for contacts with promiscuous females and often for extra earnings through overtime.

Long-haul trucking in particular, which involves out-of-town driving, boasts all of the above "rewards" in addition to a general high status in the truckers' world.

Thus truck driving tends to select men who claim they "can't stand indoor work", who want a sense of independence on the job, are mechanically inclined, and also value a sense of belonging. As an occupational group, truckers share a common work experience and a system of values and work codes that serves along with their union and its drinking club – in the east-end slums of Toronto – to integrate them more than many lower status work groups. One pub manager spoke of the drivers who regularly gather in his pub: "They come in and they laugh it up. They talk to one another over the tables, maybe three or four tables away; there seems a much closer association than among other groups. They seem to have more things to talk about." Those issued with distinctive uniforms by their companies, Loblaw drivers for instance, especially give signs of a strong sense of status and group unity.

Certain aspects of truck driving are functional to the value system of the young Anglo-Saxons in the lower Ward, for example, the convenient location of the work itself. This fits in with the common emphasis placed on avoiding great effort, and also facilitates identification with the neighbourhood and its small insulated social world. Relative freedom on the job and lack of careful supervision also permit a casualness of attitude that accords well with the social temper of the lower Ward and its norm of impulse gratification. The appeal of the excitement and danger involved in daring driving is not to be underrated, and clearly answers the conditioned need for excitement. In certain types of trucking, accidents are quite frequent. One long-haul driver told the writer: "Four of my chums have been killed in the last year. The last one was crushed while loading at the back of a truck." It is easy to see how truck driving would appeal to the youth of the lower Ward, conditioned to a life of accidents, mobility, danger, and thrills in boyhood. In fact, [this] cultural complex [surrounds] the truck driver's work life, with its considerable group identification and pub-centred recreation, its expression of impulse, and its casual acceptance of illegal violence, not excluding wildcat strikes.

W. E. Mann
"The Social System of a Slum:
The Lower Ward, Toronto"
in S. D. Clark
Urbanism and the Changing Canadian Society

vitamins, and other means of improving their endurance, alertness and punching power.

"You have to live up to being a fighter." This phrase justifies their deprivations and regulated living. There is also a cult of a kind of persevering courage, called a "fighting heart", which means "never admitting defeat". The fighter learns early that his exhibited courage – his ability, if necessary, to go down fighting – characterizes the respected, audience-pleasing boxer. He must cherish the lingering hope that he can win by a few more punches. One fighter was so severely beaten by another that the referee stopped the bout. The brother of the beaten fighter, a former fighter himself, became so outraged that he climbed into the ring and started to brawl with the referee. In another instance a boxer incurred very severe eye injury, which would have meant the loss of his sight. But he insisted on continuing to fight, despite the warnings of his seconds. When the fight was stopped, he protested. This common attitude among boxers is reinforced by the demands of the spectators, who generally cheer a "game fighter". Thus the beaten fighter may become a "crowd-pleaser" and may get matches despite his defeat. On the other hand, some fighters who are influenced by friends, by wives, or by sheer experience recognize that sustained beatings may leave permanent injuries and voluntarily quit when they are beaten. But the spirit of the code is that the boxer continue to fight regardless of injuries. "If a man quits a fight, an honest fight," claimed one fighter, "he has no business there in the first place."

Fighters who remain in the sport are always hopeful of occupational climbing. This attitude may initially be due to a definite self-centredness, but it is intensified by the character of boxing. Boxing is done by single contestants, not by teams. Emphasis is on the boxer as a distinct individual. The mores among boxers are such that fighters seldom admit to others that they are "punchy" or "washed-up". One fighter said: "You can tell another fighter to quit, but you can't call him punchy. If you do, he'll punch you to show you he still has a punch." He has to keep up his front.

Further, the boxer is involved in a scheme of relationships and traditions which focus upon building confidence. The boxing tradition is full of legends of feats of exceptional fighters. Most gymnasiums have pictures of past and present outstanding boxers on the wall, and identification with them comes easy for the incoming fighters. Past fights are revived in tales. Exceptional fighters of the past and present are compared and appraised. Second, the individual boxer is continually assured and reassured that he is "great" and that he is "coming up". As a result, many fighters seem to overrate their ability and to feel that all they need are "lucky breaks" to become champions or leading contenders. Many get self-important and carry scrapbooks of their newspaper write-ups and pictures.

As most bouts are unpredictable, boxers usually have superstitions which serve to create confidence and emotional security among them. Sometimes the manager or trainer uses these superstitions to control the fighter. One fighter believed that, if he ate certain foods, he was sure to win, because these foods gave him strength. Others insist on wearing the same robe in which they won their first fight: one wore an Indian blanket when he entered the ring. Many have charm pieces or attribute added importance to entering the ring after the opponent. Joe Louis insisted on using a certain dressing room at Madison Square Garden. Some insist that, if a woman watches them train, it is bad luck. One fighter, to show he was not superstitious, would walk under a ladder before every fight, until this became a magical rite itself. Consistent with this attitude, many intensify their religious attitudes and keep Bibles in their lockers. One fighter kept a rosary in his glove. If he lost the rosary, he would spend the morning before the fight in church. Although this superstitious attitude may be imported from local or ethnic culture, it is intensified among the boxers themselves, whether they are white or Negro, preliminary fighters or champions.

When a fighter likes the style, punch, or movement of another fighter, he may wear the latter's trunks or one of his socks or rub him on the back. In training camps some fighters make a point of sleeping in the same bed that a champion once occupied. For this reason, in part, some take the names of former fighters. All these practices focus toward the perspective of "filling the place" or taking the role of the other esteemed fighter. Moreover, many fighters deliberately copy the modes of training, the style, and the general movements of role-models.

As fighters, in the process of training, become keyed to a finely balanced physical and emotional condition and frequently are irritable, restless, and anxious, they also grow dependent and suggestible. The superstitions and the reassuring statements of the trainer and manager both unwittingly and wittingly serve to bolster their confidence.

Before and during the bout, self-confidence is essential. Fighters or their seconds try to unnerve the opponent. They may try to outstare him or may make some irritating or deflating remarks or gestures. In the ring, tactical self-confidence is expressed in the boxer's general physical condition and movements. His ability not to go down, to outmaneuver the other contestant, to change his style in whole or in part, to retrieve his strength quickly, or to place the opponent off-balance inevitably will affect the latter's confidence. A fighter can *feel* whether he will win a bout during the early rounds, but he is always wary of the dreaded single punch or the unexpected rally.

Boxers become typed by their style and manner in the ring. A "puncher" or "mauler" differs from a "boxer" and certainly from a "cream puff", who is unable to hit hard. A "miller", or continual swinger, differs from one who saves his energy by fewer movements. A "butcher" is recognized by his tendency to hit hard and ruthlessly when another boxer is helpless, inflicting needless damage. A "tanker" is one who goes down easily, sometimes in a fixed fight or "set-up". The "mechanical" fighter differs from the "smart" fighter, for among the "smart" fighters are really the esteemed fighters, those who are capable of improvising and formulating their style, of devising original punches and leg movements, of cunningly outmaneuvering their opponents, and of possessing

The Teacher

In any analysis of the school as a social system, and of the teacher's role within it, it is important to note the declining rewards in the actual teaching situation. The "natural-born teacher" can no longer use his or her art without having learned "techniques" from the expert. And the teacher who is content to devote the whole of his or her attention to teaching tends to be regarded by his colleagues as old-fashioned. Some of these teachers may be markedly oriented towards subject-matter, bent on strict discipline, and somewhat apart from the prevailing staff camaraderie. Should these tendencies go too far, the teachers in whom they are unduly obvious may not be considered good material for promotion....

The teacher, at the beginning of his career, must strike a delicate balance vis-à-vis the power structure. He must please his Principal, the Director of Education, the provincial government inspectors, and finally the more peripheral yet potent Board of Education. He has to accomplish his end without antagonizing any of the numerous specialists encompassing his path, both within and marginal to the school system....

Like his opposite number, the budding junior executive, if he tries too hard, he [the teacher] runs counter to the prevailing tabu on competition and also the society's maturity values which call for a high degree of independence and individuality. Yet if he does not try at all, he runs the risk of being thought apathetic, "unco-operative", or lacking in professional interest....

The teacher is more akin to the social worker than to the lawyer or doctor, who, in Western society, are in the front ranks of those who set the professional norms. And, in addition, the parents, who are the indirect clients of the teacher in the school situation, are, also and at the same time, the tax-payers from whom the teacher ultimately derives his salary — and not a fee!

John Seeley, R. Alexander Sim, and
Elizabeth Loosely
Crestwood Heights

The Ad Man

The role of an advertising man is painted in a rather negative fashion by Joseph Bensman in his book *Dollars and Sense*. He describes the career as a response to the questions: "Would you recommend advertising as a career to the son of a dear friend?" and "Under what circumstances would you recommend it?"

Bensman feels that if the son has true talent or creative ability in any field, advertising is the last place for him to be. The constant pressure of committee politics and decision-making would be destructive of his creative talent. Each time a new assignment is taken on, the creative person could feel that he has betrayed his talent.

Advertising requires "strong defenses, toughness, nerve, and the willingness to exploit oneself and others", and the kind, gentle, ethical person would find himself in continual situations of emotional stress. The successful advertising man would need a "healthy constitution" and the capacity for hard, but not necessarily meaningful, work. He would need the ability to handle himself under pressure, to be tactful, and to enjoy superficial social relationships. But most of all, he must be motivated by a desire for financial success and power.

The role of the advertising man is a direct reflection of the material values of our society. "Advertising simply accepts the world as it is, and then makes it even more so."

The Role of the Professional Thief

The professional thief has a complex of abilities and skills, just as do physicians, lawyers, or bricklayers. The abilities and skills of the professional thief are directed to the planning and execution of crimes, the disposal of stolen goods, the fixing of cases in which arrests occur, and the control of other situations which may arise in the course of the occupation. Manual dexterity and physical force are a minor element in these techniques. The principal elements in these techniques are wits, "front", and talking ability. The thieves who lack these general abilities or the specific skills which are based on the general abilities are regarded as amateurs, even though they may steal habitually. Also, burglars, robbers, kidnappers, and others who engage in the "heavy rackets" are generally not regarded as professional thieves, for they depend primarily on manual dexterity or force. A few criminals in the "heavy rackets" use their wits, "front", and talking ability, and these are regarded by the professional thieves as belonging to the profession. . . .

The professional thief, like any other professional man, has status. The status is based upon his technical skill, financial standing, connections, power, dress, manners, and wide knowledge acquired in his migratory life. His status is seen in the attitudes of other criminals, the police, the court officials, newspapers, and others. The term "thief" is regarded as honorific and is used regularly without qualifying adjectives to refer to the professional thief. It is so defined in a recent dictionary of criminal slang: "Thief, *n.*, A member of the underworld who steals often and successfully. This term is applied with reserve and only to habitual criminals. It is considered a high compliment." . . .

the compensatory hostility, deadly impulsiveness, and quick reflexes to finish off their opponents in the vital split-second.

Boxers have to contend with fouls and quasi-fouls in the ring. At present, these tactics seemingly are becoming more frequent. They may have to contend with "heeling", the maneuver by which the fighter, during clinches, shoves the laced part of his glove over the opponent's wound, particularly an "eye" wound, to open and exacerbate it, with "thumbing" the eye, with "butting" the head, with having their insteps stepped on hard during clinches, with punches in the back of the head or in the kidneys, or with being tripped. These tactics, which technically are fouls, may be executed so quickly and so cleverly that the referee does not detect them. When detected, the fighter may be warned or, at worst, may lose the round. The boxers are thus placed in a situation fraught with tension, physical punishment, and eventual fatigue. They may be harassed by the spectators. Their protection consists of their physical condition and their acquired confidence. Moreover, the outcome of the fight is decisive for their status and self-esteem.

The boxer's persistent display of aggression is an aspect of status. Thus two boxers may be friends outside the ring, but each will try to knock the other out in a bout, and after the bout they may be as friendly as competition permits. Furthermore, the injury done to an opponent, such as maiming or killing, is quickly rationalized away by an effective trainer or manager in order to prevent an excess of intense guilt, which can ruin a fighter. The general reaction is that the opponent is out to do the same thing to him and that this is the purpose of boxing: namely, to beat the opponent into submission. The exception is the "grudge fight", in which personal hostility is clearly manifest.

In a succession of bouts, if the fighter is at all successful, he goes through a fluctuating routine, in which tension mounts during training, is concentrated during the fight, and is discharged in the usual celebration, which most victorious fighters regard as their inevitable reward. Hence many boxers pursue a fast tempo of living and spend lavishly on clothes, women, gambling, and drink, practices seemingly tolerated by the manager and encouraged by the persons who are attracted to boxers. Many boxers experience intense conflict between the ordeals of training and the pursuits of pleasure.

The boxers who remain in the sport believe that they can ascend to the top because of the character of the boxing culture, in which the exceptional boxer is emphasized and with whom the aspiring boxer identifies. When the boxer ceases to aspire, he quits or becomes a part-time boxer. Yet the aspiring hopes of many boxers are not unfounded, because climbing in the sport does not depend upon ability only but also can be a result of a "lucky break".

Boxers live in a wide social milieu of trainers, managers, and promoters. The boxer and trainer usually form the closest relationships in the boxing milieu. At one time, many managers were trainers, too; and a few owners of local gymnasiums still combine these roles, but their number has declined. Furthermore, the relationships between boxer and trainer are becoming increasingly impersonal. Consequently, the careful training and social intimacy which characterized the conditioning of many boxers by trainers in the past has also declined.

One boxer has characterized managers as follows: "Some managers are interested in the money first and the man second; other managers are interested in the man first." Our observations lead us to infer that the vast majority of managers at the present time are in the first category. They regard boxing as a business and the fighter as a commodity and are concerned mainly with making money. To do so, they are compelled to please the promoters and to sell their fighters' abilities to the promoters. Unless the manager is also a trainer, he is not concerned with the techniques of boxing, except to publicize his charge and to arrange matches which will bring the most revenue.

Some managers will encourage fighters to borrow money from them and usually will not discourage them from squandering their earnings. One manager stated characteristically: "It's good to have a fighter 'in you' for a couple of bucks." By having fighters financially indebted to them, they have an easy expedient for controlling individuals who are unusually headstrong. Some fighters are in the continual process of regarding every fight as an essential means for clearing their debts.

Legally managers cannot receive more than one-third of the fighters' purses, but many do not conform to this rule. Frequently, they take one-half of the purse, or they may put their fighters on a flat salary and get the rest. Some managers tell their preliminary fighters that the purse was less than it was actually and thus keep the rest for themselves.

As many ruthless individuals and petty racketeers who know little about boxing are increasingly drawn into this sport with the prime purpose of making money quickly, boxers tend to have little, if any, protection from managers except that provided by boxing commissions, whose rules can be evaded without difficulty. Moreover, it is extremely difficult for a boxer to climb or get important matches unless he has an effective manager.

The boxer's relationship with the promoter is usually indirect. Yet the promoter is the most influential person in the boxing hierarchy. He is primarily a showman and businessman, emotionally removed from the fighter, and regards him chiefly as a commodity. His aim is to get the most from his investment. Thus the "show" comes first, regardless of the boxer's welfare. To ensure his direct control over many boxers, the promoter, who legally cannot be a manager, may appoint one or a series of "managers" as "fronts" and thus get shares of many boxers' earnings, as well as controlling them. Furthermore, he can reduce the amount of the fighter's share because the "front" manager will not bargain for a larger share. In effect, most boxers are relatively helpless in dealing with promoters, especially at the present time, because of the monopolistic character of boxing.

When a potentially good fighter wants to meet leading contenders, the manager may have to "cut in" the promoter or "cut in" some other manager who has connections with the promoter. Thus the mobility of the fighter depends in large part upon the manager's relationship to the promoter. When the manager does

Professional thieves disagree as to the extent of gradations within the profession. Some thieves divide the profession into "big-time" and "small-time" thieves on the basis of the size of the stakes for which they play, on the preparations for a particular stake, and on connections. A confidence man who regarded himself as "big-time" wrote as follows regarding a shoplifter:

> While he undoubtedly was a professional thief, I should a few years ago (before he was committed to prison) have been ashamed to be seen on the street with him. I say this not out of a spirit of snobbishness but simply because for business reasons I feel that my reputation would have suffered in the eyes of friends to be seen in the company of a booster (shoplifter).

On the other hand, the thief who wrote this document insisted that there are no essential gradations within the profession:

> I have never considered anyone a small-time thief. If he is a thief, he is a thief — small-time, big-time, middle-time, Eastern Standard, or Rocky Mountain, it is all the same. Neither have I considered anyone big-time. It all depends on the spot and how it is handled. I recall a heel touch (sneak theft) at ten one morning which showed $21 and three hours later the same troupe took off one for $6,500 in the same place. Were they small-time in the morning and big-time in the afternoon? . . .

This difference in opinion is quite similar to the difference that would emerge if lawyers or doctors were discussing the gradations within their professions. In any case there is pride in one's own position in the group. This pride may be illustrated by the action of Roger Benton, a forger, who was given a signed blank check to fill out the amount of money he desired; Benton wrote a big "Void" across the face of the check and returned it to the grocer who gave it to him. He explains, "I suppose I had too much professional pride to use it — after all I was a forger who took smart money from smart banks, not a thief who robbed honest grocerymen." . . .

The following explanation of the emphasis that thieves place on punctuality is an illustration of the way consensus has developed:

> It is a cardinal principle among partners in crime that appointments shall be kept promptly. When you "make a meet" you are there on the dot or you do not expect your partner to wait for you. The reason why is obvious. Always in danger of arrest, the danger to one man is increased by the arrest of the other; and arrest is the only [accepted] excuse for failing to keep an appointment. Thus, if the appointment is not kept on time, the other may assume arrest and his best procedure is to get away as quickly as possible to save his own skin. . . .

One of the most heinous offenses that a thief can commit against another thief is to inform, "squeal", or "squawk". This principle is generally respected even when it is occasionally violated. Professional thieves probably violate the principle less frequently than other criminals for the reason that they are more completely immune from punishment, which is the pressure that compels an offender to inform on others. Many thieves will submit to severe punishment rather than inform. Two factors enter into this behaviour. One is the injury which would result to himself in the form of loss of prestige, inability to find companions among thieves in the future, and reprisals if he should inform. The other is loyalty and identification of self with other thieves. The spontaneous reactions of offenders who are in no way affected by the behaviour of the squealer, as by putting him in coventry, are expressions of genuine disgust, fear, and hatred. Consensus is the basis of both of these reactions, and the two together explain how the rule against informing grows out of the common experiences of the thieves. . . .

The professional thief in North America feels that he is a social outcast. This is especially true of the professional thieves who originated in middle-class society, as many of them did. He feels that he is a renegade when he becomes a thief. It has been said that the thief is looking for arguments to ease his conscience and that he blocks off considerations about the effects of his crimes upon the victims and about the ultimate end of his career. When he is alone in prison, he cannot refrain from thought of such things, and then he shudders at the prospect of returning to his professional activities. Once he is back in his group, he assumes the "bravado" attitudes of the other thieves, his shuddering ceases, and everything seems to be all right. . . .

The thief must come into contact with persons in legitimate society in order to steal from them. While, as a pickpocket, he may merely make physical contact with the clothes and pocketbooks of victims, as a confidence man he must enter into intimate association with them. This intimacy is cold-blooded. The feelings are expressed as by an actor on a stage, with calculations of the results they will produce. He is like a salesman who attempts to understand a prospective customer only as a means of breaking down sales resistance and realizing his own objective of increased sales. . . .

More specifically, the organization of professional thieves consists in part of the knowledge which becomes the common property of the profession. Every thief becomes an information bureau. For example, each professional thief is known personally to a large proportion of the other thieves, as a result of their migratory habits and common hangouts. Any thief may be appraised by those who know him, in a terse phrase, such as "He is O.K.", "He is a no-good b——", or "Never heard of him". The residue of

not have this acceptable relationship and is unwilling to "cut in" a third party, he will not get the desired matches.

The punitive character of boxing, as well as the social relationships in the boxing milieu, affects the boxer-participants during and after their careers in the ring.

First, the physical effects of boxing, which are intrinsic to the sport, operate to the boxer's detriment. Although boxers may cultivate strong bodies, the direct and indirect injuries from this sport are very high. In addition to the deaths in the ring, one estimate is that 60 per cent of the boxers become mildly punch-drunk and 5 per cent become severely punch-drunk. The severely punch-drunk fighter can be detected by an ambling gait, thickened or retarded speech, mental stereotypy, and a general decline in efficiency. In addition, blindness and visual deficiency are so pervasive that eye injuries are considered virtually as occupational casualties, and misshaped noses and cauliflower ears are afflictions of most boxers who are in the sport for five or more years. Despite these injuries, attempts to provide safeguards, such as head guards, have been opposed by the fans and by many boxers because such devices presumably did not "protect" and did not fit into their conceptions of virility and presumed contempt for punishment.

Second, the boxing culture tends to work to the eventual detriment of the boxer. Many boxers tend to continue a particular fight when they are hopelessly beaten and when they can become severely injured. Many boxers persist in fighting when they have passed their prime and even when they have been injured. For example, one boxer, blind in one eye and barred from fighting in one state, was grateful to his manager for getting him matches in other states. Another old-time boxer has admitted characteristically: "It's hard to quit. Fighting gets into your blood, and you can't get it out." Many fighters try to make one comeback, at least, and some fight until they are definitely punch-drunk.

Boxers find further that, despite their success in the sport, their careers terminate at a relatively early age. As their physical condition is so decisive to their role, when they feel a decline in their physical prowess, they tend also to acquire the premature feeling of "being old". This attitude is reinforced by others in the sport who refer to them as "old men", meaning old in the occupation. As boxing has been the vocational medium of status attainment and as they have no other skills to retain this status, many boxers experience a sharp decline in status in their postboxing careers. As an illustration, of ninety-five leading former boxers (i.e., champions and leading contenders), each of whom earned more than $100,000 during his ring career, eighteen were found to have remained in the sport as trainers or trainer-managers; two became wrestlers; twenty-six worked in, "fronted for", or owned taverns; two were liquor salesmen; eighteen had unskilled jobs, most commonly in the steelmills; six worked in the movies; five were entertainers; two owned or worked in gas stations; three were cabdrivers; three had newsstands; two were janitors; three were bookies; three were associated with the race tracks (two in collecting bets and one as a starter); and two were in business, one of them as a custom tailor. In short, the successful boxers have a relatively quick economic ascent at a relatively young age in terms of earning power. But the punitive character of the sport, the boxers' dependence upon their managers, and their carefree spending during their boxing careers contribute to a quicker economic descent for many boxers. Their economic descent is accompanied by a drop in status and frequently by temporary or prolonged emotional difficulties in readjusting to their new occupational roles.

Social role of the housewife

Helena Z. Lopata

How many times has the woman of the house said, "I'm just a housewife"? Those few plaintive words suggest not only an attitude but also a social role. This article will describe how the role of housewife develops and changes. In modern North American society a young woman usually enters upon the role of housewife when she marries. It is a role for which she is not adequately trained in school, as many interviews with women have suggested. Although each young girl has probably lived in a home run by her mother until the time of her marriage she has not been deeply involved in its operation. The Canadian and American systems of education and occupation remove a girl from the home for most of her conscious hours – starting at the age of five. While she may receive some training in home economics, homemaking skills as such are not usually a part of the school program and her leisure time is usually taken up with school, work, boys, and leisure-oriented activity. Each teenager then tends not to be a role but an individual.

The process of becoming a housewife includes the phase of learning the various skills used in maintaining a home and relating to those people who are involved in its maintenance such as the milkman and the store keeper. The newly married girl must shift her identification from the stress upon the location of the self outside the home in a life role such as office worker, teacher, or secretary and place the emphasis on the self inside the home. The newly married girl may for a while continue to work or go to school and thus for the first few months or years of her married life have outside roles apart from that of housewife. Living in her own place is important as is her relationship to her husband and her feelings about that relationship. Gradually the newly-wed experiences a growing awareness of her complexity of duties involved in the role of being a wife. She must budget, she must purchase, she must deal with people as a homemaker and if she is working her money will increasingly go into the house, whereas before marriage her salary could be spent on personal adornments or things that she wanted. Now resources are given generally to fixing up the apartment or house. Gradually the self begins to be expressed inside the house and the house takes on a symbolic representation of the housewife and her relationship in the home.

such appraisals is available when a troupe wishes to add a new member, or when a thief asks for assistance in escaping from jail.

Similarly, the knowledge regarding methods and situations becomes common property of the profession. "The lunch hour is the best time to work that spot." "Look out for the red-haired saleslady – she is double-smart." "Never grift on the way out." Similar mandates and injunctions are transmitted from thief to thief until everyone in the profession knows them. The discussions in the hangouts keep this knowledge adjusted to changing situations. The activities of the professional thieves are organized in terms of this common knowledge.

Informal social services are similarly organized. Any thief will assist any other thief in a dangerous situation. He does this both by positive actions, such as warning, and by refraining from behaviour that would increase the danger, such as staring at a thief who is working. Also, collections are taken in the hangouts and elsewhere to assist a thief who may be in jail or the wife of a thief who may be in prison. In these services reciprocity is assumed, but there is no insistence on immediate or specific return to the one who performs the service.

The preceding description of the characteristics of theft suggests that a person can be a professional thief only if he is recognized and received as such by other professional thieves. Professional theft is a group-way of life. One can get into the group and remain in it only by the consent of those previously in the group. Recognition as a professional thief by other professional thieves is the absolutely necessary, universal, and definitive characteristic of the professional thief. This recognition is a combination of two of the characteristics previously described, namely, status and differential association of professional thieves.

Selection and tutelage are the two necessary elements in the process of acquiring recognition as a professional thief. These are the universal factors in an explanation of the genesis of the professional thief. A person cannot acquire recognition as a professional thief until he has had tutelage in professional theft, and tutelage is given only to a few selected from the total population. . . .

Selection is a reciprocal process, involving action by those who are professional thieves and by those who are not professional thieves. Contact is the first requisite, and selection doubtless lies back of the contacts. They may be pimps, amateur thieves, burglars, or they may be engaged in legitimate occupations as clerks in hotels or stores. Contacts may be made in jail or in the places where professional thieves are working or are spending their leisure time. If the other person is to become a professional thief, the contact must develop into appreciation of the professional thieves. This is not difficult, for professional thieves in general are very attractive.

They have had wide experience, are interesting conversationalists, know human nature, spend money lavishly, and have great power. Since some persons are not attracted even by these characteristics, there is doubtless a selective process involved in this, also. . . .

An emergency or crisis is likely to be the occasion on which tutelage begins. A person may lose a job, get caught in amateur stealing, or may need additional money. If he has developed a friendly relationship with professional thieves, he may request or they may suggest that he be given a minor part in some act of theft. He would, if accepted, be given verbal instructions in regard to the theory of the racket and the specific part he is to play. In his first efforts in this minor capacity he may be assisted by the professional thieves, although such assistance would be regarded as an affront by one who was already a professional. If he performs these minor duties satisfactorily, he is promoted to more important duties. During this probationary period the neophyte is assimilating the general standards of morality, propriety, etiquette, and rights which characterize the profession, and he is acquiring "larceny sense". He is learning the general methods of disposing of stolen goods and of fixing cases. He is building up a personal acquaintance with other thieves, and with lawyers, policemen, court officials, and fixers. This more general knowledge is seldom transmitted to the neophyte as formal verbal instructions but is assimilated by him without being recognized as instruction. However, he is quite as likely to be dropped from participation in further professional activities for failure to assimilate and use this more general culture as for failure to acquire the specific details of the techniques of theft. . . .

A person who is a professional thief may cease to be one. This would generally result from a violation of the codes of the profession or else from inefficiency due to age, fear, narcotic drugs, or drink. Because of either failure he would no longer be able to find companions with whom to work, would not be trusted by the fixer or by the policemen, and therefore he would not be able to secure immunity from punishment. He is no longer recognized as a professional thief, and therefore he can no longer be a professional thief. On the other hand, if he drops out of active stealing of his own volition and retains his abilities, he would continue to receive recognition as a professional thief. He would be similar to a physician who would be recognized as a physician after he ceased practice. . . .

The thief is relatively safe in his thefts for three reasons: First, he selects rackets in which the danger is at a minimum. The shakedown (extortion from other criminals) is safe because the victims, being themselves violators of the law, cannot complain to the police. The confidence game is safe for the same reasons, for the victims have entered into collusion with the thieves to defraud someone else and were themselves

Gradually the roles which cluster around being a wife become centred and the former roles of daughter, worker, colleague, or student tend to take on less importance or to lose their former significance. The role of housewife or homemaker and of consumer–purchaser are gradually pushed into the foreground.

The birth of the first child creates a dramatic change in a woman's life. Former roles must be dropped and a shift in focus to a cluster of roles concerning the housewife's activities become accepted. Because of the utter dependence of a new-born upon an adult for constant twenty-four hour care, the number of activities outside the house must be decreased and the housewife finds herself confined to a variety of housekeeping activities. Often inexpertly and alone she must cope with a large number of new sets of duties and new role relations begin to develop. The husband now becomes a father of the child and must relate to his spouse as a wife and also in her new role as a mother. Oftentimes the shift in attention caused by the new baby pushes the role of wife to the background temporarily and occasionally permanently. It could be said that a peak stage of being in the role of a housewife is reached when a woman has several small children. The role of housewife is determined by a combination of factors such as the number and ages of the children, their needs, the size of the house and what must be done to keep it maintained, the number of persons helping in the performance of duties and the type of assistance each provides, such as servants, relatives, friends, neighbours, as well as the number of labour saving devices and conveniences designed to decrease the effort or time required in doing housewife work. The role of housewife then can be performed in a variety of styles and in a greatly complex or in a simplified way.

When the last small child has entered school many women anticipate time of relaxation – "time for myself" – they say. This is the fullhouse stage of the housewife's role. An opportunity to get outside the house, to strike up new relationships, to take courses, to do things which have been impossible because of the care required by small children, while hoped for is often not possible. While the children may be more capable of looking after themselves and controlling their activities, the housewife's role may in fact become more complex. New relationships with other people are begun such as playmates, playmates' parents, neighbours, scout leaders, teachers who may make special demands upon the children requiring more work from the mother. The role of supervising teenage children often leads many mothers to feel that they are very busy, not necessarily in the activities of supervision, but in the worry and concern that goes along with having teenage children.

The role of the housewife may be affected very much by the career cycle of her husband in a situation where the husband is advancing in his career and where there is a good deal of affluence. In this situation the role of housewife may in fact require work to do as the result of the objects and appliances which are purchased either for beauty or for status. At the same time, there is an outside/inside relationship developing with the children and the husband. As the children develop interests and orientations outside the home and as the father continues to work and to identify with his occupation, the housewife may be the only person who is basically located inside the house. She can continue to focus on any of her three roles of wife, mother, or housewife; indeed many women talk about their identity in terms of the family. It is common in this situation for a housewife to say that she is a cook for the family or sews for the family or waits for the family to come home. Other women undertake full time employment and begin to centre their roles outside the house once again, and some women never become "inside located" as has been described earlier. Rather after the birth of the children these women return rapidly to an outside orientation, whether because of a need for financial support or through career interests. Many women find an important place for themselves by roles related outside the home once the family has begun to develop an outside orientation.

Once the family has grown and the children begin to leave the home for university or for work or to get married, a whole new stage in the housewife's social role begins. The role of housewife is a shrinking one at this stage as the family gradually leaves and the house is once more occupied by the wife and husband. The housewife may encounter some difficulty in shifting her role as a housewife since she may not easily be able to relate outside the home whereas her husband is likely for a while to continue high involvement in his role as worker. Women in a high socio-economic bracket find this is a good time in their lives since they are able to go where they like and do what they like and have financial resources. Women in a lower socio-economic bracket find that they encounter feelings of unimportance or uselessness. Dissatisfied with life they take a somewhat negative view at times. A source of some satisfaction for some women at this stage is the role of grandmother where a woman enjoys children and finds satisfaction in being grandmotherly. For others, however, the distance which the children may live from the home coupled with the problem of travelling to and fro may diminish very much the role of grandmother. In these years there is a gradual aging and a new change in the relationship of the housewife and her role, particularly when her husband, no longer employed and probably retired, begins to focus inside the home, whereas previously he had been focusing his role outside at work.

The last role of the housewife is usually widowhood since statistically most women will out-live their husbands. Here the housewife is the only person in the house and her performance of the role is in terms of providing accommodation and support to visiting relatives, perhaps children or grandchildren and the performing of the role as hostess. This role lasts until the death of the housewife or until the time she breaks up her household and moves into a residence being run by someone else, be it an offspring or paid administrator. During this time the woman sees a decreasing number of persons. Society expects a lessening contribution from her while it increases her rights. No-one seriously expects the old widow or the old woman to be given a role outside her home. The end result of this process of adjustment in the performance of her

defrauded in the attempt. Stealing from stores is relatively safe because the stores are reluctant to make accusations of theft against persons who appear to be legitimate customers. Picking pockets is relatively safe because the legal rules of evidence make it almost impossible to convict a pickpocket. The professional thief scrupulously avoids the types of theft which are attended with great danger and especially those which involve much publicity. The theft of famous art treasures, for instance, is never attempted by professional thieves. It would probably not be especially difficult for them to steal the treasures, but it would be practically impossible, because of the publicity, for them to sell the treasures. It is significant that the two most famous thefts of art treasures in the last century — Gainsborough's "Duchess of Devonshire" and Da Vinci's "Mona Lisa" — were not motivated by the expectation of financial gain.

Second, by training and experience the professional thief develops ingenious methods and the ability to control situations. A thief is a specialist in manipulating people and achieves his results by being a good actor. Third, he works on the principle that he can "fix" practically every case in which he may be caught. . . .

Cases are fixed in two ways: first, by making restitution to the victim in return for an agreement not to prosecute; second, by securing the assistance of one or more public officials by payment of money or by political order or suggestion. These two methods are generally combined in a particular case.

The victim is almost always willing to accept restitution and drop the prosecution. This is true not only of the individual victim but also of the great insurance companies, which frequently offer rewards for the return of stolen property with an agreement not to prosecute and are thus the best fences for stolen property. The length of time required for the prosecution of a case is one of the reasons for the willingness of the victim to drop the prosecution. At any rate, the victim is more interested in the return of his stolen property than he is in maintaining a solid front of opposition against theft. He tries to get what he can, just as the thief tries to get what he can; neither has much interest in the general social welfare.

Edwin Sutherland
The Professional Thief

John R. Howard defines the term "hippie" to include a number of different categories of behaviour. His simplest form of analysis includes four types of hippies:

1) *The visionaries*. He feels that the visionaries gave birth to the hippie movement. They had a vision of people "grooving together". They attempted to remove those things that had set up barriers between people and among people in the past: property and ownership, prejudice, and ideas of what is normal and what is immoral. The visionaries typically have been frustrated by other groups in the areas they have inhabited and many have moved on to other stages of development. The current move toward rural communes is an example of this trend.

2) *The freaks and heads*. This group of hippies attempts to find its goals under the influence of drugs. Almost a religion with its rituals has been established around the use of drugs such as LSD. The explanation for the use of drugs is to provide a greater understanding of oneself and the world. The pattern of use of drugs of the heads (the users of marijuana) and the freaks (the users of the extremely dangerous drug group—amphetamines) seems to relate to the available supply of drugs on the market. Because of the almost random use of all kinds of drugs, many of these hippies have suffered severe emotional let-downs, and in some cases, death.

3) *The plastic hippies*. These are not real hippies but individuals who spring up in every movement to take advantage of it as a fad. They are exploiters of the hippies, the people who dress like hippies and assume the same kinds of behaviour, but for the purpose of gaining a financial return. They sell the love beads, the headbands, the leather clothes, the glasses that help define people as hippies.

4) *The midnight hippies*. These are individuals who never had the opportunity to participate in activities such as those in which the hippies are involved, and who turn to the hippie culture at a later stage in their lives. Because they had no hippie scene to turn to, they finished school and moved into the job world. The midnight hippie is often drawn from the university world and helps make a case for the hippie way of life in the "straight" world.

John R. Howard
The Flowering of the Hippie Movement

role as old person and widow really means that there is no role expected of her, she is not considered as a person having to or needing to be vitally concerned with any role. The role of wife and mother have already been left behind entirely or significantly. The role of worker and association member are no longer a source of action and identity. The role of daughter as well as many others are impossible to maintain. Finally a right which is often taken away from the aging housewife is that of running her own home or deciding the duties she should undertake to run it. When this happens she loses one of the important rights by which house-wives contrast this role to that of working outside, the right to be her own "boss" and plan her own work.

Our society has not come to grips with the problems of role transition in old age. Means and mechanisms of helping the old people to make a transfer from one role to another or of providing some status in being old are essential.

The hippies of Yorkville

Frank Longstaff

(Mr. Longstaff spent three months in Yorkville as a participant-observer of the scene. The following selection is taken from his report of his activities there.)

In major metropolitan centres in both Canada and the United States, certain parts of the city are being over-run by teenagers. The "beats" of New York's Greenwich Village are moving to the East Side as the longhairs begin to take over the Village. In Los Angeles, the once exclusive Sunset Strip has gone the same way, as have parts of North Beach in San Francisco. Toronto has experienced part of the same social movement and over the past three years Yorkville, which was once a colourful, but relatively quiet, university-oriented area, has become the domain of youth.

The reason for this phenomenon is not at once clear. It appears to be a reflection of rapid change in our society, both social and technical, combined with increased teenage affluence and freedom. Technical changes, complex as they are, are at least predictable. The social changes which are by-products of the technical are not so predictable and society is not so prepared for them. Youth is much quicker to pick up new manners and morals because it is not so committed to the old.

Knowledge is expanding so rapidly that children often become experts in areas where their parents are poorly informed. Thus the aura of infallibility that parents once had is now challenged. The lessons of the past are often no longer applicable today because conditions are changing so rapidly.

Ten years ago Yorkville already had overtones of non-conformity and a reputation as a centre for the young when it was a Coffee House area haunted by university students. There was the nucleus of certain entertainment facilities in its folk-singing clubs and the rest of the area thrived on the offbeat. Thus this new influx did not cause alarm. For the most part it still doesn't. Yorkville has long been a collection of specialty shops catering to the sophisticated.

Demographically as well, the area is suited for this kind of development. Toronto is the hub of Ontario, indeed of English-speaking Canada, and so draws people from coast-to-coast. Yorkville's position in the centre of the city, on both subway lines, makes it virtually minutes away from almost any part of Toronto. It is an old residential area close to the University of Toronto. Housing facilities catering to young people, rooms and flats with non-bourgeois and often absentee landlords, are long established. In so many ways it is a natural area, not only for rebellious youth leaving home, but for relatively contented youth looking for an evening's entertainment.

Yorkville has developed a flavour of its own, one of informality and friendliness augmented by the excitement generated by a crowd. Toronto has a reputation for being a cold city and yet in the Village visitors remark on the friendliness of the people. Conversations are easy and spontaneous among complete strangers. People are more relaxed with those around them.

Many different kinds of people make use of the Village. I have found it useful to employ the distinctions used by those in Yorkville itself. They break things up into 5 groupings which are easily identifiable, although boundaries are sometimes fuzzy. The first are the "Villagers" themselves, youths living in or close to the area, who spend time there daily and who have adopted something of an anti-middle class value system. Villagers feel that society will not leave them alone because its members, its parents and teachers, have been challenged and rejected and because it is jealous of the Villagers' free and easy, irresponsible way of life.

There are about two to three hundred Villagers living in and around Yorkville, one-third to one-quarter of whom are girls. As often as not the Villagers came originally from outside Metropolitan Toronto, from urban rather than rural centres. Many are from Montreal and Ottawa and even as far away as Halifax and Vancouver. Yorkville, thanks to the press, has become well-known across the country and this, coupled with the fact that Toronto is the centre of English-speaking Canada, makes it a gathering point for youth of a similar bent from coast-to-coast.

Those from Metropolitan Toronto who have come to live in Yorkville are more likely to be from the well-to-do residential parts of Metro, Etobicoke, North York, and Scarborough, etc., than from the Downtown areas. The area draws suburban 'teens with middle-class backgrounds, rather than the under-privileged from the slums.

This is a young group. Most of those living in Yorkville fall into the 17–20 age bracket. There are few who are younger and those that are there are often a source of concern to the main group. Not only is there a feeling that such people are too inexperienced to handle a Village kind of life safely and satisfactorily, but there is also concern that the more very young people living in Yorkville, the more likely will be interference from society at large.

There are also some residents in their middle and late twenties who have an association with Yorkville but are not really con-

Teeny-boppers

[In some circles this term refers only to young high school girls. Here it has been used (or misused) throughout to refer to both sexes.]

Like Villagers, their background is usually a middle-class one. But few teenagers come to Yorkville from downtown areas of Toronto. Social workers from the Regent Park and Allen Gardens areas in the east and the lower ward in the west indicate that their people have been in Yorkville once or twice but just don't like it or the people there. In fact, they recognize it as a middle-class area and discuss it in "we–they" terms.

While Villagers go to Yorkville mainly for negative reasons, that is, to avoid the regimentation of home and school, teeny-boppers go there mainly for the activities available. Music, both rock and folk, is one of the big drawing cards, with the discotheques being particularly popular. Mostly, however, they go because Yorkville is "where it's at" – it's the place to go. They enjoy being in an area where their peers set the standards. The crowds are exciting and there is always an excellent chance of meeting interesting people of the opposite sex.

It is prestigious for teenagers to go to Yorkville. They feel special in school on Monday morning when they can talk about their Saturday night jaunt at Boris' or the Purple Onion. To go there is to be socially active and socially aware. And there are parts of the Village which exist especially for teeny-boppers.

Teeny-boppers are not disgruntled rebels of the Village mould. For the most part they are typical high school students who live at home, take a relatively active part in school affairs, are interested in the kind of music being played. They also have money to spend and the urge to spend it. They are not frequent, regular visitors to Yorkville, but rather socially mobile youth who rate an occasional night in the Village in the same class as school dances, shows, and suburban parties. Yorkville has a place in their social whirl; it is not the whole thing.

One of the most important points to arise from this study deals with Villager/teeny-bopper relations. Each recognizes the existence of the other. Teeny-boppers have a certain amount of respect for Villagers' individuality but have really no desire to emulate them. They are happy with home and school (or not so unhappy that they are ready to do without the accompanying benefits and security). Villagers, on the other hand, look upon teeny-boppers as fools and suckers, as representatives of middle-class society.

Greasers

Greasers are also a small group but to a certain extent are responsible for drawing attention to Yorkville over the summer, for they were catalysts in the highly publicized ruckus at the end of May. The term "greaser" applies to the working-class, motorcycle-gang type of youth. They are usually older than Villagers and teeny-boppers, being in their late teens and early 20s, they are early high school drop-outs and most have blue-collar jobs. Their background is a working-class rather than a middle-class one. They are interested in Yorkville because of its crowds and excitement and they go there for a little "action". They are not there as a form of social protest like the Villagers or because of an interest in music and discotheques like the teeny-boppers. While in Yorkville they stay pretty close to their motorcycles, either driving them up the street, or sitting on them in one of the parking lots.

Those who come specifically looking for "action" or a bit of a fight don't usually find it, and when they do it's with members of another gang from another part of the city, rather than with Villagers, teeny-boppers, or tourists.

The Saturday-night ruckus of May 28th was caused by one of the few Villager-greaser mixups. On the Friday night before, greasers had found some Villagers alone in side alleys and cut their hair. On the Saturday night, Villagers were ready for more trouble and, around midnight, a scuffle broke out between two Villagers and two greasers. The police soon appeared on the scene and the greasers, who have had long experience with them, ran and were lost in the crowd. The Villagers, with their middle-class backgrounds, did not know enough to get away quickly and one was arrested for causing a disturbance. As the police led their captive off, they were challenged by the crowd, so they called in for reinforcements. This drew every policeman in Yorkville to the corner of Yorkville and Avenue Road on the double and the crowd, seeing them go, and sensing the excitement, followed, pushing out on to Avenue Road and blocking traffic in both directions.

The aftermath of this one incident has been felt in Yorkville ever since, and the people affected have been, for the most part, Villagers rather than greasers, for with one notable exception, the motorcycle groups have been leaving the Village alone.

The exception is an important one. The Vagabonds, a motorcycle club, has moved into the Yorkville area and has found its niche there. The hostility between Villagers and greasers that had been present before does not exist where the Vagabonds are concerned. Rather, they live in a state of peaceful co-existence with cooperation, but few friendships, crossing the group lines. The Vagabonds have established the Village as their area and keep other motorcycle groups, those who had caused trouble earlier, out.

sidered Villagers. Most of these have lived in the area for some time – at least a year – and many have an occupational link with Yorkville. They are Bohemian and creative in outlook and often committed to writing or some form of art or music.

The middle-class background of Villagers is evident not only in terms of area of origin, but in other fields as well. Villagers are school dropouts, but at the Grade XII and XIII levels rather than Grade IX and X. Not only are Villagers advanced educationally but some also have hopes of continuing their education at university at a later date. They value education and realize that it is a key to independence in the future.

Another indication of the middle-class background of Villagers is their attitude toward violence and toward the police. In look and actions they are not physically aggressive. They do not engage in fights and rumbles. No one need be afraid to walk the streets of the Yorkville area at any hour of the day or night. In the time spent in the area, I saw one or two scuffles among those looking for such action, but no fights. At no time was a tourist threatened with violence.

As for the Villagers' attitude toward the police, it did not have the same fear and avoidance patterns as found among the slum youth. Villagers are more likely to taunt the police than to avoid them and when they feel the police are intimidating them they organize committees, stage protest marches, and inform the newspapers. In other words they use avenues of protest that lower class teenagers are not aware of or would not employ.

Villagers come to Yorkville more for negative than positive reasons. For the most part they come to get away from what they consider a suffocating, conformity-demanding society. Some of them are people who couldn't "make it" in the competition of conventional society and while a few of these find a niche in Yorkville's undemanding anonymity, for the most part they don't "make it" in the Village either. They find no more comfort here than they did outside. Girls more than boys appear to be of this weak, lost variety, perhaps because our society is more protective of the female and so she is less able to succeed on her own.

But while a few are of this struggling misfit category, a few are obviously neurotic, most appear to be relatively strong competent people. To begin with they have shown the strength required to make the first big step away from a secure and materially privileged home. There has been a breakdown of communications between the generations so that neither one understands the other. The young feel that excessive restrictions are placed upon their mode of behaviour and that parents are pushing them toward goals they have no desire to attain. For them, their parents have ceased to become guides and influences but only suppliers of money and resources.

The school system is also a source of frustration from which Villagers seek to escape. Boards of Education which regulate length of hair and style of dress or refuse to let children go home for lunch quickly lose the respect of some of their pupils. Most Villagers claim to have become disillusioned, not with education but with school. While realizing the importance of formal educa

on as an aid in achieving desired goals, the manner in which for-
ıal education is dispensed is a formidable barrier.

In the above I do not mean to imply that all Villagers are tal-
ınted under-achievers who cannot do well because of a poor school
ystem. Some are legitimate dropouts of limited academic means
ho have come to Yorkville for other reasons. Some are university
ıudents, able to find a sympathetic niche in their universities, who
ome to try out Yorkville for a summer or who live there in the
inter while attending the University of Toronto. But, neverthe-
ıss, for most Villagers, the school system has been too tight, too
egimented, and they have felt they had to get out.

While Villagers come to Yorkville for negative reasons associ-
ted with home and school, there are positive points which serve
ɔ attract them as well. The chief of these is that the Yorkville area,
s manners and customs, is dominated by kids rather than by
dults. They escape external authority imposed upon them and
ve by their own rules. Patterns of behaviour must still fall within
esignated bounds to be accepted in the Village (these bounds are
astly different from those outside) but there is much more flexi-
ility, much less uniformity. Generally, there is a certain amount
f conformity to styles of grooming (long hair) and dress (jeans
nd boots, sandals or bare feet), to night-time activities, and in atti-
ıde toward the world outside. But variations are frequent and
ccepted. Some don't have long hair or sloppy clothes; some have
egular jobs; not all are running away from home and/or school.
he main drawing point is the fact that Yorkville is the centre for
outh with similar social viewpoints, a place of informality and
on-conformity for those tired of formality and conformity, a place
f acceptance and status for those who are rejecting or being re-
ected (or both) in other places.

Poverty is a way of life for Villagers. Often it is looked upon as a
irtue. It is not a grinding or insecure kind of poverty – few, if any
f these kids have ever been neglected materially and there is
lmost always security in the knowledge that the poverty and the
ay in the Village are only short-run. But nevertheless, it influ-
nces the manner of living common to those in Yorkville. Jobs are
egarded in a fairly neutral way. The money they provide is nice,
ut it doesn't really matter if you don't work steadily, so long as
ou have access to some money most of the time, enough to cover
ɔod, rent and incidentals, regardless of the source. Males often
ave trouble getting jobs because of their long hair – most employ-
rs demand a haircut and at the time this appears to be too great a
acrifice. The jobs that are available are usually menial and not
ɔo well paying. Because of financial hardships, and since almost
veryone is in need at one time or another, an inter-dependence
merges. Many commodities such as housing, food, clothes, cig-
rettes, money in general, are shared and those who have help
hose who have not, knowing that next week the shoe may be on
he other foot. The resulting cohesiveness is not an over-demand-
ng one, however. Usually a Villager is known only by his first
ame and in some cases an alias is used. Such a practice makes it
ıuch easier for him to compartmentalize his life inside and outside
he Village and also makes it easier for him to make a cut with

The Vagabonds have been accepted in Yorkville and, in fact, perform an important service
there. Not only do they keep other troublesome
elements out, but in squabbles between different
elements of Villagers, they are often called in as
arbitrators and enforcers of the Village code. The
size and strength of this club, combined with its
interest in the area, make it fairly efficient in this
role.

Weekenders

Weekenders form a small group which is somewhere in transition between teeny-boppers and
Villagers. Like teeny-boppers, they are still living
at home or at least outside of the Yorkville area,
but their visits to the Village are much more frequent, coming two or three times a week, and
occasionally they will find a room to share with
some Villagers where they can stay on a Friday
or Saturday night. They have established contact
with the Villager group and like them. They also
share much of the Villagers' anti-middle-class
outlook and value system or at least pay lip-
service to it, although they don't always back
this up with the same amount of participation.
Some help out Villagers by selling copies of
Satyrday, the Village newspaper, and turning over
part or all of the profits to them.

Weekenders are in a position on the fringe of
Village society. They try to emulate Villagers'
dress and grow their hair as long as they can get
away with at home. They try to play down the fact
that they don't actually live in Yorkville to the
extent that they will get off the subway a stop
early and walk in rather than be seen coming out
of the entrance to the Bay Street station on
Bellair. But they are accepted by Villagers only to
a limited extent, because they haven't made the
physical break with their old community and
because they are not there all the time.

There are not many weekenders – perhaps one
to two hundred at a given time – and needless to
say, only a small percentage make the step from
weekender to Villager. Just as most Villagers soon
tire of the Yorkville way of life, so do weekenders.
Because it is not a complete experience for them,
it often takes weekenders longer to give up on
the area, but the pattern is the same nonetheless.

Tourists

Tourists, the infrequent visitors to Yorkville who are not aware of the subtleties of the youth culture, are also important ingredients in the Yorkville recipe, and can find a great deal of interest and entertainment there. There are generally two kinds of tourists – adults and university students.

The adults put the area to use both day and night. During the daytime they enjoy browsing through the various specialty, antique, and fashion shops situated on Yorkville and Cumberland Streets, and on Old York Lane which runs between the two. The open patios of the coffee houses provide a place to relax for shoppers and business executives alike.

Sophisticated restaurants also draw an adult clientele to Yorkville. Such establishments serve excellent dinners and are also popular for after-theatre refreshments. Some adults also visit coffee houses featuring folk music, but this is more popular with university students (or people in their early 20s).

Yorkville used to be a university-oriented area and since the younger element has taken it over, university students don't quite know what to think and certainly don't understand it. Because there is little left in the area for them, they feel it has been wasted and mourn the change. But they still lay claim to a few bits of real estate in the area.

The only other preserve left open to the average university student are the coffee houses that provide entertainment.

Why condone this rot and filth that is "hippie" in this beautiful city of ours? Those who desecrate our flag, refuse to work, flaunt their sexual freedom, spread their filthy diseases and their garbage in public parks are due no charitable consideration. The already overloaded taxpayer picks up the bill.

If every city so afflicted would give them a bum's rush out of town, eventually with no place to light, they might just wake up to find how stupid and disgusting they are. Their feelings of being so clever and original might fade into reality. They might wake up and change their tactics.

(From "Letters to the Editor" in an American newspaper.)

In summary, the hippies have commented powerfully on some of the absurdities and irrationalities of the society. It is unlikely that the straight will throw away his credit cards and move to a rural commune, but it is equally unlikely that he will very soon again wear the emblems of his straightness with quite so much self-satisfaction.

John R. Howard
The Flowering of the Hippie Movement

Yorkville when he decides this is what he wants to do.

During the day, before the sundown onslaught of tourists and teeny-boppers, Yorkville is a relatively quiet but unique street. There are well-to-do customers of the carriage trade visiting their favourite boutiques and there are junior executives escaping from their Bloor Street office buildings for coffee in the sunshine at the Penny Farthing. There are also Villagers, sitting on the fence in front of the Grab Bag. Of those without a regular job, few get up before 10 or 11 o'clock, and the day is passed in a relaxed, casual manner. Often someone is there with a guitar or harmonica, playing mostly for himself but arousing the interests of others anyway. On some days a trip to Toronto Island is planned but this is infrequent behaviour and surprising enough, Villagers show little mobility within the city itself. They are interested only in what the Village has to offer. The day is passed, then, almost as if it were killing time. They have created a youth village ruled by primary ties of neighbourhood. They sit and talk, mostly about Yorkville, what other Villagers are doing, complain about police or political action directly affecting their group, voice protests about a society which they have tried to escape for a while and which Villagers feel is jealous of the irresponsible Yorkville way of life.

As the crowds begin to build up in the evening, Villagers become a little more obscure – they have little desire to mix with the infiltrating teeny-boppers. Many disappear back to their, or others', rooms where parties are planned.

The average length of stay for Villagers in Yorkville is not long, usually about two or three months. In the time that I was in the area, a three-month period, I noticed almost a complete turnover. Where they go when they leave Yorkville is not always easy to ascertain; however, most indications are that they go back into the middle-class society from which they came. But it is with a different outlook and a little different status. They begin to appreciate their parents' positions and their parents usually afford them more freedom and individuality. A few people leave Yorkville in worse shape than when they went in.

Some of the more confirmed Villagers move on as a matter of principle, just to keep rambling. Usually the next stop along the line for the few confirmed Villagers is Vancouver or Greenwich Village, although the latter sometimes presents a problem because longhairs often are turned back at the border.

Living in the Village then is usually a fairly short-term sort of thing. Villagers wake up one morning and decide that they have had enough of it, enough living in crowded conditions, enough self-induced poverty. But they are not sorry that they have had the experience. For many of them it is a chance to mark time and catch their breath, it is a vacation from organized society, a needed moratorium. Most of all it is a time when they are able to do things on their own and able to learn from their own mistakes. Those who are more committed to the Village, who spend more than a few months there or who move around the circuit are those who find some occupational reason for staying. They become professional Villagers. Few follow this course.

three   Roles and their status

"Every soldier carries a marshal's baton in his knapsack."
                    Napoleon
'A man who has a million dollars is as well off as if he were rich."
                    John Jacob Astor

For centuries society has been divided into the rich and poor, the ruler and ruled, the owner and tenant, the lord and peasant, the educated and uneducated. Each of those terms creates a mental picture in your mind of a person with a certain place in society, under certain obligations, and with certain privileges. The rich enjoy a certain life style of big cars, chauffeurs, large houses, fine clothes, good food and drink, exotic travel and leisure activities. The poor are poorly dressed; they live in small or inadequate housing; they don't have cars; their diet is meagre and plain. The casual observer would be able to rank the rich and the poor easily: one high and one low. You could say upper class and lower class, and for those in between, middle class. Layering or stratifying people is common to every society. In India for example, there is a caste system in which movement up or down is virtually impossible. An individual is by birth placed in a caste and behaves according to others' expectations of that caste. In Canada our system is a class system within which there is movement both up and down. Status in terms of prestige, rights, and obligations is rewarded frequently on the basis of economic success, but social and political success are related. In our society it is assumed that a person who has ability and is willing to work hard will achieve success and the status that goes with it. Achieved status is typical in a modern industrial society where specialization and scholarship combine to create new occupations hitherto unknown, such as astronaut, computer systems analyst, and ecologist. In folk societies, status is generally ascribed – that is, positions are inherited, with the young reared from birth to carry on the same activities that were carried on by their mothers and fathers.

A social class has characteristics that separate its members from other classes. There is a consciousness by members of the class that they are different from others, and that some behaviours peculiar to that class are not shared to the same extent by others. Class membership is often classified according to such standards as wealth, education, occupation, living accommodation, cultural pursuits, and types of possessions such as appliances, cars, and clothes. The following selections deal with aspects of social class. The first is an encounter between teenagers from Don Mills, a middle-class Toronto suburb, and Cabbagetown, a low socio-economic area, in which students exchange views on the life styles of poverty and affluence. This is followed by a study done in an Ontario high school, where the activities of students are considered in terms of their social-class background. The next selection presents an analysis of the corporate leaders of Canada, in which their background and social interactions are explored to show how they are selected and how they maintain their positions at the top. The fourth article illustrates the way in which people in various occupations view their work. The concluding article deals with spending behaviour and social class. This study shows how buying habits indicate social-class background, and how marketing techniques are designed to take advantage of this knowledge.

The Prestige Occupations in Canada

The scores represent adjusted average rankings to fit in a range from 0 to 100. The raters were selected to represent a national sample. (793 were used.) The raters were asked to rank the occupations on the basis of their social standing.

Provincial premier	89.9	Bookkeeper	49.4
Physician	87.2	Locomotive engineer	48.9
Member of the Canadian Senate	86.1	Advertising copy writer	48.9
Member of Canadian House of Commons	84.8	Owner of a food store	47.8
University professor	84.6	IBM keypunch operator	47.7
Member of Canadian Cabinet	83.3	Insurance agent	47.3
County court judge	82.5	Real estate agent	47.1
Lawyer	82.3	Railroad conductor	45.3
Mayor of a large city	79.9	Machinist	44.2
Architect	78.1	Farm owner and operator	44.1
Physicist	77.6	Firefighter	43.5
Psychologist	74.9	Playground director	42.8
Chemist	73.5	Plumber	42.6
Civil engineer	73.1	Tool and die maker	42.5
Biologist	72.6	Bank teller	42.3
Bank manager	70.9	Typist	41.9
Colonel in the Army	70.8	Welder	41.8
Owner of a manufacturing plant	69.4	Service station manager	41.5
Druggist	69.3	Travelling salesman	40.2
General manager of a manufacturing plant	69.1	Barber	39.3
Veterinarian	66.7	House carpenter	38.9
High school teacher	66.1	Baker	38.9
Airline pilot	66.1	Receptionist	38.7
T.V. star	65.6	Telephone operator	38.1
Author	64.8	Disc jockey	38.0
Registered nurse	64.7	T.V. repairman	37.2
Accountant	63.4	Bricklayer	36.2
Public relations man	60.5	Mailman	36.1
Draughtsman	60.0	Bus driver	35.9
Public school teacher	59.6	Sheet metal worker	35.9
Manager of a real estate office	58.3	Clerk in an office	35.6
YMCA director	58.2	Beauty operator	35.2
T.V. announcer	57.6	Butcher in a store	34.8
Commercial artist	57.2	Steel mill worker	34.3
Air hostess	57.0	Trailer truck driver	32.8
Sculptor	56.9	Used car salesman	31.2
Building contractor	56.5	Cashier in a supermarket	31.1
Advertising executive	56.5	House painter	29.9
Funeral director	54.9	Cook in a restaurant	29.7
Professional athlete	54.1	Private in the Army	28.4
Superintendent of a construction job	53.9	Assembly line worker	28.2
Computer programmer	53.8	Construction labourer	26.5
Manager of a supermarket	52.5	Taxicab driver	25.1
Musician	52.1	Logger	24.9
Policeman	51.6	Filling station attendant	23.3
Construction foreman	51.1	Farm labourer	21.5
Foreman in a factory	50.9	Waitress in a restaurant	19.9
Airplane mechanic	50.3	Laundress	19.3
Electrician	50.2	Janitor	17.3
		Garbage collector	14.8

Peter Pineo and John Porter
The Prestige of Occupations in Canada

The day that Cabbagetown met Don Mills

Following are excerpts from a conversation between two girls from Don Mills and two boys from Cabbagetown, who met in Don Mills to discuss the differences in their way of life for the CBC radio program, *Concern*.

DON MILLS: I don't know that much about Cabbagetown compared to Don Mills, except that people here have more money. That probably makes a big difference. But Don Mills is the only place where I've lived.

CABBAGETOWN: What I wanted to ask was when I say to you that I'm from Cabbagetown, what's that mean to you? And not just people being richer.

DON MILLS: When I think of Cabbagetown, I think of open windows, hot air, strong smells of people and cooking. People know each other when they walk in the street. They are more friendly; they say hello. Not so much a physical proximity but closeness in a social way.

CABBAGETOWN: All the kids in Cabbagetown, even me and everybody, are ignorant to things. We just don't know nothing. I didn't know that Don Mills existed or this kind of area existed or anything like that until I went in to a free school. It is really strange, the kids here can talk to somebody. They can have a conversation with somebody like a teacher. The people I know couldn't speak with anybody like that. I wouldn't know what to say. People start talking about, like legislature and that kind of thing. I didn't know what the word meant and I still don't, actually. It is really different. Like kids here read all these books.

DON MILLS: Not everybody, though.

CABBAGETOWN: No, but kids get to read these better books. Like kids here (Don Mills) at 12 or 13 start reading about Greek psychology or whatever it's called. I didn't know that existed until maybe a month ago. And there are a whole bunch of other things where people just don't know what is happening – don't know how anything is run. All they know is that they are living in an area that is poor. They don't have much money and that is it.

DON MILLS: There's an awful lot of kids here that are just interested in sports at school and they don't know about anywhere else in Toronto. They don't leave Don Mills.

CABBAGETOWN: But I mean they're smarter in a conversation about things. I mean they're intellectual. They know more words, more bigger words.

DON MILLS: They may know more words but they don't always think that much. Some guys are really stupid. Just money, just cars, that's it. They couldn't talk to you about life. They wouldn't know what to say. They've never thought about such things.

CABBAGETOWN: Another thing, in Cabbagetown to be accepted by everybody you've got to fight, you've got to be one of the gang. Like say you live on Carlton street and you want to hang around with the guys. You've got to show them you're tough, you've got to steal, you've got to beat up people.

DON MILLS: The only fights that I know that ever happened in Don Mills are like everybody knows it's going to happen at 3:30 across from the school. And you wouldn't believe it, like 300 kids come to watch and usually it's a big guy beating up a little guy. It's a big put-on and the worst anybody ever gets is a bloody nose.

CABBAGETOWN: They're not real fights. They don't really want to kill or hurt. Guys in Don Mills talk it out. We fight it out because we can't talk it out.

DON MILLS: Obviously, by the way you're talking, fighting gives you a feeling of power.

CABBAGETOWN: I don't think the kids in Don Mills have as their ambition in life to make lots of money. I say a lot of them want to get away from it. They leave home where their parents want to buy them out. Whereas the kids at Cabbagetown, their dream is to make it rich and make lots of money and they never do.

DON MILLS: There is a big difference in money in Don Mills. Like there are some people who have an awful lot of money. And it gets into real problems, like clothes, who has more clothes.

CABBAGETOWN: To us clothes really matter a lot, too. I would be shy to go to school, because of the clothes. I remember just before winter would set in, and I would still be wearing this sweater. In that cold, I'm tough, you know. Like we are really freezing but we had to wait until my father got the extra money to buy us a coat or a ski jacket or something like that. People in Don Mills wear pants with patches on purpose because it looks cool. And to us patches are ugly.

DON MILLS: I think in Don Mills everyone's trying to be the same.

CABBAGETOWN: The difference between the houses and other things are just unreal. Like, okay, my mother and father got a house in Cabbagetown, this big house and they started renting out rooms and guys started to come from New Brunswick and you know my mother was keeping people, right? My brother and I would be sleeping on these little cot beds in the hall and all these guys were coming up from New Brunswick, these young guys who wanted to make it in Toronto and the trouble is they go to Rose's place and they all live upstairs and I'd be sleeping with cousins of mine I didn't even know. We never had a bed, you know, I mean a real bedroom because they were renting out the other rooms to make money. The whole thing of going into houses here, like your place for instance. It's really beautiful. Like compared to my house, it's unreal. My house, not that it's dirty or anything, but you know, we don't have really fancy furniture. It's comfortable and it's old furniture, kinda ripped at the edges here and there and when I go into a house like yours it's really strange. It just freaks you right out. I never used to bring any friends of mine home, especially the ones who I thought were middle-class from somewhere outside in Scarborough or some place. I was really embarrassed to bring friends around, only people I knew and I had to see their place first to make sure that it was something like my place. We're renting the house and the outside is filthy. It hasn't been painted for the last 20 years and there are 20 houses all stuck together and all the same color. When you walk inside the hall is kinda dirty. The

On what bases are people classified? This is where some of the disagreement over definition enters, with experts arguing over what is the "right" basis on which to classify people. Various criteria for stratification have been considered important from time to time and from place to place. These are the major ones:

authority
power (political, economic, military)
ownership of property
income (amount, type, sources)
style of life
occupation or skill, and achievement in it
education, learning, wisdom
divinity, "control" over the supernatural
place in "high society", kinship connections, ancestry (i.e., inherited position)
ethnic status, religion, race

Despite anecdotes about harried business executives and unhappy suburban housewives, most people would probably agree that conditions are more stressful for those at the bottom of our society than for those nearer the top. With least share in the available resources of society, persons of low status seem virtually guaranteed more than their share of misfortune.

Barbara Snell Dohrenwend
and Bruce P. Dohrenwend
Social Stress

Other differences between social classes have been reported. As measured by income, for example, it is clear that upper-class persons live longer than those in the lower classes. People in the lower classes are sick more often, and for longer periods, than those in the upper class. Certain mental illnesses appear more frequently among lower-class groups. Kinsey reports social-class differences in sexual behaviour.

Frank Jones
Introduction to Sociology

Modern societies maintain considerable institutionalized inequality in the absence of a class
system.

Dennis Wrong
The Oversocialized Conception of Man

Every known human society, certainly every
known society of any size, is stratified.

The hierarchical evaluation of people in different
social positions is apparently [natural to] human
social organization. Stratification arises with the
[simplest] division of labor and appears to be
socially necessary in order to get people to fill
different positions and perform adequately in
them.

Kingsley Davis
Human Society

The lower-class individual lives in the slum and
sees little or no reason to complain. He does not
care how dirty and dilapidated his housing is
either inside or out, nor does he mind the inadequacy of such public facilities as schools, parks,
and libraries: indeed, where such things exist he
destroys them by acts of vandalism if he can.
Features that make the slum repellent to others
actually please him. He finds it satisfying in
several ways.

Edward C. Banfield
The Unheavenly City

landlord doesn't give you any paint, and it's not your home. You
rented the house so you're not going to spend a fortune just to fix
it up.

DON MILLS: My family considers our home here in Don Mills as sort
of like a work home. It's like a base for the kids to go to school
from and come back. And it is a base for my father and it is nice
because it's where my mother wants it. But all our interior decorat-
ing and all the things we like and love we put up in our cottage up
north. That's the home that everyone loves. Not here.

CABBAGETOWN: A lot of guys in Cabbagetown and a lot of girls are
doing dope now and the reason is just to be hip you know. It's not
really to get turned on, have a beautiful trip or whatever it is; it's
cool to get stoned. Now they all meet and they buy 10-24s and all
kinds of acid and they get stoned and drunk.

DON MILLS: I didn't think there was that much dope in Cabbagetown because dope costs.

CABBAGETOWN: But they steal for it. Like friends of mine, just
broke into a jewelry store on Parliament Street, they broke into
that store about 20 times.

DON MILLS: At our school they held a student-parent-teacher night.
It was organized by a social worker and he organized this thing.
Only three kids showed – three high school kids. There were about
12 parents and the teachers. They thought that the parents
wouldn't be the ones to show up because they would be nervous
about coming into the school and everything. It was kind of sad to
watch the parents. They were so eager to try to grasp the situation.
They had no comprehension. My parents pretty well know because I talk to my parents. But I know kids that don't talk to their
parents. You know, what's your parents? They're the ones that
feed you. Your dad gives you the car or gives you an allowance and
that's about it.

CABBAGETOWN: Do you ever drink with your parents? Like have
really wild parties and all get drunk together?

DON MILLS: Not yet.

CABBAGETOWN: Like, we've been doing it for a long time and it's a
laugh for my father too, you know. First time I drank I think I was
about 11 or 12. It's a laugh to give me a bottle of wine and get all
drunked up and get a real big hangover.

DON MILLS: My parents rarely go to parties. Once a year and it's
always a military thing because my father was a colonel. They go
to the armories and they come home by 11.

CABBAGETOWN: Our parties last about all night, sometimes until
seven o'clock in the morning.

DON MILLS: I think you guys would hate me if I was sort of conde-
scending and say well, you know, I've got it better than you. I'll
chip in for you. Would you like that?

CABBAGETOWN: I don't mind now because I've learned where I
stand from going to this free school. I've learned an awful lot and
it doesn't bother me. I know that I'm not middle class and I know

hat I'll never be a lawyer and I know that my little brother will ever be a lawyer and so it doesn't really matter.

ON MILLS: But I think that, really, people in Don Mills are pretty gnorant of people in Cabbagetown. And people in Cabbagetown re pretty ignorant of people in Don Mills. You may envy us and e may not think much about you. We just don't associate – and hat's really bad. Just not knowing about places like Cabbagetown, bout places like Don Mills.

CABBAGETOWN: I've been brought here from Cabbagetown. The Don Mills people talk about Cabbagetown, right? But it is really trange being used like that – people wanting to know about the lums. But I've never heard of anybody from Don Mills being alled down to Cabbagetown to tell about Don Mills.

ON MILLS: I think it's kind of a good thing that kids, most kids, lon't want to stay in Don Mills. When they leave Don Mills hey're going to find out that there is a bigger world.

CABBAGETOWN: The kids in Don Mills want to leave, and the kids rom Cabbagetown want to come to Don Mills to live.

Social class and secondary school behaviour

A. J. C. King

This is a report of a study that was designed to look at the relationship between the social-class background of students and the activities in which they became involved while in secondary school. The following areas were selected for study: 1) the courses students choose, 2) the importance and prestige of extracurricular activities such as football teams and camera clubs, and the participation of students in these activities, 3) the participation of the parents of the students in community activities, 4) the way in which students are viewed by their teachers, 5) the dating behaviour of students and their attendance at dances, and 6) student misbehaviour. In all cases, an attempt was made to determine the relationship between the student's social background and the above activities.

The study took place in a high school in a small Ontario community (population 13,000) located on the shores of Lake Ontario. The population of students involved was 535, of which 251 were girls. More than 90 per cent of the students who were in attendance at the school lived in the community and the remainder were bused in to the school.

It was necessary to determine the social-class background of each of the students involved in the study. In order to do this, the researcher obtained information on 1) the occupation of the fathers of the students, 2) the extent of education of the fathers, and 3) the value of the residence in which the students lived. Using these three pieces of information, each of the students was placed into a social class. Five social classes were used for this purpose. The upper class included the children of executives, and professionals such as lawyers and doctors. The upper-middle class

Child Rearing Patterns

Patterns that help the achievement of children

1) Child given freedom within clear limits to explore and experiment

2) Wide range of activities guided by parents

3) Planning for the future and a strong belief in long-term goals

4) Gradual training and preparation for life as an independent person

5) Parents provide models for children in terms of education and occupation

6) Thinking based on solid evidence

7) A great deal of talking among family members

Patterns associated with children of low-income parents

1) Child given limited opportunity to explore (partly because of overcrowded conditions)

2) Unvaried lives led by parents – a distrust of the new and unknown

3) A feeling that the individual has little control over his future, coupled with a tendency to be unconcerned

4) A tendency for abrupt changes in a person's status (from school to work) – some loss of control by parents

5) Pattern of parents' failure in school and in their jobs – tendency to rely on personal qualities rather than learned skills

6) Mechanical, rigid thinking

7) Little talking among family members

Adapted from the work of
Catherine S. Chilman

We have observed that a student at a given status level is more likely to expect to attend college, to have a strong desire to go to college when he does expect to go, to want to go when he does not expect to, and actually to attend when his best friend does rather than does not plan to attend college. When the student and his friend both plan to go, he is more likely to attend if his best friend does.

James C. Coleman
The Adolescent Culture

Thus our educational system, which next to the family is the most effective agency in teaching good work habits to middle-class people, is largely ineffective with underprivileged groups. Education fails to motivate such workers because our schools and our society both lack real rewards to offer underprivileged groups. Neither lower class children nor adults will work hard in school or on the job just to please the teacher or boss.

Allison Davis
Social-Class Influences Upon Learning

Inasmuch as adolescents are excluded from equal participation in the social, economic, and political activities of the larger society, the school provides the only highway by which young people may make the journey to adulthood. As such, the school, particularly the high school, represents the only formally designed link between adolescent status, and projected adult careers.

John I. Kitsuse and Aaron V. Cicourel
The Educational Decision-Makers

included the children of engineers, pharmacists, educational administrators, successful businessmen, and executives. Since there was such a small representation of students from the upper class, it was decided to combine the upper class with the middle class when the information was analyzed. The lower-middle-class group included the children of people who owned small businesses and farms, as well as the children of salesmen and other clerical workers. Included in the upper-lower-class group were the children of skilled manual workers, semi-skilled employees, factory and construction workers, and town labourers. However, this group also included a percentage of low-paid clerical and sales workers. Most of the lower-lower-class parents were classified this way because of their lack of formal education and the low value of their housing. Many of them have similar occupations to those in the upper lower classes, such as factory and construction workers. When all the students were classified, it was found that 13 per cent were placed in the upper-middle class, 26 per cent in the lower-middle class, 55 per cent in the upper-lower class, and 6 per cent were placed in the lower-lower class.

Most of the information was collected by way of a questionnaire that was filled out by the students. The questionnaire included items on the activities in which the students had participated in school, whether or not they had attended school dances, whether or not they had dated and who their dating partners were, whether their parents participated in community activities, and the type and place of work of the parents. Each student was also asked to rate the prestige of extracurricular activities in the school on a rating scale from 1 to 5. Each teacher was asked to rate his students on the following five factors: attentiveness, attitude toward authority, dependability, behaviour in class, and motivation. Information on the courses in which the students were enrolled and records of any misconduct were obtained from the school files.

The Findings

It was found that there was a relationship between the courses the students were enrolled in and their social class. The five-year (university-bound) program attracted a greater proportion of students from the upper classes than from the lower classes, and naturally the four-year (non-college-bound) courses attracted more lower-class students than upper-class students. Many people attempt to explain this on the basis of marks and performance on intelligence tests, based on the assumption that lower-class students are more likely to have a lower IQ and obtain lower marks than upper-class students. Although there was evidence that this was the case to some extent, it was not sufficient to explain the course choices of the students. It appears that something in the background and social relations of students from the upper classes encourages them to select the university-bound program to a greater extent than is the case for students from the lower classes.

It was anticipated that there would be substantial differences between classes in the extent to which students participated in the extracurricular program of the school. This was based on the conention that students from the lower classes are less likely to have the support of their parents and friends with regard to school activities, and are more likely than upper-class students to find their recreational pleasures outside of school. This is in part related to the lesser education of their parents, and the need their parents felt to find recreation outside of school. *Table 1* shows that upper-class students were far more likely than lower-class students to participate in the extracurricular program of the school. The upper-middle-class students were three times as likely to participate than the lower-lower-class students.

The students in the school tended to rate the prestige of the extracurricular activities very similarly. *Table 2* shows the ranking the students assigned to the various activities in the school. It is interesting to note the high status of the athletic and student government activities, and the relatively low status of the clubs associated with school subjects such as Math and French. However it is very clear that the students share a common feeling about the prestige of the activities. When the social-class background of the students in each of the groups was considered, no noticeable relationship was found between the prestige of the club and the percentage of students from each social class participating in it. It should be remembered, however, that the upper-class students are more likely to be involved in extracurricular activities in any case.

It was also found that the students' participation in the extracurricular activities of the school paralleled very closely the participation of their parents in the activities of their community. The father of the one lower-class student who gained a position in the student government was the only lower-lower-class parent who had a position in the community. It does appear that the tendency of parents to participate is conveyed to their children in some way in the home.

The teachers tended to rate the lower classes of students lower than the upper classes of students on the factors of attentiveness, attitude toward authority, dependability, behaviour in class, and motivation. When this relationship was investigated in some detail, it was found that it was more closely related to the academic achievement of the students. But it was still true that there was a tendency for the upper-class students to receive more positive ratings than the lower-class students, even when their marks were approximately the same. This suggests that the teachers might have an unfair bias toward lower-class students. There is probably some truth in this statement, but it may very well be caused by the more defensive attitude of the lower-class student who, by background, is more unsure of himself in an atmosphere for which his parents have been unable to prepare him.

It was found that students tended to date students from their own social class. Of course, this is associated with the neighbourhoods in which the students live, but interestingly, when the student had more than one date with a person, there was a greater tendency for the second date to be with someone from the same class. This suggests that the students are more likely to find something in common with someone from the same social class, but

Table 1
Participation in Extracurricular Activities by Social Class

Lower-lower class	27%
Upper-lower class	45%
Lower-middle class	70%
Upper-middle class	84%

Table 2
Rank-Order of Extracurricular Activities by Prestige

1. Students' Council
2. School Magazine
3. Boys' Football
4. Boys' Basketball
5. Boys' Athletic Association
6. Track and Field
7. Girls' Athletic Association
8. Girls' Basketball
9. Girls' Volleyball
10. Drama Club
11. Wrestling
12. Science Club
13. Camera Club
14. Badminton Club
15. Curling Club
16. Math Club
17. French Club
18. Chess Club

Table 3
Percentage of Students from
Each Social Class Who
Attended the School Formal

Lower-lower class	9%
Upper-lower class	18%
Lower-middle class	34%
Upper-middle class	43%

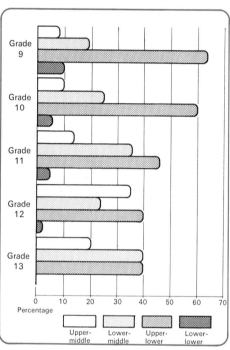

Figure 1   The student population in each grade
by social class (per cent)

... school creates what I have called the essential nightmare. The nightmare must be dreamed in order to provide the fears necessary to drive people away from something (in our case, failure) and toward something (success). In this way, children, instead of loving knowledge, become embroiled in the nightmare.

Jules Henry
Culture Against Man

these dating habits might also reflect the parents' influence. "Going steady" occurred slightly more often among the lower-class students, but not significantly so.

One can readily see from *Table 3* that attendance at the school formal was closely related to the social class of the students. The students from the lower classes are less likely to attend than students from the upper classes. Certainly an explanation might be found for this in terms of the lack of money for a ticket and the other expenses associated with a formal, but records of attendance at the regular school dances, which were relatively inexpensive showed the same tendency.

When the school discipline records were investigated, it was found that a definite relationship existed between the social-class background of the students and the frequency of referrals to the vice-principal for disciplinary reasons. The lower the social class of the student, the greater was the likelihood that he would be referred to the office for disciplinary reasons. Although "lateness to class", "misconduct in class", and "gum chewing" were not clearly associated with the social-class background of the students "homework not done", "truancy", and "no equipment" clearly were. Students who were referred to the office on numerous occasions for disciplinary reasons were far more likely to come from the lower classes than from the upper classes. It would appear either that the lower-class students are not well prepared for adjustment to school by their home backgrounds, or that they tend to become hostile toward school as a result of what takes place there. Not too surprisingly, boys run into far more difficulty than girls in the area of discipline.

This study clearly points out that the social-class background of students has implications for their adjustment to and acceptance of school. *Figure 1* shows the breakdown of each grade in the school by the social-class background of the students. The low representation of the upper-lower and lower-lower classes in Grades 11, 12, and 13 suggests that the dropout rate is much higher for students from these social classes. Part of the adjustment problem of the lower-class students to school is related to the middle-class orientation of many school teachers and the great value they place on education. For many teachers, school is a route to higher status, but for many lower-class students, whatever success has been achieved by their parents has been in spite of their level of education and not on account of it. Whatever reasons there are for these differences among students, if we value education as a worthwhile activity for all, we must attempt to create an educational environment in which every young person can appreciate and value the educational experience.

Profile of a corporate executive

Every village, town, and city has citizens who would be described as "prominent". Local doctors, lawyers, successful merchants, and small manufacturers could be thus described. Yet, in Canada, there are a few very large corporations, banks, and insurance companies where the top positions are filled by men who could be said to form the "economic elite" of the nation. Again, every nation of the world has a national economic elite, and indeed, a few men are of world importance. Henry Ford III and Aristotle Onassis are good examples. The prominent sociologist John Porter has said there are about 985 people in Canada's economic elite who hold power positions in Canada's largest national business enterprises.

A look through any library could yield a host of books to help the reader succeed. Dale Carnegie's book, *How to Succeed in Business*, has long been the Bible of the businessman, followed more recently by Robert Townsend's *Up the Organization*, a humorous but informative book about the world of business. The rich leather furniture, polished oak panels, executive suites and chauffeur-driven limousines suggest to some observers that the rewards of this "life at the top" are worth achieving. Years ago, Horatio Alger books told how hard-working newsboys came to be publishers of newspapers and railway porters became railway tycoons. But does it really happen that way? Professor Porter's study would suggest a different reality.

Looking for a moment at the average important executive, this picture emerges. He probably was born in this country to a family of upper-middle-class, English background. His father was probably a lawyer, doctor, or successful businessman. He may have attended a private school in either Ontario or Quebec, and then gone on to a certain school in the "Headmasters Association", such as Trinity College School, Upper Canada College, Lower Canada College, or St. Andrews.

Our executive will more often than not be an Anglican, the religion of 25.5% as opposed to 14.7% for the population as a whole. At university he will have studied engineering or science (about 20% of the elite have) or law (14%) or, in the case of an insurance company executive, actuarial science or commerce and finance (17%). He probably attended McGill University, Queen's University, or the University of Toronto. During his school days, the corporate executive will have known many of his present corporate colleagues. He will tend to have a great deal in common with them, possessing a relatively common educational background and set of social values. According to Professor Porter, of 611 members of the elite, 135 or 22% inherited their positions.

As a corporate executive, he will hold an official title: vice-president, president, or chairman of the board. He will also be the director of several other corporations besides the one for which he "works". The corporation probably has been established in business for some time.

The executive's life style will be reflected in the location of his residence, usually a house in a "good" district in Toronto, Montreal, or Vancouver. He belongs to several clubs, where he associates with others who are at the same socio-economic level. In

The Sinking of the Titanic and Social Privileges

Travel at the turn of the twentieth century reflected the social stratification of society. Trains offered three classes of accommodation – first, second, and third. Ships were also divided into first, second, and third or steerage classes. The poor, mainly immigrants, going to North America, were housed on the lower decks, usually at the stern. The cost and comfort of travel varied according to the class of accommodation purchased. On board ship, a first-class passenger had a spacious cabin and suite. The upper decks and public rooms were reserved for his use. Each class below first had less space and less luxurious accommodation. In steerage, there would be as many as seven or ten people in one cabin and only a small area of deck on which to walk.

The White Star liner "Titanic" was a symbol of British craftsmanship, engineering skill, and design. In accommodation she reflected the society of the day, with luxury for the wealthy and crowded conditions for the poor. When in 1921 the "Titanic" sank on her maiden voyage, there were 2,200 passengers aboard and only 1,200 spaces in the lifeboats, so that only 30 per cent of her total capacity, including the crew, could be accommodated.

While the rule "women and children first" applied, statistics reveal that women and children who were first- and second-class passengers survived the disaster in greater numbers than did the third-class women and children. Of 143 women in first class, four were casualties (2.8 per cent), three of these "by choice". Of 93 women in second class, there were 15 casualties (16.1 per cent), but of the 179 women in third class, 81 were lost (45.3 per cent). Only one of the 29 children in first and second classes died, but 53 of the 76 children in third class died.

The Board of Inquiry that investigated the disaster ruled that there should be more lifeboat spaces available on passenger ships. The above statistical analysis of survival by class was never brought to the attention of the Board of Inquiry. As Walter Lord has said in his book, *A Night to Remember*, "The night was a magnificent confirmation of 'women and children first', yet somehow the loss rate was higher for third-class children than for first-class men. It was a contrast which would never get by the social consciousness of today's press."

Toronto, the York, National, and Ontario Clubs attract the economic elite; in Ottawa, the Rideau Club; in Montreal, the St
James Club, and the Vancouver Club in Vancouver – all provide
an opportunity for old friends to meet and converse with people
of common outlook.

When the corporations are examined closely, the directorships
are seen to be held by a relatively few people, each of whom fill
several such positions. Each corporation has directors chosen because they represent regional interests, yet each has heavy representation from the class that Professor Porter has called the "economic elite". Several law firms in both Toronto and Montreal hold
a large number of directorships in common, through partners in
the legal firm who are associated with the corporations through
the legal service they have provided.

The corporate leader usually holds a number of positions in
charitable or philanthropic institutions. The business organizations are pleased to have their prominent men act as patrons of art
galleries, the Symphony Orchestra, and the ballet, as well as serving
for community groups such as the United Appeal, the Red Cross
or the Boy Scouts. The prestige of being asked to participate and
then in performing a highly competent job for these groups, also
brings prestige and favourable comment about the executive and
his industry. The boards of governors of the various universities
also invite corporate executives to participate, and they accept in
large numbers.

This description of the decision-makers of industry and finance
is a generalized one. Not all corporate executives are Anglican, or
university graduates, or members of clubs, or on the board of
governors of a university. The evidence does suggest that this is
the general profile of the corporate leader, however, with room for
many individual exceptions. In the banks for example, a significant number of top executives have not attended university; this
suggests that a person could expect to rise from the teller's cage to
the executive suite. But there is a trend toward the requirement
for more and more specialized training or expertise for a person to
qualify for a top position with a bank.

Yet, throughout the economic elite, there is a pattern of cross-
membership and a common background and outlook. In school,
marriage, business, and society, the thread of association is maintained within a relatively small group.

Social class, type of work, and work satisfaction

There are many people who explain the success of others in terms of the cost to their happiness. They say if you have to work too hard to be successful, it is not worth it. And there is no reason why you cannot be poor and happy, is there?

In fact, work satisfaction differs considerably according to occupation. Perhaps not surprisingly, the highest percentage of satisfied workers is usually found among professionals (such as doctors, lawyers, engineers, architects) and businessmen, and the lowest percentage is usually found among labourers (such as factory and construction workers).

The following material has been prepared by extracting information from a number of studies done on this subject. This information suggests to us that high-status jobs are more attractive to people and more personally satisfying than are low-status jobs.

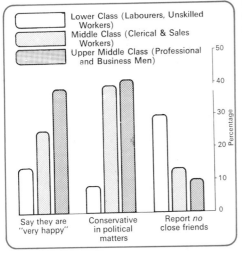

Work satisfaction, political beliefs, and closeness of friendships among lower, middle, and upper-middle class occupations

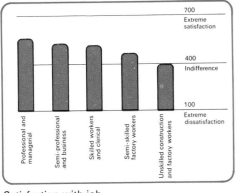

Satisfaction with job

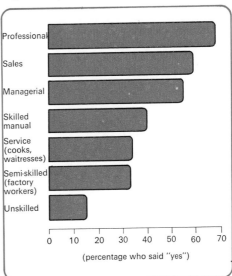

"If you inherited enough money to live comfortably, would you stay in the same kind of work?"

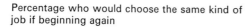

Percentage who would choose the same kind of job if beginning again

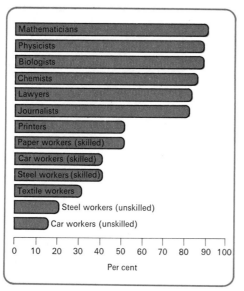

Per cent
Mathematicians
Physicists
Biologists
Chemists
Lawyers
Journalists
Printers
Paper workers (skilled)
Car workers (skilled)
Steel workers (skilled)
Textile workers
Steel workers (unskilled)
Car workers (unskilled)

0 10 20 30 40 50 60 70 80 90 100
Per cent

The plain truth is that factory work is degrading. It is degrading to any man who ever dreams of doing something worthwhile with his life; and it is about time we faced the fact. The more a man is exposed to middle-class values, the more sophisticated he becomes and the more production-line work is degrading to him. The immigrant who slaved in the poorly-lighted, foul, vermin-ridden sweatshop found his work less degrading than the native-born high school graduate who reads Judge Parker, Rex Morgan, M.D., and Judd Saxon, Business Executive, in the funnies, and works in a fluorescent factory with ticker-tape production-control machines.

Harvey Swados
The Myth of the Happy Worker

The work isn't hard, it's the never-ending pace. . . . The guys yell ''hurrah'' whenever the line breaks down. . . . You can hear it all over the plant.
The job gets so sickening – day in and day out, plugging in ignition wires. I get through with one motor, turn around, and there's another motor staring me in the face. It's sickening.

Charles R. Walker and Robert H. Guest
The Man on the Assembly Line

Social classes and spending behaviour

Pierre Martineau

It has been argued that there cannot be a class system existent in North America when most individuals do not have the slightest idea of its formal structure. Yet in actuality every individual senses that he is more at home with and more acceptable to certain groups than to others. In a study of department stores and shopping behavior, it was found that the Lower-Status woman is completely aware that, if she goes into High-Status department stores, the clerks and the other customers in the store will punish her in various subtle ways.

"The clerks treat you like a crumb," one woman expressed it. After trying vainly to be waited on, another woman bitterly complained that she was loftily told, "We thought you were a clerk."

The woman who is socially mobile gives considerable thought to the external symbols of status, and she frequently tests her status by shopping in department stores which she thinks are commensurate with her changing position. She knows that, if she does not behave in a certain manner to the clerks, if she is awkward about the proper cues, then the other customers and the clerks will make it very clear that she does not belong.

In another study, very different attitudes in the purchase of furniture and appliances involving this matter of status were found. Middle-Class people had no hesitancy in buying refrigerators and other appliances in discount houses and bargain stores because they felt that they could not "go wrong" with the nationally advertised names. But taste in furniture is much more elusive and subtle because the brand names are not known; and, therefore, one's taste is on trial. Rather than commit a glaring error in taste which would exhibit an ignorance of the correct status symbols, the same individual who buys appliances in a discount house generally retreats to a status store for buying furniture. She needs the support of the store's taste.

In a very real sense, every one of us in his consumption patterns and style of life shows an awareness that there is some kind of a superiority–inferiority system operating and that we must observe the symbolic patterns of our own class.

Choice of Store

A number of studies were undertaken to determine the relationship between social class and spending behaviour. All of these studies reveal the close relation between choice of store, patterns of spending, and class membership. Such questions were asked in the total metropolitan area as:

"If you were shopping for a good dress, at which store would you be most likely to find what you wanted?"
"For an everyday dress?"
"For living room furniture?"
"At which store do you buy most of your groceries?"

To assume that all persons would wish to shop at the glamorous High-Status stores is utterly wrong. People are very realistic in the way they match their values and expectations with the status of the store. The woman shopper has a considerable range of ideas about department stores; but these generally become organized on a scale ranking from very High-Social Status to the Lowest-Status and prestige. The social status of the department store becomes the primary basis for its definition by the shopper. This is also true of men's and women's apparel stores, and furniture stores, on the basis of customer profiles. The shopper is not going to take a chance feeling out of place by going to a store where she might not fit.

No matter what economics are involved, she asks herself who are the other customers in the store, what sort of treatment can she expect at the hands of the clerks, will the merchandise be the best of everything or lower priced and hence lower quality? Stores are described as being for the rich, for the average ordinary people, or for those who have to stretch their pennies.

Did you know, for example, that bus vacationers tend to be "somewhat hostile, belligerent, impulsive types", while train vacationers are "quiet, passive, very sensitive individuals who like to be left alone to meditate and philosophize"?

The swingers are the air travellers, who are "particularly active, inquisitive, confident types", according to the survey material, "much more so than auto vacationers".

The people who really are with it are the Canadians who travel abroad, for this, in the view of the survey of 5,995 people, takes a great deal of courage and confidence. "The farther Canadians travel on vacation, the greater their self-confidence, reflected in leadership and ascendance, and their trust in others."

Men who travel to sports events, festivals and other special attractions are outgoing, sociable, active types, but at the same time they display "a certain amount of emotional instability". Women at the same events tend to display "dominance and leadership".

Canadians who spend their vacations visiting relatives and friends are inclined to be passive and slow-moving while those who head for a vacation spot are more active, sociable, have more depth and enjoy a sense of good health.

Cottagers, in the surveyors' opinion, "are fairly thick skinned and are not concerned with their health". They are also more inclined toward overt activity than toward thoughtfulness.

Tenters and campers, according to this survey, are unusual only on the stability dimension which suggests they are moody, quiet and tend to worry.

Many outdoor activities, the survey material states, must offer solitude and some form of escape because "they seem to attract individuals who are also somewhat asocial and lacking in confidence, a combination of emotional instability, defensiveness and distrust of others".

"Travellers are clearly more active, outgoing and inquisitive than people who do not take any holidays."

(From a survey made by the Canadian Government Travel Bureau.)

The most important function of retail advertising today, when prices and quality have become so standard, is to permit the shopper to make social-class identification. This she can do from the tone and physical character of the advertising. Of course, there is also the factor of psychological identification. Two people in the same social class may want different stores. One may prefer a conservative store, one may want the most advanced styling. But neither will go to stores where they do not "fit", in a social-class sense.

In contrast to the independent food retailer, who obviously adapts to the status of the neighborhood, the chain grocers generally invade many income areas with their stores. Nevertheless, customer profiles show that each chain acquires a status definition.

While the national brand can and often does cut across classes, one can think of many product types and services which do have social class labels. The Upper-Middle Class person rarely travels by bus because none of his associates do so, even though there is certainly nothing wrong with this mode of transportation. On the other hand, even with low airline fares, one does not see many factory workers or day laborers on vacation around airports. Such sales successes as vodka and tonic water, and men's deodorants and foreign sports cars, were accomplished without benefit of much buying from this part of the market.

Communication Skills

There is also a relation between class and communication abilities which has significance for marketing. The kind of supersophisticated and clever advertising which appears in *Toronto Life* and *Saturday Night* is almost meaningless to Lower-Status people. They cannot comprehend the subtle humor; they are baffled by the bizarre art. They have a different symbol system, a very different approach to humor. In no sense does this imply that they lack intelligence or wit. Rather their communication skills have just been pressed into a different mold.

Here again style of advertising helps the individual to make class identification. Most of the really big local television success stories in large metropolitan areas have been achieved by personalities who radiate to the mass that this is where they belong. These self-made businessmen who do the announcing for their own shows communicate wonderfully well with the mass audience. While many listeners switch off their lengthy and personal commercials, these same mannerisms tell the Lower-Status individual that here is someone just like himself who understands him.

Social Research, Inc., has frequently discussed the class problem in marketing by dividing the population into Upper-Middle or quality market; the middle majority which combines both the Lower-Middle and Upper-Lower; and then the Lower-Lower. The distinction should be drawn between the Middle Classes and the Lower-Status groups. In several dozen of these store profiles, there is scarcely an instance where a store has appeal to the Lower-Middle or Upper-Lower classes with anything like the same strength.

It would be better to make the break between the Middle Class, representing one-third of the population, and the Lower-Status or Working-Class or Wage-Earner group. This permits some psychological distinctions to be drawn between the Middle-Class individual and the individual who is not a part of the Middle-Class system of values.

Who Saves, Who Spends?

Another important set of behavioral distinctions related to social-class position was revealed in the "save-spend aspiration" study. The question was asked: "Suppose your income was doubled for the next ten years; what would you do with the increased income?" This is a fantasy question taken out of the realm of any pressing economic situation to reflect aspirations about money. The coding broke down the answers to this question into five general categories: (1) the mode of saving, (2) the purpose of saving, (3) spending which would consolidate past gains, meet present defensive needs, prepare for future self-advancement, (4) spending which is "self-indulgent-centered", (5) spending which is "house-centered".

Here are some of our findings. The higher the individual's class position, the more likely is he to express some saving aspirations. Conversely, the lower his class position, the more likely is he to mention spending only. Moreover the higher the status, the more likely is the individual to specify *how* he will save his money, which is indicative of the more elaborate financial learning required of higher status.

Proceeding from the more general categories (such as saving versus spending only) to more specific categories (such as non-investment versus investment saving and the even more specific stock versus real estate investment, etc.) an increasing sharper class differentiation is found. It is primarily *noninvestment* saving which appeals to the Lower-Status person. Investment saving, on the other hand, appeals above all to the Upper-Status person.

Investors almost always specify how they will invest. And here in mode of investment are examples of the most sharply class-differentiated preferences. Intangible forms of investment like stock and insurance are very clearly distinguished as Upper-Status investments. Nearly four times as many Upper-Middles select insurance as would be expected by chance, whereas only one-fifth of the Lower-Lowers select it as would be expected by chance. By contrast, Lower-Status people have far greater preference for tangible investments, specifically ownership of real estate, a farm, or a business.

To sum up, Middle-Class people usually have a place in their aspirations for some form of saving. This saving is most often in the form of investment, where there is a risk, long-term involvement, and the possibility of higher return. Saving, investment saving, and intangible investment saving – successively each of these become for them increasingly symbols of their higher status.

The aspirations of the Lower-Status person are just as often for spending as they are for saving. This saving is usually a noninvestment saving where there is almost no risk, funds can be quickly converted to spendable cash, and returns are small. When the

The absence of classes helps to account for the relative invisibility of the poor, for the poor tend to be conscious of their situation only as individuals. They do not identify as members of a group that shares similar characteristics. Consequently, they do not act as a group politically, thereby making their weight felt. Similarly, other individuals in society fail to recognize the existence of any distinct group of poverty-stricken individuals. Part of this is due to the lack of action on the part of the poor, and part is a result of the fact that others also do not identify as members of some group with similar economic interests.

Bernard S. Phillips
Sociology: Social Structure and Change

Lower-Status person does invest his savings, he will be specific about the mode of investment, and is very likely to prefer something tangible and concrete – something he can point at and readily display.

Turning from mode of saving to purpose of saving, very significant class relationships are likewise evident. Consider the verbalization of saving purpose. Lower-Status people typically explain why one should save – why the very act of saving is important. On the other hand, Middle-Class people do not, as if saving is an end-in-itself, the merits of which are obvious and need not be justified.

Spending is the other side of the coin. Analysis of what people say they will spend for shows similar class-related desires. All classes mention concrete, material artifacts such as a new car, some new appliance. But the Lower-Status people stop here. Their accumulations are artifact-centered, whereas Middle-Class spending-mentions are experience-centered. This is spending where one is left typically with only a memory. It would include hobbies, recreation, self-education, and travel. The wish to travel, and particularly foreign travel is almost totally a Middle-Class aspiration.

Even in their fantasies, people are governed by class membership. In his daydreaming and wishful thinking, the Lower-Status individual will aspire in different patterns from the Middle-Class individual.

Psychological Differences

This spending-saving analysis has very obvious psychological implications to differentiate between the classes. Saving itself generally suggests foresightedness, the ability to perceive long-term needs and goals. Noninvestment saving has the characteristics of little risk-taking and of ready conversion, at no loss, into immediate expenditures – the money can be drawn out of the account whenever the bank is open. Investment spending, on the other hand, has the characteristics of risk-taking (a gamble for greater returns) and of delayed conversion, with possible loss, to expenditures on immediate needs.

Here are some psychological contrasts between two different social groups:

Middle-Class

1) Pointed to the future
2) His viewpoint embraces a long expanse of time
3) More urban identification
4) Stresses rationality
5) Has a well-structured sense of the universe
6) Horizons vastly extended or not limited
7) Greater sense of choice-making
8) Self-confident, willing to take risks
9) Immaterial and abstract in his thinking
10) Sees himself tied to national happenings

Lower-Status

1) Pointed to the present and past
2) Lives and thinks in a short expanse of time

3) More rural in identification
4) Nonrational essentially
5) Vague and unclear structuring of the world
6) Horizons sharply defined and limited
7) Limited sense of choice-making
8) Very much concerned with security and insecurity
9) Concrete and perceptive in his thinking
10) World revolves around his family and body

Conclusion

The essential purpose of this article was to develop three basic premises which are highly significant for marketing:

1) *There is a social-class system operative in metropolitan markets, which can be isolated and described.*

2) *It is important to realize that there are far-reaching psychological differences between the various classes.* They do not handle the world in the same fashion. They tend not to think in the same way. As one tries to communicate with the Lower-Status group, it is imperative to sense that their goals and mental processes differ from the Middle-Class group.

3) *Consumption patterns operate as prestige symbols to define class membership, which is a more significant determinant of economic behavior than mere income.* Each major department store, furniture store and chain-grocery store has a different "pulling power" on different status groups. The usual customers of a store gradually direct the store's merchandising policies into a pattern which works. The interaction between store policy and customer acceptance results in the elimination of certain customer groups and the attraction of others, with a resulting equilibration around a reasonably stable core of specific customer groups who think of the store as appropriate for them.

Income has always been the marketer's handiest index to family consumption standards. But it is a far from accurate index. For instance, the bulk of the population in a metropolitan market today will fall in the middle-income ranges. This will comprise not only the traditional white collar worker, but the unionized craftsman and the semiskilled worker with their tremendous income gains of the past decade. Income-wise they may be in the same category. But their buying behavior, their tastes, their spending-saving aspirations can be poles apart. Social-class position and mobility-stability dimensions will reflect in much greater depth each individual's style of life.

four   *Stereotyping and prejudice*

It is said that the Irish are superstitious and sentimental while the Scottish are canny and thrifty with their money. When an individual talks about a group of people in such general terms, he is stereotyping or attributing characteristics to the individuals who make up that group. The exploitation of stereotyping can be seen in the propagandists' characterization of Germans during World War II as "cruel, fierce, and hysterical enemies", and then ten years later, as "hardworking" and "dependable NATO allies". Often a stereotype is based on very narrow experience with members of a group, but more often it is learned through family and peer group influences. People categorize other individuals and attribute general characteristics to them, forming an opinion that will have implications for the way in which they will treat these individuals.

Stereotyping is closely related to prejudicial behaviour. When an individual applies negative stereotypes to others, his behaviour may reflect his belief. He may avoid their company, make unflattering remarks, and attempt to deny equality of access to employment, housing, and opportunity. He may likewise be prejudiced toward a person or group as a result of a positive stereotype. The manager of a company may always hire boys from Scotland because his stereotype dictates that they are thrifty and hardworking. Thus his behaviour is prejudiced in their favour. He may similarly never hire boys from North Toronto, because he feels that as a group they are pampered and lazy. Thus his behaviour is prejudiced against them.

The first selection that follows deals with the way in which individuals attribute characteristics to others. The second selection deals with the way in which marketing research reveals consumer prejudice, and how this influences the sale and marketing of goods.

The vicious circle of discrimination

What we think of other people

O. Klineberg

About a year ago I was in London at the invitation of British psychologists and sociologists in order to lecture on "National Stereotypes". Throughout the preceding day, during which I was undoubtedly made more sensitive by my preoccupation with this topic, I kept running into examples of such stereotyped thinking.

In my hotel, I heard someone say, "Oh, she has that Scottish stubbornness, you know." A book review in a newspaper used the phrase, "With true Gallic wit". At the theatre that evening, during the interval, I caught part of a conversation in which a pretty girl said to her escort, "I know that all Americans have a 'line' "; and in a mystery story that I read before retiring there was a reference to "typical German thoroughness".

These are all instances of those "pictures in our heads" to which Walter Lippman gave the name of stereotypes. They are typical of the ease with which most of us generalize about national or ethnic groups, usually without even stopping to think where such "information" comes from, and whether it represents the truth, the whole truth, or anything like the truth.

There are certainly very few, if any, among us who have not succumbed to the temptation to stereotype nations. One might almost describe the tendency as inevitable, or at least very nearly so. We *know* that Englishmen are reserved, and Irishmen pugnacious; we have heard it all our lives; besides most people agree with us. If we are asked, however, *how* we know, we would not easily find a suitable answer.

One of the earliest careful studies of this tendency was made by Katz and Braly, in 1932, in connexion with the stereotypes held by Princeton University students. The technique was simple.

Each student was given a list of traits, and a list of nationalities; from the first list he chose the five traits which he regarded as characteristic of each national or racial group.

The results showed a fair degree of unanimity, e.g., out of 100 students, 78 described the Germans as "scientifically minded", and 65 described them as "industrious"; 53 students used the adjective "artistic" for the Italians; the same percentage described the English as "sportsmanlike"; 79 agree that the Jews were "shrewd" and 54 stated that the Turks were "cruel"; 84 regarded Negroes as "superstitious", and 75 described them as "lazy".

We may summarize the results in a slightly different manner by indicating the three or four characteristics most commonly ascribed to each nationality.

Americans	Industrious Intelligent Materialistic Ambitious	Germans	Scientifically minded Industrious Stolid
Chinese	Superstitious Sly Conservative	Irish	Pugnacious Quick-tempered Witty
English	Sportsmanlike Intelligent Conventional	Italians	Artistic Impulsive Passionate
Negroes	Superstitious Lazy Happy-go-lucky	Japanese	Intelligent Industrious Progressive
Turks	Cruel Religious Treacherous	Jews	Shrewd Mercenary Industrious

A recent study of the stereotypes of German students at the Free University of Berlin by Sodhi and Bergius showed a similar willingness to stereotype nations and on the whole, comparable results. Americans, for example were described as sportsmanlike, democratic, materialistic; the Italians, as warm-blooded, musical, lighthearted; the Chinese as poor, inscrutable, modest; the Germans as conscious of duty, loving their homeland, intelligent; the English as proud of their nation, bound by traditions, sportsmanlike. There were some variations between the German and the American stereotypes, but on the whole the overlapping is considerable. . . .

Few people realize how much the existence of stereotypes may color our relations with other people, even to the extent of seeing them differently as a result. Psychologists have long known that

Inter-group prejudice is universal wherever groups are brought into contact as groups, and only a utopian can cherish the hope that any reform of society or re-education of man can wholly eradicate it.

Robert M. MacIver
Society : Its Structure and Changes

So subtle and swift is the process of acquiring prejudiced attitudes that we may safely say that for the most part they are caught rather than taught.

Gordon W. Allport
ABC's of Scapegoating

In a study reported by Kenneth B. Clark and Marnie B. Clark, two hundred and fifty white and Negro nursery school children were asked to make evaluations of dolls by way of a group of requests:

1) Give me the doll that you like to play with.
2) Give me the doll that is a nice doll.
3) Give me the doll that looks bad.
4) Give me the doll that is a nice color.

The overall finding was that the majority of Negro children preferred the white doll and rejected the coloured doll. Thus, not only were the children able to distinguish between the two categories of white and coloured, but they placed the white at the top and the coloured below. In other words, they ranked these categories as well as separating them.

This ranking process seemed to have some impact on a number of the children. The request, "Give me the doll that looks like you", was the last one in the experiment: the children had already made known their likes and dislikes. When this question was asked, some of the children who were free and relaxed at the beginning of the experiment broke down and cried or became somewhat negative. Two children ran out of the testing room convulsed in tears. Only two-thirds of the children had identified themselves as coloured. For example, a seven-year-old Northern child with skin of a light colour went to great pains to explain that he was actually white but: "I look brown because I got a suntan in the summer." When the child places himself in a low-status category, there is a tendency for this to disturb him emotionally. Indirect evidence for this is provided by the high proportion of "don't know" and "no" responses when "the doll that looks bad" was called for.

The social disease of prejudice is sinister. It issues in inequalities, exclusions, denials, and rejections :

This is the social disease which every year affects more people than infantile paralysis, cancer, and tuberculosis, all combined.

Sterling W. Brown
Primer in Intergroup Relations

Rabbie's Reds and Greens

Jaap Rabbie, conducting experiments on intergroup conflict at the University of Utrecht, has been amazed by the ease with which conflict and stereotype develop. He brings into an experimental room two groups and distributes green name tags and pens to one group, red pens and tags to the other. The two groups do not compete; they do not even interact. They are only in sight of each other while they silently complete a questionnaire. Only 10 minutes are needed to activate defensiveness and fear, reflected in the hostile and irrational perceptions of both "reds" and "greens".

A. G. Athos and R. E. Coffey
Behavior in Organizations

Prejudice and discrimination are not innate but are learned, usually within the family and often without conscious intent. Here is a summary of some research evidence, from *Human Behavior* by B. Berelson and G. A. Steiner :

Prejudices are usually acquired slowly and over a period of time. The child acquires his ethnic values and racial attitudes as he learns other social lessons, from adults, from his peers, and from his life experiences. Groups that are segregated in schools or in the community he assumes are inferior because society treats them as inferiors. Few parents actually teach their children to be prejudiced. However, their own attitudes and behavior, their restrictions on the playmates of their children, and the tendency to stereotype all individuals of a given racial or religious group with certain physical, behavioral, and mental characteristics result in a pattern of prejudice which their children imitate. It is not the parents' attitudes alone, but the whole home influence that is responsible for the development of prejudice.

It appears that prejudiced people tend to recall unpleasant childhood experiences with members of minority groups, but that seems to be more a rationalization after the fact of prejudice than a cause of it.

our perceptions of the external world, and particularly of human beings, are determined not only by what is *out there*, but also by what is *in ourselves*. What we see is determined in part by what we expect to see. If we believe, for example, that Italians are noisy, we will have a tendency to notice those Italians who are indeed noisy; if we are in the presence of some who do not fit the stereotype we may not even realize that they, too, are Italians. If someone points that fact out to us and says, "Look, those people are Italians, and they are not noisy", we can always dismiss them as exceptions.

Since there is no limit to the number of cases that can be so dismissed, we may continue to cling to the pictures in our heads, in spite of all the facts to the contrary. This does not always happen. Stereotypes do sometimes change in the light of new experience, and evidence for this is presented later. If we have had them for a long time, however, we surrender them with great reluctance.

A number of significant investigations have shown in a very dramatic manner how our stereotypes may determine our perceptions. Some years ago Allport and Postman, psychologists at Harvard University . . . studied some of the phenomena associated with the spread of rumours, making use of a technique known as "serial reproduction", a very simple device which anyone can use with a group of friends in his own home. They showed a picture to one student, and he described to a second student what he saw in the picture. The second then told a third what the the first had told him; the third told the fourth and so on, through a series of 8 to 10 reproductions. Then a comparison was made between the final result and the original presentation.

One of the pictures used in this investigation showed a scene in a subway in which, in addition to a number of people seated, there were two men standing, one a white, the other a Negro. The white was dressed in working clothes, with an open razor stuck in his belt. It so happens that the stereotype of the Negro held by some people in the USA includes the notion that Negroes carry with them an open razor, of which they make ready use in an argument.

The psychologists were able to demonstrate that in half of the groups who served as subjects in these experiments, before the end of the series of reproductions had been reached, the razor had "moved" from the white man to the Negro. In some instances, the Negro was even represented as brandishing the razor violently in the face of the white man. This does not mean that half of the subjects in the experiment saw the Negro with the razor, since if only one person in the chain made this error, it would be repeated by those that followed. Interestingly enough, this did not occur when the subjects were Negroes (who rejected the stereotype), or young children (who had not yet "learned" it).

Another study points in the same direction. A group of college students were shown photographs of 30 girls, and asked to judge each photograph on a 5 point scale, indicating their liking of the girl, her beauty, her intelligence, her character, her ambition, and her "entertainingness". Two months later, the same students were again shown the same photographs, but with surnames added. For some of the photographs Jewish surnames were given, such as Rabinowitz, Finkelstein, etc.; a second group received Italian names, such as Scarano, Grisolia, etc.; a third group Irish surnames, such as McGillicuddy, O'Shaughnessy, etc.; a fourth "old American" names like Adams and Clark.

The investigator was able to demonstrate that the mere labelling of these photographs with such surnames definitely affected the manner in which the girls were perceived. The addition of Jewish and Italian names, for example, resulted in a substantial drop in general liking, and a similar drop for judgment of beauty and character. The addition of the same names resulted in a rise in the ratings for ambition, particularly marked in the case of the Jewish surnames. It seems clear that the same photographs *looked different* just because they could now be associated with the stereotype held by these students.

Stereotypes frequently change. In some cases it may be argued that this corresponds to a real change in the characteristics of the people; in others, however, it seems much more likely to be due to external circumstances which have little or nothing to do with the group concerned. The Dutch sociologist, Shrieke, has, for example, made a collection of some of the descriptive phrases applied to the Chinese during the course of their residence in the state of California.

When the Chinese were needed in California, in order to carry on certain types of occupation, they were welcome there; during that period, newspapers and journals referred to them as among "the most worthy of our newly adopted citizens", "the best immigrants in California", they were spoken of as thrifty, sober, tractable, inoffensive, law-abiding. This flattering picture prevailed over a considerable period of time, but around 1860, presumably because economic competition had grown much more severe, there was a marked change in the stereotype of the Chinese. The phrases now applied to them included: "a distinct people", "unassimilable", "their presence lowered the plane of living", etc. They were spoken of as clannish, criminal, debased, servile, deceitful, and vicious.

This startling change can hardly be accounted for by any real modification of the characteristics of the Chinese population of California. The most acceptable explanation is that when it became advantageous to reduce the competition from the Chinese, the stereotype was altered in a direction which would help to justify such action. In this historical case it seems reasonable to conclude that the change in the characteristics ascribed to the Chinese throws doubt on the notion that stereotypes must necessarily contain some truth. . . .

One of the most amusing examples of a stereotype which has apparently developed without any kernel of truth emerges from an investigation by Schoenfeld on stereotypes associated with proper names. Here again the technique used was a simple one. The American students who served as subjects in this study were given a list of eight proper names and a list of eight adjectives; their task was to "match" or pair each name with the adjective regarded as most appropriate.

Pressed to tell what Chinese people really think of Americans, a Chinese student reluctantly replied, "Well, we think they are the best of the foreign devils." This incident occurred before the Communist revolution in China. Today's youth in China are trained to think of Americans as the *worst* of the foreign devils.

Gordon W. Allport
The Nature of Prejudice

Studies of the development of prejudice in children show that young children who have not yet been involved in prejudiced behavior patterns, may pick up prejudiced talk, but this doesn't affect their unprejudiced behavior. Later, after having become involved in prejudiced behavior patterns, they may pick up democratic language in the schools or elsewhere, but this doesn't affect their prejudiced behavior.

Earl Raab and Seymour M. Lipset
Prejudice and Society

In the mid-1940s, a Canadian researcher, S. L. Wax, attempted to find out how summer resorts would respond to requests for reservations from individuals of two different backgrounds. He wrote to approximately 100 summer resorts that had advertisements in Toronto newspapers.

To each of these hotels and resorts he wrote two letters, mailing them at the same time, and asking for room reservations for exactly the same dates. One letter he signed with the name "Mr. Greenberg", the other with the name "Mr. Lockwood". Here are the results:

To Mr. Greenberg:
    52 per cent of the resorts replied;
    36 per cent offered him accommodation.

To Mr. Lockwood:
    95 per cent of the resorts replied;
    93 per cent offered him accommodation.

As you can see, nearly all of the resorts in question welcomed Mr. Lockwood as a correspondent and as a guest; but nearly one-half of them failed to give Mr. Greenberg the courtesy of a reply, and only slightly more than one-third apparently were willing to receive him as a guest.

None of the hotels knew Mr. Lockwood or Mr. Greenberg. For all they knew, Mr. Greenberg might have been a quiet, orderly gentleman, and Mr. Lockwood a rowdy drunk. The decision was obviously made not on the merits of an individual, but Mr. Greenberg's supposed membership in a minority group.

A researcher asked 110 American businessmen and schoolteachers about the degrees of social intimacy to which they were willing to admit certain ethnic groups. The degrees of social distance employed were to close kinship through marriage, to my club as personal chums, to my street as neighbours, to employment in my occupation, to citizenship in my country, to my country as visitors only, and exclusion from my country. By weighting these seven classifications, the researcher obtained the following preferential rating of 23 ethnic groups:

Canadian	22.51
English	22.35
Scottish	20.91
Irish	19.38
French	18.67
Swedish	16.20
German	14.95
Spanish	14.02
Italian	8.87
Indian	7.30
Polish	6.65
Russian	6.40
Armenian	6.16
German-Jewish	5.45
Greek	5.23
Russian-Jewish	4.94
Mexican	4.57
Chinese	4.12
Japanese	4.08
Negro	3.84
Mulatto	3.62
Hindu	3.08
Turkish	2.91

Prejudices which are most productive of hostile action, i.e., discrimination, arise out of ignorance and hostility. If there is knowledge rather than ignorance, we have judgment instead of prejudice; and if we have friendliness rather than hostility, the prejudice is of the harmless variety.

Sterling W. Brown
Primer in Intergroup Relations

Among the more common strategies devised to lure us are: building self-images of ourselves into their product (playful gasolines for playful people); reminding us that their product can fill one of our hidden needs (security, self-esteem); playing upon our anxiety feelings; offering us ways, through products, to channel our aggressive feelings; selling us sexual reassurance; encouraging impulse buying; conditioning the young; selling us status symbols; making us style-conscious and then switching styles.

Vance Packard
The Hidden Persuaders

Since there were 120 students, and eight names, the results to be expected by chance alone, that is to say, if no stereotype existed, would be 120 divided by eight, or 15 for each name. The actual results showed that 63 out of the 120 judges matched Richard with "good looking"; 58 judged Herman to be "stupid"; 59 judged Rex as "athletic"; 71 associated Adrian with "artistic"; and 104 agreed that Cuthbert was "a sissy". In a similar experiment with American girls judging feminine names, 54 regarded Minnie as stupid; 60 saw Linda as sophisticated; 69 said that Mary was religious; 58 that Maisie was talkative; and 73 that Agatha was middle-aged.

Although this study was done with American students, it seems quite certain that comparable stereotypes would be found in languages other than English. . . .

Stereotyped thinking may be almost inevitable, but there is good evidence that it can at least be reduced, if not eliminated. . . .

Who buys what? Projective techniques in marketing research

Mason Haire

For the purposes of experiment a conventional survey was made of attitudes toward Nescafé, an instant coffee. The questionnaire included the questions "Do you use instant coffee?" (If No) "What do you dislike about it?" The bulk of the unfavorable responses fell into the general area "I don't like the flavor". This is such an easy answer to a complex question that one may suspect it is a stereotype, which at once gives a sensible response to get rid of the interviewer and conceals other motives. How can we get behind this facade?

In this case an indirect approach was used. Two shopping lists were prepared. They were identical in all respects, except that one list specified Nescafé and one Maxwell House Coffee. They were administered to alternate subjects, with no subject knowing of the existence of the other list. The instructions were "Read the shopping list below. Try to project yourself into the situation as far as possible until you can more or less characterize the woman who bought the groceries. Then write a brief description of her personality and character. Wherever possible indicate what factors influenced your judgment."

Shopping List 1
  Pound and a half of hamburger
  2 loaves Wonder bread
  bunch of carrots
  1 can Rumford's Baking Powder
  Nescafé instant coffee
  2 cans Del Monte peaches
  5 lbs. potatoes

Shopping List 2
    Pound and a half of hamburger
    2 loaves Wonder bread
    bunch of carrots
    1 can Rumford's Baking Powder
    1 lb. Maxwell House Coffee (Drip Ground)
    2 cans Del Monte peaches
    5 lbs. potatoes

Fifty people responded to each of the two shopping lists given above. The responses to these shopping lists provided some very interesting material. The following main characteristics of their descriptions can be given:

1) 48 per cent of the people described the woman who bought Nescafé as lazy; 4 per cent described the woman who bought Maxwell House as lazy.

2) 48 per cent of the people described the woman who bought Nescafé as failing to plan household purchases and schedules well; 12 per cent described the woman who bought Maxwell House this way.

3) 4 per cent described the Nescafé woman as thrifty; 16 per cent described the Maxwell House woman as thrifty. 12 per cent described the Nescafé woman as a spendthrift. 0 per cent described the Maxwell House woman this way.

4) 16 per cent described the Nescafé woman as not a good wife; 0 per cent described the Maxwell House woman this way. 4 per cent described the Nescafé woman as a good wife; 16 per cent described the Maxwell House woman as a good wife.

A clear picture begins to form here. Instant coffee represents a departure from "home-made" coffee, and the traditions with respect to caring for one's family. Coffee-making is taken seriously, with vigorous proponents for laborious drip and filterpaper methods, firm believers in coffee boiled in a battered sauce pan, and the like. Coffee drinking is a form of intimacy and relaxation that gives it a special character.

On the one hand, coffee making is an art. It is quite common to hear a woman say, "I can't seem to make good coffee", in the same way that one might say, "I can't learn to play the violin". It is acceptable to confess this inadequacy, for making coffee well is a mysterious touch that belongs, in a shadowy tradition, to the plump, aproned figure who is a little lost outside her kitchen but who has a sure sense in it and among its tools.

On the other hand, coffee has a peculiar role in relation to the household and the home-and-family character. We may well have a picture, in the shadowy past, of a big black range that is always hot with baking and cooking, and has a big enamelled pot of coffee warming at the back. When a neighbor drops in during the morning, a cup of coffee is a medium of hospitality that does somewhat the same thing as cocktails in the late afternoon, but does it in a broader sphere.

These are real and important aspects of coffee. They are not physical characteristics of the product, but they are real values in

In a study conducted by Westfall, one hundred subjects were asked to characterize the owners of different makes of automobiles by selecting the appropriate adjectives from a long list. On first thought one says, "What a ridiculous task. Any make of car is driven by millions of people and they must run the gamut." Still, when you think about it, we do have notions about Cadillac owners which are different from our notions about Chevrolet owners and it turns out that many other people have the same notions. Here are some characterizations on which there was substantial agreement:

Cadillac owners	Rich, high class, famous, fancy, important, proud, superior
Buick owners	Middle class, brave, masculine, strong, modern, pleasant
Chevrolet owners	Poor, ordinary, low class, simple, practical, cheap, thin, friendly
Ford owners	Masculine, young, powerful, good-looking, rough, dangerous, single, loud, merry, active
Plymouth owners	Quiet, careful, slow, moral, fat, gentle, calm, sad, thinking, patient, honest

These stereotypes are not simply inferences as to socio-economic status from the price of the car. There were great differences in belief about owners of the low-priced three: Ford owners were virile, youthful, and adventurous; Plymouth owners were stodgy but sensible; Chevrolet owners were just plain cheap.

Some Personality Differences
Associated with Model of Car Owned *

Characteristic	Convertible	Standard or compact
Active	13.3	11.5
Vigorous	11.3	10.5
Impulsive	12.5	11.1
Dominant	12.6	11.8
Stable	11.2	11.9
Sociable	13.5	12.2
Reflective	8.6	9.3
No. of cases	62	169

* The higher the score, the greater the tendency to show the personality characteristic.

the consumer's life, and they influence his purchasing. We need to know and assess them. The "labor-saving" aspect of instant coffee, far from being an asset, may be a liability in that it violates these traditions. How often have we heard a wife respond to "This cake is delicious!" with a pretty blush and "Thank you – I made it with such and such a prepared cake mix." This response is so invariable as to seem almost compulsive. It is almost unthinkable to anticipate a reply "Thank you, I made it with Pillsbury's flour, Fleischman's yeast, and Borden's milk." Here the specifications are unnecessary. All that is relevant is the implied "I made it" – the art and the credit are carried directly by the verb that covers the process of mixing and processing the ingredients. In ready-mixed foods there seems to be a compulsive drive to refuse credit for the product, because the accomplishment is not the housewife's but the company's.

In this experiment, as a penalty for using "synthetics" the woman who buys Nescafé pays the price of being seen as lazy, a spendthrift, a poor wife, and as failing to plan well for her family. The people who rejected instant coffee in the original direct question blamed its flavor. We may well wonder if their dislike of instant coffee was not to a large extent occasioned by a fear of being seen by one's self and others in the role they projected onto the Nescafé woman in the description. When asked directly, however, it is difficult to respond with this. One cannot say, "I don't use Nescafé because people will think I am lazy and not a good wife." Yet we know from these data that the feeling regarding laziness and shiftlessness was there. Later studies showed that it determined buying habits, and that something could be done about it.

Analysis of Responses

Some examples of the type of response received will show the kind of material obtained and how it may be analyzed. Three examples of each group are given below.

Description of a woman who bought, among other things, Maxwell House Coffee

"I'd say she was a practical, frugal woman. She bought too many potatoes. She must like to cook and bake as she included baking powder. She must not care much about her figure as she does not discriminate about the food she buys."

"The woman is quite influenced by advertising as signified by the specific name brands on her shopping list. She probably is quite set in her ways and accepts no substitutes."

"I have been able to observe several hundred women shoppers who have made very similar purchases to that listed above, and the only clue that I can detect that may have some bearing on her personality is the Del Monte peaches. This item when purchased singly along with the other more staple foods indicates that she may be anxious to please either herself or members of her family with a 'treat'. She is probably a thrifty, sensible housewife."

Descriptions of a woman who bought, among other things, Nescafé Instant Coffee

"This woman appears to be either single or living alone. I would guess she had an office job. Apparently, she likes to sleep late in the morning, basing my assumption on what she bought such as Instant Coffee which can be made in a hurry. She probably also has peaches for breakfast, cans being easy to open. Assuming that she is just average, as opposed to those dazzling natural beauties who do not need much time to make up, she must appear rather sloppy, taking little time to make up in the morning. She is also used to eating supper out, too. Perhaps alone rather than with an escort. An old maid probably."

"She seems to be lazy, because of her purchases of canned peaches and instant coffee. She doesn't seem to think, because she bought two loaves of bread, and then baking powder, unless she's thinking of making cake. She probably just got married."

"I think the woman is the type who never thinks ahead very far – the type who always sends Junior to the store to buy one item at a time. Also she is fundamentally lazy. All the items, with the possible exception of the Rumford's, are easily prepared items. The girl may be an office girl who is just living from one day to the next in a sort of haphazard sort of life."

As we read these complete responses we begin to get a feeling for the picture that is created by Nescafé. It is particularly interesting to notice that the Nescafé woman is protected, to some extent, from the opprobrium of being lazy and haphazard by being seen as a single "office girl" – a role that relieves one from guilt for not being interested in the home and food preparation.

The references to peaches are significant. In one case (Maxwell House) they are singled out as a sign that the woman is thoughtfully preparing a "treat" for her family. On the other hand, when the Nescafé woman buys them it is evidence that she is lazy, since their "canned" character is seen as central.

In terms of the sort of results presented above, it may be useful to demonstrate the way these stories are coded. The following items are extracted from the six stories quoted:

Maxwell House	*Nescafé*

1) practical
   frugal
   likes to cook
	1) single
	   office girl
	   sloppy old maid

2) influenced by
   advertising
   set in her ways
	2) lazy
	   does not plan
	   newlywed

3) interested in family
   thrifty
   sensible
	3) lazy
	   does not plan
	   office girl

Items such as these are culled from each of the stories. Little by little categories are shaped by the content of the stories themselves. In this way the respondent furnishes the dimensions of analysis as well as the scale values on these dimensions.

Several of the techniques being used on us by certain of the advertising men (and their scientific allies), however, do give cause for concern. These are the techniques designed to catch us when our conscious guard is down. Here are some of the types of operation I have in mind.

1) Appeals designed to play upon our hidden weaknesses. At one of America's largest advertising agencies, staff psychologists have been exploring the subconscious of sample humans in order to find out how to shape messages that will have maximum impact with people of high anxiety, body consciousness, hostility, passiveness, and so on.

2) Strategies involving the manipulation of children. The agency just mentioned also conducted a study of the psyche of straight-haired small girls to find how best to persuade them and their mothers that the girls might feel doomed to ugliness and unhappiness if they were not somehow provided with curly hair.

   The most inviting opportunity to manipulate children for profit, of course, is via television. Five-year-old children, admen have learned, make mighty fine amplifiers of singing jingles (beer or cigarettes included). They can be taught to sing them endlessly with gusto around the house all day long and, unlike the TV set, they can't be turned off.

3) The deliberate sale of products for their status-enhancement value. Automotive advertisers have hammered so long and loud on the theme of bigness that many Americans feel socially insecure in a small or medium-sized car (unless it is their second car or a chic foreign-made car).

4) The creation of illogical, irrational loyalties. This occurs most conspicuously in the promotion of gasolines, cigarettes, whiskeys, detergents. The research director of a leading advertising agency which has made a study in depth of cigarette smoking states that 65 per cent of all smokers are absolutely loyal to one brand of cigarettes, even to the extent of walking down five flights of stairs to buy their own brand rather than accept another brand offered by a friend. About 20 per cent are relatively loyal. Yet he found in tests where cigarettes were masked that people could identify their brand by only 2 per cent better than chance. He concluded: "They are smoking an image completely."

Vance Packard
The Hidden Persuaders

Some of the techniques used to probe consumer motives have been borrowed straight from psychiatric clinics and sociological laboratories: the depth interview (a miniature psychoanalysis without the couch), projective picture and word association tests, galvanometers (lie detectors), hypnosis, and social-layer analysis. When our motives are fathomed the experts then shape and bait psychological hooks which will bring us flopping into their corporate boats.

Vance Packard
The Hidden Persuaders

Second Test

It is possible to wonder whether it is true that the criticism that is heaped on the Nescafé woman comes from her use of a device that represents a shortcut and labor-saver in an area where she is expected to embrace painstaking time-consuming work in a ritualistic way. To test this a variation was introduced into the shopping lists. In a second experiment one hundred and fifty housewives were tested with the form given above, but a sample was added to this group which responded to a slightly different form. If we assume that the rejection in the first experiment came from the presence of a feeling about synthetic shortcuts we might assume also that the addition of one more shortcut to both lists would bring the Maxwell House woman more into line with the Nescafé woman, since the former would now have the same guilt that the Nescafé woman originally had, while the Nescafé woman, already convicted of evading her duties, would be little further injured.

In order to accomplish this a second prepared food was added to both lists. Immediately after the coffee in both lists the fictitious item "Blueberry Fill Pie Mix" was added. The results are shown in the accompanying table.

It will be seen immediately, in the first two columns, that the group to whom the original form of the list was given showed the same kind of difference as reported above in their estimates of the two women. The group, given an additional prepared food to consider, however, brought the Maxwell Coffee woman down until she is virtually undistinguishable from the Nescafé woman. There seems to be little doubt but that the prepared-food-character, and the stigma of avoiding housewifely duties is responsible for the projected personality characteristics. . . .

Table 1
Personality Characteristics Ascribed to Users of Prepared Foods

If they use	No prepared food (Maxwell House alone)		Nescafé (alone)	
They are seen as:	No.	%	No.	%
Not economical	12	17	24	32
Lazy	8	11	46	62
Poor personality and appearance	28	39	39	53
N =	72		74	

If they use	Maxwell House (plus pie mix)		Nescafé (plus pie mix)	
They are seen as:	No.	%	No.	%
Not economical	6	30	7	35
Lazy	5	25	8	40
Poor personality and appearance	7	35	8	40
N =	20		20	

five   *The influence of the group*

Rarely does a person perform a role in isolation; indeed, most of our identity is experienced in terms of other people or groups. Thus a hockey player identifies himself in part with his team; a son identifies himself in relation to his father, mother, brothers, and sisters. A businessman identifies himself in part with his business associates. The group provides support to its members but it also regulates behaviour. Certain people will have more influence than others in a group, and at times, the leadership function of a group will rotate. Take for example a group of explorers in the Arctic following an Eskimo guide. The party at that time is under the influence and leadership of the guide. Back at the research station, the guide reverts to his old role of advisor and helper, and someone else becomes the leader. Within a group there are pressures to force conformity or encourage a certain behavioural pattern.

Group membership carries certain obligations and rights. Leadership of a group also involves rights and obligations for the leader, whose action is controlled to some degree by the limits set by the group. Identity in the group will be evidenced by certain behavioural clues: dress (for example, the old school tie), language (choice of vocabulary), taste (appreciation of some things, rejection of others), outlook (as in political or social views). Membership within a group gives a member some sort of satisfaction – be it status, or fulfillment of personal needs – and a basic sense of identity.

Each one of us belongs to a myriad of groups. Some are permanent, such as the family, others are temporary, such as a casual card-game partner or a summer resort acquaintance. Work groups are part of most people's experience. Most employees of large organizations experience membership in various work groups from the advisory group to the president, to the social and flower committee. Membership in some groups brings more prestige than does membership in others.

People behave differently in different groups depending on the circumstances. A gentle, kind man who loves his family can, in other circumstances (for example, in a mob), cry for vengeance, or shout "Kill him", "Lynch him", "Teach him a lesson". When people behave collectively, their behaviour can differ tremendously. A group of pickets can become part of a riot, a group of spectators at a hockey game can become a mob, a group of students can erect barricades and begin anti-government riots. People under certain conditions can behave unpredictably: a "fun" crowd can turn ugly, or a mob can turn peaceful and then disperse.

The first selection in this section is a report on research conducted by Solomon E. Asch. It effectively demonstrates that certain individuals under the influence of group pressure will support a point of view that they know to be incorrect. The second selection is an excerpt from the classic study of gang behaviour, *The Corner Boys* by William F. Whyte. The members of the gang are shown to operate under the powerful influence of gang, rather than personal, values. The final selection focuses on riot behaviour and shows how a mob acts almost as a single individual.

Group influence

Solomon E. Asch

The following experiment demonstrates the influence that groups can exert upon their individual members. It shows that even relatively mild forms of group pressure can force certain persons to lie about situations that are obvious under ordinary circumstances, and, in effect, to call white black. How does one explain the errors of perception and judgment that were observed in the study? What are some of the personal and social causes of the differences among peoples' responses to group pressure? Is there anything in the structure of society, the patterns of friendship, or the processes of education that may contribute to the study's outcome? What, if anything, can the social sciences do to enhance the validity of human perceptions, and should anything be attempted in this regard?

The study was set up in a very simple manner. We placed a person by himself among a group of people who contradicted him about an obvious easily seen matter of fact. The situation to be judged was present and could be seen by everyone present.

The individual persons in the groups were required to announce their judgments publicly. This situation caused conflict for the individual as was intended. The object of the study was to trace the course and outcome of the conflict, and to observe how changes in certain of the conditions of the experiment affected the individual who was being contradicted.

Plan of Investigation

The plan of the investigation required a special kind of majority group, one that cooperated with the experimenter. The members of this group had been instructed in advance to announce judgments (from time to time) that were in fact wrong, and to do so unanimously. This was a *wrong* majority. One person in the group did not know that the group was set up to contradict him. Thus, whenever the larger group and the individual were in disagreement, the group was lying and the individual was reporting faithfully.

The task was one of matching the lengths of lines. The group was shown a line, which we will call the standard, and next to it three lines of clearly different lengths, one of which was equal to the standard. The instructions were to select, from among the three comparison lines, the one equal to the standard. The comparison lines were numbered I, II, and III, and the members of the group announced their judgments, by calling out the correct number, in the order in which they were seated. When the judgments were completed, one set of lines was removed and replaced by a new set of standard and comparison lines (see *Figure 1*).

The individual was seated toward the end of the group. He always heard all but one of the majority report their judgments before his turn came to respond.

The task of determining which of the lines was the same was easy since the comparison lines clearly differed in length. The errors of the majority group were considerable, ranging between ¾ inch and 1¾ inches. Further, the majority was not consistent in its errors on successive occasions; it both underestimated and overestimated.

The subjects were male college students, ranging in age from 17 to 25; the average age was 20. The members of the majority, who numbered in size from 7 to 9, were also students drawn from the

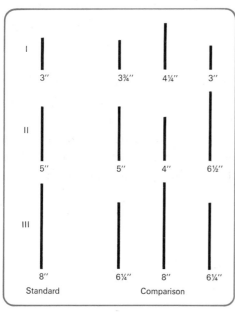

Figure 1   Critical comparisons

same institutions. There were 123 persons who played the individual or minority role in the groups.

Contradictory Demands of Situation. This situation placed contradictory demands upon the individual. On the one side was a clearly seen comparison of lines which he had tried to judge correctly. On the other side was the unanimous opinion of a majority of other students whose competence and trustworthiness he had reason to take for granted. Further, there was no possible compromise for the situation. Since there was no discussion during the experiment, there was no possibility of persuading or being persuaded. The contradiction was also in an important respect understandable; as long as the subject did not know the setup, and this was the rule, there was no possibility of explaining the disagreement. Finally, the subject was under the necessity of making a decision. He could not escape, postpone, or delegate responsibility.

The individual who was being set up could stand by the evidence of his eyes but this was the same as declaring that the unanimous majority was in error. Or he could follow the majority, but this he could do only by holding back the truth of his own eyes.

Results

The main results are summarized in *Figure 2.* 1) Let us note first that a group of individuals who made the comparison of lines without being misled was overwhelmingly accurate; under this condition errors made up less than 1 percent of all comparisons. 2) In the set-up situation there was a large percentage of erroneous comparisons: one-third of the comparisons were errors in the direction of the majority group. This is an important result when one considers the nature of the task and the fact the individuals were university students. 3) Perhaps more significant was the great range of individual differences. A number of the individuals were not influenced by the majority throughout the experiment; others varied between the majority and their own view; still others went with the majority as often, or almost as often, as the conditions permitted. The information concerning individual differences appears in *Table 1*.

Those individuals who were not influenced by the majority in the early part of the experiment tended to remain that way and similarly for those who went with the majority at the outset.

Effects of Changes in the Size of the Majority. The effect here described was also studied with majorities differing in size. In a series of experiments we varied the size of the opposition from 1 to 15; each situation required, of course, different individuals. The result may be summarized as follows: 1) The full effect was obtained with a majority of three. An increase of majority beyond this point, up to the limit of 15, failed to change the effect. 2) An opposition of two reduced the influence on the individuals one-third. 3) An opposition of one produced a small but telltale effect (3% errors).

From these findings we may draw a few conclusions. First, the sheer size of the majority group, while an important condition, is

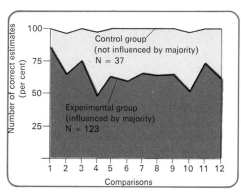

Figure 2   Correct estimates on successive
comparisons

Table 1
Numbers of Errors Made by the
Experimental and the Control Groups
in their Comparisons of
the Lengths of Lines

	Control group (Not influenced by contradicting majority)	Experimental group (Influenced by contradicting majority)
No errors	35	29
1 to 3 errors	2	35
4 to 7 errors	0	24
8 to 12 errors	0	35
	——	——
	37 persons	123 persons

not wholly decisive. Beyond a point that is soon reached, further increases of size are without effect. Second, the study shows that there were individuals who acted more independently against an opposition of 15 than others who faced an opposition of 2.

In another series of experiments the conditions described earlier were retained exactly, except for one detail. There were now two individuals placed into the set-up situation, opposed by a majority of seven to nine. In short, we altered the situation of the individual by putting him in the position of a minority of two. The seemingly small change had quite an effect; indeed, it robbed the majority of most of its power. Although the individuals continued to face the opposition of a substantial majority, in the presence of a partner they were far less likely to be influenced by the majority.

There were very few individuals who went with the majority more than two or three times when another person sided with them. The majority was still exerting an effect, but one that had been drastically reduced.

We conclude that the weakness of the minority-of-one condition is to be traced to the special quality of loneness it created. The presence of one other voice testifying to the individual's sense of rightness was enough to strengthen and protect him from the opposition of an opposed majority.

We have spoken of a special, indeed an unusual, situation. We have studied conformity to the group under highly special conditions, and we would expect different results under different conditions. It is not hard to think of free thinking that is irresponsible or of conformity to the group that requires courage. Nevertheless, the observations of this study tell us something about social life.

There are circumstances when the welfare of the individual and the group requires that each should act according to his conviction. Indeed, a human community depends on its members to contribute of their thinking and feeling. When this source of mutual correction and enlightenment is weakened, the social process is disturbed at its foundations; both the individual and the group are damaged.

The corner boys

William F. Whyte

Close friendship ties already existed between certain of the men, but the Nortons, as an organization, did not begin to function until the early spring. It was at that time that Doc returned to the corner. Nutsy, Frank, Joe, Alec, Carl, and Tommy had a great respect for Doc and gathered around him. Angelo, Fred, and Lou followed Doc in making the corner their headquarters. Danny and Mike were drawn to Norton Street by their friendship for Doc and by the location of their crap game, right next to "the corner". Long John followed Danny and Mike.

The men became accustomed to acting together. They were also tied to one another by mutual obligations. In their experi-

In his article, "An Approach to the Study of Communicative Acts", Theodore Newcomb has said that there is a tendency for people to move into groups and this has the effect of increasing the values that the group shares. But if a group is not comfortable for a person, he will continue to be on the lookout for another set of friends. They could be in part inside his present group or outside the group. This tendency on the part of human beings leads some scholars to talk of a human need for "support for basic beliefs". A society meets this need in its members by sorting itself into smaller groupings which share similar feelings and beliefs.

nces together there were innumerable occasions when one man would feel called upon to help another, and the man who was aided would want to return the favor. Strong group loyalties were supported by these reciprocal activities.

There were distinctions in rank among the Nortons. Doc, Danny, and Mike held the top positions. They were older than any of the others except Nutsy. They possessed a greater capacity for social movement. While the followers were restricted to the narrow sphere of one corner, Doc, Danny, and Mike had friends in many other groups and were well known and respected throughout a large part of Cornerville. It was one of their functions to accompany the follower when he had to move outside of his customary social sphere and needed such support. The leadership three were also respected for their intelligence and powers of self-expression. Doc in particular was noted for his skill in argument. On the infrequent occasions when he did become involved, he was usually able to outmaneuver his opponent without humiliating him. I never saw the leadership three exert their authority through physical force, but their past fighting reputations tended to support their positions.

Doc was the leader of the gang. The Nortons had been Doc's gang when they had been boys, and, although the membership had changed, they were still thought to be Doc's gang. The crap game and its social obligations prevented Danny and Mike from spending as much time with the Nortons as did Doc. They were not so intimate with the followers, and they expected him to lead.

Long John was in an odd position. Though he was five years younger than Doc, his friendship with the three top men gave him a superior standing. As Doc explained:

It's because we've always catered to Long John. When we go somewhere, we ask Long John to go with us. We come up to him and slap him on the back. We give him so much attention that the rest of the fellows have to respect him. . . .

One evening in the fall, Doc scheduled a bowling match against the Italian Community Club, which was composed largely of college men who held their meetings every two weeks in the Norton Street Settlement House. The club was designed to be an organization of well-educated and superior men, although Doc was a member, and Angelo, Lou, and Fred of the Nortons had been voted in upon his recommendation. The other Nortons felt that the club was "high-toned", and around the corner it was known as the 'Boys' Junior League''. They were a little flattered that members of their group could mix with such a club, but their opinion was formed largely from the personalities of Chick Morelli, the president, and Tony Cardio, another prominent member, both of whom they considered snobbish and conceited. Consequently, the Nortons took this match very seriously. . . .

Feeling ran high. The Nortons shouted at the club bowlers and made all sorts of noises to upset their concentration. The club members were in high spirits when they gained an early lead but had little to say as the Nortons pulled ahead to win by a wide margin. . . .

The Small Group

There are certain conditions under which people in small groups will act in a similar way and agree what is "right" to think about and support. Some of these are as follows:

1) The more attractive the group is to its members, and the more important its goals, then the stronger the desire for the individual to remain in it and to depend on it.

   In such cases, the group members are likely to change their own opinions to those held by the group and to try to convince other people regarding the wisdom of those opinions. This is particularly true of cliques in schools where students appear to have a strong need to belong. They will often change strong beliefs that they have learned from their parents in order to be part of such cliques.

2) The more unified in feeling the group is on some issue, such as concern for the poor or the mistreatment of fellow students, the stronger the feeling of being part of a group.

   A cause often acts to cement a group of individuals together. This occurs when labour unions picket together, and when students hold a protest march. In most cases, when the cause loses importance, the group is weakened and tends to pull apart.

3) The more common the background of the members of the group, the greater the likelihood that they will remain together and share the same feelings.

   In school, cliques are usually composed of students from the same part of town, or with the same interests. There are usually two main cliques in a high school – one based on the athletic skills of its members (star football and basketball players) and the other composed of students from upper-class or upper-middle-class homes. Cliques made up of students with both athletic and social class credits are quite influential in school activities and are difficult to join.

4) The more a group member's opinions are expressed in a group, the more likely that he will conform to the opinions of the group. It is quite natural that the spokesman of any group, clique, or gang will be required to convey the group's beliefs in an accurate way to other people. When you talk of your group, you must expect to defend its actions and beliefs. The member of a motorcycle gang must support that gang in public or he will be rejected from the gang.

5) The more favourably the group members think of each other, the more they spend time together, and the more they share decision-making, the closer they will become and the stronger the feeling of "we-ness" that will result.

Men and women in our society seem to need the support and comfort of group activities in their everyday life. However, the individual must be careful not to sacrifice strong personal beliefs for the short-term security of a group that may break up when a certain cause loses its importance. The individual is then left without the support of the group and without personal beliefs.

What Is the Ideal Group Size?

The size of a group determines to a considerable extent what happens in that group. In a group of two we usually find quite a bit of tension and emotion. There is a tendency to avoid disagreement, but at the same time, there is a high possibility of deadlock. In groups of two there is a tendency for one person to take on a more active role, while the other behaves passively but with the power of veto. If the two people are husband and wife, there is not usually support for either person's point of view, and because this is a long-term relationship, mutual tolerance is necessary for survival.

In groups of three, a situation of two against one usually arises. It is most often the strongest two against the weakest. This is a steady form of grouping, although there may be a shifting of partners. In a study of three-man groups conducted by Theodore Mills, it was found that the two more active members form the pair and the least active member becomes the third party:

In larger sized groups it has been found that there is more disagreement in even-numbered groups (4, 6, 8) than in odd-numbered groups (5, 7, 9) because it is possible to form smaller groupings of equal size. It appears that the most satisfying size for effective decision-making and for the personal satisfaction of the members is five. Five allows a 2:3 division into smaller groups, which provides support for the minority group members. A group of five provides stimulation for the members since it is small enough for all to participate and for all to be recognized.

Theodore Mills
Sociology of Small Groups

The Community Club match served to arouse enthusiasm for bowling among the Nortons. Previously the boys had bowled sporadically and often in other groups, but now for the first time bowling became a regular part of their social routine. Long John, Alec, Joe Dodge, and Frank Bonelli bowled several nights a week throughout the winter. Others bowled on frequent occasions, and all the bowlers appeared at the alleys at least one night a week.

A high score requires several spares and strikes. Since a strike rarely occurs except when the first ball hits the kingpin properly within a fraction of an inch, and none of the boys had such precise aim, strikes were considered matters of luck, although a good bowler was expected to score them more often than a poor one. A bowler was judged according to his ability to get spares, to "pick" the pins that remained on the alley after his first ball.

There are many mental hazards connected with bowling. In any sport there are critical moments when a player needs the steadiest nerves if he is to "come through"; but, in those that involve team play and fairly continuous action, the player can sometimes lose himself in the heat of the contest and get by the critical points before he has a chance to "tighten up". If he is competing on a five-man team, the bowler must wait a long time for his turn at the alleys, and he has plenty of time to brood over his mistakes. When a man is facing ten pins, he can throw the ball quite casually. But when only one pin remains standing, and his opponents are shouting "He can't pick it", the pressure is on, and there is a tendency to "tighten up" and lose control.

When a bowler is confident that he can make a difficult shot, the chances are that he will make it or come exceedingly close. When he is not confident, he will miss. A bowler is confident because he has made similar shots in the past and is accustomed to making good scores. But that is not all. He is also confident because his fellows, whether for him or against him, believe that he can make the shot. If they do not believe in him, the bowler has their adverse opinion as well as his own uncertainty to fight against. When that is said, it becomes necessary to consider a man's relation to his fellows in examining his bowling record.

In the winter and spring of that year bowling was the most significant social activity for the Nortons. Saturday night's intra-clique and individual matches became the climax of the week's events. During the week the boys discussed what had happened the previous Saturday, and what would happen on the coming Saturday. A man's performance was subject to continual evaluation and criticism. There was, therefore, a close connection between a man's bowling and his position in the group.

The team used against the Community Club had consisted of two men (Doc and Long John) who ranked high and three men (Joe Dodge, Frank Bonelli, and Tommy) who had a low standing. When bowling became a fixed group activity, the Nortons' team evolved along different lines. Danny joined the Saturday night crowd and rapidly made a place for himself. He performed very well and picked Doc as his favorite opponent. There was a good-natured rivalry between them. In individual competition Danny usually won, although his average in the group matches was no better than that of Doc. After the Community Club match, when Doc selected a team to represent the Nortons against other corner gangs and clubs, he chose Danny, Long John, and himself leaving two vacancies on a five-man team. At this time, Mike, who had never been a good bowler, was just beginning to bowl regularly and had not established his reputation. Significantly enough, the vacancies were not filled from the ranks of the clique. On Saturday nights the boys had been bowling with Chris Teludo, Nutsy's older cousin, and Mark Ciampa, a man who associated with them only at the bowling alleys. Both men were popular and were first-class bowlers. They were chosen by Doc, with the agreement of Danny and Long John, to bowl for the Nortons. It was only when a member of the regular team was absent that one of the followers in the clique was called in, and on such occasions he never distinguished himself.

The followers were not content with being substitutes. They claimed that they had not been given an opportunity to prove their ability. One Saturday night in the late winter, Mike organized an intra-clique match. His team was made up of Chris Teludo, Doc, Long John, himself, and me. Danny was sick at the time, and I was put in to substitute for him. Frank, Alec, Joe, Lou, and Tommy made up the other team. Interest in this match was more intense than in the ordinary "choose-up" matches, but the followers bowled poorly and never had a chance.

After this one encounter the followers were recognized as the second team and never again challenged the team.

On his athletic ability alone, Frank should have been an excellent bowler. His ball-playing had won him positions on semi-professional teams and a promise – though unfulfilled – of a job on a minor-league team. And it was not lack of practice that held him back, for, along with Alec and Joe Dodge, he bowled more frequently than Doc, Danny, or Mike. During the winter Frank occupied a particularly subordinate position in the group. He spent his time with Alec in the pastry shop owned by Alec's uncle, and, since he had little employment throughout the winter, he became dependent upon Alec for a large part of the expenses of his participation in group activities. Frank fell to the bottom of the group. His financial dependence preyed upon his mind. While he sometimes bowled well, he was never a serious threat to break into the first team.

Some events of the early summer cast additional light upon Frank's position. Mike organized a baseball team of some of the Nortons to play against a younger group of Norton Street corner boys. On the basis of his record, Frank was considered the best player on either team, yet he made a miserable showing. He said to me, "I can't seem to play ball when I'm playing with fellows I know, like that bunch. I do much better when I'm playing for the Stanley A.C. against some team in Dexter, Westland, or out of town." Accustomed to filling an inferior position, Frank was unable to star even in his favorite sport when he was competing against members of his own group.

One evening I heard Alec boasting to Long John that the way he was bowling he could take on every man on the first team and

Seating the Group for Effectiveness and Satisfaction

W. E. Vinacke studied the effects of seating arrangements on group effectiveness and satisfaction. He used four types of seating arrangements involving groups of five people: circle, chain, "Y", and wheel.

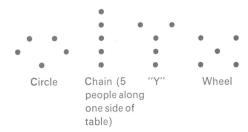

Circle   Chain (5 people along one side of table)   "Y"   Wheel

In the experiment, the groups were required to put several bits of information together to solve a problem.

It was found that the "wheel" was most efficient in problem-solving and produced the least number of errors. The "Y" came next, followed by the "chain" and the "circle". The "chain" was the most unpredictable of the formations.

In terms of enjoyment and satisfaction with the activity, it was found that the members of the "circle" reported the most enjoyment and the members of the "wheel" the least enjoyment. But the members of the "circle" liked their group less than did the others.

The group members were more inclined to see one of their members as the leader in the "wheel" and least likely in the "circle". Remember no leaders were established at the start of the activity. The more remote a group member was from the centre of group activity, the less likely he was to be satisfied. This was particularly true for those at the bottom end of the "Y" and on either end of the "chain".

On the basis of this study and the work of other researchers in this field, it appears that if you want a specific job to be done, a "wheel" set-up is most effective, with a leader and a division of labour. If group involvement and personal satisfaction is more important to you, then the "circle" set-up is most effective.

W. E. Vinacke
Foundations of Psychology

The Committee as a Group

Unlike groups that are established to meet the needs of individuals, committees are usually established to meet the needs of organizations. Churches, businesses, clubs, and government all use committees for such purposes as collecting information, making recommendations, and doing certain jobs. There are situations where a committee would be appropriate for action, and other situations where a committee would be completely inappropriate. Some advantages and disadvantages of committee activities are listed below.

Advantages

1) A group of people bring a great deal more experience and judgement to a problem than can a single individual. The group can bring together more possibilities and evaluate these from a broad range of experience.

2) A committee allows different groups to be represented in decision-making. It is easy to neglect certain points of view when something is being done, and the committee provides an opportunity for the involvement of major interests.

3) A committee makes it possible for information to be communicated to people who do not usually meet each other on a day-to-day basis. Two-way conversations are often possible in committees when they would not be possible otherwise.

4) Jobs that require the working together of different groups can be coordinated through a committee. Each member of the committee is knowledgeable about certain activities not well known to other group members. Problems can be anticipated better.

5) Since committees involve more people in decision-making, the individuals involved are more highly motivated to work harder. Effective organizations usually involve as many people as possible in their decision-making activities.

lick them all. Long John dismissed the challenge with these words, "You think you could beat us, but, under pressure, you die!"

Alec objected ·vehemently, yet he recognized the prevailing opinion of his bowling. He made the highest single score of the season, and he frequently excelled during the week when he bowled with Frank, Long John, Joe Dodge, and me, but on Saturday nights, when the group was assembled, his performance was quite different. Shortly after this conversation Alec had several chances to prove himself, but each time it was "an off night", and he failed.

Carl, Joe, Lou, and Fred were never good enough to gain any recognition. Tommy was recognized as a first-class bowler, but he did most of his bowling with a younger group.

One of the best guides to the bowling standing of the members was furnished by a match held toward the end of the season. Doc had an idea that we should climax the season with an individual competition among the members of the clique. He persuaded the owners of the alleys to contribute ten dollars in prize money to be divided among the three highest scorers. It was decided that only those who had bowled regularly should be eligible, and on this basis Lou, Fred, and Tommy were eliminated.

Interest in this contest ran high. The probable performances of the various bowlers were widely discussed. Doc, Danny, and Long John each listed his predictions. They were unanimous in conceding the first five places to themselves, Mark Ciampa, and Chris Teludo, although they differed in predicting the order among the first five. The next two positions were generally conceded to Mike and to me. All the ratings gave Joe Dodge last position, and Alec, Frank, and Carl were ranked close to the bottom.

The followers made no such lists, but Alec let it be known that he intended to show the boys something. Joe Dodge was annoyed to discover that he was the unanimous choice to finish last and argued that he was going to win.

When Chris Teludo did not appear for the match, the field was narrowed to ten. After the first four boxes, Alec was leading by several pins. He turned to Doc and said, "I'm out to get you boys tonight." But then he began to miss, and, as mistake followed mistake, he stopped trying. Between turns, he went out for drinks, so that he became flushed and unsteady on his feet. He threw the ball carelessly, pretending that he was not interested in the competition. His collapse was sudden and complete; in the space of a few boxes he dropped from first to last place.

The bowlers finished in the following order:

1. Whyte	6. Joe
2. Danny	7. Mark
3. Doc	8. Carl
4. Long John	9. Frank
5. Mike	10. Alec

There were only two upsets in the contest, according to the prediction made by Doc, Danny, and Long John: Mark bowled very poorly and I won. However, it is important to note that neither Mark nor I fitted neatly into either part of the clique. Mark associated with the boys only at the bowling alleys and had no recognized status with the group. Although I was on good terms with all the boys, I was closer to the leaders than to the followers, since Doc was my particular friend. If Mark and I are left out of consideration, the performances were almost exactly what the leaders expected and the followers feared they would be. Danny, Doc, Long John, and Mike were bunched together at the top. Joe Dodge did better than was expected of him, but even he could not break through the solid ranks of the leadership.

Several days later Doc and Long John discussed the match with me.

Long John: I only wanted to be sure that Alec or Joe Dodge didn't win. That wouldn't have been right.

Doc: That's right. We didn't want to make it tough for you, because we all liked you, and the other fellows did too. If somebody had tried to make it tough for you, we would have protected you. . . . If Joe Dodge or Alec had been out in front, it would have been different. We would have talked them out of it. We would have made plenty of noise. We would have been really vicious. . . .

I asked Doc what would have happened if Alec or Joe had won.

Doc: They wouldn't have known how to take it. That's why we were out to beat them. If they had won, there would have been a lot of noise. Plenty of arguments. We would have called it lucky – things like that. We would have tried to get them in another match and then ruin them. We would have to put them in their place.

Every corner boy expects to be heckled as he bowls, but the heckling can take various forms. While I had moved ahead as early as the end of the second string, I was subjected only to good-natured kidding. The leaders watched me with mingled surprise and amusement; in a very real sense, I was permitted to win.

Even so, my victory required certain adjustments. I was hailed jocularly as "the Champ" or even as "the Cheese Champ". Rather than accept this designation, I pressed my claim for recognition. Doc arranged to have me bowl a match against Long John. If I won, I should have the right to challenge Doc or Danny. The four of us went to the alleys together. Urged on by Doc and Danny, Long John won a decisive victory. I made no further challenge.

Alec was only temporarily crushed by his defeat. For a few days he was not seen on the corner, but then he returned and sought to re-establish himself. When the boys went bowling, he challenged Long John to an individual match and defeated him. Alec began to talk once more. Again he challenged Long John to a match, and again he defeated him. When bowling was resumed in the fall, Long John became Alec's favorite opponent, and for some time Alec nearly always came out ahead. He gloated. Long John explained: "He seems to have the Indian sign on me." And that is the way these incidents were interpreted by others – simply as a queer quirk of the game.

Disadvantages

1) Committee work usually takes a great deal of time and time tends to be valuable in most organizations. Since some meetings are wasteful of time, there is the feeling that the time could have been used more productively.

2) It is in the nature of committees to come to decision points with members taking opposing views. This lack of decisiveness is not only time-consuming, but also it inevitably leads to compromise.

3) Compromising is a skill one learns very quickly in committee work. This can result in decisions that are really acceptable to none of the members. It often means that a decision is made that is least disagreeable to most of the committee members.

4) It is often difficult to determine where the responsibility lies with a committee. If the activities of a committee are unsuccessful, it is hard to pinpoint the factors that led to the problem.

People use committees in different ways. In some cases, the disadvantages are used as advantages. Some individuals who wish to delay a decision on an important issue use a committee for this purpose. And if one wishes to hide the responsibility for certain decisions, it is possible to bury the decisions in the activities of a committee.

Disasters

The response of people to a peacetime disaster, such as a tornado or a flood or a large explosion, typically takes the following form:

(a) People who have previously experienced a disaster tend to respond appropriately to an advance warning; people who have not had such experience tend to respond to the warning by seeking other cues that allow them, in effect, to disregard the warning. Just as there is a tendency to underplay the likelihood of the event's occurring at all, so there is a tendency to underestimate its destructiveness afterwards.

Many people tend to deny or disbelieve information that danger is near at hand. They seize on any vagueness, ambiguity, or incompatibility in the warning messages enabling them to interpret the situation optimistically. They search for more information that will confirm, deny, or clarify the warning message, and often they continue to interpret signs of danger as signs of familiar, normal events until it is too late to take effective precautions.

(b) There is very little panic during and immediately after the disaster.

The notion that people typically "panic", become "hysterical", or "go to pieces" in the presence of danger is not supported by disaster research findings. . . . Although some cases of individual or small-group panic have occurred in disasters, its frequency and significance in disaster have been grossly exaggerated. It is a rare response rather than a typical one.

Usually, there is much more traffic *to* the scene of disaster than *from* it.

(c) An informal but effective and highly solidary social organization arises soon after the disaster to deal with the consequences, even in isolated communities, and the leadership is more likely to come from those with most stake in the community – heads of families, for instance, rather than single men. At this time the normal social distinctions are sharply lessened, but gradually reappear with the passage of time. Only later do conflicts arise over alleged inequities in handling the consequences.

The widespread sharing of danger, loss, and deprivation produces an intimate, primary group solidarity among the survivors, which overcomes social isolation and provides a channel for intimate communication and expression and a major source of physical and emotional support and reassurance. . . . The social disorganization that occurs in disaster is essentially a social disorganization of secondary group life. . . . Except momentarily, it does not disorganize primary-group life. On the contrary, this is

It is significant that, in making his challenge, Alec selected Long John instead of Doc, Danny, or Mike. It was not that Long John's bowling ability was uncertain. His average was about the same as that of Doc or Danny and better than that of Mike. As a member of the top group but not a leader in his own right, it was his social position that was vulnerable. . . .

Riots

Kurt Lang and Gladys Engel Lang

(When people are in a crowd, they can often express feelings that they are unable to show when they are in a small group. They tend to use the crowd as a shield: the expression of their personal feelings can be swallowed up in the overall activity of the crowd. It has been said that crowds take on the characteristics of a single person and become predictable on this basis, but there is very little evidence to support this point of view.

Crowds provide an opportunity for individuals to express some of their real feelings. Sometimes these feelings become enormously exaggerated because they are shared and reinforced by other members of the crowd. It is this type of pattern that leads to uncontrollable riots. The following examples of riot behaviour have been taken from the book Collective Dynamics *by Kurt and Gladys Lang. The examples clearly show how the crowd situation makes it possible for individuals to give vent to anger and hostility in a way that they would not find possible under normal circumstances.)*

The Rome Lynching

This riot grew out of the trial of Pietro Caruso, Rome's police chief during the final months of the German occupation. He was the first Italian accused of collaboration to be brought before the tribunal for punishment of Fascist crimes. A major charge against him was that he had provided 50 of the 320 hostages whom the Nazis executed at the Ardeatine caves. Relatives of the victims of that atrocity were invited to be spectators at the trial, which was to be held starting September 18, 1944, at the Palazzo di Justizia facing the Tiber River at the foot of the Umberto Bridge.

Thousands of people gathered in front of the palace from the early morning hours on. The police cordons were quickly broken by the mob which pressed on, howling, to the entrance. The big hall on the first floor was already jammed with authorized spectators and newspapermen. At 9:30 A.M., just as the presiding judge was about to enter the courtroom, the mob rioted into it, overturned tables, and surged toward the judges and correspondents. All semblance of order disappeared.

Everybody, including the *carabinieri* (the state police), sought shelter wherever it could be found. Caruso had not yet been brought up from the cellar where he was hidden. The mob, believing him to be in the anteroom, clamored for his appearance.

Pollock, British police chief for the American Military Government, and Mario Berlinguer, the Italian official in charge of the prosecution of Fascist crimes, both tried to calm the crowd.

After a half-hour of exhortation from these two officials, the fury of the crowd seemed to abate somewhat. An announcement was made that the trial would be postponed. The crowd might have dispersed then if two women had not pointed out Donato Carretta among the witnesses. Carretta had been the vice-director of the prison in which the hostages were held prior to their execution. He had been one of Caruso's right-hand men, but he was scheduled to be a major prosecution witness. Some young men grabbed and hit him. He was dragged and kicked downstairs into the main entrance hall of the palace. There a few *carabinieri* made a halfhearted attempt to usher Carretta out and away from his attackers. Near the entrance a young man jumped him while his back was turned, knocking him down. Others immediately started kicking and beating him. Carretta got up and ran but was trapped at the end of the courtyard. A lieutenant in the *carabinieri* made two attempts to have Carretta driven away in a car. Both drivers, one American and one British, refused. Herbert Matthews, reporting the incident, states: "When I bitterly kept telling the crowd around me that this was worse than fascism and that Italy would get a black name throughout the world – some shamefacedly admitted this was bad."

By this time Carretta was unconscious. For a while the crowd stood around the body on the street. One young girl – well-dressed and looking like a student, who had been one of the ring-leaders – kept kicking Carretta. Finally someone shouted, "Throw him into the Tiber!" The limp body was dragged, not lifted, across the wide street to the bridge, then heaved into the water some thirty feet below. The shock of cold water apparently revived Carretta, who managed to crawl to the bank and hang on, half in the water just below the bridge. Some of the mob got a rowboat, went up to him and pushed him back into the water. Whenever he tried to make the bank again, they stopped him with their oars.

Hundreds and then thousands of persons crowded the embankments and the Sant' Angelo Bridge, some hundreds of feet away. There were many women. Many of the men as well as the women were middle-class or lower middle-class. "This was no mob of hooligans," said Matthews. Some were horrified. When one woman hysterically protested, she had to be rushed away lest the crowd mob her. Many laughed gleefully as they watched.

Carretta died as he floated under the Sant' Angelo Bridge. Some howling men dragged the body out of the water and along the ground right to the near-by Regina Coeli prison. There they strung up the body. By this time the crowd had swelled to an estimated seven thousand. They believed Caruso was inside, but the prison police managed to keep the doors closed and took down Carretta's body. Then the crowd dispersed without any further violence.

It is ironic to note that a rumor quickly spread that Caruso had been killed; many people in the crowd probably did not know who was the actual victim of their lynching.

strengthened, and this in turn constitutes the nucleus out of which the society can once again reconstitute itself and develop a new complexity of organization.

(d) The first reaction is typically concern for the safety of one's family and other intimates and then for the larger community – even on the part of those with community responsibilities, who often feel caught in this cross-pressured situation. In general, there is less feeling of self-interest and more concern for the community than exists in normal times.

The net result of most disasters is a dramatic increase in social solidarity among the affected populace during the emergency and immediate post-emergency periods. The sharing of a common threat to survival and the common suffering engendered by the disaster tend to produce a breakdown of social distinctions and a great outpouring of love, generosity, and altruism. During the first days and weeks following a major community-wide disaster, people tend to act toward one another spontaneously, sympathetically, and sentimentally, on the basis of common human needs, rather than in terms of pre-disaster differences in social and economic status.

(e) Most people experiencing a severe disaster soon suffer some kind of emotional or physical upset – nausea, diarrhea, "nerves", or the like – that continues to some degree for days or even weeks. But such transitory reactions do not incapacitate most of the sufferers from responding realistically to the event and its aftermath; moreover, they rarely arrive at chronic states of severe mental disturbance.

(f) The farther people are from the scene of disaster, the less accurate their information about it and the less their concern for the victims.

(g) For the victims themselves, the disaster remains for years a major event in their lives.

A re-study of a midwestern river town conducted more than 15 years after a severe flood in 1937 showed that the disaster was still a salient fact in the life of the community. People tended to date events in terms of the disaster; their memories of the happenings in the flood remained vivid; and they still identified many of their fellow inhabitants in terms of the kind of social role (rescue worker, helper, etc.) that they played in the disaster.

The continuing public recognition of the disaster as an important juncture in human experience also provides a form of social absolution: people are permitted to make a clean break with the past and take a fresh start in reorganizing their lives.

Below is a list of conclusions reached by other researchers on the subject of disasters:

Mass panic is a phenomenon that occurs rarely and only under certain circumstances. . . . Few actual cases of looting can be discovered. . . . Stricken populations are not a "dazed, helpless mass", but help themselves and perform rescue and welfare tasks. . . . There are only isolated examples of breakdown of moral codes. (Charles E. Fritz, "Disaster", in Robert K. Merton and Robert A. Nisbet (eds.), *Contemporary Social Problems*.)

The social group organization does not break down but is strengthened. . . . There is no significant increase in psychoses and psychoneuroses. (National Research Council, "A Brief Review of Salient Specific Findings on Morale and Human Behavior Under Disaster Conditions", unpublished memorandum.)

Emotional after-effects are widespread but relatively mild and transitory. . . . Morale and optimism soon rebound and are abnormally high in some respects. . . . The big problem of crowd control is not flight of the victims from the disaster area, but a convergence of people to the disaster area from the outside.

The Shanghai Riot

The long lasting Shanghai riot began in the early morning of November 30, 1946, when a number of relatives of street vendors who had been arrested appeared at the police station with food parcels for the prisoners. Altogether six hundred vendors had been picked up for continuing to operate in the Lonza and Whangpoo districts of Shanghai in violation of the recent police decrees. Many of these vendors were refugees driven out of their native villages or off their farms, either by unsatisfactory conditions or by fear of conscription. According to some reports, the police had merely asked relatives to line up in orderly fashion, but some of them, wearied of their long wait, had begun to protest and to mill around the police desk.

About 8:00 A.M. a crowd, composed of relatives of the prisoners, staged a presumably spontaneous demonstration outside the police station. About five or six hundred people were present. A rumor started that six of the street hawkers had died in the prison as a result of beatings and brutal treatment. All morning the crowd milled around the police station. Shortly before noon the crowd grew more clamorous. Bricks, stones, and bottles were heaved at the police. The police responded by arresting several "agitators" in the crowd, whom they pulled, one by one, into the station, beating them as they were being dragged. One young man in an overcoat grabbed a policeman's lapel and took down his number after he had beaten one person. This young man, too, was dragged into the station. A *China Press* reporter followed this man into the building but was ordered out.

By this time the crowd had grown to several thousand. At 2:00 P.M. a fire hose played streams of water against the crowd. The crowd backed away slowly, never ceasing to yell. Every time the water was turned off, the angry crowd closed in upon the police station. This went on for two hours. Once the crowd wrested the nozzle from the firemen and played the water on the policemen, who succeeded in dispersing them.

At 4:45 P.M. three city councilors arrived. One of them told the police not to beat a man while dragging him into the police station. At 5:20 P.M. K. C. Wu, then mayor of Shanghai, entered the police station amidst sporadic shouts. Members of the crowd entered several near-by buildings. The crowd was finally dispersed by machine-gun fire followed by a police charge, with bayonets and clubs, against the crowd.

Thereafter the crowd began its rampage of Shanghai. It filled the streets, wrecked store windows along the Nanking road, insisting that shops close in sympathy with the rioters. One printing shop was burned to the ground. A subsequent report by the mayor alleged that the demonstrators sent children to ask shopowners to close, and that these children were each rewarded with five-thousand Chinese dollars.

A streetcar was overturned. Automobiles were wrecked. Another crowd formed around the Lonza police station. The wrath of the crowd was not turned against foreigners, but some said they had been struck in the face by ruffians who held up their cars. Some of these attackers were said to have shouted, "Down with

Nanking! Chou En-Lai (Chinese Communist leader) is right!"

That evening Wu, in a broadcast, announced the release of all vendors. Rioting nevertheless continued until early morning. The next day rioting was less spontaneous and was organized at particular points. Shops were closed when riot leaders threatened to smash them if they reopened. The police cordoned off the downtown areas. In the afternoon three trucks with demonstrators tried to enter the race course to hold a meeting. This establishment, traditionally closed to Chinese, was guarded by United States military personnel who turned back the trucks.

The rioting seems finally to have stopped after Wu spoke on the radio again that evening. He said nobody had been killed during the riots and that all vendors had been released. A delegation of vendors had come to him with a written declaration disclaiming responsibility for the riot. In all, 221 persons had been arrested. Finally, he said he was ordering the police to shoot to kill anyone creating disturbances or carrying arms without authority.

The Montreal Hockey Riot

This riot really began when Clarence Campbell, president of the National Hockey League, after a full hearing, announced the suspension of French-Canadian hockey hero Richard, "The Rocket", for the remainder of the hockey season. The reason: he had engaged in violence against both an opposing player and an official who tried to restrain him.

Canadians take their hockey seriously, and the Montreal club was then leading second-place Detroit by only two points. Quite naturally feelings ran high because Richard, the star player on whom the Montreal Canadiens depended, was the cherished idol of all the Montreal fans. Few voices, either English or French Canadian, publicly supported a decision made by an English-Canadian against the player whose suspension more than ever made him the champion of French Canada.

Before noon, partisans with placards hailing Richard and condemning Campbell appeared in front of the Forum, where the Canadiens played. The numbers swelled throughout the afternoon and they obviously received general support. While newspapers and radio stations headlined every new development, the crucial question soon boiled down to this: would Campbell dare to make a public appearance at the game? One Montreal paper reported an attempt to buy up a block of seats near Campbell to be occupied by a special delegation of hecklers. A local radio station expecting trouble, sent a mobile sound unit to the scene.

Two hours before the game was to start, the demonstration was in full swing. About this time, youngsters wearing black motor cycle jackets began to join in. They were allegedly brought in by trucks. Besides the demonstrators, estimated at about six hundred, thousands were outside the Forum seeking admission to the game. As the Forum loudspeaker announced that there were no more seats, one of the demonstrators shouted, "We don't want seats. We want Campbell," a cry that was enthusiastically taken up.

Campbell, escorted by a police inspector, reached his seat inside the Forum just as Detroit scored a second goal against Montreal.

Behaviour in Disasters

In Bootle, England (population 55,000) people were bombed every night for a week during World War II. At the end of this time, only 10 per cent of the houses had escaped serious damage. In spite of the bombing, one-quarter of the population remained asleep in their homes during the raids. In London, only 37 per cent of the mothers and children who could leave the city actually did leave it during the bombing crisis. And even when the bombing was at its heaviest, people were drifting back into the city as fast as others were being moved out.

This was also found to be true in Japan and Germany when those countries were being heavily bombed during World War II. It appears that human beings have a very strong tendency to continue doing what they have been doing in the past rather than start up new activities. In Port Jarvis, New York, during a flood crisis, it was reported that most of the inhabitants fled when they heard that a dam had broken. In fact, only about one-quarter of the inhabitants left. Neither was there any evidence of great panic among those who did leave. People tended to remain with their own families and many lent a helping hand to other groups of people.

Surprisingly, after a disaster, people usually work out their own problems. Recently, a heavy wind storm in Sudbury, Ontario, caused deaths and considerable damage to homes in the area. Many families were left homeless. Naturally, the Red Cross and other public authorities attempted to house the homeless. But for the most part, friends, neighbours, and other family members took in the homeless. Friendship and family ties do not usually weaken during disaster periods. Disaster provides a rare opportunity for people to show the importance of family and friends.

Panic Behaviour

The conditions that produce panic behaviour in people can be viewed as a series of building blocks, with each one adding to the problem. Panic can be defined as "a group of persons fleeing from something as a result of a hysterical belief". The following five steps can be seen as the building blocks of panic behaviour.

1) *The situation* must be suitable for panic behaviour – such as an impending flood or stock market disaster. The escape routes must be few in number and they must not be completely open nor completely closed. There must be other people in the same situation so that the panicky reactions can be shared.

2) *Strain* is involved in the second step. There must be a feeling that something is about to happen almost immediately. People must be unsure about the outcome of the situation. The strain occurs in part because the individuals feel powerless to do anything. Interestingly, those individuals who are most likely to panic tend to be churchgoers, women, those with low status, and the emotionally or physically ill.

3) *Anxiety* – a general feeling of tenseness – is a necessary ingredient. The expectation that something is about to happen makes exaggeration possible.

4) *A specific threat* – in the form of something happening that transforms vague anxiety into fear – is the next step. Suspicions are confirmed, perhaps by word that the water is rising rapidly and the river is threatening to overflow, or that a once-secure stock has faded badly on the stock market. For a group of politicians who fear an assassination attempt, the backfire of a nearby car could change their fear into panic. Sometimes the incidents that trigger panic behaviour are quite unimportant in themselves.

5) *Preparation for flight* – someone starts to run and others join in – is a phase that consists of two steps. First, the individuals respond to the event (the flood warning, the stock dropping, the backfire of a car). Then there is the emotional response when others are seen panicking. Fear begins to feed and grow on the fear of others. Even after the first flight, there are usually secondary panic behaviours.

He was immediately recognized and greeted with catcalling. Campbell, rather than the game, became the focus of attention.

Spectators had apparently come prepared. In addition to programs, bottles, and rubber boots, Campbell was showered with eggs, tomatoes, and all sorts of vegetables. Every time Detroit scored a goal – they scored two more during the first period – the crowd vented its anger on him.

The police, especially detailed on this night to protect Campbell, did little to interfere with the crowd. A young man who stepped up to Campbell and struck him was allowed to get away. Another, who squashed a couple of tomatoes against his shirt front, was arrested only after Campbell kept on urging the police to take action. The three hundred or so ushers, policemen, firemen, etc., whose duty it was to maintain order in the Forum were hardly in evidence.

At 9:11 P.M., after the end of the first period, the crowd began to close in on the N.H.L. official. They surrounded his box, and there was no one to restrain them.

The explosion of a tear-gas bomb by a person never identified saved Campbell at that critical moment. People did not know what had happened. They thought it was fire or that the ammonia pipes under the ice had sprung a leak. Panic was prevented only by the police and firemen, who now intervened decisively, keeping all doors open. Fans were turned on to disperse the fumes. In the confusion Campbell and his party escaped into the first-aid center, not far from where he had his seat. The fire department stopped the game, and Campbell ruled it forfeit to Detroit.

Until the frightened and excited fans poured out, the crowd outside had been neither destructive nor in any way out of control. But as soon as their numbers swelled, the mood changed entirely. Demonstrators hurled overshoes, chunks of brick, and whatever ammunition they could find at the Forum. Doors were torn off their hinges. Several people were injured.

The police were reluctant to apply force because of the number of women and children in the crowd. Consequently the corps of rioters, after discharging their ammunition, could always find safety in the crowd.

By 11:00 P.M. the crowd was estimated at more than ten thousand. They first besieged the stadium, but soon began to attack the ground-floor stores of the Forum. Rioters heaved rocks through windows and looted the stores, taking mostly small objects not easily traceable. Along Montreal's main shopping street, some fifty stores were damaged and looted. By the end of the riot there were two hundred and fifty police, including twenty-five radio patrol cars, on the scene. Five hundred policemen attending an employees' association meeting two miles away were never called. The reason, as the Montreal police chief explained later: "More police would only have provoked the crowd."

All the while, Montrealers tuned in to CKVL enjoyed on-the-spot radio coverage. Some time after midnight the radio stations were prevailed upon to cease broadcasting the trouble. By 1:00 A.M. police, forming a solid chain, gradually drove the crowd down St. Catherine Street. The rioting and disorder finally halted about

3:00 A.M. From all evidence, most of the troublemakers were not hockey fans. There were many teen-agers, who, according to one witness, were being egged on by older people.

In his article, *Images of Withdrawal Behaviour in Disasters: Some Basic Misconceptions*, Enrico Quarantelli makes three important points:

1) The idea that many people run away from disaster in panic is incorrect. Some do not want to leave at all while others leave only because of their concern to find family or friends.

2) After the initial shock of the disaster, most people begin rescue and recovery operations without waiting for directions from officials.

3) The idea that rescue operations always have to be organized and controlled by officials is not the case. In fact, in most cases, such operations are too large for official agencies. If it was not for the personal responses of average citizens, disasters could be far greater.

Resources for Part 3

Banton, M. 1965. *Roles.* London, England: Tavistock Publications.

Bensman, J. 1967. *Dollars and Sense.* New York: The Macmillan Co.

Blishen, B. et al. 1968. *Canadian Society: Sociological Perspectives.* Toronto: The Macmillan Co. of Canada Ltd.

Bordua, D. J. (ed.). 1967. *The Police.* New York: John Wiley & Sons, Inc.

Clark, S. D. 1962. *The Developing Canadian Community.* Toronto: University of Toronto Press.

Coleman, J. 1961. *The Adolescent Society.* New York: The Macmillan Co. (Free Press). Don Mills, Ontario: Collier-Macmillan.

Klausner, S. Z. (ed.). 1968. *Why Man Takes Chances.* New York: Doubleday Anchor Book.

McCreary, A., Szasz, J. and G. 1968. *Adolescents in Society.* Toronto: McClelland & Stewart Ltd.

MacDonald, J. 1962. *Understanding Yourself and Your Society.* Toronto: The Macmillan Co. of Canada Ltd.

Mann, W. E. (ed.). 1968. *Canada: A Sociological Profile.* Toronto: Copp Clark.

Porter, J. 1965. *The Vertical Mosaic.* Toronto: University of Toronto Press.

Tiger, L. 1969. *Men in Groups.* New York: Random House.

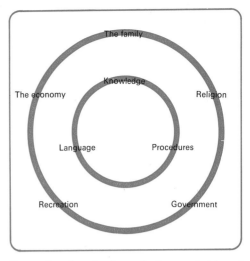

Categories of society's needs (larger circle) and the basics of culture (smaller circle)
Our social institutions are derived from inter-relationships among these factors

Part 4

The institutions of man

An institution meets one or more of the basic needs of a larger society. Each institution has its own values, roles, and regulations. Institutions shape our behaviours into common patterns, and through them we learn to know what is expected of us and how to channel others into appropriate behaviours.

The family can be seen as an institution that has, among its other purposes, the responsibilities of raising children, developing in them the beliefs and knowledge required by our society, and meeting their emotional needs. All families in Canada do not perform their functions in exactly the same way, but there are many common elements that make the Canadian family a basic social institution. Parents typically live together with their children until their children move into the work world; they are held legally responsible for their children's schooling and behaviour, and in general, remain emotionally linked to them throughout life.

Other institutions are responsible for the meeting of other kinds of needs for our society. The economy as an institution is responsible for the production and distribution of goods. The institution of law is responsible for the maintenance of order within the group. The political system is responsible for law-making and for the maintenance and continued development of our society at the municipal, provincial, and national levels. Education as an institution is responsible for the maintenance of our traditions and the preparation of children for adult life.

Social institutions are relatively stable but, over time, many changes have taken place. The school, for example, has gradually assumed more responsibility than the family for teaching children and equipping the younger generation to enter an increasingly complex society, whereas in the past (and in simple societies even today) most education took place in the home, administered by the family and other kin. However, our specialized age requires special knowledge and specialized training centres, schools, universities, and community colleges, to perform the complex educational task.

All societies have developed means of establishing rules of conduct for their members. In a tribal society, taboos and social pressure act as a control mechanism. In a complex society, political institutions have been created to control behaviour for what the majority of society agrees is the common good.

The various social institutions in our society are related to each other, and in some cases, their responsibilities overlap. But, unlike primitive societies where the family, the government, and the economy are so interwoven that it is hard to know where one starts and another leaves off, it is very easy for us to analyze our basic institutions.

It is within our social institutions that the order of our society is shaped. In fact, without the ordering of rights and responsibilities that is encouraged within our institutions, our society would be chaotic.

one   The family

On Mother's Day, the family pays homage to motherhood. A number of kind things are said and done. On Father's Day, a more recent commercially inspired event, the same sort of thing happens, and "good old" Dad is remembered. Whether the occasion is Christmas, Thanksgiving, or other holidays, the family gathers together to celebrate the event. At these times the special significance of the family as an institution is most obvious. From man's earliest beginnings, the family has been a necessary social institution. Whereas most animals can survive on their own, after a very few days or weeks, the offspring of man requires a lengthy period of special care. The stages through which an infant grows to childhood and then to adulthood involves a lengthy period of living and learning. The responsibility for the process has long been a family function.

It is inside the family circle that children first learn what is good or bad, how to behave, and the values and moral standards of the family and community. In less complex societies than ours the family performs a larger number of tasks. A young man of the Mundugamor people of New Guinea learns to hunt and to be a warrior – skills he learns from his family. In Samoa, a young girl looks after younger children in anticipation of the time when she will be a mother with her own family (although compulsory education is changing this pattern). All over the world, the family teaches customs and basic skills, provides models of behaviour, and passes on traditions and family norms from the societal ancestry. In short, the family socializes the younger generation who will, in their turn, pass on the legacy to the next generation. Even amid the stresses and strains present in our society, the family carries on its basic sustaining role. In the following selection, the life cycle of the modern Canadian family is traced, and changes in decision-making processes are noted.

The family and decision-making

Benjamin Schlesinger

In order to find out how decisions are made by the families of today, the author undertook a study of 120 couples. A long questionnaire was given to the husband and wife of each couple, and they were asked to fill them out separately. Interviews and some tape recordings supplemented the information obtained from the questionnaires.

The characteristics of the couples in the study were that all of them lived in urban areas, had been married only once, were born on this continent, and had attended college (not necessarily graduated). An effort was made to obtain couples of different age ranges, so that we could compare how decision-making patterns differ at various stages of married life. This was done by using the concept of the *family life cycle*.

The Family Life Cycle

The family life cycle begins with the marriage. The family develops as the husband and wife assume the traditional roles as father and mother with the coming of the first child. As successive

> The family is a social group characterized by common residence, economic cooperation, and reproduction. It includes adults of both sexes, at least two of whom maintain a socially approved sexual relationship, and one or more children, own or adopted. . . . Marriage defines the manner of establishing and terminating such a relationship, the normative behaviour and reciprocal obligations within it, and the locally accepted restrictions upon its personnel. . . .
>
> George Peter Murdock
> *Social Structure*

children are born, the family enlarges its roles, to bring in the additional children in the family group. Each additional member of the family brings a significant reorganization of family living.

As the children grow older, their parents are also growing older, changing in their needs and desires, their hopes and expectations, as well as their responses to the demands and pressures of growing children. At the same time, the children are constantly changing in their relationships to their parents, brothers and sisters, and other relatives.

The big, bustling years when the family life runs at a hectic pace eventually gives way to the long, slow-moving years of the "empty nest", when the middle-aged parents face the later half of their marriage as a pair, similar to the beginning of the family life cycle.

Each family grows through the years in its own particular way. On the other hand, all families will pass through the stages of the family life cycle. *Table A* shows the six stages of the family life cycle used in the study.

In each of the stages of the family life cycle, couples were questioned about their decision-making pattern, and then the six groups were compared to find the changes at different levels of married life.

What did we find? We will discuss each stage of the family cycle.

Stage I: Beginning families. It is in this stage, where one finds most joint decision-making, the highest amount of participation in decision-making discussions, the most satisfaction in the areas of decision-making used in the study, and the largest amount of consultation in decision-making. One can attribute this to the fact that the Beginning family stage is one in which the men and women are using the first two years of their married life as a period of "finding out about each other". There seems to be an unusual amount of emphasis on "considering the person" and of doing things together. It appears that it is in this stage that the couples share most of their decisions, be they very small and unimportant, or large and important. It seems to be important to "agree" with the other spouse, and not to have too many differences.

A 21-year-old newly-wed woman summed up this stage by saying, ". . . we seem to be deciding things together all the time, such as what to buy at the supermarket, the kind of drapes to get for the apartment, what friends to invite, and what kind of a car to purchase. . . . When John comes home from work, we sit down and talk about the day's activities . . . I tell him what happened in my teaching job, and he relates events at his engineering firm. . . . It's fun to do things like this . . . it helps us in our marriage."

In a popular sense this stage can be compared to a boxing bout. At the beginning of a boxing match there is usually the "sparring period", during which the two boxers appear to jab at each other, always very careful not to give away any of their "secret punches". During this sparring they observe each other, and begin to watch their opponent's techniques, and strong and weak points. They move back and forward, trying out various boxing rules and regulations to prepare for the rest of the bout which might last for ten or more rounds.

Table A
Six Stages in the Family Life Cycle

Stage		Age of Oldest Child	No. of Years Married
I	Beginning families	no children	2
II	Child-bearing families	up to 3	2–5
III	Families with pre-school children	3–6	5–10
IV	Families with school children	6–13	10–15
V	Families with teenagers	13–20	15–25
VI	Families as "launching centers"	20–27	25 plus

A comparison of methods of control used by parents in bringing up delinquent and non-delinquent boys

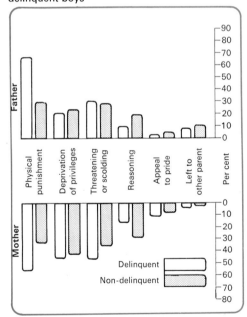

The above figure, taken from *Unravelling Juvenile Delinquency* by Sheldon and Eleanor Glueck, shows that there is usually more physical punishment in the background of delinquent boys than in that of non-delinquents

The emphasis on doing things jointly, such as decision-making and other life patterns, is strongly evident in this period, although we have had lately a great surge toward the idea of "togetherness" for the whole family life cycle. One can also assume that it is in this period that the spouses begin to discover the other person's patterns of decision-making, patterns of communication, and needs of both psychological and physical nature. There is a lot of catering to the other person. These findings would thus go along with the popular view that the Beginning family period is the most "ideal" stage of married life. However, one can look at it in a different light. The transition of bachelorhood and spinsterhood into matrimony brings with it many adjustments and role changes which have to be worked out in mutual discussion, mutual decision-making, and a general sharing of views. This "discovery" stage is one in which each spouse begins to learn the pattern of life of the other spouse. In this stage, it is possible to assume that the roles in decision-making are solidified and these roles are then kept for the rest of the family life cycle.

Stage II: Child-bearing families. Typically, it is during the second year of marriage that the family shifts into this stage. The marriage relationship is subtly and frequently dramatically changed when the first baby arrives, with its own demands. The new roles of father and mother are added to those of husband and wife. Most of the decisions now focus on the new arrival. One of the decisions is the extra financial costs which have to be met and this may result in the husband taking on extra work to supplement his present income. On the other hand, many couples begin to lower their standard of living, and to shift some of the previous expenses to the day by day costs of the baby.... There is a loss of husband-wife closeness. At night, mother is just "too tired" to go out or entertain as she did before the baby came, and it is quite possible that her fatigue carries over into all areas of the husband and wife relationship.

We found that in our study it appeared that husbands and wives shared child rearing decisions, and also actually shared the baby's care. This defies the traditional pattern of mother being the sole person who looks after the infant, while father brings home the money. A father commented, "I went to pre-natal classes with my wife, and believe it or not, when we brought our baby home, I became an expert in diapering and bathing. At night and on weekends, I help with the baby. It relieves my wife from some of the necessary duties. I must confess I rather enjoy looking after the baby...."

There is nothing feminine about a man helping with the baby, and the often heard statement that "I may hurt the baby, I am so rough" is really not true for most men. It is important in this stage not to fall into the pattern of focusing all the attention on the baby and neglecting the husband-wife relationship, because it may be a beginning of distance between the spouses, which widens as the marriage develops.

The wife has to try and pay attention to her husband, and he in turn has to be aware of the strenuous daily routine which the new

On Bringing Up Children

In his book *Human Society*, Kingsley Davis states that studies, by direct observation, of the mental health and development of children in institutions, hospitals, and foster homes make it plain that, when deprived of maternal care, the child's development is almost always retarded – physically, intellectually, and socially – and that symptoms of physical and mental illness may appear. Such evidence is disquieting, but sceptics may question whether retardation is permanent and whether the symptoms of illness may not easily be overcome. The retrospective and follow-up studies make it clear that such optimism is not always justified and that some children are gravely damaged for life. This is a sombre conclusion that must now be regarded as established.

The father is out of the house all day and therefore can be neither overlord nor companion. With the father absent, radio and television provide the mother with a watery substitute for adult companionship. A young colleague told me recently that his wife leaves the radio on all day merely to hear the sound of a grown-up voice. The continual chatter of little children can be profoundly irritating, even to a naturally affectionate person. As it is now, diapers, dishes, and the state of the baby's bowels absorb the day's quota of energy. There is scarcely any strength left for sharing emotions and experiences with the husband, for which there is often no opportunity until the late hours of the evening.

Barrington Moore
Future of the Family

First-born children, at least in our society, are probably more anxious; more dependent on others, especially in anxious situations; and more inclined to go along with the group than are other children.

B. Berelson and G. Steiner
Human Behavior

The unhappy effects of punishment have run like a dismal thread through our findings. Mothers who punished toilet accidents severely ended up with bedwetting children. Mothers who punished dependency to get rid of it had more dependent children than mothers who did not punish. Mothers who punished aggressive behavior severely had more aggressive children than mothers who punished lightly.... Harsh physical punishment was associated with high childhood aggressiveness and with the development of feeding problems.

Robert R. Sears, Eleanor E. Maccoby,
and Harry Levin
Patterns of Child Rearing

The less the affection, satisfaction of dependence, or warmth the infant and child receives (in other words, the more the reserve, neglect, or rejection), (1) the less developed is his subsequent personality likely to be and the less quickly he matures (in childhood) – i.e., the more he is apathetic, unresponsive, "vegetative", and incapable of independent action; and (2) the less strength of character and sense of self he is likely to have, leading even to the development of a psychopathic personality that feels no responsibility to others.

B. Berelson and G. Steiner
Human Behavior

In general, the unloved child tends to be an unloving adult, with a high degree of self-hatred (i.e. unlovable).

B. Berelson and G. Steiner
Human Behavior

The mechanisms of socialization are of special importance in the family. The child's first rewards and punishments, first image of himself, and first models of behaviour are experienced in the family setting, and all help to develop a "personality base", subject to subsequent influences. The child's reaction to others is partially determined by his previous relationships with parents and siblings. And, as we have observed, personality type is closely related to the socialization process itself.

Bruce Watson and William Tarr
The Social Sciences and American Civilization

mother has to follow. The house cannot always be very neat and tidy, and supper may be late. Mother does not "lie down on the job", but has to meet the immediate needs of the helpless infant. As the baby grows a little older, the couple can resume their social life to a limited degree, by allowing a baby sitter to look after the infant, while they attend a party or a play. A 24-year-old mother states:

> John and I did not go out for three months after our baby was born. We felt cooped up and blamed our baby for keeping us at home. We were tired of watching T.V., and our friends urged us to go out. Finally it got to the point where we had to go out. I cannot tell you what a difference it made to our relationship. It was like "old times". We are planning to do this regularly now.

A new baby does not mean an end to social life, and it is important to have a change in routine.

Stage III: Families with pre-school children. The children are growing up, and more and more time is spent on child rearing. Decisions have to be made. Should we send Bob to nursery school? Should we have another child? Do we need larger quarters? Should we buy a house? This stage is usually illustrated by the family who has a three year-old, and is expecting or have just had their second child. Thus they have to watch the growth of the pre-schooler, while looking after an infant with his own needs. Responsibilities in the home increase, more money is needed, and space is inadequate. The mother may especially become completely absorbed in keeping the house running and looking after the child care. A young mother said:

> It seems as if I go from diapers to picking up Joan's toys, which only a 3-year-old can throw all around. The baby has colic right now, and at night when he wakes up, our 3-year-old also wakes up. My husband comes home from work and expects the house to be clean and neat . . . he does not realize that I have a full-time job on my hands right here at home. I have become a slave to my children. . . .

Husband and wife may be moving slowly away from each other, and each appears to have found different major interests. He has his work, and mother has the children. A husband ruefully remarked, "My wife has been sloppy. She runs all day after the kids and worries needlessly. She uses Dr. Spock as her Bible, and every time there is something wrong with one of our children, she has to find it in his book, and if she does not find it, she immediately bothers our doctor. We used to have so much fun together; all her former charm and 'sexiness' seems to have gone. I feel at times like staying late at work, just so that I do not have to come into the house. . . ."

Again we find a misunderstanding of each other's roles and functions, and there seems to be a loss of communication. Husband and wife do not talk things out, but let things go which may result in bringing them emotionally apart. This misunderstanding of

ach other's role is illustrated by a personal example, when I had
o look after our 2-month-old son for a day. I was exhausted, and
was looking with great anxiety toward the return of my wife, to
ake over the tiring routine which a young infant needs. I feel that
[will never again state that "mothers have it easy, all they do is
stay home and look after kids". If you do not believe me, why not
for a day exchange jobs? Co-operation is one of the pillars of this
stage. Love of husband and wife is another element in keeping
husband-wife relationships on an even keel. Love has been defined
n so many ways, and each couple has its way of showing love. It
encompasses the wide range from caring about each other, to a
normal sexual relationship; from doing things together to celebra-
ion of anniversaries; and from recognizing that marriage is not
only for children, but for the warm and intimate relationship
which can only develop between husband and wife as they grow
together in marriage.

Stage IV: Families with school children. This stage begins with a
feeling of joy and sorrow. A housewife of 35 declares, "It's funny.
[waited anxiously for my children to begin school so that I would
have more time. Now that they have begun school, I miss them,
and am looking for something to keep me occupied. I am planning
to take on some part-time work. I used to be a very good secretary...." It is during this stage the husbands are "moving up the
ladder" in their jobs, and this requires more of their time for the
good of the Company. The slogan "Produce or Perish" is always
in the upper-mind of eager young men. A husband states, "I have
to put in more time at work, so that I will be noticed and promoted. When I get home, it is usually late, and I have work from
the office. I know it is a 'rat race', but what can I do?"

Decisions now center around discipline problems of the children, T.V. watching time, budgeting for vacations, and frequently
a move to another neighbourhood. We found here a beginning of
a division of labour in husband-wife decision-making. The husband appears to make decisions which involve expenditure of
money, such as car purchasing, purchasing of large appliances, and
payment of bills. The wife has moved into the area of household
decisions almost completely, and rarely consults her husband in
this area.

Stage V: Families with teenagers. This is the stage in which the
least satisfaction, the least joint efforts and the least consultation
in decision-making is found. A close look at this stage of the family
cycle will reveal the fact that it is at this time that the men are
usually at the height of their working form, they have usually
reached a certain plateau in the field of business or in their professional careers, and are busy concentrating a lot of their time and
energy on their work. This period is also characterized in our culture by an increase in community activities, and both men and
women are active in various community groups. The teenagers at
the same time live their own lives and are in and out of the home;
they are beginning to make a lot of their own decisions, and are
beginning to feel that their parents are "old fashioned" and can-

As compared with families today, the Canadian
families of 1864 were larger, had more intensive
relations with an extended group of relatives, had
few divorces, placed more emphasis on authority
and obedience, were less likely to act on the
premise of equality of the sexes, had a larger and
more important role for elderly parents. The
family was more often a unit of economic production and a center of religious observance. Births
and deaths were more likely to occur within the
home. Although we have no definite proof, it is
likely that "romantic love" was stressed less and
marital duty more. Both birth-rates and death-
rates were higher than now.

As the family has dropped many of its functions and activities which have been taken over
by industry, government, church, school, and
other agencies, it has become a more *specialized*
social unit. It specializes in the production and
maintenance of human personalities. Our concerns about the family reflect this historical shift.
We expect more from the family in terms of
"happiness" — of affection and sexual adjustment, of mutual understanding, of "good"
personality development in children.

If divorce has increased, so has marriage.
Decade by decade the age at marriage has
dropped and the proportion of married persons
has increased. It does not appear that the importance of the family to individual persons has
decreased. As economic and social functions,
once incorporated in the family, have dropped
away, marriage has become increasingly a matter
of individual choice, and the unit has had to
depend more than in the past upon personal
satisfactions and the individual's private sense
of obligations. The relatively isolated nuclear
family in a mobile and competitive society is
exposed to unusual strains. It is also a focus of
high expectations, both in terms of the ideals of
romantic love and companionship between husband and wife and in terms of standards for
child-rearing.

Benjamin Schlesinger
The Canadian Family: Yesterday and Today

In his book, *The Family*, William J. Goode has stated that the speed of industrialization in countries was directly related to specific family patterns. The following kinds of family changes were observed:

1) Increased freedom in the choice of a marriage partner which meant that marriage bargaining was taken from the hands of parents, marriages with large age-gaps between the partners diminished, and there develops a more consistent idea of the proper age for marriage.

2) Marriages between members of the same kinship group diminish.

3) The dowry or bride price begins to disappear.

4) The divorce rate tends to be high.

5) Where remarriage of divorcees or the widowed was unlikely, it becomes common.

6) The importance of the mother in matters of inheritance decreases.

7) The number of children per family decreases.

Over a long period, the family in Western society has come to have a different place in the individual's life, largely through the transfer of economic activities away from the home.

In the simpler society, kinship is the major channel for a range of social activities. In the modern industrial society, new institutions come to take over various economic, educational, and religious functions. But the emotional intensity within the family is probably as great now as it always was.

B. Berelson and G. Steiner
Human Behavior

not understand them in their day to day life. It is possible that this stage can be characterized as a "busyness" stage in which each member of the family has his or her interests, and the "twain do not meet". The institutions and agencies of the community have taken on much of the former home activities, and are pulling the family members in all directions. One hears often the phrase "there is so little time to do things in the family". The popular comedy pictures the family members in this stage as being always on the move, and their lack of communication is evident in that they only see each other at the dinner table, and this occasion is sometimes rare. A business junior executive comments:

> I have to produce in order to get on top ... social functions are part of my job, and I join communal organizations to meet business contacts. I am rarely home nights. My wife belongs to social agency boards, and works part-time at the Red Cross. Bob, age 14, is at an age when he spends more time with his friends than at home. Jane, age 16, has a steady boyfriend who keeps her occupied. Our home is a place to rest up, before we move to the next activity or meeting. . . .

One must consider also that by this time, the marriage has progressed for about 15–20 years, the roles have been more or less solidified, the decision-making pattern has been worked out, and each spouse has the responsibility for certain areas of decision-making. A housewife added her comments: "We used to tell each other things, and I remember that at night we would lie in bed and talk into the small hours of the morning. It was a joy to share our experiences, joys, and sorrows. Now we see each other so little, and have so little to say. Something wonderful seems to have gone out of our marriage."

Loss of communication was one of the factors which emerged from the husband-wife relationship during this stage. Decisions were being made on an individual basis, with little consultation. It is important again not to fall apart, but to remember that the husband-wife relationship needs nurturing, care, love and consideration in the same way as care of children and attention to the job in the office.

Stage VI: The launching period. An interesting fact emerged in this study about this period of the family life cycle. There appeared a return to some of the "joint" decision-making patterns, and the high amount of satisfaction and consultation in decision-making items. This was similar to Stage I. It was quite noticeable when one considers that in Stage V, the low point of the cycle emerged.

In our culture, this stage has been characterized by the terms "lonely", "retired" and "new beginning". It is in the launching stage that the spouses find themselves again in a similar position as in the beginning stage. The men are looking forward to retirement, and this may not be a good prospect for many of them, but due to our emphasis on "youth", they are forced to retire. The women have by this time involved themselves quite actively in community affairs and find that suddenly their children, whom they had considered as "babies" for many years, have left and have begun their own families. The shouting of the vibrant teenagers has stopped, the arguments are silenced, and the table is set again for two. A 50-year-old wife reminisces:

> I look around me, and I see an empty house. It seems to me it is like the beginning of our marriage 30 years ago, the two of us. So much has happened since. I wish that we can now take the promised vacation – my children live about 1000 miles away, and call once in a while. I keep active in organizational work, but I miss my children. It seems as if a bird flew out of a nest. It is not easy for a mother to see her children leave home. . . .

The spouses have a choice. One is to begin to appreciate each other again, and to "do things" together again, taking trips and going out much more. There is the possibility that they have more time, and they begin to do things about which they always had been talking, but did not do anything about.

In our mobile society, there is the chance that the children live thousands of miles away, and thus even as "grandparents", they have little to do. It is possible that it is in this stage that the spouses begin to do many more things together, and there occurs a "reorientation and appreciation" of each other.

This stage does not have to be a sad one. Many interests and plans can be carried out as two people, husband and wife. Life can be enjoyed to the fullest, and with our jet planes, any part of the globe can be visited within hours. It is not a stage for "reminiscing", but a time for increased effort to solidify the husband-wife relationship, and to enjoy each other's company. It is a new beginning, not an old ending.

Conclusion

There are some central themes running through the family life cycle in respect to decision-making. The first is that it appears as if we have a trend in decision-making which ranges from a great deal of joint decision-making in the first two stages of the family cycle, to a low ebb of joint decision-making in the families with teenage children. Then appears a renewal of joint consultation and decision-making in the Launching Stage. The second is that the husband and wife seem to participate quite actively in child rearing and thus this may be a changing trend from the traditional patterns of child upbringing. The third is that there appeared a division of labour in decision-making functions, which supports the popular view that "the wife should tend to the household business" and the husband "should not meddle with the household duties but should look after money matters".

It seemed that as children came on the scene, there was a tendency to reduce the closeness of the husband-wife relationship, and to find that slowly the spouses were drawing apart, and the focus of attention became the children. One gets the feeling that the popular conception of "togetherness" is just a myth which has been promoted by high powered advertising agencies, and which

The family and marriage exist in every known human society. B. Berelson and G. Steiner state that, in a study of 250 societies, not one exception to this rule was found. Other observations of this research team have been summarized below.

One fact stands out beyond all others, that everywhere the husband, wife, and immature children make up a unit apart from the rest of the community.

The family has this importance in human society, presumably, because it provides services without which a society could not be maintained: provision for economic support, channeling of sexual behavior, reproduction, child-rearing, placement in the class system, emotional support.

Furthermore, in all societies marriage is the preferred arrangement for having children. Even where illegitimate children are common, they are disapproved: in general, both the parents and the child are punished.

Marriage and the family, or something like these, also exist in animal species below man. In general, the more stable family units are found among the larger, the more intelligent, the slower-maturing, the longer-lived animals — that is, those most like human beings in these respects. One big difference is that within a given animal group, family life seems to be much the same, whereas it varies widely among human beings.

B. Berelson and G. Steiner
Human Behavior

No substitute has yet been found for the ties of sentiment and emotion, and, in general, those ways in which only the family can satisfy certain longings of the human heart.

K. Ishwaran
Family Life in the Netherlands

has been great material for satirical cartoons. There is little "togetherness" with each member of the family moving in different directions, with different goals, objectives and interests. What we need to do is to stand still and ask where are we running – is it necessary to take part in so many community activities? We hear so little of family gatherings, family picnics, family games. Why not return to some of these family-centered activities?

Dr. Aaron Rutledge, past President of the National Council on Family Relations, has stated that the missing ingredient in present day marriage is "nearness". He has defined it as closeness; the absence of oneliness, loneliness, of isolation. He points out that "nearness provides emotional-social-spiritual-physical nourishment for the growth, maintenance and smooth functioning of an individual". The family of today seems to have forgotten this important point.

Decision-making is a daily activity of husband and wife, and gives a good indication of their relationship in the family cycle. We need to pay more attention to family life and the constant changes in our nuclear age which affect the family members in their day by day living.

two

Education

People in all cultures have procedures for passing on their culture to the young, for guiding them toward behaviours that are socially approved. In some primitive societies, education takes place through training by adults with whom the child is in daily contact. Sometimes this is done in a systematic way, but for the most part, it occurs through imitation. In societies like ours, it is quite impossible for parents to assume the full responsibility for preparing their children for adulthood. The tremendous variety of jobs required by our complex society, the vast cultural heritage, and the wide array of expected behaviours have required that a separate institution be established – the educational system.

The educational system in Canada has changed substantially during the past century. The rural one-room school has given way to larger elementary schools. High schools and universities have become accessible to everyone, rather than just to the religious and economic elite. Programs have been expanded to include specific job preparation, as well as "education" in the broad sense. Education is valued so highly that in most Canadian provinces young people are required to remain in school until age sixteen.

While in some societies education acts to maintain differences among people, in our society education can provide opportunities for improvement in status and income. In Canada, the extent of a person's education is closely related to his financial success, and as a result, diplomas, certificates, and university degrees have become union cards to the job world. Sadly, the work that is done to obtain a diploma is often unrelated to the position that requires the diploma.

Also, education has come to take on a custodial, or "baby-sitting", function for our society. Many parents are anxious to get their children into school at an early age so that their educational process can begin earlier and, incidentally, so that their children are taken off their hands for an even longer period of their childhood. This can contribute to conflict between home and school on certain issues for children. It also forces the children to attach considerably more importance to the approval of their friends and classmates than they would otherwise.

In the last few years, educational change has accelerated in Canada. The following selection deals with the responses of students to changes that have been initiated in an Ontario school.

The student response to change in the schools

A. J. C. King

Education in North America has gone through many different stages of development. Although the number of young people staying in school for longer periods of time has been steadily increasing, in two other respects there have been a series of swings back and forth between two main viewpoints. Firstly, there has been the swing from the idea of education as job training or training for life to education for the full development of each person's potential. In the late 1950s, when the Russians sent up "Sputnik" to move ahead of the West in the race for space, there was an immediate adjustment in the schools. The emphasis was placed on mathematics and sciences to encourage more young people to become scientists and engineers. In recent years, the tremendous costs

> Human history becomes more and more a race between education and catastrophe.
>
> H. G. Wells
> *The Study of History*

The Critics of Education

It is probably safe to say that publicly supported educational programs can never be flexible and varied enough to meet the needs of all citizens. Thus it is not surprising to find that education has been the target of critics throughout the world. No matter what approach to education is attempted, there will always be someone to take the opposing view. The following quotations are examples of the kinds of criticisms education has received over the years.

Our high schools have cost much money. They are architecturally splendid, full of expensive equipment, replete with swimming pools, libraries, gymnasiums, staffed by people who think they are worth a minimum of $8,100 and a maximum of $17,100.

Yet if their net effect is to bore children, to kill in them the spark of curiosity, to make them wish they were almost anywhere else, then they are a very costly failure.

(An editorial that appeared in the Toronto *Globe and Mail*, November 10, 1970.)

The solution which I am urging is to eradicate the factual disconnection of our subjects which kills the vitality of our modern curriculum. There is only one subject matter for education, and it is Life in all its manifestations. Instead of this single unity, we offer children — Algebra, from which nothing follows; History, from which nothing follows; Geometry, from which nothing follows; Science, from which nothing follows; a couple of languages, never mastered; and lastly, most dreary of all, Literature, represented by plays of Shakespeare, with philogical notes and short analyses of plot and character to be, in substance, committed to memory.

Can such a list be said to represent Life, as it is known in the midst of living it? The best thing that can be said of it is, that it is a rapid table of contents which a deity might run over in his mind while he was thinking of creating a world and had not yet determined how to put it together.

Alfred North Whitehead
Science and the Modern World

In such a school, the children, like butterflies mounted on pins, are fastened each to his desk, spreading the useless wings of barren and meaningless knowledge which they have acquired.

Maria Montessori
The Absorbent Mind

of the Vietnam war and space exploration have forced a rethinking of our educational values. Currently the emphasis is on the student as an individual. The goal is to allow each person to meet his needs rather than meet the needs of larger society. We went through this stage in the 1920s, under the influence of the great philosopher-educator John Dewey. It seems inevitable that we swing back and forth between these two views of the purpose of education. Ideally, of course, we must fall somewhere in between, since education will probably continue to be linked to job preparation in some form.

Secondly, and closely tied in, is the move from teacher-centred education to student-centred education. In teacher-centred education the teacher, as the representative of the local board of education, imposes the learning experience on the student, with very little opportunity provided for students to make real decisions. In student-centred education, the student makes a majority of the educational decisions that affect him. Again, ideally, the educational system should fall somewhere in between these two extremes. There are some learning experiences that a society requires of all its young people, and there are many optional experiences from which the student can select those that are appropriate for him.

In recent years the high school system in Ontario has moved through a stage of vocational-type schooling. Students were required to enrol in university-bound (5-year) programs or non university-bound (4-year and 2-year) programs in one of three branches – Arts and Science, Business and Commerce, or Science and Technology. Educational critics have complained that this has led to a social class system in the high schools, with the four-year, and two-year students at the bottom. In response to the complaints of these critics and as part of the general trend in North America, there has been a move to more student-centred programs with an emphasis on the student as an individual. Elements of vocational training are still present but have been minimized. The following selection is a chapter from a study of a school undergoing the changes to a more student-centred type of program. For purposes of comparison, another school that has been relatively successful with the more vocationally oriented program is also described.

The innovative school (we have called it Clearview) is located in a large Ontario city and offers an individual timetable that is computer-processed for each student. The students make their subject selection from a wide variety of courses offered at different levels of difficulty. Each course is assigned a number of credits, and in order to graduate, a student must obtain a specified number of credits. He is required to repeat or change only those subjects in which he has been unsuccessful. In Clearview, student discipline has been made the responsibility of the individual teacher to a much greater extent.

The other school (we have called it Greendale) is located in the same city, just a few miles from Clearview. Students select a program of studies (for example, the four-year Arts and Science program) and for the most part remain with one group of students throughout the school day. Both schools have an enrolment of approximately 1,100 students.

This part of the report deals with the reactions of the students f Clearview High School to the changes that have taken place ere. A general picture of both schools from the students' point f view is also provided. It was expected that when the students ere given greater responsibility in the choice of their subjects and ersonal behaviour as well as a more individualized program, they ould achieve at a higher level and receive greater satisfaction om their total school experience. (The information used in this udy was obtained from interviews with students and from a ques- onnaire administered to all students in both schools in the Spring f the school year.)

The students from Clearview High School were asked what they ought of the changes that had been made in their school. More an 90 per cent of the students interviewed made favourable eneral comments and followed up by listing certain advantages f the changes. The following quotations are representative of the ositive reactions:

I think they're really good because they can help lots of people. (Grade 9, 4-year girl)

Well, I would have flunked this year if they didn't have it here. (Grade 10, 5-year boy)

It's a lot better than the other system. A student can advance at his own rate. (Grade 11, 5-year boy)

The main factors pointed out by the students were the follow- ng:

) Each student is treated as an individual and not just as part of a larger class.

) Because each class is made up of a different group of students throughout the school day, it is possible to meet and become friends with more students.

) The competitiveness that is present when the class remains to- gether throughout the school day is not as much of a problem – the student does not have to be at the bottom of his class in all subjects.

) It is not necessary to repeat a subject that has been successfully completed.

) Students can choose their courses from a larger number of options.

) Students have greater freedom from rules and regulations gov- erning behaviour than they have had before and than they have in other high schools.

) It is not as easy for teachers to identify students as members of a poor class or to link a class with one of the branches or pro- grams.

A small number of students were critical of the changes, often or the same reasons that caused other students to react positively.

Last year when we went to class we would follow people around and I got in a whole lot of classes where I like the kids,

It is quite possible that much of our current educa- tional system is engaged in preparing young people for "jobs" that simply will not exist in our society by the time these students come into the marketplace. It is equally possible that a goodly segment of the "jobs" being performed in our economy today are simply atavisms of 19th century concepts of work which have little economic, social, or even personal value today, and will have even less value in the future as our developing technology changes the nature of the use of human energy.

Don Fabun
The Dynamics of Change

Education has not yet caught up with the fact that the educational pattern of the past, in which it was assumed that the old know and the young must learn, is no longer valid.

We are teaching young people to respect authority at a time when authority is no longer possible, and when we ought to be struggling together to understand the world in which we live. We still say to them, *listen and learn*, rather than *strive with us*.

Robert Theobald
Cybernation, Immediate Threat and Future Promise

Professor O. K. Moore of Yale University has shown that even two and three year olds of average intelligence can learn to read, write and type. Public schools have been wasting valuable years by postponing the teaching of many important subjects on the grounds that they are too difficult.

Charles E. Silberman
Crisis in the Classroom

Regulations governing dress and grooming may be trivial. What is not trivial is that submission to such regulation teaches students that they have no rights or dignity. The very triviality of the regulations makes them more effectively humili- ating. Most adolescents would accept and even welcome adult direction in matters of grave consequence. But I would maintain that the real function of these regulations is to humiliate, to show any adolescents with too much autonomy what happens to wise guys and trouble makers.

Edgar Friedenberg
Coming of Age in America

but this year I don't know half the people in the class. (Grade 9, 5-year girl)

One often gets the almost eerie impression of huge clouds of educational reform drifting back and forth from coast to coast and only occasionally touching down to blanket an actual educational institution.

National Education Association Journal

I think they are moving too fast. The students don't have enough to say about everything. They are trying to be first or something like this. I don't know what they are trying to prove. (Grade 10, 4-year boy)

Well, sometimes the credit system gets complicated and if you miss out on something you might have to spend another year at school to catch up. My brother's friend got messed up and he even did another credit. (Grade 10, 5-year boy)

I don't think it is any good. It is the same as before. You might as well just get your Grade 12. In Grade 13 you have to have so many credits for university – so you are getting pretty much the same deal really, right? (Grade 11, 5-year boy)

Many of the students in the senior grades were sorry that the changes had not come sooner:

The credit system is all right, but they started it at the wrong time for myself and a lot of others. (Grade 13 boy)

Teenagers are captive in a school system. Their actions and behaviour are observed and recorded. Unlike their elders they are compelled by law to be captive. They cannot protect themselves from such systematic scrutiny. "The system" is put ahead of the rights of the individual.

Tim Reid
in Tim and Julyan Reid (eds.)
Student Power and the Canadian Campus

But they were also worried about getting caught in the change-over from one system to another:

I think that for a student starting Grade 9, this is a good school, but the changes this year were too great for Grade 13 students. (Grade 13 girl)

We are sort of caught up in the pinch between the credit system and the system of the previous four years. (Grade 13 boy)

When asked which students would particularly benefit from the changes, a large number of students responded that the good and poor students would probably benefit most. A number of students felt quite strongly that the lazy student would suffer in a system that left so much up to the individual.

Satisfaction with Subject Choice

Students at Clearview had the opportunity of selecting their program from a wider variety of courses than did students at Greendale. In order to determine whether it was possible for students to obtain the subjects that they wished, all students were asked "Were you able to take the subjects that you wanted to take?" The responses to this item are presented in *Table 1*. Although satisfaction was generally quite high in both schools for students in five-year programs, a slightly greater proportion of five-year program students from Clearview than from Greendale were able to take the subjects that they wished. Four-year program students from Greendale were quite a bit less satisfied with their subject choice than the four-year students from Clearview. An analysis of timetables for students of both schools indicated that students from Clearview had come up with a much greater variety of time tables than had students from Greendale.

Table 1
"Were you able to take the subjects that you wanted to take?"

| | Clearview | | Greendale | |
	5-Year	4-Year	5-Year	4-Year
	%	%	%	%
Yes	60	53	56	42
Yes, nearly all	33	32	35	40
No	7	15	9	18

Differences Between Four- and Five-Year Program Students

One of the most severe criticisms of the kind of school program represented by Greendale was that it created a social-class system in the high school based on the three major programs (2-, 4- and 5-year) and the three branches (Arts and Science, Business and Commerce, Science and Technology). It was hoped that the changes introduced at Clearview would help reduce the social stigma attached to four-year program students, by providing an opportunity for students from four- and five-year programs and across the three branches to mix together in classes and to compete as team-mates in an extracurricular program based on a house system.

There was evidence of quite a bit of intermixing of students from the various programs and branches, but the great majority (74%) of five-year program students took all five-year courses. Twenty-six per cent of the five-year students were enrolled in one or more four-year courses (46% of this group were enrolled in four-year typing). Forty per cent of the four-year students were enrolled in one or more five-year courses.

The individual student timetables were more effective in providing a mix of students from the different branches than from the four- and five-year programs (see *Table 2*). The following comment is typical of the responses of students to the question, "Do you think it makes any difference whether you are in Arts and Science, or in Technical or in Commerce?"

Well, it doesn't really matter now because the classes are mixed. There's some Commercial, some Arts and Science, some Technical, but before there was all Technical in one group and then they'd say, "Okay, here's those big bullies, I'm going to have to study with them," and they are in a miserable mood before you even get there. Well, I don't go for that. But now it's mixed up and you can't really say, "Here's the Technical boys," because there's Technical and there's Arts and Science, and there's Commercial, and they're all in one class. The switch is pretty good. (Grade 10, 4-year boy)

Figure 1 presents the responses of students to questionnaire items bearing on differences between four- and five-year program students. Although the use of such items in questionnaires may encourage students to exaggerate or even create differences that may not exist, there is very little doubt that in the Province of Ontario there are very real status differences between four- and five-year program students.

It can be seen from *Figure 2* that a large number of students from both Clearview and Greendale saw differences between the attitudes held by students and teachers toward four- and five-year program students. Apparently students were more likely to see four- and five-year program students differently than were teachers. Four-year program students were far more likely than five-year program students to feel that four-year students are as intelligent as five-year students. Clearview four- and five-year program students responded similarly to the items on students' and teachers' attitudes toward four- and five-year students, but four-year

Table 2
Extent of Intermixing of Students from the Three Branches at Clearview High School

Program of enrolment	Percentage taking one or more courses in other programs		
	Arts and Science	Business and Commerce	Science and Technology
Arts and Science (73%)	—	26	2
Business and Commerce (15%)	95	—	—
Science and Technology (12%)	84	7	—

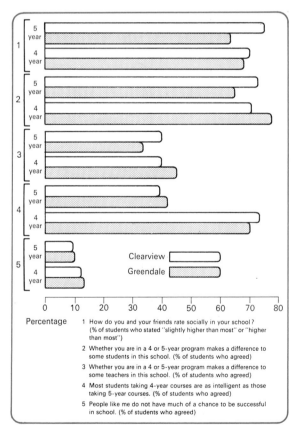

Figure 1 Students' perceptions of differences between four and five-year program students

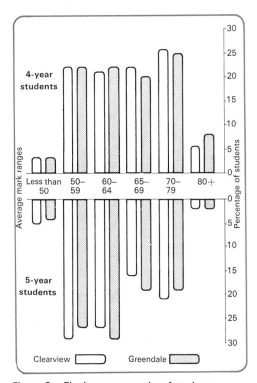

Figure 2   Final average marks of students

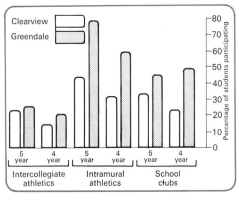

Figure 3   Participation in extracurricular
activities

students at Greendale were more likely to note differences than were five-year students at Greendale. Five-year students at Clearview were more likely to note differences between four- and five-year students than were five-year students at Greendale, but four-year students at Greendale were more likely to note differences than were four-year students at Clearview. This presents an interesting paradox: whereas the four-year student at Clearview appears less sensitive to differences between four- and five-year program students than the four-year student at Greendale, his five-year program counterpart is more sensitive to the differences than the five-year student at Greendale. When the responses of four- and five-year students were combined, differences between the two schools were not pronounced. Five-year students at Clearview did feel somewhat more successful socially than did Greendale five-year students, and four-year students at Greendale were more inclined to feel that being "in a four-year or a five-year program makes a difference to some students".

There is very little evidence to suggest that status differences between four- and five-year program students have decreased significantly at Clearview with the introduction of the changes. The schools, of course, still reflect the larger society with its basically competitive structure. When teachers and students label students, the sorting of students into the various job categories is simplified for society. Indeed, if status were not determined in school on the basis of four- and five-year program differences, it would surely take some other similar form, probably just as harmful to the students on the bottom of the scale. However, the advantage of the individualized educational system is that it helps obscure differences among students for a good part of their time in school.

When looking at the school marks of the students at Clearview, it must be remembered that the school still operates under the same general conditions within the larger educational system as it has in the past. This means that the school is expected to produce a certain number of successful students. Therefore the teachers will probably feel pressure to give failing grades to about as many students as they have in the past. Also, since the marking in many secondary school subjects allows for the bias of teachers, it would be hard to know whether an increase in student marks was caused by improved student performance or by the fact that the teachers think the changes are good and mark accordingly. In view of these considerations, we did not expect large increases in student marks as a result of the changes at Clearview. However, neither could the changes be justified if there was an apparent lowering of academic achievement throughout the school. Although an increase in the overall achievement of students was a long-term objective of the changes at Clearview, in the early stages it was hoped that there would be an increase in responsible behaviour on the part of students as well as an increase in their satisfaction with school.

The final average-mark was used as the indicator of student academic achievement. The percentages of students enrolled in four- and five-year programs at Clearview and Greendale High Schools who indicated their averages fell within the stated mark ranges are presented in *Figure 2*. It is obvious that the differences between the two schools were relatively small. An analysis of school records for the previous four years indicated that in both schools students received approximately the same pattern of final marks.

Participation in Extracurricular Activities

Many educators feel that a sound extracurricular program helps a school to encourage in students a feeling of being part of the school, including its academic purposes, as well as to provide for the development of student interests. In fact, many students tend to describe their schools in terms of the effectiveness of its extracurricular program.

Figure 3 presents a picture of the extent of participation of students in the extracurricular programs of Clearview and Greendale High Schools. The voluntary participation of students in the extracurricular programs at Greendale High School is extremely high and the program itself is quite extensive. It has been found that four-year program students are far less likely than five-year program students to participate in the extracurricular programs of high schools in this province. It is quite remarkable that Greendale High School has achieved such a high level of four-year student participation in particular. Participation in extracurricular activities is average at Clearview and not particularly high for four-year program students.

General Attitude Toward School

In this section, the way in which the student sees his school and his teachers in comparison with other schools is considered. Also an attempt is made to identify the factors related to the students' satisfaction or dissatisfaction with school and to determine whether these factors are associated with the changes that were introduced in Clearview High School.

Figure 4 clearly shows that the students in both schools view their teachers very similarly. At the same time, however, it is quite clear that the schools represent two different approaches to school organization. The responses to the questionnaire item, "The teachers in this school take the side of the administration", indicate that the teachers at Greendale support the principal and vice-principal in matters of discipline to a greater extent than do teachers at Clearview. The responses to the item, "The rules that I have to follow in class vary from teacher to teacher", suggest that discipline at Clearview is more likely to be the responsibility of each individual teacher. Responses to the item, "If a student talks back to a teacher in this school he will get sent down to the office", suggest that insolence is more likely to be handled within the classroom at Clearview than at Greendale.

In *Figure 5*, items dealing with general student reaction to their schools are presented. The majority of students in both schools would rather remain in their own school than change to another school. However, fewer students from Clearview would rather go to another school. School spirit was quite a bit higher at Greendale than at Clearview and this appears to correspond with the

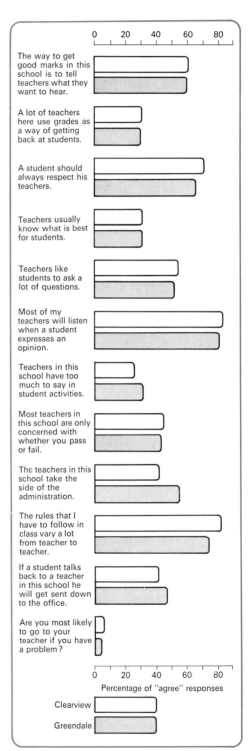

Figure 4   Students' perceptions of teachers

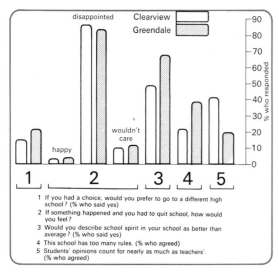

Figure 5   Students' general attitudes toward
their school

higher participation in extracurricular activities and the success-ful intercollegiate sports program at Greendale. It appears that the term "school spirit" tends to reflect the participation in extra-curricular activities and general involvement in intercollegiate sports, rather than the way the school is organized to help learning take place. Students from Greendale were more inclined to say that their school had too many rules and less inclined to feel that students' opinions counted for nearly as much as the teachers'. It was quite clear that there were not only organizational differences between the schools but also basic differences with regard to the amount of freedom and responsibility given to students.

The students who were interviewed were asked, "How would you compare your school with other schools in the city?" This question was designed to obtain a general impression of how students describe their school to others, not only to provide a comparison between the schools, but also to determine whether Clearview students included some evaluation of the changes in their responses to a general question.

The students from Greendale were generally favourable in their impressions of the school, but their responses appeared to be quite varied and, to some extent, were not specific.

> It's a pretty good high school and it doesn't have – I don't think it has – as many drugs going around and stuff like that. (Grade 9, 4-year girl)

> I'd rather go to Greendale because my brother was here and he said it was great. (Grade 9, 4-year girl)

> I like it here. I mean there are a lot of schools that are better, but I like it here. (Grade 10, 5-year boy)

When the students of Greendale were more specific, they saw the major favourable features as good school spirit and good teachers. As had been noted previously, this school spirit appears to be a product of a well-developed extracurricular program and considerable success in intercollegiate athletics:

> The sports program is really good and the teaching system isn't bad. (Grade 9, 5-year boy)

> We have over thirty sports activities. (Grade 9, 4-year boy)

> Sports and the teachers are good. (Grade 9, 4-year boy)

> Sports – they have a great variety of them and I like the way they are set up and the teachers seem to be pretty good. (Grade 9, 5-year boy)

> They have pretty good teachers and school spirit is high. (Grade 9, 5-year boy)

Almost all quotations regarding school spirit and the extra-curricular program came from boys. Substantially fewer girls at Greendale commented favourably on the program.

The students interviewed at Clearview High School were more appreciative of their school than were the students at Greendale. Their responses to the school comparison question tended to be more specific and were more related to academic aspects of the program:

It is a little better because, you know, the other schools don't have the credit system. It is a little more advanced. You have got more choice and more courses. (Grade 10, 5-year boy)

We have the credit system and you can go at your own rate, and if you are smart, you can get ahead. I think that's good because in other grades in the other schools everybody has to sort of compete with everybody, but here you can go at your own rate. Well, you do have to compete, too, but well, you know. (Grade 11, 4-year girl)

Well, I'd rather be at Clearview because of the systems they have here and the subject promotion and this sort of thing. Because I would be a grade behind right now if there weren't subject promotions, because I am dragging a couple of subjects. (Grade 11, 5-year boy)

I wouldn't want to go to any other school because at Clearview you have got so much scope. You can take whatever you want and you can change from year to year, and in every class you enter there are different kids, and from the social point of view, I think that's good. (Grade 12, 5-year boy)

It's better than most of them because of the credit system and the system of individual timetables. (Grade 12, 5-year boy)

Most of the students interviewed at Clearview felt that the discipline in their school was more student-centred than at other schools and provided for greater individual student freedom:

I like it because it kind of makes you feel freer, like you are not stuck with something, and we have lots of activities to do. (*Q: What do you mean, freer?*) Well, it's just the sensation you get when you walk around the halls, and you are not with the class or something. (Grade 10, 5-year boy)

We went down to another school one afternoon when we had a day off here, and it was like a jail. The teachers watch every move and there is no freedom there. Here you can more or less do what you want. (Grade 10, 4-year girl)

They haven't got too many rules, not like some of the other schools, and academically, I think they have got a good layout. The people know their business. (Grade 10, 4-year boy)

I went to another school, but here you get to do things more freely. At the other school, every time you turned round there was a teacher standing in front of you telling you something. (Grade 10, 4-year boy)

I think that Clearview is an experimental school. I haven't heard of any other schools that have as much freedom as the students here or have as many courses put to them. (Grade 10, 5-year boy)

Well, the students are a lot more free. They are allowed to organize their own things. I think that Clearview is a lot better off than other schools because I think they are a little more strict in all other schools. (Grade 11, 5-year boy)

Personally, I wouldn't want to go to any other place because

Where the old type of school was a monument to the efficacy of learning in a puritanically ugly environment, the new school stresses social learning in an atmosphere of lightness, color, and accepted and self-conscious modernity. The contrasting types of school building are eloquent reminders of the general cultural shift from production for acquisition and saving, to consumption for conspicuous display and spending, a transition which has also manifested itself in house decoration and architecture, and which is backed by all the forces of present-day advertising.

John Seeley, R. Alexander Sim, and Elizabeth Loosely
Crestwood Heights

Dr. Wilder Penfield has said that you can become educated by reading, travel, and talking with intelligent, experienced people. I would go right along with this; you must attend university if you want a degree, but if you simply want an education, there's no necessity to go near one. Go instead to the public library, where you'll find all the truly great teachers who ever lived. Hit the road for a year and find out something about yourself. Talk to older people who've had some experience of life. Get a job, any job, and learn on it.

Richard J. Needham, Columnist
Toronto *Globe and Mail*

Canadians appeared to believe, more emphatically than did Americans, that the public school should serve the individual; Americans believed, on the other hand, that it should serve society. Canadians, as a group, assigned considerably higher priority than did Americans to knowledge, scholarly attitudes, creative skills, aesthetic appreciation, and morality, as outcomes of schooling. Americans emphasized physical development, citizenship, patriotism, social skills, and family living much more than did Canadians.

Lawrence W. Downey
"A Canadian Image of Education"
Canadian Society : Sociological Perspectives

The radical educator Peter Marin has said that North American schools are based on three particular things :

1) Our puritanical vision of "sinners" or "savages" in which human impulse is not to be trusted and must therefore be controlled or trained.

2) The necessity of assimilating great masses of immigrants from many different backgrounds, using the schools to provide a common experience for all.

3) The need for energy and labour to run the machines of industry. The State, needing workers, educates persons to be technically competent but conforming and dependent on authority.

Clearview is freer, is not as strict as other schools, and well, kids are really relaxed. I find they are not afraid to speak their minds. At Clearview you feel more grown up. (Grade 12, 4-year boy)

Being here, you get sort of spoiled to this system. Like, I have talked to other kids from other high schools and it would be terrible going there. (*Q: How?*) Like, everything just seems as though it is not relaxed like at Clearview. The teachers are far more friendly than at other schools. (Grade 12, 4-year boy)

Well, the kids from outside will tell you it's slack because of the way in which we can subject promote and so on. Everyone says, "Oh, Clearview, that's an easy one", but it's not true. You have to get your subjects but they think that you can take any subject that you want and really you can't. I think Clearview is the best school in the city. (Grade 12, 5-year girl)

Student critics of Greendale were few in number and tended to focus their complaints on rules and comparisons with Clearview:

Well, the discipline is a little overboard. Really, I mean you've got to get a pass to go out of the room and you've got to ask permission to go to the bathroom; you are eighteen and you have to ask permission to go to the bathroom. There are just too many rules, and it makes people want to rebel against them. (Grade 10, 5-year boy)

About the same as other schools, I guess, except that you are not freer. The teachers are too strict here. (Grade 10, 4-year boy)

There aren't as many options here as there are in other schools, such as Clearview. (Grade 9, 5-year boy)

Teachers don't pay much attention to the individual student, it is the class as a whole. (Grade 10, 4-year boy)

The small number of student criticisms of Clearview tended to be directed toward a general lowering of standards:

Well, I would rather go to (a nearby school). It's got a higher standard of education and the commercial course is better. (Grade 10, 4-year girl)

(*Q: What do you mean it's not the best?*) Academically, I mean. Some schools have a higher academic standing. (Grade 11, 5-year boy)

It's very slack and, you know, there's hardly any rules at all and you don't really feel you have to do it if you have an assignment. (Grade 12, 4-year girl)

This school is known as a reject school, anybody can come here. (Grade 13, 5-year boy)

Discipline

As has been previously noted, school discipline at Greendale is well organized and effectively coordinated throughout the school.

Discipline at Clearview appears to be less consistent from teacher to teacher and to have less coordination from the administration of the school. What patterns of discipline problems emerge as a product of these different strategies of dealing with student problems? In order to shed some light on this issue, the school discipline records kept by the vice-principals of Clearview and Greendale were analyzed.

In *Table 3* the percentages of students from four- and five-year programs referred to the offices of the schools for discipline are presented. It is obvious that the total number of students referred to the office was very similar in the two schools. However, at Clearview, four-year program students were more likely to be referred for discipline. This tends to support the suggestion that students who are not highly motivated are more likely to abuse the increase in freedom, if we accept the idea that four-year students are less motivated than five-year students.

In *Table 4* students referred for disciplinary reasons have been placed into three main categories. The category "academic rule violation" refers to the offences that occur in the classroom and bear directly on the process of learning. It includes such items as work not done, not trying, not keeping up, and not having the right equipment. The category "teacher conduct violation" includes such offences as truancy, skipping classes, lateness, smoking, fooling in the halls, fighting, stealing, and clothing or general appearance violations.

Students from Clearview were more likely to be referred in the category of "general rule violation" than were students from Greendale. Referrals for truancy and skipping classes were far more common at Clearview, according to the records, while referrals for in-class disturbances were less common at Clearview. Teachers at Clearview were likely to be less happy with the treatment of an office referral than were teachers at Greendale, and consequently, they were probably less inclined to send students to the office for problems that occurred in their classes.

The multiple offender, that is, the person who was sent to the office more than once, was far more common at Clearview than at Greendale. This was probably related to the way in which the problem student was treated when he was sent to the office. It appears that his treatment was more severe at Greendale and therefore he was less likely to be sent back to the office.

Dropouts

If a student is dissatisfied with school and if he is past the legal age of required attendance, he has the option of leaving school. Information on the number of school dropouts was obtained from school records, and reasons for withdrawing, and attitude toward school were obtained from a telephone survey of those students who withdrew from the two schools.

The number of dropouts from the two schools was similar, and for both schools, fewer students had dropped out than was the case in previous years. Generally speaking, dropouts from Clearview were less likely to blame the school for their withdrawal than were dropouts from Greendale.

Table 3
Percentage of Students by Program Sent to Office by Teachers for Misbehaving

School	5-Year %	4-Year %	Mean %
Clearview	10	19	13
Greendale	12	13	12

Table 4
Categories of Office Referrals

	Clear-view %	Green-dale %
Academic rule violation	11	13
Teacher conduct violation	24	32
General rule violation	65	55

The Future of Education

Contrary to the expectations of many, the computer may make classroom teaching more, rather than less, an individual affair. And in doing so it will facilitate learning at a speed and depth of understanding that now seem impossible to achieve.

Patrick Suppes
Saturday Review

The very first casualty of the present-day school system may well be the whole business of teacher-led instruction as we know it.

Marshall McLuhan and George B. Leonard
Look Magazine

The school composed chiefly of classroom is obsolete. In schools of the future, upwards of one half of the student's time may be spent in the library, in science laboratories, or in other workrooms where he can search for knowledge, analyze data, reflect upon the ideas which he is encountering, and put his conclusions in writing.

Francis S. Chase
University of Chicago

We must recognize that the student is already "working" at least as relevantly as the man in the factory. The time has come when we must introduce the concept of a student salary, starting possibly at 14, and increasing with age, payable to all students attending high school or university. . . .

Robert Theobald
*Cybernation, Immediate Threat and
Future Promise*

Two other anachronisms that haunt today's educational process also relate to our agrarian past. The typical school day may run from 8.30 to 3.30. This is to allow Johnny to do the morning chores before leaving for school, and to get back home in the afternoon in time to bring in the firewood, slop the pigs, round-up the cows, and bring in water for the early evening supper (since there was no electric light), before dark. Johnny these days performs none of these chores in the typical urban home; but he does have a long time to "kill" between school and dinnertime. A longer school day would appear to hasten the educational process and help solve some of the problems of "juvenile delinquency".

Don Fabun
On Education

For a first grader and a kindergartener the important things about school are one's cubby-hole, one's place in line, having two crackers instead of three, and having singing after juice. The excitements are losing something, a substitute teacher, and having a birthday party.

National Education Association Journal

Summary

Most Clearview students reacted very favourably to the changes. They were particularly appreciative of the increased freedom, not only in subject choice, but also in behaviour and involvement in decision-making within the school. The students at both schools appeared to be quite satisfied with their schools, with the students at Greendale citing high school spirit, good teachers, and a strong extracurricular program as the main reasons, and the students at Clearview citing the innovations, their treatment by teachers as individuals, and freedom as the main reasons. Slightly more students from Clearview than from Greendale indicated that they were able to take the subjects that they wished to take.

It was found that participation in extracurricular activities was particularly high at Greendale for both four- and five-year students. This was probably due in part to the fact that, at Greendale, participation receives a greater weighting than winning in the intramural athletic program. Participation in the extracurricular program at Clearview was average by Ontario standards.

There was little evidence that a substantial decrease in status differences between four- and five-year program students had occurred as a result of the changes at Clearview, but there was evidence that branch differences (Arts and Science, Business and Commerce, Science and Technology) had decreased as a result of the intermixing of students. Discipline was seen as being more severe and more centrally organized at Greendale than at Clearview. The number of dropouts was similar for the two schools, but dropouts from Greendale were more likely to blame the school for their problems at school than were dropouts from Clearview.

three   *The total institution*

In some systems, the behaviour of individuals is so rigidly controlled at all times that, to all intents and purposes, its members live in total institutions. Sociologists define total institutions as closed worlds, where a number of individuals in similar circumstances are required by a formal system to perform certain tasks at specified intervals while under confinement. The individual confined to a total institution is, in effect, cut off from his larger society. A prison is the best known example of a total institution, but some mental hospitals, military recruit training camps, and ships at sea are other examples. In this situation, the individual is controlled by individuals with formal authority, such as guards and officers. There is usually an educational process in preparing individuals for life in a total institution. Soldiers are trained for battle, prison inmates learn what is required of them, and mental patients are instructed in what is expected of them.

Typically, in a total institution, an informal subculture develops among inmates to help sustain them in face of the severe requirements of the formal system. Of course, this process is carried on by the inmates themselves. It usually involves the vocation of an informal set of leaders, and strategies to ease the work load of the inmates. In the following selection we see how the new inmate is prepared for his time in a reformatory, by both the administration of the reformatory and the older experienced inmates.

Life in a reformatory

W. E. Mann

The emergence of an inmate way of life and its acceptance by many prisoners is intimately related to the manner in which the inmates at Guelph reformatory tend to come mainly from the lower-class or working-class. The successful preparation of new inmates (fish) to the inmate way of life and much of the form that it takes is dependent to a high degree upon their experiences in the working classes. This background emphasizes violence, personal freedom, and the immediate satisfaction of impulses. Statistics on jobs and educational background suggest that a predominantly lower-class and working-class background characterizes the inmate group at Guelph. It may be expected, then, that a substantial number of the inmates have been exposed to techniques of petty crime, to certain basic attitudes which are hostile to society which are common to the lower-class and the criminal culture, and to significant defensive explanations about police, social workers, clergy, and psychiatrists. The fact that a great majority of Guelph's prisoners were convicted of at least two illegal offences before they were imprisoned also indicates some acquaintance with delinquent values. B and E (break and enter) artists, thieves, and assault offenders, who make up over 75 per cent of the institution's members, are more likely to have such acquaintance than those convicted of white-collar crimes or simple (joy ride) car thefts.

The length of term and number of terms served also affect the extent to which inmates adopt the way of life of the reformatory. Interviews indicate that repeaters, especially those serving a third or fourth term, have learned and accepted a great proportion of the way of life and its values. It is these who teach the new prisoners, acting in a way like their parents. Long termers serving 12 to 24 months likewise tend, other things being equal, to identify strongly with the inmate way of life. But even first timers serving short terms of five or six months usually move significantly toward the inmate norm and value system. Usually, only those serving the very short three-month term can avoid the impact of the inmate society and its socializing agents. Apart from class factors, age and marital status are significant. Men over 30 and those with strong home ties are more resistant to the socializing pressures. The influence of a stable home life and settled habits block rapid and sweeping changes in the prisoners.

Analysis of the way in which new prisoners are taught must begin by an examination of certain common pre-Guelph experiences that prepare the inmates to accept the standards and ways of the inmate community. First, a majority of inmates have a history of membership in cliques, "partnerships", or small gangs in which lying, stealing, drinking, and concealment devices designed to fool the police and other representatives of the community are common. Though not necessarily participants in the type of gang common in the depression days of the 1930's, the majority of inmates have experienced, usually before the age of 12, some personal ties with one or more such groups. Secondly, from 30 to 40 per cent of the fish coming to Guelph have previously spent up to a year in juvenile correctional institutions. Even before arriving at such institutions juveniles are often held for a week or more in detention homes where they may associate with a ready-made group whose underground code favours lying, conniving, and anti-authority attitudes.

At the provincial juvenile institution for those 13 and older, inmates often learn certain basic aspects of the criminal way of life, including techniques of thieving, conning the guards, conniving, and avoiding imposed work. They also may develop an interest in some criminal values and a certain psychological immunity to such normally disturbing experiences as brutal beatings. One informant told how he learned at a juvenile institution that the correct way to handle anyone who rats to the police is to "smash" him at the earliest opportunity.

When "graduates" of juvenile institutions first enter Guelph they already know quite a few prisoners and, what is equally useful, have some know-how by which to discriminate among the various types. As one such prisoner intimated: "A guy is away ahead if he goes in and knows somebody already there. This guy briefs you on what smocks and boots are worth, gives you the score on gambling and makes it so you won't get pushed around." Thus, prior experience in a correctional institution helps in avoiding some of the penalties of being a novice, and may accelerate identification with the inmate way of life.

Imprisonment in a county jail may have similar results. Thus, the experience of being locked up in the county "bucket", as it is called, and faced with trial and a possible sentence turns the prisoner's thoughts to how he will get along, if sentenced, in

Guelph. Because many young lower-class youths are caught with the evidence and do not seek a lawyer they tend to expect a term of imprisonment when first in the county jail. One inmate noted, "From the time you get sentenced you begin thinking of what you will do in the institution. Your mind wanders to Guelph till you get there." Many fish in this situation, surrounded by a great assortment of jail repeaters, will turn to jail inmates of more experience and higher status for advice on or the "scoop" about Guelph. Again owing to the minimum of recreational facilities provided – cards and checkers – and the prisoner's disinterest in the offerings of the library, much of their day is spent in conversation, which revolves around such topics as sex, crime, tricks of fooling the police and magistrates, and the merits and demerits of the province's main correctional institutions. Besides hearing how to pull "good scores" new prisoners may rub shoulders with rounders and members of the underworld, men who uphold anti-social, anti-police, and anti-middle-class attitudes and values. One young fellow elaborates:

> I met him in the county jail – he had been there before – and he told me a few things I didn't know, like what to do when you pull a score or when you get snaffled (picked up by the police). I was never to sign a statement or never to plead guilty when arrested and he told me different things to do to get out on bail.

Practical warnings like "Don't talk to anybody in a crowd unless you really know them", and "Watch out for the finks or they'll turn you in before you've had a chance to think", are common. In addition, one young inmate confided, "The older men, they usually kid you along and try to make you real scared." But the older men will also give useful advice to the fish. Here is one first offender's description:

> I received advice from an old guy in the jail who had spent seven years in the pen. . . . He talked quite well . . . he told me to be sure to make friends as quickly as possible because I might need them. Also, he said, make sure you talk to the right people, find out, watch and see who is a wheel and then get to know him, just enough to say hello to him and be sure to say hello two or three times a day. This gives anybody who is watching the impression that you have friends and that they had better not make a go at you.

In short, depending on his length of stay, which may range from a few days to two months, and the size and type of jail, a first offender may experience and learn things that will simplify entry into and adoption of the Guelph inmate way of life.

Further initiation into the institution's life is provided when the prisoner is handcuffed and shipped down with other prisoners in the bus. A busload or "chain" usually consists of 25 to 30 prisoners. The bus ride, depending on the location of the county jail, the weather, and the route, may be short or may last several days. Handcuffed in pairs, the bus riders are drawn together by their common fate and fears, and some new friendships are begun.

Sociologist Erving Goffman states that the "total institution" has the following characteristics:

1) All aspects of life are conducted in the same place and under the same single authority.

2) Each phase of the member's daily activity is carried on in the immediate company of a large group of others, all of whom are treated alike and required to do the same thing together.

3) All phases of the day's activities are tightly scheduled, with one activity leading at a prearranged time into the next, the whole sequence of activities being imposed from above by a set of regulations and a group of officials.

4) The various enforced activities are brought together into a single plan that is designed to fulfill the official aim of the institution.

5) There is a sharp split between the supervisors and the inmates.

6) Information concerning the fate of the inmate is often withheld from him.

7) The work structure in the total institution, geared as it is to a twenty-four-hour day, demands different reasons for work than exist in society-at-large. Working for money and status does not make a lot of sense to prisoners in jail.

8) There are usually real or symbolic barriers indicating a break with the society "out there".

If we look at the activities of a sailor aboard ship, we can see that in many ways he is part of a total institution. Louis A. Zurcher, Jr., notes that on American ships:

. . . all aspects of life aboard a vessel at sea are carried out within the limits of bow and stern, beam, and bilges to foretruck. Authority of the Captain is absolute, by law and by custom, and drifts down to the sailors through the chain-of-command. (All commanding officers of naval vessels, regardless of their actual rank, are called "captain".) He has total responsibility for and to the men and the ship. His influence spreads over *all* activities of the crew. Nothing the Captain says or does is taken impersonally. The sailor salutes other officers aboard only the first time he meets them during the day. He salutes the Captain every time he meets him.

It is almost impossible for the sailor at sea to be alone. He goes through each day's routine in close company with his "shipmates". He works with them, eats with them, showers with them, participates in recreation with them, and sleeps stacked in a compartment with them.

Each day is tightly scheduled by a "plan of the day", which is mimeographed and posted daily on bulletin boards throughout the ship. The "plan of the day" specifies all the day's activities from reveille until taps: what and when ship's work will be, what uniforms will be worn during which time of the day, what time meals will be taken, who will be on duty and who will be at liberty, what the evening's entertainment will be. At the bottom of the plan are listed by name those individuals the Captain has seen fit to promote, and those whom he has seen fit to punish.

Louis A. Zurcher, Jr.
"The Sailor Aboard Ship"

Conversation revolves around the institution, its rules and restrictions, on who might be seen there, and on devices for "making out", that is, adjusting. Formal rules and regulations are discussed and memorized. The same group goes through three weeks of classification procedures together and its members, particularly the first timers, may hang together for their first month or two and jointly accept increasing amounts of the inmate way of life, thus reinforcing its impact.

A succession of experiences in the first few weeks impresses upon the rookie that he has entered a new and distinctive community and that if he fails to observe the formal regulations of the authorities and the norms of the inmate group serious trouble awaits him. In the Superintendent's speech of "welcome" he is warned not only that he is now in a prison and not a "boy scout camp", but also that he has to watch out for other inmates, and avoid their schemes. Yet it is quickly apparent that not all the prison's rules and penalties are covered in the issue rule sheet and that to find out what is legitimate and illegitimate one has to depend upon other inmates.

Like recruits in the army, newcomers at Guelph learn to watch and copy others. As one man put it: "When you first go in, the thing to do is to do exactly as the man beside you and the man in front of you does. Always follow the man in front." In self protection, new inmates stick close to those with whom they came in, or to acquaintances from their home town, or to members of their racial group. Indeed they soon discover that they need some friends not only for protection but for comfortable survival as well. From warnings by guards that inmates in reception are occasionally conned out of their new-issue cigarette lighters, rookies become aware of their vulnerability and eager for tips on what to watch out for from fellow inmates or officials. Hence, an urgent need to find out what is going on drives them to seek acquaintance with one or two experienced inmates and consciously or unconsciously to fall in with some of the existing norms and practices for getting along.

Various official reception procedures, which begin on the first day, prepare the fish to accept prison life. Among other things, he is given a short haircut, known as the "Whiffle", which takes about three weeks to grow out and identifies newcomers to guards and inmates alike. It has several useful purposes: one ex-inmate explained, "On two occasions I became lost in the institution, and if it hadn't been for my high haircut I might have been charged with being in an unauthorized place." This ready identification helps to unify newcomers as a group and may assist them in learning how to deal with the con lines and exploitative manoeuvres of more seasoned prisoners. Being easily identified, of course, the haircut may mark him out as "easy bait".

Certain reception procedures involve a thorough-going humiliation of new inmates. Already degraded and stigmatized by the trial and imprisonment in the county jail, they are stripped, searched, finger-printed, man-handled, and deprived of almost all personal possessions. At the same time they find themselves shouted at and ordered around by the guards and generally treated as untrustworthy. Freedom to choose their clothing, toilet articles, food, or work is gone. The daily regime, controlled by a host of rules and regulations, many of which seem senseless, also reminds them that their total round of life is now beyond their own control. Though such humiliation will affect men differently, for many it strengthens feelings of inferiority and hostility to authority. For many it also leads to a search for "angles" and ways around the many rules. The rookie is on his way to discovering that almost everyone resorts to lying and evasions when possible. In general, the totally policed set of rules arouses an interest in the patterned ways of escaping from the work, the hated PT, and the custodial supervision which are available and well-developed in the inmate way of life. Thus, this early and repeated experience of personal mistreatment and hostility to rules and officials propels the new inmate in the direction of some of the central attitudes and values of the inmate society. In addition the rookie is likely to look for guidance from the older prisoners about what to say and not to say to guards and how to describe them behind their backs. Notably, he is told that various degrees of trouble are applied to prisoners who tell officials of important events or tricks in the inmate community. In short, patterns of relations with the guards are already laid down in the inmate's world and provide him with ready-made, easily used ways of response. Again, finding himself in a group engaged in a cold war with officials, he learns that when someone has been beaten up, it is safer not to ask "Who fixed that fellow and why?" In fact, he notes it is usually best to mind his own business, "to keep one's ears and eyes open but one's mouth closed". In sum, the necessity of attaining a tolerable existence, combined with the insecurity of his status as a newcomer, usually force the fish quickly to adopt a number of basic rules, judgments, and norms set up in the inmate way of life.

Reception over, new inmates not sent to the nearby minimum-security institution at Brampton are plunged fully into the Guelph routine, going either to a cell or to a dorm and, after a Work Board, participating in the daily work programme. Sending good reform risks to Brampton means concentrating the more uncooperative and less educable persons at Guelph. Though this helps the adjustment of the Brampton inmates, the classification process may help to consolidate the Guelph inmates into a community of similar types. In the complex life of the institution most first termers are at once placed on one of the lowest rungs in the ladder. Unless they have close friends among wheels or solid types, and can play that kind of role, they are accorded goof status. Rank among rounders on the outside (the street) counts for little. Here is how one inmate expressed it: "Maybe in the town he came from he was right up there, but in the joint, he isn't. There's wheels from every place in there but only some of them are wheels in there."

The rookie's adjustment to the role-playing and beliefs characteristic of the prison is aided by his separation from the law-abiding society outside. Such separation includes the physical isolation of prisoners, their wearing of a special uniform, and their demeaning treatment as convicts. They are allowed a minimum of contact with the outside world. Permitted to write one weekly one-page letter, which is then censored, they find it difficult to maintain a correspondence with more than two or three relatives or friends. (This regulation is evaded by some who send out illegal notes called "kites" through co-operative guards.) Many inmates keep in touch with only one person, some with none, and their communications, though perhaps maintaining a friendship, rarely touch on or initiate important social norms or activities characteristic of the "street". Again, inmate chats with visitors are usually so short and infrequent that outside interests and realities easily grow dim. Rules governing the receiving of contemporary Canadian magazines such as *Maclean's*, or the daily newspaper mean that only a small fraction of inmates regularly see such printed media. In fact, apart from the weekly movie and the daily radio broadcast there is little in the prison's weekly round to remind the inmates that the world outside still exists. The occasional Sunday visit of a girls' choir from an evangelical church adds a welcome but incongruous touch to the otherwise drab and restricted routine. The absence of discussion groups, educational films, or television, or regular contact with the law-abiding community completes the inmates' isolation from conventional norms and interests and indirectly aids in the building up of a distinctive inmate culture.

Though administrative regulations and policies effectively cut off most inmates from regular means of identification with beliefs, standards, groups and persons who uphold conventional anti-criminal norms and goals, placing young inmates in work groups of various kinds exposes them to the norms and goals of experienced prisoners, repeaters, and older men. Each work group has its own work standards and methods of stalling, its own peculiar privileges or opportunities for conniving or stealing, and its own place within the status hierarchy of good or poor "goes". This is, of course, not unlike a department in a large corporation. The difference is that the official heads of Guelph work gangs, the guards, have few incentives to offer – and none of them financial – to secure the worker-inmates' compliance with goals of production or responsible labor. Instead of being trained, as is the official hope, in good work habits, the young rookie is liable to learn how to fit in with the institutionalized stalls, how to help smuggle contraband, such as goodies from the kitchen, and how important it is to stay in solidly with one's work group. Because the great majority of inmates find their work boring or unrewarding, many fish will follow the pattern of filling in empty time on the job with conversation on crime, or with conniving or various kinds of gambling.

Specific types of work gangs can play a crucial role in an inmate's learning and accepting the rules. Some gangs develop among their members relatively little pressure to accept criminal mores. For instance small-farms and teamster gangs are small units operating far from the main body of prisoners and their daily isolation from the exercise yard and the main inmate group tends to weaken the pull of the prison way of life. Jobs in the tailor shop, where prison garments are made, are considered women's work and are accorded the lowest status in the inmate ranking system. Few if any inmate leaders or aggressive "solid type" bearers of the

The Army

The army, of course, is another example of the total institution. In Frank Jones' study, "Socialization of the Infantry Recruit", we can see the role superiors play in this process in the Canadian Army. The persons responsible for the new recruits naturally act in ways that separate them, usually by establishing their superiority. Jones noted that all instructors of new recruits acted in such a way as to indicate that they had a great deal of knowledge that the recruit had yet to acquire. During question periods, the instructors would deliberately select recruits who could not answer questions correctly. This made it possible for the instructor to demonstrate his knowledge without allowing the more capable recruits a chance to show what they knew. Some teachers in our educational system do the same thing. Often when an instructor accidentally made an error and then discovered it, he would ask the recruits whether he was right or wrong. Although both the instructor and recruits knew it was wrong, this strategy saved the instructor from appearing incompetent

nmate culture are found in the shop and, because great care is exercised by the administration to prevent stealing, inmates are usually unable to take out shop valuables for contraband sale. On the other hand, work gangs high in status, in solid-type membership, and in opportunities for stealing and for wheeling and dealing, are significant in preparing prisoners for the inmate culture and value system. Two of these are the kitchen, which may employ in all up to forty men, and the buller or main work party which often numbers over a hundred. "The kitchen is the control centre for all foods and favours, the cookies and the ice cream and the oranges, etc. . . . A job in the kitchen gives you a great deal of control and a great deal of opportunity to buy favours and to wield influence." On the buller, the inmates' sense of belonging to a tough 'solid' bunch managed by the real wheels explains much of its influential role. Only physically strong prisoners can hold their own in heavy work and a certain kind of prisoner therefore finds his way into this gang which develops practices and standards highly integrated with inmate patterns of conniving, fighting, and self-promotion. Contraband is passed around, rules are broken, and malingering and conniving are common. Moreover, in order to keep control of this large group its inmate leaders, usually wheels, are often accorded considerable power by the guards in charge. So great is inmate influence that, contrary to regulations, two prisoners may be allowed to have a fight supervised by the guard, or a guard may throw down his cap and fight an inmate. In short, to be on the buller generally means to be in or close to the solid group and brings some status and valuable friendships. Thus, inmates desiring higher status are brought into line fairly easily. Fear of physical pressure cannot be altogether discounted. In contrast to the buller, whose members tend to hang together a good deal in off hours, members of most other gangs disperse in the evenings into other social groups.

Adjusting to the work groups often helps fish to be absorbed into the inmate community, as does placement in a dorm of thirty-three other prisoners – the experience of roughly half of the inmates. In a dorm the average fish has little choice but to adjust his ways to the group already there. "You've got to kinda fit into their pattern. They are used to doing things in a certain order. . . ." In such a small group, refusal to accept ways of dress, language, and behaviour can hardly go unnoticed. New inmates are also put through a series of testing experiences, both verbal and physical, designed to discover their courage and fighting ability, shrewdness, social skills, and loyalty to the prisoners' code. Failures can lead to psychological or physical punishments, while success guarantees fuller acceptance.

In the dorm, a rookie member may be forced to take on more than his share of sweeping and also have to act "six" (call out six, meaning nix, when a guard is seen coming), which can be both tiresome and risky. However, by conformity he may earn some status, avoid these "Joe" jobs, and perhaps get "cut in" on a profitable contraband "deal" being promoted by dorm associates.

As has been noted, because legal dorm recreation is confined to reading, checkers, and chess, much free time is devoted to conver-

The authors of *The American Soldier* point out that the army was a new world for most civilian soldiers, and draw attention to three important respects in which it differed from civilian institutions:

(i) its authoritarian organization, demanding rigid obedience;
(ii) its highly stratified social system, in which hierarchies of deference were formally and minutely established by official regulation, subject to penalties for infraction, on and off duty;
(iii) its emphasis on traditional ways of doing things and its discouragement of initiative.

Michael Banton
Roles: An Introduction to the Study of Social Relations

sation, and inmates spin endless stories about illegal exploits imaginary and actual. The concentration on crime in these stories reflects the fact that the only significant behaviour pattern all inmates share is illegal activity. Such conversation may seduce listeners into exaggerating their criminal experience, fighting successes, physical toughness, or loyalty to the prisoners' code. A dorm thus exposes the new inmate to a wide range of information and tricks about crime which may well excite his imagination and interest. In addition, his own conversational involvement is likely slowly to shift his values in the direction of clever operating.

The process of conforming to the inmate value system typically begins with the learning and use of the prison language. Although not as extensive as in the "Bib House" (provincial penitentiary) the prison argot at Guelph includes dozens of words identical or nearly identical with those in use in other North American institutions. The new vocabulary is absorbed in part by sheer exposure. "You hear it and you get to know what they're saying. If you don't know you just ask them. Being exposed to it, you just pick it up.... The new inmate, he picks it up because he's continually around the guys that are using it." It is usually the younger prisoners who pick up and use the language with enjoyment and ease while some of the older men "tend to keep to themselves a bit and loathe the way they (the main body of prisoners) like to talk". One older inmate pointed out, "I did try to avoid it but occasionally we would use a word from the jargon because it was quick and easy and everybody knew it, but I don't think I ever fell into that kind of talk." Besides being suited to the situation, the inmate vocabulary, including much blasphemy and obscenity, acts as a convenient sign of identification with the inmate way of life.

Plunged into work gang and dormitory, after three weeks in the joint and beginning to learn the language, the newcomer also has to pick up certain details of the economy and its operation. He learns how much various items of contraband cost in cash or "bales" of tobacco, how he can convert eight bales for $1.00, and what the going price of such items as a cross and chain is. His eyes are opened to ways of gambling with bales of tobacco, to places to hide extra bales, and to ways of carrying around money hidden on various parts of the body. Learning the various tricks of fooling the administration is part of "learning the ropes".

Learning the ropes includes coming to understand many individual items of the inmate culture. The newcomer discovers that thievery is commonplace and that one cannot afford to leave things around unguarded. Slippers, for example, if worn to PT and not closely watched, would be stolen. Yet the inmate code opposes thieving and if someone is caught stealing he is usually quickly and brutally punished. The rookie also discovers that fights are part of the daily routine and that when a big fight is on, "anything goes". He will observe that if an inmate fails to stand up for himself he invites further trouble, and that it is smart in a fight to hit the person first and hard and so end the business in a hurry. Brutality is common. "I learned to think nothing of kicking a guy in the face," said one inmate. Again highly colourful and exaggerated stories about criminal, sexual, or conning achievements are en-

The following excerpt from an article about sailors on board ship describes how initiation ceremonies are used to help group morale after long periods at sea.

Initiations are . . . held every time a sailor is promoted. Only those who hold a rating equal to or above his can serve in the initiation, which usually consists of a chase, a capture, and a dunking. The promotee's new insignia is "pinned on" his shoulder by a number of fists. In return for his recognition, he must give all his peers and superiors cigars. The promotion initiation for chief petty officers is far richer, calling for the initiate's wearing of some clownish costume for twenty-four hours, the standing of absurd watches (i.e., guarding the ship's fog whistle), and finally, the reading, with all hands at quarters for muster, of a document which acknowledges the older chiefs' acceptance of this lowly initiate into their ranks.

The most impressive and the most complete initiation ceremony of all, however, is the elaborate program involved in *crossing the line*.

The night before the ship is scheduled to cross the equator, a colorfully costumed "Davy Jones" crawls, amid a glare of spotlights and great fanfare, out of a hawse pipe (where the anchor hangs), and demands to see the Officer of the Deck. He quizzes this officer about the name of the ship and its destination, then demands to see the Captain. When the Captain comes to the bridge, Davy Jones reads him a summons from Neptunus Rex, the King of the Sea, ordering the Captain to prepare for a visit from His Royal Highness on the following morning. Davy Jones then takes his leave.

On the following morning, Davy Jones reappears and announces that Neptunus Rex is about to make his entry. The Flag of Neptunus Rex is run up, the ship is stopped dead in the water, and all hands are ordered to fall in at quarters for muster. Neptune (usually played by a senior chief) makes his grand entry with his retinue (played by other enlisted men): Amphitrite, the Royal Baby, the Royal Chaplain, the Royal Navigator, Neptune's Officer of the Day, Judges, Attorneys, Barbers, Doctors, Bears, and Police. After informing the Captain that the Royal Navigator will take over the ship, Neptune ascends his throne and commands that the initiation of the "polywogs" begin. (All personnel

countered and most inmates tend to develop a certain cynicism about "good" lines. The rookie who observes inmates being "marked in" by con artists "grinding a buck" may learn to see through much of the flim-flam and pick up simple con lines himself; or if already somewhat skilled he may learn new and better tricks from the more experienced.

Spotting the exchange of contraband in the exercise yard and elsewhere, the newcomer will discover which inmates can arrange trades, and later try to arrange simple deals himself, for example, to exchange tobacco for clean shirts or slippers. Eventually he may graduate to enjoy the satisfaction of "dealing" and take on the role of a wheeler and dealer. The scarcity of cash – forbidden completely by the authorities – tends to accentuate the importance attached to money. Prisoners with money command respect. Among many inmates conversation concentrates on clothes and cars, and men buck for status by describing the things they possessed or claim to have possessed before coming in. Exposure to enthusiastic and repeated discussions of the enjoyments provided by money, clothes, and cars increases the desire to have impressive things and contributes to efforts at slick operating. Inmates are constantly confronted by various betting and gambling practices which also strengthen the slick operating and fast-buck idea with its contempt for hard work and middle-class hopes for a career. The fish will also observe the ways in which inmates resist the orders of the guards. They will also hear of or be exposed to protection rackets, and may have to buy protection. In sum, the rookie inmate finds himself in a community in which techniques and norms of thievery, illicit trading, gambling, lying, scheming and manipulating, malingering, self-promoting, cynicism, fighting, and violence are common and even regularized.

Learning to cope with these and other such social patterns is the fate of all newcomers to Guelph. Adjustment occurs much faster than the usual adjustment of a stranger to a new community. "You catch on fast at Guelph or else," inmates agree. "For instance, when I first went in there, they took me for 27 bales (of tobacco) in gambling and I didn't even know what was going on. ... Finally I got onto it, it took time, but I got onto it." A fifth-floor man amplified the rigors of the learning process: "When the new men come in the wheels take them for everything that they've got, which isn't much, such as tobacco, razor blades, etc. They haven't got much choice because if they don't give it to them, they just take it off them anyway, the hard way." Thus, the first timer is often one man against the crowd.

Acceptance, at least outwardly, of the prisoner's code is also strongly pressed upon the new inmate by the values promoted by the experienced prisoners and seldom criticized openly. Key items are statements such as "We've gotta stick together", "Help the underdog", "Never trust the guards or the administration", "Don't let the guards put anything over on you", and "Working is for dopes". New inmates discover that disregarding these articles of faith brings penalties. A man may be labelled a rat or a Square John or a goof. Ratting is often dealt with by physical actions. Being friendly with guards – unless one is a wheel – usually leads

who have crossed the equator, and can prove it by showing certificates, are "shellbacks", and are members of the retinue. Those who have not crossed the equator are called "polywogs", and are about to undergo a hazing that will make them fit subjects for Neptune's kingdom.) Summonses usually have been issued the night before, ordering the polywogs to appear before the court and answer charges made against them (often dealing with physical characteristics or personal idiosyncrasies of the victims). The polywogs are always found guilty as charged, and sentenced to such things as a dunking into a tub filled with salt water and garbage, hair clipping, kissing the Royal Baby's belly (he is always the fattest shellback on board). Officer polywogs are also sentenced, but usually to more sophisticated punishments – i.e., polishing brass in the chief's quarters.

After the ceremony is completed, usually by noon of the same day, all hands are shellbacks, and the initiates are given their certificates of membership. The spirit of unity abounds. This event will be talked about, relived, many times in the future, and each time it will thus reinforce the cohesion of the crew. So important is this occasion for the sailor that squadrons of ships have been known to sail for days just north of the line, waiting for favorable initiation weather before crossing.

Here is an operation of the informal organization that is wide enough in scope to encompass the entire vessel, and to "usurp" the power of the Captain. It is seen, however, that this ceremony is given full cooperation by the formal organization – a "we feeling" crew better carries out the formal goals of the ship. One ship's Captain, writing aboard a U.S. Navy vessel over a hundred years ago, says of the ceremony:

> Its evil is [short-lived], if an evil there be, while it certainly affords Jack [the sailor] a topic for a month beforehand and a fortnight afterwards; and if so ordered as to keep its monstrosities within the limits of strict discipline, which is easy enough, it may even add to the authority of the officers, instead of weakening their influence.

Louis A. Zurcher, Jr.
"The Sailor Aboard Ship"

to verbal criticism or "centring out", being singled out by a number of prisoners for humiliating remarks. Among the solid types other basic values include "Don't let anyone push you around", and "Have heart (courage)" and "Always back up your pals when they're in trouble". To gain full acceptance by this class of inmate the new inmate must in due course demonstrate loyalty to these stiffer values.

A significant kind of relationship occurs when a new inmate enters into a buying relationship, under pressure, with a "protector" or "protectors". In essence, this means he has to get money regularly, either through visitors, "drops", gambling, or stealing, and hand it over to his protector. From twenty to over a hundred of the younger, less robust, and less experienced new inmates get involved in such a relationship. The way it happens is described by an unusually articulate inmate:

> Immediately the typical 17-year-old arrives he is bait for the upper strata of the inmate group. Upon his first appearance in the exercise yard, a competition almost develops among them as to who will own and influence him. This is usually not too overt, though sometimes it is. He can, within a matter of hours, have taken from him his lighter, his ration of tobacco, or if it's in the winter time, and he happens to have a fairly good smock, this may be changed for a more beaten-up sort of thing.... He then realizes that he can't by himself exist in this prison, because these "exchanges" are always made by two or three people at a time. He may be physically fairly powerfully built, but he has no chance against odds of three or four to one. So he can either look for some sort of protection or it can be offered to him.... When he is approached by some person who offers him protection for possibly a fee or a service, he may have to steal in order to protect himself.... Practically every adolescent who goes in for the first time feels he is immediately dependent upon other influences in order to just exist.... He finds he has to steal to live, he has to evade a lot of regulations and in a period of six months he hasn't got much further than learning how to steal pretty effectively from the government, that is, taking things from the institution.

The significant thing at Guelph and most other North American prisons is that the inmate group dominates the socializing process, while the administration, in the absence of clear-cut reform policies and adequate qualified staff, carries on at best a rearguard, defensive action. This is not to say that the large majority of inmates accept the values of the criminal culture. Some find it to their advantage "to play it cool". When one three-timer ex-inmate was asked how he would advise a rookie to steer clear of criminal influences, he answered, "I'd tell him to just use his head and not to be taken in by all these guys. Play it cool. There's a time and place for everything."

four   *The business organization*

The economy consists of a number of institutions that are involved in the production and distribution of various goods and services. Factories, mills, farms, and mines produce the goods sought by our society. Trains, trucks, planes, and boats, and the tracks, roads, and routes associated with them, distribute the goods. Exchange of goods is made possible through money, and this service is supported by banks and other financial institutions. Advertising firms encourage the exchange of money for goods. Many other institutions surround the economic market-place; entertainment, repair firms, and cleaning establishments are some examples.

Money has provided the basis for exchange of goods throughout the world. It makes it possible to place a value on each product. It provides freedom for the buyer and seller to negotiate, since they are not required to trade one product evenly for another; this tends to remove somewhat the personal relationship from economic activities. And, of course, money has given us our banks and stock exchange.

While people are primarily motivated to participate in economic activities by the prospect of making money, they also work to gain more prestige, influence, friendship with others, and of prime importance, a sense of being useful. The humorous selection that follows presents various strategies for *avoiding* promotion.

Creative Incompetence: The Peter Principle

Dr. Laurence J. Peter

Raymond Hull

(The Peter Principle states that a person will move up in an organization until he reaches a position where he cannot perform the job effectively. Therefore, we stop in our advancement at that point where we are unable to do the job that is expected of us. This is because we advance to another job only when we are doing our present job effectively.)

Does my exposition of the Peter Principle seem to you like a philosophy of despair? Do you shrink from the thought that final placement, with its wretched physical and psychological symptoms, must be the end of every career? Emphasizing these questions, I should like to present the reader with a knife that allows him to cut through this philosophical Gordian knot. . . .

"Surely," you may say, "a person can simply refuse to accept promotion, and stay working happily at a job he can do competently."

An Interesting Example

The blunt refusal of an offered promotion is known as Peter's Parry. To be sure, it sounds easy enough. Yet I have discovered only one instance of its successful use.

T. Sawyer, a carpenter employed by the Beamish Construction

Always do one thing less than you think you can do.

B. M. Baruch

Better to light a single candle than to curse the Edison Co.

Dr. Lawrence J. Peter
Raymond Hull
The Peter Principle

Company, was so hard-working, competent and conscientious that he was several times offered the post of foreman.

Sawyer respected his boss and would have liked to oblige him. Yet he was happy as a rank-and-file carpenter. He had no worries: he could forget the job at 4:30 p.m. each day.

He knew that, as a foreman, he would spend his evenings and weekends worrying about the next day's and the next week's work. So he steadily refused the promotion.

Sawyer, it is worth noting, was an unmarried man with no close relatives and few friends. He could act as he pleased.

Not So Easy for Most of Us

For most people, Peter's Parry is impracticable. Consider the case of B. Loman, a typical citizen and family man, who refused a promotion.

His wife at once began to nag him. "Think of your children's future! What would the neighbours say if they knew? If you loved me, you'd want to get ahead!" and so on.

To find out for sure what the neighbours would say, Mrs. Loman confided the cause of her chagrin to a few trusted friends. The news spread around the district. Loman's young son, trying to defend his father's honor, fought one of his schoolmates and knocked out two of the other boy's teeth. The resulting litigation and dental bills cost Loman eleven hundred dollars.

Loman's mother-in-law worked Mrs. Loman's feelings up to such a pitch that she left him and secured a judicial separation. In his loneliness, disgrace and despair, he committed suicide.

No, refusing promotion is no easy route to happiness and health. I saw, early in my researches, for most people, *Peter's Parry does not pay*!

An Illuminating Observation

While studying hierarchal structure and promotion rates among the production and clerical workers of the Ideal Trivet Company, I noticed that the grounds around the Trivet Building were beautifully landscaped and maintained. The velvety lawns and jewel-like flower beds suggested a high level of horticultural competence. I found that P. Greene, the gardener, was a happy, pleasant man with a genuine affection for his plants and a respect for his tools. He was doing what he liked best, gardening.

He was competent in all aspects of his work except one: he nearly always lost or mislaid receipts and delivery slips for goods received by his department, although he managed requisitions quite well.

The lack of delivery slips upset the accounting department, and Greene was several times reprimanded by the manager. His replies were vague: "I think I may have planted the papers along with the shrubs." "Maybe the mice in the potting shed got the papers."

Because of this incompetence in paper work, when a new maintenance foreman was required, Greene was not considered for the post.

Two researchers told their subjects the story of John, a foreman who was promoted to divisional head but who continued to wear foreman's clothes to the factory instead of a business suit. After several months of this the other divisional heads started to avoid him. What, the research workers asked, would happen? Thirty-six per cent of their sample said that John would be demoted or transferred; 25 per cent that he would be discharged or allowed to leave; 14 per cent that he would get no further advancement; 11 per cent that he would voluntarily accept demotion; 6 per cent that he would quit. In short, over nine-tenths of the sample believed that a failure to dress as expected would adversely affect the occupational mobility and the future of the man in question.

Michael Banton
Roles: An Introduction to the Study of Social Relations

I interviewed Greene several times. He was courteous and co-operative, but insisted that he lost the documents accidentally. I questioned his wife. She told me that Greene kept comprehensive records for his home gardening operations, and could calculate the cost of everything produced in his yard or greenhouse.

A Parallel Case?

I interviewed A. Messer, shop foreman at Cracknell Casting and Foundry Company, whose little office seemed to be in grotesque disorder. Nevertheless, my time-and-motion study showed that the tottering piles of old account and reference books, the cardboard cartons bursting with tattered work sheets, the cabinets over-flowing with unindexed files and the sheaves of long-disused plans pinned to the walls were really not a part of Messer's basically efficient operation.

I could not tell whether he was or was not consciously using this untidiness to camouflage his competence, in order to avoid promotion to general foreman.

Madness in his Method?

J. Spellman was a competent school-teacher. His professional reputation was high, yet he never got the offer of a vice-principalship. I wondered why, and began to make inquiries.

A senior official told me, "Spellman neglects to cash his pay checks. Every three months we have to remind him that we would like him to cash his checks, so that we can keep the books straight. I just can't understand a person who doesn't cash his checks."

I questioned further.

"No, no! We don't distrust him," was the reply. "But naturally one wonders whether he has some private source of income."

I asked, "Do you suspect that he might be involved in some illegal activities?"

"Certainly not! A good man! A sterling reputation!"

Despite these disclaimers, I drew the inference that the hierarchy cannot trust a man who manages his finances so well that he does not rush to the bank and cash or deposit his pay check in order to cover his bills. Spellman, in short, had shown himself incompetent to behave as the typical employee is expected to behave; hence he had made himself ineligible for promotion.

Was it *only* coincidence that Spellman was happy in his teaching work, and had no desire for promotion to administrative duties?

Is There a Pattern?

I investigated many similar cases of what seemed to be deliberate incompetence, but I could never certainly decide whether the behaviour was the result of conscious planning, or of a subconscious motivation.

One thing was clear: these employees had avoided advancement, not by refusing promotion – we have already seen how disastrous that can be – but by contriving never to be offered a promotion!

Bureaucracy and Democracy in the Voluntary Association

According to Alvin Gouldner, the idea that bureaucratic modes of organization arise inevitably in all spheres of life, and that they inevitably subvert democratic values, is widespread among social scientists:

It is the pathos of pessimism . . . that leads to the assumption that organizational constraints have stacked the deck against democracy. . . . It is only in the light of such a pessimistic pathos that the defeat of democratic values can be assumed to be probable while their victory is seen as a slender thing, delicately constituted and precariously balanced. . . .

Wrapping themselves in the shrouds of nineteenth-century political economy, some social scientists appear to be bent on resurrecting a dismal science. Instead of telling men how bureaucracy might be mitigated, they insist that it is inevitable. Instead of explaining how democratic patterns may, to some extent, be fortified and extended, they warn us that democracy cannot be perfect. Instead of controlling the disease, they suggest that we are deluded, or more politely, incurably romantic, for hoping to control it. Instead of assuming responsibilities as realistic clinicians, striving to further democratic potentialities wherever they can, many social scientists have become morticians, all too eager to bury men's hopes.

Alvin W. Gouldner
"Metaphysical Pathos and
The Theory of Bureaucracy"
American Political Science Review, Vol. 49

If reserved detachment characterizes the attitudes of the members of the organization toward one another, it is unlikely that high *esprit de corps* will develop among them. The strict exercise of authority in the interest of discipline induces subordinates, anxious to be highly thought of by their superiors, to conceal defects in operations from superiors, and this obstruction of the flow of information upward in the hierarchy impedes effective management. Insistence on conformity also tends to engender rigidities in official conduct and to inhibit the rational exercise of judgment needed for efficient performance of tasks.

Peter M. Blau
Bureaucracy in Modern Society

Eureka!

This is an infallible way to *avoid the ultimate promotion*; this is *the key to health and happiness* at work and in private life; this is *Creative Incompetence.*

A Proven Policy

It does not matter whether Greene, Messer, Spellman and other employees similarly situated are consciously or unconsciously avoiding the ultimate promotion. What does matter is that we can learn from them how to achieve this vitally important goal. ("Vitally important" is no figure of speech: the correct technique may save your life.)

The method boils down to this: *create the impression that you have already reached your level of incompetence.*

You do this by exhibiting one or more of the non-medical symptoms of final placement.

Greene the gardener was exhibiting a mild form of Papyrophobia. Messer, the foundry foreman, to a casual observer, seemed to be an Advanced Papyromaniac. Spellman the schoolteacher, procrastinating over the deposit of his pay checks, showed a severe, though unusual, form of the Teeter-Totter Syndrome.

Creative Incompetence will achieve best results if you choose an area of incompetence *which does not directly hinder you in carrying out the main duties of your present position.*

Some Subtle Techniques

For a clerical worker, such an unspectacular habit as leaving one's desk drawers open at the end of the working day will, in some hierarchies, have the desired effect.

A show of niggling, officious economy – the switching off of lights, turning off of taps, picking up paper clips and rubber bands off the floor and out of wastebaskets to the accompaniment of muttered homilies on the value of thrift – is another effective maneuver.

Stand Out from the Crowd

Refusal to pay one's share of the firm's or department's Social Fund; refraining from drinking coffee at the official coffee break; bringing one's own lunch to a job where everyone else eats out; persistent turning off of radiators and opening of windows; refusing contributions to collections for wedding and retirement gifts; a mosaic of standoffish eccentricity (the Diogenes Complex) will create just the modicum of suspicion and distrust which disqualifies you for promotion.

Automotive Tactics

One highly successful department manager avoided promotion by occasionally parking his car in the space reserved for the company president.

Another executive always drove a car one year older, and five

---

David McClelland's research work on the development of economies in various countries has led him to some interesting conclusions. He feels that the individual's desire for achievement is of critical importance when explaining why nations rise and fall. Civilizations do not rise and become successful only because they have minerals and other raw products, factories trade routes, and markets, but mainly because of the spirit in men that takes advantage of these resources.

McClelland feels that this desire to achieve is most often found among businessmen. It is not profit by itself that makes the businessman go, but a strong desire to achieve something and to do a good job. Profit is only one way of knowing whether a good job has been done or not. But profit is not necessarily the goal itself.

McClelland and his colleagues took examples of the popular writings of the past and present in various countries. They used poems, songs, plays, and stories for this purpose. They estimated the concern each country had for achieving by analyzing these materials. In most situations they found that a high level of concern for achievement is followed 50 years later by rapid economic growth and prosperity.

McClelland summarizes his feelings as follows (in "Business Drive and National Achievement", *Harvard Business Review*):

If there is one thing that all this research has taught me, it is that men can shape their own destiny, that external difficulties and pressures are not nearly so important in shaping history as some people have argued. It is how people respond to those challenges that matters, and how they respond depends on how strong their concern for achievement is. So the question of what happens to our civilization or to our business community depends quite literally on how much time tens of thousands or even millions of us spend thinking about achievements, about setting moderate achievable goals, taking calculated risks, assuming personal responsibility, and finding out how well we have done our job. The answer is up to us.

hundred dollars cheaper in original price, than the cars of his peers.

Personal Appearance

Most people agree *in principle* with the dictum that fine feathers don't make fine birds, but *in practice* an employee is judged by his appearance. Here, then, is ample scope for Creative Incompetence.

The wearing of unconventional or *slightly* shabby clothes, irregularity of bathing, *occasional* neglect of haircutting or *occasional* carelessness in shaving (the *small* but conspicuous wound dressing adjoining a *small* blob of congealed blood, or the small patch of stubble missed by the razor) are useful techniques.

Ladies may wear *a shade too much* or *too little* makeup, possibly combined with the *occasional* wearing of an unbecoming or inappropriate hair style. Overly strong perfume and overly brilliant jewelry work well in many cases.

More Real-life Examples

Here, for your guidance and inspiration, are some superb instances of Creative Incompetence which I have observed in my studies.

Mr. F. proposed to the boss's daughter at the firm's annual Founder's Birthday Party. The girl had just graduated from a European finishing school, and F. had never seen her before that occasion. Naturally, he did not get the daughter and naturally, too, he rendered himself ineligible for promotion.

Miss L., of the same firm, contrived to offend the boss's wife at the same party by imitating the older woman's peculiar laugh within her hearing.

Mr. P. got a friend to make *one* fake threatening phone call to him at the office. Within earshot and sight of his colleagues, P. reacted dramatically, begged for "mercy" and "more time" and pleaded, "Don't tell my wife. If she finds out this will kill her." Was this just one of P.'s typically stupid jokes or was it an inspired piece of Creative Incompetence?

An Old Friend Revisited

I recently reviewed the case of T. Sawyer, the carpenter whose successful use of Peter's Parry I described at the beginning of this chapter.

In the last few months he has been buying cheap paperbound copies of Henry D. Thoreau's *Walden* or *Life in the Woods* and giving them away to his workmates and superiors, in each case with a few remarks on the pleasures of irresponsibility and the joys of day labor.

He follows up the gift with persistent questioning to see whether the recipient has read the book and how much of it he has understood. This meddlesome didacticism I denominate *The Socrates Complex.*

Research indicates that employees who have no opportunity for close social contact find their work less satisfying, and this lack of satisfaction often reflects itself in lower production and higher turnover and absenteeism. Many years ago Elton Mayo observed that employees in a textile plant who worked at isolated jobs were highly dissatisfied and consistently failed to meet production standards. Staggered rest periods helped a little. But when the company permitted these workers to take rest periods *as a group*, production and satisfaction both increased. Another company, where the girls worked in small, isolated booths, had the same experience. When management put the glass partitions between the booths, the rate of turnover and the number of grievances both dropped sharply. Similarly, researchers in hospitals have discovered that maids feel uncomfortable when they work only in the company of high-status personnel (doctors, nurses, etc.) with whom they cannot associate with ease. Several hospitals have found that when three or four maids are grouped together as a team, turnover falls and a much better job is done.

George Strauss and Leonard R. Sayles
Personnel: The Human Problems of Management

Sawyer reports that the offers of promotion have ceased. I naturally felt a little disappointment at the disappearance of the only living example of a *successful* Peter's Parry (successful in the sense that it had averted proffered promotion without causing him unhappiness). Yet this disappointment was counterbalanced by pleasure at seeing an elegant proof of the fact that

Creative Incompetence beats Peter's Parry every time!

An Important Precaution

A thoughtful study of the concept will give you plenty of ideas for developing your own form of Creative Incompetence. Yet I must emphasize the paramount importance of *concealing the fact that you want to avoid promotion*! As camouflage, you may even indulge in the occasional mild *grumble* to your peers: "Darned funny how *some* people get promotion in this place, while others are passed over!"

Dare You Do It?

If you have not yet attained final placement on Peter's Plateau, you can discover an irrelevant incompetence.

Find it and practise it diligently. It will keep you at a level of competence and so assure you of the keen personal satisfaction of regularly accomplishing some useful work.

Surely creative incompetence offers as great a challenge as the traditional drive for higher rank!

It is one thing to offer to pay the worker for his education outside the plant; it is quite another to motivate him to obtain more education. Many of the workers as a result of their previous experience with educational institutions probably became convinced of either the lack of importance of further education or their own inability to be successful in the academic environment. It is not an easy matter to induce someone who already has had unsuccessful educational experiences to try once more.

Harvey Swados
The Myth of the Happy Worker

Resources for Part 4

Berton, P. 1965. *The Comfortable Pew.* Toronto: McClelland & Stewart Ltd.

Canadian Teachers Federation. 1970. *The Poor at School in Canada.*

Elkin, F. 1968. *The Family in Canada.* Ottawa: Vanier Institute of the Family.

Meiklejohn, P. J. 1969. *The Family.* Toronto: McClelland & Stewart Ltd.

Packard, V. 1968. "Life of the Executive." *The Pyramid Climbers.* Greenwich Conn.: Fawcett World.

Vaughan, F., Kyba, P., Dwivedi, O. P. (eds.). 1970. *Contemporary Issues in Canadian Politics.* Scarborough, Ontario: Prentice-Hall (Canada) Ltd.

Part 5
The problems of man

The Greeks had a word for it – Utopia. Literally translated from the Greek, Utopia means "nowhere" and is used in a philosophic sense to denote a perfect system that affords an ideal existence for everyone. For several centuries, philosophers and scientists have searched for such an idyllic state, and some people still believe that Utopia is possible. Indeed, some men continue to kill one another to prove that a better world is just around the corner. For some, the ideal is a world free of war, for others a world free of poverty and disease, and for still others, a world free for democracy, liberty, and individual enterprise.

In recent years, the very existence of man has been jeopardized by his own acts and inventions. Centuries ago, when famine, disease, and predatory animals threatened him, man was able to survive through his ability to make use of that uniquely specialized organ – the brain. Of course, many scientists say he still can survive, but an increasing number of scientists feel it may be too late. Man must face a growing technology that has complicated his social relations. Problems of living space, food distribution and production, energy sources, and a despoiled environment cannot be ignored any longer. It has become clear that the magnitude of some of these problems requires concerted international action. Canada's former Prime Minister, Lester B. Pearson, has warned us of the dangers of the growing gap between the rich and poor nations: "With these disparities there can be no stability or security or peace in the future".

The following section represents an attempt to bring into greater focus some of the more critical problems facing mankind today.

one   *Living in a complex world*

Each generation inherits problems from the past, adds problems of its own, and creates others for future generations. Man is a gregarious being: he tends to seek out relationships with other men. Modern technology has had profound effects on men's relationships with society and with himself.

The term "alienation" has been coined to refer to a human condition in which man has lost a sense of purpose for his life, in which he feels unrelated to other men and his own work, in which he feels alone. In our first selection, "Adolescence in a Changing World", the conditions that contribute to adolescents' confusion about adult life are considered. These conditions lead to normal adjustment for some, alienation for others, and a strong negative reaction by others. Following this article, a series of extracts is presented in which we extend and develop the themes of alienation, student unrest, and the effect of automation on our lives. The section concludes with a brief article by David Riesman on the problems created for work-oriented man in a society that is becoming more and more leisure-oriented.

Adolescence in a changing world

The adolescent today faces a shifting, complex world from which he must create his own unique adult identity. The period of adolescence can be seen as a changeover from childhood to adulthood – a stage between the carefree fun-orientation of the child to the responsibility and dedication of the adult. In our Canadian society, the time taken for this voyage from childhood through adolescence varies considerably with the individual. For some young people, marriage and entrance to the work world take place before the age of 20, and yet for others, it is delayed through long training periods.

In more primitive cultures, the shift from childhood to adulthood takes place in elaborate ceremonies – we call them "rites of passage". There is no doubt in the minds of the young people involved that they have attained adulthood. For boys, typically, it is necessary to go through a series of activities (such as staying out for two nights by oneself without food) that are often dangerous physically and usually awarded with an item of clothing, a tattoo, or some symbolic indication that they have become a man. For girls, the timing of the ceremony is usually related to the onset of menstruation (the ability to have children). In some cases, this occasion is celebrated as a wondrous event and the young girl is glorified in a celebration, but in others, the young girl is hidden away from the eyes of her people until she is "clean" again. However, there is a great difference between the swift rite of passage of the primitive tribe and the slow, tedious, confused period of time the young Canadian adolescent must go through.

The strains of this time period have resulted in many interesting behaviours in young people. It appears that adolescence in Canadian society is beginning at an increasingly earlier age. Students in elementary schools take on the symbols (long hair, unusual clothing, special vocabulary) and behaviour of their older brothers

[Western society saw] the rise of completely new industries which concocted a "youth culture" catering exclusively to the younger generations who had the money to buy the gadgets and other products specially produced for them. This youth culture rejected the adult world and the adult rationale; it stressed change and novelty in clothing and other apparel, initiation rites, the cult of speed and violence, the thrill of being "with it", and the teenage idols instead of the time-honoured heroes (James Dean, West Side Story, etc.).

Adults felt strange in this new world of "young" music, "young" records, "young" clothing, "young" hairstyles, "young" cigarettes, "young" drinks, the "young" look, etc. Radio and TV stations were literally invaded by advertising programmes trumpeting the new mood. And the world was divided between the teenage "in-group" and the old fogey "out-group".

All this was the work of adults who looked upon youth as just one big potential market. And it is saddening to reflect that the first important surveys of youth carried out in Europe were actually market studies.

Marcel Hicter
"The Angry Generation"
UNESCO Courier, April 1969

One cannot, therefore, on looking at these young people in all the glory of their defiant rags and hairdos, always just say, with tears in one's eyes: "There goes a tragically wayward youth, striving romantically to document his rebellion against the hypocrisies of the age." One has sometimes to say, and not without indignation: "There goes a perverted and willful and stony-hearted youth by whose destructiveness we are all, in the end, to be damaged and diminished."

George F. Kennan
The Radical Vision

Long hair on young men has probably caused more family quarrels during the past years than any other single subject, and while father may still scream about the length of his son's locks, the old man has been letting his own grow a bit on top and discovered that longer sideburns are really quite becoming.

Frances Moffat
What the Hippies Gave Us

Our youngsters do not hate us adults, or even dislike us particularly and even the most militant of them are not primarily interested in putting us down . . . but they have learned that they cannot trust us, because we have never had any respect for them and very little for the principles by which we pretend to govern our lives and theirs.

Paul C. Harper, Jr.
Who Am I?

Many are indeed "dropping out" of the ordinary life styles of the sterile "middle class": get up in the morning, go to work for eight hours, come home and watch television until the week is over, and then the weekend of fun and games ends, and the cycle starts all over again. The denial of this sterile way of life and the search for a new "life style" is a threat to the existing society.

Excerpt from a student newspaper
(quoted in) Orrin E. Klapp
Collective Search for Identity

and sisters. Mixed parties and dances now take place among pre-teenage children, along with cigarette smoking and even some use of drugs. Interestingly, many parents encourage their children into early adulthood by holding parties where dancing is an important feature, and in the case of girls, encouraging them to use make-up and to wear brassieres. Also there is evidence that young people are becoming physically mature earlier.

At the other end of this process, we have seen an increase in the time young people remain in school: it is now expected that most young people will graduate from high school. Students are encouraged to remain beyond high school, made more possible by the opening of community colleges in addition to the traditional universities, nursing schools, trade schools, and teacher-training institutions. To be a psychiatrist, a person typically must graduate from high school, take B.A. courses for three or four years, and then enter a four-year medical program, followed by a one-year internship, and then up to five years of psychiatric training. Under these conditions, a person could remain in school until he is 30 years old, before starting work for the first time. With this example in mind, it is obvious that we cannot pinpoint the time at which the adolescent becomes an adult as the time at which he begins working.

Our technology has made it possible for young people to remain out of the work world for longer and longer. The needs of industry require that we produce competent technicians and specialists, and this means that young people must train for much longer periods. This delay has made it possible for certain young people to postpone their official move into adult life and to continue the process of looking for their personal identity. Some of these young people become "hippies" or "radicals", but others just remain in school because it is expected and because it is less threatening than going out into the real world.

Popular opinion holds that adolescents have developed their own culture, including language, beliefs, and life style. Studies have shown that young people tend to value athletic and social activities more than regular school work. They worship sports heroes who combine athletic skill with the "swinger" image – for example, Joe Namath and Derek Sanderson. This means that, to many young people, academic work is not considered to be as important as athletic pursuits. In a superficial sense it is true, in that young people generally do not hold the good academic student in high regard, but practically speaking, they do recognize the value of school as a route to a good job. Some Canadian research has found that, in spite of a superficial commitment to the athletic type of image, most young people still value the hard work and thrift that leads to a good job and the status that this brings.

Recent studies have led us to believe that older youth are tremendously influential in determining the way of life of younger teenagers. Today it appears that variations in clothing, social habits, and general behaviour appear first in the hippie and university student and then filter down to the teenagers in the secondary schools. Perhaps one of the most important changes that has taken place in Canadian youth is an increased social concern for the welfare of others. This seems to be a product of the idealism of youth – the ideal of helping out one's fellow man. While this is often encouraged by adults, it rarely results in action. In response to this concern, young Canadian students have travelled to the southern United States to participate in campaigns intended to improve the U.S. racial situation. They have picketed the Russian and American embassies to protest the invasion of Czechoslovakia and the war in Vietnam, as well as many other issues. Even within the schools, there has been a demonstrated concern about the quality of the food in the cafeteria or the dismissal of a janitor, with students picketing or walking out. To some people it seems as if today's youth are desperately seeking a cause – *any* cause – through which they can demonstrate their social concern, and that they might follow *any* leader. These people cite such instances as mass walkouts in Ontario schools when the school year was lengthened by a few days.

With the advent of television, young people are able to obtain information on what is happening throughout the world, and they are able to find causes to fight for on a much larger scale. Young people tend to reject national differences and to fight against prejudice and discrimination – feelings shared by young people throughout the world. Some researchers see it as a world-wide conflict between young people and their parents, and perhaps this is true. The actions of young people are often explained by parents as "a phase they are going through", but it is more than a phase. The young, with their actions given importance by the mass media, have in fact changed society, made society more aware of common world problems, such as those faced by the poor and the underprivileged.

It is interesting to look at the universities, which have been the source of much of this social concern, and to see the kinds of students who are in the forefront of change – notably those enrolled in such programs as English, history, modern languages, psychology, sociology, economics, and political studies; students enrolled in the sciences, law, education, and medicine appear to be generally satisfied with the "status quo". This is also true in the high schools, where students in the vocational schools and those enrolled in technical and commercial courses are less likely to be involved in demonstrations. It appears that those who are more likely to get jobs are less likely to want to change society – a fact that was particularly evident in the early stages of student unrest. But the feeling of concern for others and the thought that the world is a place that we all must share and grow in has come to involve all kinds of students in all programs in all schools.

This concern also has been directed toward educational institutions. Schools and courses have been called irrelevant, and depending on your definition of relevant, this criticism *can* be applied to many of our courses and programs. Canadian young people want to apply education to all social problems. They want the "ivory tower" university, where ultimate forms of truth are sought, to be replaced by an institution that attacks today's problems – pollution, overpopulation, and so on.

In behaviour between the sexes, many of the older traditions

. . . ugly satanic old idleness is now rechristened "leisure". . . . Now if a boy loafs around the pornography rack at the drug store, it is merely because he has a "leisure time problem". The solution is not to put him to work . . . but to encourage him to take up the oboe or start a bee colony. In this way, we say he uses his leisure "creatively".

Russell Baker
"Observer: Rich Richard's Almanac"
The New York Times

You can't fill the heads of young lovers with "buy me the new five-hundred-dollar deep-freeze and I'll love you" advertising propaganda without poisoning the very act of love itself; you can't hop up your young people with sadism in the movies and television and train them to commando tactics in the army camps, to say nothing of brutalizing them in wars, and then expect to "untense" them with Coca-Cola and YMCA hymn sings.

Orrin E. Klapp
Collective Search for Identity

The student radical is saying that humanity somehow has been tempted away from an understanding of itself. It has forgotten its own authentic sense of being human. The ailing adults of our society, while they admit this in their cups or in that moment of honesty between waking and sleeping, are not willing to admit it in a practical way. They put off the day of reckoning by inventing categories into which they can fit student thought and action and thereby hopefully "know" it and control it, resting easily with their former preserves of authority and influence.

Gerald F. McGuigan
Student Protest

If an affluent society is to survive it must undergo a value revolution which will make . . . human values pre-eminent over production values. . . . The nature of contemporary urban society makes this increasingly necessary. . . . Earlier alternative bases of family solidarity are disappearing. . . . commitment is an increasingly crucial bond. Increasingly, the family is the only security base available to man today.

Charles W. Hobart
"Commitment, Value Conflict and the Future of the American Family"
Journal of Marriage and Family Living

The younger generation, brought up on participation and engagement in the whole world through television, has gone through a radically different socialization process compared with the older generation. In their eyes, private preserves of wealth, knowledge, food and industrial resources are primitive. For the older generation, participation may mean merely sharing what they own "by their own rights" and on their own terms, with others who have not.

Gerald F. McGuigan
Student Protest

The most incurably frustrated – and, therefore, the most vehement – among the permanent misfits are those with an unfulfilled craving for creative work. Both those who try to write, paint, compose, etcetera, and fail decisively, and those who after tasting the elation of creativeness feel a drying up of the creative flow within and know that never again will they produce aught worthwhile, are alike in the grip of a desperate passion. . . . Their unappeased hunger persists, and they are likely to become the most violent extremists in the service of their holy cause.

Eric Hoffer
The True Believer

In one sense, my feeling for these people [hippies and flower children] is one of pity, not unmixed, in some instances, with horror. I am sure that they want none of this pity. They would feel that it comes to them for the wrong reasons. If they feel sorry for themselves, it is because they see themselves as the victims of a harsh, hypocritical and unworthy adult society. If I feel sorry for them, it is because I see them as the victims of certain great and destructive philosophic errors. . . . One of these errors – and it is one that affects particularly those who take drugs, but not those alone – is the belief that the human being has marvelous resources within himself that can be made available to him merely by the passive submission to certain sorts of stimuli. . . . Well, it is true that human beings sometimes have marvelous resources within themselves. . . . But it is not true that they can be released by hippie means.

George F. Kennan
The Radical Vision

have been rejected. Hypocrisy, taking advantage of others, and using people as things, have been pushed aside and replaced by caring for, trusting, and loving other people. This is directly related to the concern for the social welfare of people not only in Canada, but throughout the world. There is a new concern for openness in all human dealings – in government, in business, in education, and in religion.

One of the symbols of rejection of adult values is the clothes that young people wear. As a reaction against adult society's desire to acquire new things of all kinds, young people wear old clothes bought at thrift stores and from Salvation Army outlets. When students started to dress as they did back in the 1920s and 1930s, manufacturers recognized that the thrift stores could not supply enough of this kind of clothing, so they began producing clothes that *look* old and used. In this way, young people directly influence current fashions. Although only a small proportion of young people adopt the dirty, ungroomed look of the hippie, this strikes at the heart of the traditional Canadian, for it is in this way that the young people can demonstrate so visibly the problems of the poor and underprivileged.

For some young people, this search for new meanings in life has led them away from the older, more traditional religions. In many cases, the established religions have been pushed aside to be replaced by new religions. It is not the beliefs and values encouraged by the traditional churches that have been questioned, but the way in which the young people see these churches operating. Far Eastern religions, such as Zen Buddhism and Hinduism, and even witchcraft have been supported by groups of young people. Perhaps the most moving example of this new religious faith are the events of such festivals as Woodstock, where there was a strong feeling of togetherness and concern for others. Sadly, in subsequent rock festivals we have had almost as much evidence of violence and criminal behaviour as we have had of love and togetherness. Young people have tried to make a distinction between a religion that means going to church and a religion that means living in a certain way. They have been striking out against the religious establishment and traditional authority by demanding that people *live* their religion, not just *believe* it.

The music of young people reflects this concern for the welfare of others and the way of life of their parents. Songs have been written about the poor and about minority groups, such as Indians, that present their problems. The way of life of middle-class man, with his concern for a large house, cars, and appliances, is criticized again and again in modern popular song. Many of the songs encourage revolution and violence to fight the evil seen in the world.

Electrically amplified instruments, such as guitars and organs, and throbbing rhythms are used in different patterns and forms to pound out social comment. The rock musical "Hair" with its songs – Aquarius, Good Morning Star Shine, and Let the Sun Shine In – support faith in understanding and concern for others and a willingness to work together to solve the problems of the world. This music provides a common basis for meeting and discussion for the young. In some ways, the songs seem to be written to discourage adult listening – the simple, repetitive lyrics, the heavy rhythms, and the coarse, loud sounds are intolerable for adults whose musical tastes have refined over the years. For young people who are just developing musical appreciation, repetitive songs and heavy beats actually are quite useful. Their parents' opposition to their music simply serves to bring young people even closer to each other, while possibly widening the understanding gap between them and the adult world.

There is even some evidence that adolescents are changing their ideas about the kinds of jobs they hope to hold in adult life. Many Canadian young people have had a relatively great amount of freedom and an "easy" life unmarred by serious deprivation of necessities. However, for many parents, regular meals, proper clothing and accommodation, and steady jobs could not be taken for granted in their youth – or even in their adulthood – which probably has contributed to their desire to acquire things. Young people, in reacting against this acquisition of material things – many of which seem to be unnecessary – have decided that life is not a search for things but an opportunity to enrich their emotional and intellectual experiences. They want to avoid the "nine-to-five" rat-race that appears to have entrapped their parents. They view the world of big business as being full of dishonesty, distortion of values, and exploitation of people. Their idea of a job is one in which *they* set the working conditions and hours, and money is only of secondary importance. To them, the most important aspects of the job are the opportunity to display creativity and to obtain personal fulfillment.

Young people are critical of the "red tape" of the complex bureaucracy in modern business and government. They want to share in decision-making and to be involved in a personal way. Their interest in involvement takes them to service jobs – helping out in disadvantaged areas – to teaching jobs all over the world, and to political action. The world of music has become more important as a career possibility as the interest in rock music grows. Job security and opportunities for advancement seem to be less important for some than interesting, creative work, particularly if the work is socially relevant.

While U.S. problems, such as the Vietnam war and racial conflict, encouraged Canadian youth to be more politically active, these also demonstrated that Canada was quite different from the United States. Young people in the United States tend to focus on U.S. problems, while Canadian youth tends to focus on world-wide problems. The floods in Pakistan and the Biafran wars were of far greater significance to Canadian youth than to U.S. youth; in fact, Canadian youth seems to be more involved with U.S. problems than with Canadian problems. Canada has tended to identify with the United States not only for economic reasons, but also because the United States represented the "pioneering spirit" and "equal opportunity for all". But recent difficulties in the United States have tarnished this image for Canadians, particularly for young Canadians, and an attempt is now being made to develop a uniquely Canadian image. Here we have a basic conflict for young people: on the one hand, we have the move toward a world-

We are intensely aware, in a way perhaps not possible for the older generation, that humanity stands on the edge of a new era. Because we are young, we have insights into the present and visions of the future that our parents do not have. Tasks of an immense gravity wait solution in our generation. We have inherited these tasks from our parents. We do not blame them so much for that – the problems come from human failings – but we do blame them for being unwilling to admit that there are problems or for saying that it is we who have visited these problems on ourselves because of our perversity, ungratefulness and unwillingness to listen to "reason".

David Zirnhelt
in Gerald F. McGuigan
Student Protest

What happens when, as some have predicted, two per cent of the American population is employed in producing the necessities of life, and 98 per cent is not? How, indeed, can we hope to live meaningful lives in an "economy of abundance"? The tragedy is not, as some seem to believe, that this way of life may come about well within our lifetimes; the tragedy is that, knowing this, we are doing little or nothing to prepare ourselves or the younger generation to cope with it.

Don Fabun
The Dynamics of Change

I would submit that if you find a system inadequate, it is not enough simply to demonstrate indignation and anger over individual workings of it. If one finds these conditions intolerable, and if one considers that they reflect no adequate expression either of the will of the majority or of that respect for the rights of minorities which is no less essential to the success of any democratic system, then one places upon one's self, it seems to me, the obligation of saying in what way this political system should be modified, or what should be established in the place of it, to assure that its workings would bear a better relationship to people's needs and people's feelings.

George F. Kennan
The Radical Vision

wide culture of the young, and on the other, a move toward the development of a truly Canadian identity.

This is a very difficult time in which to grow up. When the traditions and way of life of the old are met with the idealism and enthusiasm of youth, sparks are bound to fly. Personal values are difficult to establish when information is conflicting. Alienation from others and loss of purpose can occur. But a view of life that values individual differences and preaches love and concern for others can be very sustaining in times of personal stress. It may be that our Canadian youth can help to make the world a better place for everyone to live in, if they hold true to their purposes.

Alienation

The junior executive said, "I'm tired of the rat race." The auto worker talking to a fellow worker said, "You know, I looked in the mirror when I was shaving and said, 'Joe, do you know what you're going to do today? Yeah! I'm going to bolt on car tires.' I realized that whether I'm here or not, that old line keeps on moving." The old man put it this way: "Nobody cares about anybody any more." Each person was talking about his feelings of alienation in a world in which the individual has seemingly lost his place. Big industry, big government, big stores, huge apartment buildings, computer letters and computer billing – all seem to have left the individual at the mercy of impersonal machines and, even worse, impersonal human relations.

The Dean of Yale Business School, Chris Argyris, recounts the story of talking to an auto worker who complained about his factory job. Argyris asked the man if the company should tell him that his job was meaningless, thankless, requiring no skill or intelligence. The worker surprised Argyris by his reply: "If they did, it would be the first time they levelled with me." A great number of people, both young and old, are feeling left out and hostile toward the society that has left them out. Students feel a need for greater involvement in school and in the choice of more "relevant" courses. Those in large schools complain that they feel hurt by the system, which seems impersonal in nature and unmindful of their individual needs.

These feelings of uneasiness and unhappiness can be described as feelings of alienation. Among the poor, feelings of alienation arise from the sense that they are victims of a cumbersome, insensitive bureaucratic welfare system. Many women feel alienated when they see themselves and other women offered inferior positions in business and subjected to unequal laws. As our society grows larger and more automated, as more people are left out or drop out, feelings of alienation can be expected to increase. The following excerpts suggest the nature and extent of alienation.

Sociologist Bernard S. Phillips lists five key aspects of the condition known as alienation:

1) *Powerlessness*. When a worker does not have control over his own labour and is required to do things under the control of a system of higher officials, or worse, under the control of automated machinery, he becomes more and more dependent, he cannot do his job unless all other pieces and supervision are present. He feels trapped, unable to do anything beyond the minimum requirement of his work. He feels he has no influence on the kind of work he does or in the totality of the product with which he is associated.

2) *Social isolation*. As a result of not being involved in one's own work because of certain alienating forces, an individual may withdraw from many other aspects of his life. He may not participate in voluntary organizations, the church, or even recreational activities with his family. The feeling of isolation in his work carries over to all aspects of his life.

3) *Meaninglessness*. When a worker cannot see how his work relates to other phases of the production of a product, he cannot see how it relates to his own personal development. Because he is unable to find meaning in his work, he rejects it from his consciousness.

4) *Work as a means to other ends*. Work that is not perceived as meaningful for itself must be seen by the worker as a way of reaching other personal goals. He is doing something he does not like to do in order to obtain something he wants. This manipulation of his own life justifies for the alienated man his manipulation of others.

5) *Self as product*. Perhaps the most serious stage in alienation is the point at which the individual sees himself as a product, and in his relationship with other people, he sells himself as well as whatever other ideas or commodities he is trying to sell. By defining himself as a fixed product, he is prevented from developing himself in many other ways.

"The Alienated" are those people who have been excluded or who have excluded themselves. They are the thousands of bored workers who find that what they are doing is monotonous or degrading or both. They are the young people who either commit "senseless acts of violence" or simply "don't care about anything" or who "care about everything, too much". They are the idle, lonely old who feel the world has left them behind.

Ned E. Hoopes
Who Am I?

There are further defects in an approach which sees the typical worker as an automaton, frustrated from the time he starts work until the quitting whistle blows. Most men have a realistic opinion of their strengths and weaknesses . . . they know how hard their fathers had to work to support their families, so if their own lot is easier, they are likely to be reconciled to it. . . . But they are not industrial slaves, as Marx called them, nor are they company serfs, forced to do what the employer wants. . . .

Eli Ginzberg
The Study of Human Resources

In what does this alienation of labour consist? First, that the work is *external* to the worker, that it is not part of his nature, that consequently he does not fulfil himself in his work but denies himself, has a feeling of misery, not of well-being, does not develop freely a physical and mental energy, but is physically exhausted and mentally debased. The worker therefore feels himself at home only during his leisure, whereas at work he feels homeless. His work is not voluntary but imposed, *forced labour*. It is not the satisfaction of a need, but only a *means* for satisfying other needs. Its alien character is clearly shown by the fact that as soon as there is no physical or other compulsion it is avoided like the plague. Finally, the alienated character of work for the worker appears in the fact that it is not his work but work for someone else, that in work he does not belong to himself but to another person. . . .

Karl Marx
Das Kapital

Human relations are essentially those of alienated automatons, each basing his security on staying close to the herd, and not being different in thought, feelings, or action. While everybody tries to be as close as possible to the rest, everybody remains utterly alone, pervaded by the deep sense of insecurity, anxiety and guilt which always result when human separateness cannot be overcome.

Erich Fromm
The Art of Loving

Erich Fromm feels that western man sees life in terms of a market wherein an exchange of goods takes place. All transactions with other people or things are considered from the point of view of buyer and seller relationships. Even in his closest relationships, such as love relations, western man values the other person in terms of appearance, personality, and desirability on these particular markets. Each person enters into a market contract on the basis of exchange of personality packages — each one hoping that he has obtained a fair exchange if not a bargain.

"Like, it's a slow, systematic, deliberate thing, you know? It's a changing of love into hate. I mean, alienation isn't always conscious, but it's there all the same — turning one man away from another." He might have been speaking as well for a whole group of individuals who have lost their sense of personal sameness and of historical continuity — a large and varied number of human beings who have either isolated themselves or been estranged from contemporary society.

Ned E. Hoopes
Who Am I?

"Alienation . . . is not a happening, man, it *is*!" said the bearded boy with long hair and dirty fingernails, as he tried to define a term that is currently much in vogue.

Ned E. Hoopes
Who Am I?

Youth unrest

The youth revolution is first of all a revolution in numerical terms. In Canada, the United States, and Western Europe, the under-twenty-five age groups are important consumers. In financial terms, the youth market is worth cultivating, and so the constant outpouring of entertainment, music, and cinema for youth continues. New youthful fashions fill the stores, educational institutions are expanded, and older men and women try to look young, encouraged by TV commercials that show forty-year-old housewives passing for teenagers. What youth thinks or doesn't think, likes or doesn't like, has become something of a preoccupation in politics, business, and the family.

The world is no longer simple; old solutions do not quite fit new problems; old relationships are subtly changed by a large youthful population whose impact is as irresistible as a tidal wave. On either side of the generation gap stand the adults bewildered by their offspring, and youth bewildered by their parents. The media — radio, television, newspapers – are ready to interpret the one group to the other, but the net result seems to be less and less communication for both.

Youth does care – about peace, about ecology, about human values – and, in their way, so do parents. Yet many misunderstandings underlie their relationships. The older generation finds itself hard pressed to defend its past actions which have contributed to present problems. Indeed, the very large youthful population itself has been created by the older generation.

The first institution to undergo scrutiny is the school, since it is the only institution that youth knows from the ground up. In schools, the young question as they have been taught to do, often embarrassing the educational authorities. At university, articulate spokesmen – some chosen, some self-appointed – speak for youth. Often the listener is confused by the variety of criticisms and by the contradictions put forward. How, the authorities ask, can you negotiate with someone who presents non-negotiable demands? The following quotations illuminate some of the problems.

I'll take the student power movement seriously when it has and uses the authentic instruments of power – prisons, torture chambers, machine guns. Until then, it's just a kid's game of hopscotch.

I'm not frightened by the new generation. I've seen teenagers by the thousands, from one end of Canada to the other, and the vast majority of them are as timid and docile as their parents.

Richard J. Needham, Columnist
Toronto *Globe and Mail*

Certainly, protest would be less common if the restraints of religion and authority of the family had remained as great as they were just 10 or 20 years ago. The rapid growth of mass communication media and the knowledge explosion have had considerable influence in teaching our youth to question authority, whether it be parents, the church, the university or the printed page.

Seymour L. Halleck
in Gerald F. McGuigan
Student Protest

The assumption on the part of the middle-aged is that given long enough the children will learn through bitter experience that the older generation was right after all. This approach sees students somehow fitting into established categories of growth between childhood and adulthood. In fact, they are not.

Gerald F. McGuigan
Student Protest

When the older generation claims that the young really do not try to understand what is being said, this is the first and most total misunderstanding of all. The younger generation knows perfectly well what their elders only too clearly are saying – and they are rejecting it. In the present unrest there is something much more profound at work than the differences between generations. These disturbances register a deeper-seated protest, one pointing to the creation of a new set of values. It is not that students are rejecting old values out of hand and not wanting to put anything in their place, but they simply see the old attitudes as inadequate and even dangerous. What they seek is a reassertion of human values.

Gerald F. McGuigan
Student Protest

Students are most likely to protest in a coherent, organized and rational manner when they are aware of the causes of oppression in their lives. The task of university administrators is that of deciphering and responding to those student needs that are powerful and real, and [of] dealing firmly but kindly with student demands based on unrealistic and personal misconceptions. While deans and administrators must examine each student position on its merits, they must also be aware that many proponents of that position are driven by personal needs which are beyond their power to gratify by administrative decision.

Seymour L. Halleck
in Gerald F. McGuigan
Student Protest

Automation : help or hindrance to modern society ?

In his book, *Profiles of the Future*, Arthur C. Clarke, who has been quite accurate with his scientific forecasts, claims that man's job as the dominant species on this planet is near its end. He feels that man will soon be surpassed by ultra intelligent computers. There will come a time when the machines will become capable of improving themselves.

Automated abundance is supposed to change all this because it will relieve man of the burden of work. But as long as we are primed to work towards the production of goods and as long as we maintain an attitude that only the result counts, we may break down under the burden of leisure and abundance. If, as stated above, abundance is our ideal and work the only legitimate way of passing one's time, the accomplishment of abundance can only lead to . . . disintegration, boredom, and nihilism.

Walter A. Weisskopf
Brief on the Economics and Psychology of Abundance

If we take a hard unromantic look at the golden age itself, we are struck with the incredible naivete of these scientists. They say, for example, that they will be able to shape and reshape at will human emotions, desires, and thoughts and arrive scientifically at certain efficient, pre-established collective decisions. They claim they will be in a position to develop certain collective desires, to constitute certain homogeneous social units out of aggregates of individuals, to forbid men to raise their children, and even to persuade them to renounce having any. At the same time, they speak of assuring the triumph of freedom and of the necessity of avoiding dictatorship at any price. They seem incapable of grasping the contradiction involved, or of understanding that what they are proposing, even after the intermediary period, is in fact the harshest of dictatorships. In comparison, Hitler's was a trifling affair. That it is to be a dictatorship of test tubes rather than of hobnailed boots will not make it any less a dictatorship.

Jacques Ellul
The Technological Society

Consider the argument that since we mastered the first Industrial Revolution, we will not have any enduring trouble with the second. . . . Let me mention three (unsolved) consequences of the first Industrial Revolution . . . the increasing gap between developed and have-not nations . . . the growth in some cases of slums and poverty . . . alienation from and breakdown of earlier more stable systems of value and faith.

Donald N. Michael
Some Speculations in the Social Impact of Technology

The full significance of automation is not only that it may eliminate some jobs, but also that it eliminates an entire class of jobs, leaving the displaced worker without a place in the occupational structure. This clearly points to the close connection between the process of automation and the revolution of human rights. For example, many of the ameliorative programs of job retraining, or reducing high school dropout rates, often result in preparing people for occupations that are being rapidly eliminated. One result of this situation is that programs designed to deal with poverty and unemployment are ineffective because they are unrealistically connected to the economic system.

Robert Perrucci and Marc Pilisuk
The Triple Revolution

By the year 2000, computers are likely to match, simulate, or surpass some of man's most "human-like" intellectual abilities, including perhaps some of his aesthetic and creative capacities, in addition to having some new kinds of capabilities that human beings do not have. These computer capacities are not certain ; however, it is an open question what inherent limitations computers have. If it turns out that they cannot duplicate or exceed certain characteristically human capabilities, that will be one of the most important discoveries of the twentieth century. . . .

Herman Kahn and A. J. Wiener
"The Human Ecosystem"
The Contemporary Scene

The future of leisure

David Riesman

(Our time on earth has for so long been associated with work that we have been unable to accept the idea of leisure as a way of life. The retired often die quickly without the stimulation of work; the young turn to "kicks" of all kinds. With the expectation that all of us will have more free time in the near future, we must learn to make healthier use of our leisure. David Riesman discusses this unusual problem.)

I recently had the opportunity to talk about the future of leisure with some thoughtful union leaders and adult educators. They were looking forward, in dismay as much as in hope, to a far shorter working week and a less demanding working day. They were asking specialists on leisure how these vacua of time and energy could be filled with more creativity and less boredom. They were saddling leisure with the burden which indeed it did carry for a small minority of the leisure class in some aristocratic eras – the burden of supporting life's total commitment and significance. Suggestions were made for better adult education courses, even for sabbaticals for everybody or short periods of residence in an Aspen-like setting. And one leader spoke of efforts to link workers possessing underused craft skills with groups such as nursery schools possessing substandard facilities – groups which could greatly benefit from the energies and capabilities of people who would in their time build jungle gyms, chairs, or other needed equipment. But it was clear from the tone of the meeting that these notions, valuable as they were, could not even claim the status of palliatives. It was not that they could not (given workers as they now are) compete with commercial recreation or polishing the car, but also that they did not provide the "moral equivalent of work". We can see in the bored teenagers who don't like school, and are already sated with sex unmitigated by love, what leisure is like for most people when life lacks the accent and structure given it by work – not simply stand-by "work" but some effortful and periodically challenging activity.

In the studies of unemployed men made during the great depression, the observation of the demoralizing nature of being without work was often made, but it was sometimes assumed that this was mostly a matter of status and of poverty which forced the unemployed man to hang uselessly about the house. And in the studies of men who have retired, the same theme recurs. They are demoralized because the job gave status and income, and also because they grew up in a work-minded era and were not prepared for the age of leisure. I myself had thought that when a whole generation had been reared which was not driven to work by the agreed-upon motives of hunger and gain – often unconsciously driven because work-mindedness was instilled, so to speak, with mother's bottle feeding on schedule – such people could retire more comfortably than the elderly now do because they would have been preparing for it all life long. Presently, however, I am inclined to believe that work is still necessary because our inven-

The leisure problem is fundamental. Having to decide what we shall do with our leisure is inevitably forcing us to re-examine the purpose of human existence, and to ask what fulfillment really means . . . this involves a comprehensive survey of human possibilities and methods of realizing them; it also implies a survey of the obstacles to their realization.

Julian Huxley
The Future of Man

When the great classifier and assigner of categories, Aristotle, took a look at work, he could assign it no very high value, except as a way to achieve leisure, or to *not* work. "Nature," he wrote, "requires that we should be able, not only to work well, but to use leisure well. Leisure is the first principle of all action and so leisure is better than work and is its end. As play, and with it rest, are for the sake of work, so work, in turn, is for the sake of leisure."

Don Fabun
The Dynamics of Change

To hold a job means to have status, to belong in the way of life. Between the ages of twenty-five and fifty-five, that is, after school age and before retirement age, nearly 95 per cent of all males work and about 35 per cent of all females. Various studies have portrayed the unemployed man as confused, panicky, prone to suicide, mayhem and revolt. Totalitarian regimes seem to know what unemployment can mean; they never permit it.

Sebastian de Grazia
Of Time, Work, and Leisure

Work occupies fewer hours in the lives of everyone; what work there is grows less like work every year. . . . Compared to the day's work that confronts most of mankind every morning, most [North Americans] are not engaged in work at all.

Gerard Piel
"The End of Toil"
The Nation 1961

As the world moved out of what we now consider primitivism and into more organized social structure, there grew up the myth of some "Golden Age" which was, perhaps, founded on some lingering memory of the good old days when the concept of work did not exist. All the ancient voices, whose thin dry sounds have come down their thousands of years to become the conscience of us all, considered work at best a necessary evil.

Don Fabun
The Dynamics of Change

tiveness has not found ways of relating masses of men to creative activity or to each other outside of work. Though the artist, of whatever sort and for whom there is no real division between work and play, indicates what may someday be possible, even the artist, whatever his ideology of *l'art pour l'art*, needs usually to feel he is being of some use – if only in acting out a counterpoint to Philistine utilitarianism.

The European-American society which discovered the Protestant Ethic turned work and play into opposites, something that could not have been understood by the Medieval craftsmen. The 19th century inner-directed man felt that he should work in order to "make a living". Then, paradoxically, he succeeded in making such a good living that he produced an economy of abundance in which his grandson is no longer able to work all his life, but must spend some of his years in retirement, although he still believes that work is a good thing in itself, and he is suspicious of play. Thus we are now faced with the fundamental question – Can men be happy in any other way than in work?

Robert J. Havighurst
*The Nature and Values of
Meaningful Free-Time Activity*

A man who has worked long hours all his life will be bored if he becomes suddenly idle.

Bertrand Russell
"In Praise of Idleness"
in E. Larrabee and R. Meyersohn (eds.)
Mass Leisure

The Puritan concept . . . is now and will increasingly be out of touch with the real world. Productivity is such that our economy can produce all the things the society needs with only a fraction of the total labor force. By 1975, no more than one-quarter of the labor force will be directly involved in manufacturing products, mining, growing crops, constructing buildings.

Michael Silva
Careers Today

Work is the [opposite] of free time. But not of leisure. Leisure and free time live in two different worlds. We have got in the habit of thinking them the same. Anybody can have free time. Not everybody can have leisure. Free time is a realizable idea of democracy. Leisure is not fully realizable and hence an ideal not alone an idea. Free time refers to a special way of calculating a special kind of time. Leisure refers to a state of being, a condition of man which few desire and fewer achieve.

Sebastian de Grazia
Of Time, Work, and Leisure

The salient fact about leisure is that it is growing much faster than is our capacity to use it wisely.

James Charlesworth
"A Comprehensive Plan for the Wise Use of Leisure"
Leisure in America : Blessing or Curse ?

In many low-energy societies the concepts of work time and free time hardly exist. A man does what is expected of him, which we westerners may refer to as the performance of ritual or ceremony, domestic duties, production, military service, etc. What is expected may also include the occupation of time in conversation, sleep, recreation, singing and dancing, or what-not.

A man in such a culture may feel as constrained by necessity to do one as the other. It is only when we classify his time into categories meaningful to us that work becomes defined. But if we say that he is working only when he is gaining sustenance, then many "primitive" men had far more work-free time than we have.

Fred Cottrell
The Sources of Free Time

Life can be lived in a meaningful or meaningless way. Time can be spent meaningfully or not. To use it meaningfully is to spend it in a way which contributes to the fulfillment of life, which may be considered as an experience of completion, a hoped-for satisfaction, toward which we have directed our lives. Fulfillment can be experienced in different forms and at different times. All through life, people experience smaller or larger fulfillments, in consequence of events or accomplishments which seem to answer needs or hopes, desires or expectations. . . .

Dr. Charlotte Buhler
Aging and Leisure

Ironically, the people with the most free time are often the ones least equipped to handle it. A survey reported in *McCall's* recently showed the new leisure bringing more chaos than comfort to the lives of many union members on a 30-hour week. Those who were not moonlighting were often turning to beer, long naps, often moping around the house.

The other side of the paradox is that the people who could most profitably use more time to pursue a wide spectrum of interests — the more highly educated, cultured and interested members of top management, for example — will be the least likely to get it.

Phyllis Daignault
"New Markets in Time"
Sales Management
June 18, 1965

As the author of the letter to Kazakhstanskaya *Pravda* recently observed :

. . . the reduction of the working day has found many people unprepared. . . . Vodka is the cheapest and simplest form of amusement, and this is a very important factor, especially for young people.

"Kazakhstan Alcoholics Face Compulsory Treatment"
Current Digest of the Soviet Press

The danger is not that we won't toughen up or work harder. The danger is that the idea of leisure will be mistaken or dropped. If it is mistaken for free time, it will be thought of as the opposite of work, as unproductive, and even as weakening us for the forthcoming struggle with whomever it is we shall end up struggling.

Sebastian de Grazia
Of Time, Work, and Leisure

two
Our threatened world

Man's history can be seen as a series of conquests of nature, and to a great extent, man has learned to control and exploit his environment. But nature is designed to exist in a delicate interplay of its components, and man has developed to such a stage with his technologies and massive populations that his influence has shattering implications for the fragile network of nature and the future existence of mankind.

In recent years, man has witnessed the deaths of birds and animals from the use of pesticides, and of fish from mercury pollution caused by wastes of the chemical and pulp and paper industries. Man has suffered at the hand of his fellow man, deliberately in the atom bombing of Hiroshima, and accidently through the use of drugs such as thalidomide (the use of this drug by pregnant women in many cases resulted in the birth of severely deformed children). The competitive business system that has contributed to the affluence of North American society also has contributed to many of our ecological problems, as a result of its attempts to produce better and better products, often at the expense of the environment. (Ecology is the study of relationships between an individual and his total environment. As used here, the word "environment" includes other individuals, animals, plants, nonliving matter, and even such conditions as climate and altitude.)

The following selections are designed to emphasize the magnitude of the decisions we must face to ensure the continuation of mankind. The relationship between world population and available resources is considered in the first selection. The next two selections depict the potential impact of nuclear warfare. The concluding extracts deal with the implications of carelessly disturbing the ecological balance between man and nature.

The present rate of population increase is brought into sharp focus by the following statistics. The world now adds a net of close to 200,000 people, or a new London, Ontario, every *day*; close to six million people, or a new Moscow, every *month*; and close to seventy million people, or a new Brazil, every *year*.

Herman Kahn and A. J. Wiener
"The Human Ecosystem"
The Contemporary Scene

With almost a third of the earth's land area tilled or in pasture, with a fifth in the grip of snow and ice, and with mountains, inhospitable plateaus, deserts and arid zones accounting for another two-fifths, the reserves available for tillage comprise a mere 950 million acres. One hundred and twenty-five million of these acres need to be brought under cultivation each year just to take care of the minimum food needs of the annual 70-million increase in human numbers.

George Borgstrom
Too Many: A Study of the Earth's Biological Limitations

Population and resources: the coming collision

For nearly three decades, men have believed that a distribution of wealth could be achieved among nations while populations continued to grow and per capita incomes continued to rise in the West. The holy grail of "development" under these circumstances has seized the imagination and drawn forth the labors of people in rich and poor countries alike. It is a near-universal hope that modern technology, injected into ancient systems of agriculture, manufacturing, mining and transportation, will transform peasant societies into forward-looking states with rapidly rising standards of living. Such transformations, it is believed, will narrow the economic gap between rich and poor countries at ever-higher levels of income for both.

For many North American economists, this idea has dimmed of late, but it is still appealing. In their view, any progress made by Asians, Africans, and Latin Americans will depend on how swiftly these people can apply the American economic philosophy: *Make all things useful and profitable, and life will take care of itself.* It is remarkable how powerful a hold this dynamic, narrowly effective approach has had on cultures other than the one that nursed it into vigor.

But the idea of gap-closing, population growth and ever-rising production is an illusion from which the world may now be awaking, for its three elements are not supportable in a world with limited resources. It is madness to assume that the West, which already imports more minerals, fuels and proteins than it exports, can continue to gain wealth and simultaneously help other regions approach its own standard of living. "... before any area can reach the per capita energy and mineral consumption rate of the United States, it must first build up its industry to that level. Were the whole world to have done this ... the presently estimated world supply of the ores of most industrial metals, producible by present technology, would have been exhausted well before such a level of industrialization could have been reached." [M. King Hubbert, Geologist.]

It is equal madness to assume that the global resource base can long sustain an additional 2 or 3 billion people while the per capita consumption of fuels, minerals and food increases. Today a new relationship exists between wealth and population. The richer a society wishes to become, the fewer additional people it can support in conditions of freedom and health.

And it is a final madness to assume that the global environment – the thin, fragile earth surface – can long endure the kind of development we have talked about for the last twenty-five years. The signs of ecological breakdown are everywhere apparent in our estuaries, rivers, airsheds and wildlife populations.

Of course, we cannot be certain that a new generation of technological triumphs will not provide a growing world population with materials and energy at a low level of environmental damage. But the record of the recent past is sobering on this point. Man's technological skills have grown steadily, yet pollution and the disruption of natural cycles have mounted year by year, spreading from local crisis areas to encumber the whole planet. The dream of high-energy "development" for all the world dies slowly because its roots lie deep in the psychology of Western man – especially North American man. Virtually the entire history of North America has unfolded during an era of unprecedented resource exploitation by Europeans and their descendants. It is difficult for us to emerge from the mentality of this era which has left us in a privileged 'position in world trade and wealth. But the global collision between population and resources as well as between dream and reality is so imminent that our most cherished economic assumptions are now being openly challenged.

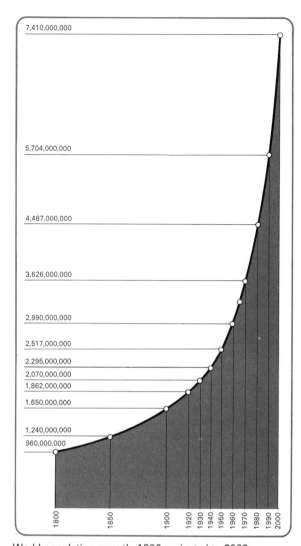

World population growth, 1800 projected to 2000

The explosion and its aftermath

Scientists' Committee for Radiation Information

As the bomb explodes, the sky fills with a bluish-white glare. A man standing 60 miles away would see a fireball 30 times brighter than the noonday sun – a fireball hot as the center of the sun.

The fireball rapidly expands until it is 4½ miles wide. As it expands, it begins to rise, scorching an ever-widening area. Meanwhile, if the explosion was a ground *surface burst*, the fireball has

The hardest choices are those between alternatives which both seem right and good. Today we face such a dilemma. Do we wish to see an ever-rising human population? Do we wish to go on getting and spending at ever-higher levels?

Or, as we prefer to believe about ourselves, do we truly seek a more equitable world in which all people can claim their due share of the earth's bounty? We cannot have it both ways. We and our descendants are fated to make a painful choice.

Charlton Ogburn, Jr.
Population Bulletin
Vol. XXVI, No. 2, June 1970

Overpopulation

On the biological level, advancing science and technology have set going a revolutionary process that seems to be destined for the next century at least, perhaps for much longer, to exercise a decisive influence upon the destinies of all human societies and their individual members. In the course of the last fifty years extremely effective methods for lowering the prevailing rates of infant and adult mortality were developed by Western scientists. These methods were very simple and could be applied with the expenditure of very little money by very small numbers of not very highly trained technicians. For these reasons, and because everyone regards life as intrinsically good and death as intrinsically bad, they were in fact applied on a world-wide scale. The results were spectacular. In the past, high birth rates were balanced by high death rates. Thanks to science, death rates have been halved but, except in the most highly industrialized countries, birth rates remain as high as ever. An enormous and accelerating increase in human numbers has been the inevitable consequence....

To those that have, shall be given. Within the next ten or twenty years, if war can be avoided, poverty will almost have disappeared from the highly industrialized societies of the West. Meanwhile, in the underdeveloped and uncontrolled breeding societies of Asia, Africa, and Latin America the condition of the masses (twice as numerous, a generation from now, as they are today) will have become no better and may even be decidedly worse than it is at present. Such a decline is foreshadowed by current statistics of the Food and Agriculture Organization of the United Nations. In some underdeveloped regions of the world, we are told, people are somewhat less adequately fed, clothed, and housed than were their parents and grandparents thirty and forty years ago. And what of elementary education? UNESCO recently provided an answer. Since the end of World War II heroic efforts have been made to teach the whole world how to read. The population explosion has largely stultified these efforts. The absolute number of illiterates is greater now than at any time.

Aldous Huxley

It comes down to this: We cannot logically hope to see a growing world population attain North American consumption levels while at the same time our own growing population seeks still greater material wealth.

Editor's Comment
Population Bulletin
Vol. XXVI, No. 2, June 1970

sucked up a vast quantity of vaporized earth and debris.

If the bomb were exploded in the *air* on a clear day, the heat would ignite a man's clothing 21 miles away and seriously burn exposed skin at 31 miles. (A contact *surface* blast would cut the distances to 13 and 19 miles.)

The matter sucked up by the fireball in a surface burst starts to condense on reaching upper air layers, five to ten miles up. It spreads out, forming a radioactive, mushroom cloud. The material in this cloud soon begins to descend as fallout.

Meanwhile, an intense pressure wave, or shock, travelling faster than sound, spreads out from the center of the explosion, crushing almost everything in its path until it gradually loses its force.

Following the shock front comes the wind of more than 1000 miles per hour. As it moves outward, the wind diminishes; behind it a vacuum develops. Then the surrounding air rushes in, fanning the fires started by thermal radiation and initial blast damage.

Soon these fires will join and develop into a firestorm that could cover an area many miles across, destroying all that will burn – structures and living things.

The blast itself, from a surface burst, would create a hole 240 feet deep, at its deepest point, and a half a mile across. Within a radius of 7.7 miles the destruction would be severe. Up to 15 miles the damage would still be heavy.

The population would face several distinct types of hazards, each of which must be coped with successfully for survival. The effects would vary somewhat, depending on whether the bomb drop were a contact surface burst or an air burst.

In summary, a surface burst produces little local fallout, more world-wide fallout, greater danger of firestorm, and more widespread blast damage.

Six types of hazards to be considered are as follows: 1) immediate thermal effects, 2) immediate nuclear radiation, 3) blast effects, 4) firestorm, 5) economic and social disruption, and 6) long-term effects.

Immediate Thermal Effects

The fireball gives off a tremendous amount of heat, or thermal energy. One can predict the extent of heat damage by noting the number of calories (unit of heat) per square centimeter of surface a given object would receive if exposed to the flash of the bomb. If the explosion occurs within the atmosphere, the energy *required* for igniting a given material is greater the larger the total energy yield of the bomb. For example, for a 20-megaton bomb, about 7 calories per square centimeter (cal/cm^2) will ignite shredded newspaper, 13 cal/cm^2 will ignite deciduous leaves. At 23 cal/cm^2 most clothing will ignite.

Flash burns are an even more probable danger than the burning of clothing. At Hiroshima and Nagasaki, flash burn casualties were *the* major problem in medical care, accounting for more than half of all deaths.

On a clear day, a 20-megaton (MT) low air burst would produce these injuries to exposed skin:

Third degree burns (12 cal/cm²) 27 miles away from the explosion
Second degree burns (10 cal/cm²) 31 miles away
First degree burns (4 cal/cm²) 45 miles away

For a surface burst these distances would drop by 40 per cent because there is less thermal energy to start with, and heat rays near the ground would not travel as far because they are absorbed and scattered by dust, water vapor and carbon dioxide. Unless medical supplies and facilities were somehow spared, the second and third degree burns would probably result in death. Such burns nearly always become infected. And radiation further reduces the chances of recovering from even minor infections.

A high altitude burst, say 20 miles up, well above most of the atmosphere, would produce even greater fire damage on earth. Atmospheric haze would reduce the range of heat damage. An explosion in clear air under a cloud layer could increase the range. A person actually seeing the flash of the bomb burst would suffer a burn on the retina, which could lead to blindness. The seriousness of the burn would depend on its size and its location on the retina. For a high burst as opposed to a surface burst the flash would be seen further away. Only sparse information about retinal burns has been declassified. However, it has been disclosed that "a megaton detonation" 40 miles high produced retinal burns in rabbits 340 miles away.

Immediate Nuclear Radiation

With a small bomb, say 20 kilotons (KT), immediate nuclear radiation is an important hazard; but with a large bomb, such as 20 megatons, it may be ignored because blast and heat effects of a 20-MT weapon are so great that they would far outweigh the immediate radiation danger. For example, 2.5 miles from ground zero the radiation intensity would be about 300 roentgens, a lethal dose for 3 to 18 per cent of those exposed. However, at that distance the 800-m.p.h. wind, the flying debris, and the flash heat would alone suffice to kill an exposed person.

Blast Effects

Blast damage to a building or other structure may result from one or several causes. First, the shock front squeezes everything in its path. A building may collapse because it is being blown over, or because the external pressure is suddenly so great that all four walls collapse inward.

Arriving with the shock front are the drag forces, in the form of a strong wind. Telephone poles and radio towers that may resist the squeezing effect of the shock front are quite vulnerable to being blown over. Within a few seconds, the shock wave and its accompanying winds have passed.

Following the shock front and drag forces, there is a reversal in pressure. Buildings now experience a partial vacuum and winds blowing back toward the center of the explosion. The stress is less, but it can add to damage on an already weakened structure. Also, the ground shock itself can knock a building down as an earthquake does.

Old-fashioned war was incompatible, while it was being waged, with democracy. Nuclear war, if it is ever waged, will prove in all likelihood to be incompatible with civilization, perhaps with human survival. Meanwhile, what of the preparations for nuclear war? If certain physicists and military planners had their way, democracy, where it exists, would be replaced by a system of regimentation centered upon the bomb shelter. The entire population would have to be systematically drilled in the ticklish operation of going underground at a moment's notice, systematically exercised in the art of living troglodytically [primitively, like cavemen] under conditions resembling those in the hold of an eighteenth-century slave ship. The notion fills most of us with horror. But if we fail to break out of the ideological prison of our nationalistic and militaristic culture, we may find ourselves compelled by the military consequences of our science and technology to descend into the steel and concrete dungeons of total and totalitarian civil defense.

Aldous Huxley
in Robert Perrucci and Marc Pilisuk
The Triple Revolution

Mankind's Inalienable Rights

1) The right to eat well.
2) The right to drink pure water.
3) The right to decent, uncrowded shelter.
4) The right to enjoy natural beauty.
5) The right to avoid pesticide poisoning.
6) The right to freedom from thermonuclear war.
7) The right to limit families.
8) The right to peace and quiet.

Paul Ehrlich

Nuclear Weapons

During the Second World War there were some great bombing raids on German cities. In one such raid, on one night, one thousand aeroplanes each carrying four tremendous one-ton block-busters destroyed much of the city of Hamburg and killed an estimated 75,000 people. If there were to be such a raid on, say, Paris today and another such 1,000-plane raid tomorrow, and then another the next day and so on day after day for fourteen years, the explosives delivered would have the power of the 20-megaton bomb.

Now, one 20-megaton bomb test in the atmosphere or at the surface of the earth liberates radioactive materials into the atmosphere which will, according to the best estimates that we can make, cause gross damage or death to 550,000 unborn children. This is the probable sacrifice of the testing of a single H-bomb by any one nation. Everyone must understand this.

If the human race survives and world population continues at a reasonable level, then I have calculated that the bomb tests carried out thus far, and amounting to 600 megatons, will in the course of time affect sixteen million children so severely that they will suffer gross physical or mental defects or embryonic, neonatal, or child-hood deaths.

We know that large amounts of high energy radiation produce cancer. If we accept the principle that high energy radiation even in small amounts is also cancerogenic – as I believe it is – then it is possible to calculate the sacrifice of human beings now living to the bomb tests.

The estimated figure is that two million human beings now living will die five, ten, fifteen or twenty years earlier than otherwise because of cancer or other diseases produced by the high energy radiation liberated in the bomb tests carried out so far. This is about one person in fifteen hundred in the world, and it gives us some idea of the nature of atomic weapons in so far as the tests go. . . .

The standard nuclear bomb today is the 20-megaton bomb. (One megaton equals a million tons.) The Soviet Union has detonated a 60-megaton bomb, which was apparently only the first two stages of a 100-megaton bomb. A 100-megaton bomb involves only about three and a half tons of explosive material and probably can be carried in a single large rocket from one continent to another. But 100-megaton bombs don't make very much sense because a 20-megaton bomb can destroy any city on earth.

My estimate is that the stockpiles of the world comprise about 16,000 of these 20-megaton bombs or the equivalent of them. Now, there aren't 16,000 large cities in the world and one might well ask why this irrationally great amount of explosive material has been produced.

The mass destruction of buildings and other objects would have produced an immense quantity of flying debris. It has been determined that chunks of flying glass and masonry could cause casualties up to 15 miles from ground zero. (A casualty is defined as "an individual sufficiently injured to be unable to care for himself and thus becomes a burden to someone else".) It should be noted that small glass fragments lodging in the eye could produce casualties at distances much greater than those cited.

There would also be a third type of blast effect – displacement, such as picking up a man and smashing him into a wall. This, too, could occur as far away as 15 miles from ground zero. A significant number of head and skeletal injuries would occur, with the extent of the injury depending on the distance traveled prior to impact.

Firestorm

A prime threat to urban populations after a thermonuclear explosion is the firestorm. Firestorm develops when a mass of fresh air breaks into a large area with a high density of fires and replaces the hot rising air. This mass of fresh air may move with hurricane velocity. The wind causes the fires to merge and encompass the entire area.

The fires can start in two ways. First, thermal radiation would ignite trash, window curtains, dry grass, leaves and, toward the interior of the fire zone, many less flammable materials. Second, the blast would upset stoves, cause electrical short circuits, break gas lines and burst underground oil storage tanks. All of these would become ignition points.

At Hiroshima, where a far smaller bomb (20 KT) was dropped, a firestorm developed and eventually covered a radius of about 1.2 miles. In Nagasaki, no firestorm developed, apparently because natural winds carried the fire into an area where there was nothing to burn. Still, all buildings in Nagasaki within 1.25 miles of ground zero were destroyed by flames.

There are, however, not enough data to justify quantitative predictions of the firestorm area.

The most complete data on firestorm casualties come from Hamburg, Germany, where a firestorm occurred on July 27, 1943, after pre-nuclear incendiary air raids. Some 60,000 persons were killed, almost as many as in the atomic bomb drop on Hiroshima.

Hamburg police engineers estimated that temperatures in the burning city blocks were as high as 800°C (about 1,500°F). Wind velocity exceeded 150 m.p.h. Hundreds of persons were seen leaving shelters as the heat became unbearable. They ran into the streets and slowly collapsed. Days after the raids ended, as home shelters were opened, there was enough heat remaining inside for the influx of oxygen to cause the shelters to burst into flames. Many bodies had been cremated.

Death from intense heat can occur in ways other than burning or disintegration. Heat stroke can occur in a temperature of 140°F. Exterior damage can close off ventilation in a sheltered area.

Also, carbon monoxide poisoning would be one of the chief types of injuries expected. In World War II it was a common cause of death in public air raid shelters and improvised home shelters.

Carbon monoxide casualties are nearly always expected in flaming buildings, where exits have been blocked by rubble. Under such conditions, a cellar protected from the blast could become a tomb. In Hamburg, it is estimated that 70 per cent of all casualties not caused by mechanical injuries or burns were brought on by carbon monoxide.

Disruption of Physical Facilities

Careful consideration of problems that arise from wide breakdown of physical facilities and social services in the event of a nuclear explosion is vitally important to any discussion of survival.

Problems of transportation facilities. This problem may be regarded in three categories: thoroughfares, fuel, and machines. Throughout the area of the 15-mile radius from ground zero, debris would clog streets with little hope of early clearance. No vehicle could be expected to pass.

Transportation equipment remaining after blast and fire would find extremely limited fuel since local supplies would be largely consumed in mass fires. The breakdown of transportation would immediately hamper or prevent rescue, evacuation, and emergency assistance measures. Later its impact would be felt in terms of the absence of such important products as food, medical supplies, and fuel – including fuel for central electric generators.

Problems of water supply. It seems probable that many water storage tanks, some mains, filtering and purification equipment and pumps would be destroyed or would become inoperable.

Problems of food supply. Food stored under normal conditions would be subject to blast and fire. Food processing plants, storage and refrigeration facilities would also be affected by blast and fire. Sheltered food supplies, if available after extensive ruin, might provide sustenance for a limited period.

Problems of housing and home fuel supplies. Those fortunate enough to have dwelling units remaining, and with a manageable radiation problem, would have a hard time during cold weather. Local supplies of fuel would probably have been destroyed and the breakdown of transportation would curtail further deliveries. Human exposure during winter months is an inevitable source of casualties.

Problems of medical facilities. The millions of dead and injured would include a sizable proportion of physicians and other trained medical personnel. Few hospitals have auxiliary power sources sufficient for more than emergency periods. Destruction of city power plants and limited fuel supplies would therefore limit an important component of hospital services. Insufficient power would affect not only light, x-ray, and other machines, but also refrigeration necessary for important drugs. The failure of transportation of medical supplies and the presumed shortage of water, raising problems of general sanitation, indicate further aggravations of the health situation in event of a 20-MT nuclear explosion.

Problems of sanitation and public health. Sources of epidemic characteristically include: uncollected refuse, sewage, uncontrol-

I shall answer this by saying that it is because the system of science education has been faulty in the past so that the people who were making the decisions could not have had a clear understanding of what they were doing – if indeed anyone did make the decisions, for there has been some doubt as to whether the development of these tremendously great stockpiles was the result of decision-making rather than some sort of accident and shifting of responsibility primarily in the United States and the Soviet Union and perhaps in Great Britain to some extent. . . .

Three hundred and twenty thousand megatons is my estimate of the size of the world's present nuclear stockpiles. If ten per cent of the stockpiles (32,000 megatons) were to be used in a nuclear war with the bombs exploded on the average within a hundred and fifty kilometres of the targets (you don't have to hit the target in order to get the result) then 60 days after the day on which the war was fought – and we assume that it would cover Europe as a whole, all the Soviet Union and the United States – of the 800 million people living in these regions, 720 million would be dead, 60 million severely injured, and there would be 20 million survivors with only minor injuries.

But these survivors would have to cope with the problems of complete destruction of all cities and metropolitan districts, and means of communication and transportation, complete disruption of society, death of all livestock, and gross radioactive contamination of all growing foods. This would be the end of this part of the world, and how great the damage would be to the rest of the world no one has been able to estimate in a reliable way. . . .

I look forward to the time when there is in existence in the world a satisfactory system of international law taking the place of war. In working to abolish war from the world we are working also for human freedom, for the rights of individual human beings. It is war, militarism, and extreme nationalism that are the great enemies of the individual human being in every country. I believe that as we achieve the goal of peace in the world and disarmament, we shall see great improvement in the social, political and economic systems of all nations and in the rights of individual human beings all over the world.

The idea of replacing war by world law is an old one and it has continued to be advanced up to the present time. Only now has the time come when it will be accepted.

Linus Pauling
(Winner of the Nobel Peace Prize
and the Nobel Prize for Chemistry)

There appear to be five main types of environmental decay, says Douglas L. Brooks. First is the decay represented by the loss of two kinds of resources: essential resources such as food, minerals, water, and living space; and desirable resources such as wildlife, play space, walking space.

A second kind of decay is represented by the increasing level of pollution, noise, and ugliness within which we are being immersed.

A third involves increasing crowding and congestion. The best example of this is the competition for space between men and their cars. Either one of these exploding phenomena can smother the continent.

The fourth variety of environmental decay can be seen in the increasing depersonalization or "thingification" of life due to the growth in size and complexity of cities, traffic, and mass communications media.

Fifth and finally, there is the environmental decay of tremendous proportions, in which inadvertent and perhaps irreversible modification of the earth's weather and climate caused by man's activities could make all the other kinds of decay of small concern. The production of carbon dioxide by world-wide burning of fossil fuels (oil, gas, and coal) promises, according to some, to so increase the heat-absorbing constituents of the atmosphere that a world-wide climatic warming may take place, perhaps melting the Antarctic and Greenland icecaps and raising the sea level by a couple of hundred feet. This might be balanced by the possible rainfall-inhibiting effect of pollution in producing clouds containing overly large numbers of abnormally small droplets which remain stably suspended in the air rather than combining to produce rain and snow. In any case, weather and climate changes of a possibly drastic nature appear to be in the making.

What causes deep concern among informed persons as the level of atmospheric carbon dioxide mounts is that the increased retention of heat in the atmosphere through the "greenhouse effect" may melt a good deal of the Greenland and Antarctic ice caps. This would raise the level of the ocean by as much as 250 feet, drowning every port city in the world and inundating every coastal plain.

J. Murray Mitchell, Jr.
Is Man's Industry Upsetting World Weather?

led vermin, contaminated water and food supplies, and lack of medical facilities. Collection and disposal of corpses would require large numbers of workers and adequate transportation facilities. Public health problems created specifically by an extensive radioactive environment have not so far been experienced. Persons suffering from exposure to radiation, however, are particularly susceptible to infection, and a population of weakened and injured survivors, as in all comparable crises, would seem to invite epidemic.

Long-term Effects

The hazards discussed in earlier sections would occur largely within days, weeks and months after the explosion. There would also be longer-term radiation effects of two types: those that affect the exposed individual (somatic effects) and those that affect his descendants (genetic effects).

These effects are not fully understood by scientists. The knowledge that does exist has been exhaustively studied, but interpretations vary and are not conclusive. The uncertainties of the biology are compounded by uncertainty about radiation doses. While these effects will not be discussed in detail here, certain observations are possible.

Virtually all scientists agree that excess exposure of a population to radiation will have harmful effects on subsequent generations. The disagreements concern the relative incidence of harmful effects. These genetic effects might include miscarriages, stillbirths, neonatal deaths, congenital malformations, reduced mental and physical vigor, feeble-mindedness, and a host of physiological diseases or malfunctions, any one of which might lead to the disablement or death of an individual.

The evidence indicates that it is unlikely that long-term exposure to radiation would result in the genetic extinction of the human species, whatever the other harmful effects might be.

There is particular concern about the effects on fertility of an exposed male generation. Men exposed to a moderately high dose of radiation followed by a continuous low dose over a period of time are likely to exhibit sterility or reduced fertility for years. The gonads are among the most sensitive to radiation of all human organs.

Among other possible somatic effects are increased incidence of leukemia and other forms of cancer, increased incidence of degenerative diseases, shortening of the life span, development of cataracts, and various adverse effects on growth and normal development, especially in embryos.

Heat pollution

Charlton Ogburn, Jr.

Heat pollution above a certain level can undoubtedly play havoc with the life of a stream. Temperature is a profound factor in the water environment. It can kill, it can affect the movement of some species, and it can regulate rates of growth, especially those associated with reproduction. It can also increase the susceptibility of water life to toxic chemicals and disease, stimulate the growth of bottom-rooted plants and thus retard flow and increase siltation, and encourage the excessive growth of algae.

Are the materially advanced nations prepared to live indefinitely in a world in which the disadvantaged five-sevenths of the human race lag far behind in the pursuit of plenty? Do they think they can live in such a world? If not, they might consider some other questions.

Can the environment sustain the stresses that would be imposed on it by power generation of the magnitude required to give a world population of five billion what we North Americans have today?

There is no simple solution for heat pollution. Ultimately, the heat that comes from fossil [coal, oil, and gas] and nuclear fuels has to radiate to space. In the meantime, we warm up. We can arrange all kinds of facilities for people, but unless we have new ways to ventilate the atmosphere, we may find the biggest problem in urban areas is excess heat. It will get hotter and hotter; we will put in more air-conditioners, which in turn will produce more and more heat. . . . We will soon have to limit the use of rivers for cooling water, which will result in more pressure for use of the ocean. In the future, the coastline will become a more and more attractive place, as we seek to use it for cooling water for power plants, navigation, and recreation. At the same time we may be seeking food from the ocean, "using" it to provide a nice climate, utilizing it for that ultimate sink in waste disposal, and it may be a source of water and minerals. [California Institute of Technology, *The Next Ninety Years.*]

It might move us to a less leisurely approach to the problem of runaway population growth. This would include a hard look at the "right" of every family to have as many offspring as it pleases. If the human race meets with disaster toward which its accelerating rate of increase seems to be rushing it, that "right" will be among the least of our possessions to be lost.

It might lead us to a deliberate policy of working more with than in disregard for nature, even if this means – for the wealthier nations that can well afford it – foregoing certain increases in consumption in order to undertake greater conservation. Efforts could be made to produce food increasingly within the natural scheme, in ways that do not require heavy power inputs or drastic disruptions of the natural economy.

It might dispose the industrialized nations to be more careful in their use of resources and to salvage more of their wastes. Some municipalities on both sides of the Atlantic are already engaged in the latter effort as a means of dealing with rising mountains of trash. We are befouling our waterways with organic wastes that might replace the nutrients which we extract from our farmlands. Nearly all the wastes of our industrial civilization, the effluents of factories, the bottles, papers, cans and car bodies, are resources we strew across the landscape at the same time that we mine the earth

By 1285 London had a smog problem arising from the burning of soft coal, but our present combustion of fossil fuels threatens to change the chemistry of the globe's atmosphere as a whole, with consequences which we are only beginning to guess. With the population explosion, the carcinoma of planless urbanism, the new geological deposits of sewage and garbage, surely no creature other than man has ever managed to foul its nest in such short order.

Lynn White, Jr.
The Radical Vision

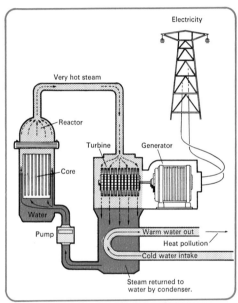

Source: Reproduced courtesy of *The National Observer.*
Boiling water reactor

The meteorologist cares about carbon dioxide for very good reasons. . . . Like water vapor, it tends to trap heat inside the atmosphere, and according to recent calculations it keeps world climate nearly 20 degrees warmer than would be the case in the total absence of the gas. More significantly, Manabe's studies also tell us that a 10 per cent increase in the atmospheric content of carbon dioxide would raise temperatures in the lower atmosphere by about one-half of a degree Fahrenheit, a figure that approaches the worldwide temperature increase actually observed since the 19th century.

J. Murray Mitchell, Jr.
Is Man's Industry Upsetting World Weather?

Disasters from Air Pollution:
an International Problem

Meuse River Valley, Belgium. In December 1930
a thick cold fog blanketed Belgium. In the 15-
mile Meuse River Valley an inversion of polluted
air took place, ending with thousands ill and
90 dead.

Donora, Pa., U.S.A. In 1948 an inversion covered
the Monongahela River valley where the industrial town of Donora is located. Six thousand
people fell ill and 20 died.

London, England. For centuries, Londoners have
known heavy fog conditions where pollution
from the soft coal used in fireplaces added to
the difficulty. In 1952 a five-day spell filled the
hospitals with thousands of people suffering illness and approximately 4,000 deaths resulted.

New York, N.Y., U.S.A. Disaster struck this city
in 1963, when 405 persons died from air pollution.

These are outstanding examples of pollution
danger, yet each day city dwellers in Montreal,
Toronto, Edmonton, Calgary, and Vancouver are
exposed to similar dangers. When inversion
problems occur in Toronto, some industries are
asked to curtail smoke. In Edmonton, a serious
inversion took place in 1970, bringing discomfort to thousands of residents just before
Christmas.

Right now we know enough about environmental reactions to remove man's dilemma from
at least the crisis category without need for any
further technological development. We know how
to stabilize soils in farm, field, and forest throughout the world. We can manage plants and animals,
wild and domestic, for high, sustained yields. We
know the source and threat of most pollutants,
and we have the technological answers (not
always "economical" ones) for abating them.

However, at this point in history, it is not a lack
of such technologies that underlies our crisis; it
is, rather, our failure to put them to work. . . .

P. A. Jordon
The Contemporary Scene

to obtain their constituents. This is currently an economical practice, but it is madness nonetheless.

It might prompt us to examine other "economies" we seek at the
expense of the environment. Radioactive products seep from nuclear reactors because trapping them would "prohibitively" raise
the cost of the electricity generated. Mountains and the forests
they support are devastated by strip-mining to keep costs of ex-
traction low. Urban sprawl consumes acreage wholesale because
land is valued in terms not of its role in the environment but of
its market price.

It might bring us to recognize that the lands and their vegetative
cover, their resources of minerals and waters, and the seas themselves, are the indispensable commons of the human species as a
whole, and that any individual or organizational proprietary
rights to any part of them are subordinate to the environmental
rights of all people, including at least our immediate heirs. The
destruction of forests and the pollution of the oceans for individual or corporate gain may impair our grandchildren's ability to
breathe. We may even come to hold that the manufacturer or
government bureaucrat responsible for the discharge of poisons
into the environment should be as accountable as if he had
dumped the crankcase drainings of his motorcar down his neighbor's well or his garbage on his neighbor's porch.

Saving our vanishing forests

Karl Heinz Oedekoven

As far back as the unknown origin of mankind, the path of human
activity has been marked by the thoughtless destruction of forest
and vegetation. Civilizations have flourished and disappeared with
a resultant depletion of trees and plants, leaving only steppe and
desert behind. Only in recent centuries has man begun to realize
that he was cutting off the branch that he was sitting on.

Man is becoming more aware today of nature's vengeance and,
at the same time, of the challenge which confronts him in preserving his dwindling natural assets while endeavouring to extend the
fertile earth which is the very basis of his existence. The demands
of an ever increasing world population make his task more and
more insistent.

The forest, our largest and most durable soil cover, was once
regarded as only an obstacle to settlement, agriculture and communications. It was recklessly burned or exploited until it suddenly became a focus of intense human interest.

Man has come to learn that the two most important elements of
his existence – soil and water – owe their stability and availability
to the presence of sufficient forest cover.

Three-quarters of the world's population are undernourished.
There is only about one acre of land per head for food production
and no less than twice this area is needed to ensure satisfactory
nutrition. The true Enemy No. 1 in the world is not a political or
military opponent, but the deterioration of the soil, the dryness,
the irresistible progress of semi-deserts and deserts.

In some countries, like the United States and the Union of

Soviet Socialist Republics, soil conservation has become almost a "State religion". In South America, all over Africa, Asia and Australia there is great concern over dangers threatening the soil.

While political leaders come and go, this destructive process of soil deterioration remains a permanent menace. Each government inherits this problem from its predecessor. Yet, even today, the efforts of many countries to remedy the situation are merely in their infancy.

We know from the experience of 500 years that the Sahara desert progresses towards the south at the rate of over three feet a year on a wide front of 2,000 miles. Lake Chad, which some decades ago was still an ideal refuge for migrating birds from Europe, is steadily diminishing in surface area and depth and its shores are turning from fertile green to steppe brown.

All far-reaching plans for the development of Africa as the "Continent of the Future", all plans for water use and industrialization will fail unless the necessary attention is paid to the importance of trees and forests.

Two extensive desert belts have developed along both sides of the equator. The one in the south reaches from Australia to South Africa and South America. The one in the northern hemisphere spreads north from China, all across Asia, North America and Mexico.

The northern belt includes those nations which, as we learned in our history classes at school, were once rulers of the world. We were puzzled to hear in geography class that large areas of these once powerful nations are now sterile. The truth is, of course, that in ancient times they were not so.

Ctesiphon and Baghdad, once centres of concentrated power, were described by Herodotus more than two thousand years ago: "Of all the countries we know this is the most suitable for growing grain. It is so well favoured that it yields two hundredfold and, where conditions are best, even three hundredfold. The ears of wheat and barley grow to the width of four fingers. But to the height of what tree millet and barley grow I shall not disclose. No one who has not seen Babylon would believe me."

For Herodotus, Babylon was the essence of fertility. He also accorded the same honour to Cinyps, a region in North Africa: "This country produces grain equal to the best I have seen for it has black soil and springs water it. The yield is equal to that of Babylon, three hundredfold under the best conditions."

Soldiers in the sandy and torrid conditions of this region (part of modern Cyrenaica) during the last war would have had difficulty in imagining that a now desolate desert was the richest of farming land two millennia ago.

There are three zones on the globe which successively were homes of dominating civilizations but where the soil became devastated in proportion to the age of their settlement.

The first zone is the desert of North Africa. In the Sahara, hundreds of archaeological finds and cave paintings indicate that this was once a flourishing country of many lakes and rivers. One cave painting shows men swimming. Imagine swimmers in the Sahara desert today!

A second zone is the continuous range of stone, salt and sand

Gordon Harrison, a program officer for the Ford Foundation, tells an interesting story about how all forms of nature are interrelated and the implications of forgetting this point.

Some years ago the World Health Organization launched a mosquito control program in Borneo and sprayed large quantities of DDT, which had proved to be very effective in controlling the mosquito. But, shortly thereafter, the roofs of the natives' houses began to fall because they were being eaten by caterpillars, which, because of their particular habits, had not absorbed very much of the DDT themselves. A certain predatory wasp, however, which had been keeping the caterpillars under control, had been killed off in large numbers by the DDT. But the story doesn't end there, because they brought the spraying indoors to control houseflies. Up to that time, the control of houseflies was largely the job of a little lizard, the gecko, that inhabits houses. Well, the geckos continued their job of eating flies, now heavily dosed with DDT, and the geckos began to die. Then the geckos were eaten by house cats. The poor house cats at the end of this food chain had concentrated this material, and they began to die. And they died in such numbers that rats began to invade the houses and consume the food. But, more important, the rats were potential plague carriers. This situation became so alarming that they finally resorted to parachuting fresh cats into Borneo to try to restore the balance of populations that the people, trigger-happy with the spray guns, had destroyed.

There is considerable scientific disagreement about the medical hazards of the new pollutants: about the effects of DDT now found in human bodies, about the diseases due to smog, or about the long-range effects of fallout. But the crucial point is that the disagreements exist, for they reveal that we have risked these hazards before we knew what harm they might do. Unwittingly we have loaded the air with chemicals that damage the lungs, and the water with substances that interfere with the functioning of the blood.

Barry Commoner
The Contemporary Scene

Pollution and Technology

Since the late eighteenth century, Europeans and North Americans have believed in progress. Belching smoke stacks polluting the English midlands, trains belching smoke across the Canadian prairies, sewage dumped into Toronto's Don River or into Lake Erie were seen as examples of "progress" in industrial expansion. Busy factories and black smoke meant high employment and full lunch pails. What was once regarded as good has become in our day a sign of corporate or managerial mismanagement.

Man made his technology. Henry Ford made it possible for virtually every man in North America to own a car. The industry grew so quickly that today our super highways seem unable to keep pace with the production of new vehicles.

The car has brought easy transportation, but at a high price. For example, traffic in central Philadelphia moves at 12 miles per hour, the same speed achieved by horse-drawn vehicles 100 years ago. The car has transformed our environment, spewing into the air carbon monoxide, lead, asbestos particles, and nitrates. The technology of the auto has proven that it is almost beyond our ability to take effective steps to control it.

Another mixed blessing of our technology has been the development of insecticides. DDT, probably the most widely accepted, has been used to control insects, but with high cost to the ecological balance. Similarly, the use of atomic energy to produce electric power appeared to be a blessing for mankind, yet the reactor is now seen as a polluter. The water used to cool the reactor is discharged heated, back into rivers and streams, affecting their ecological balance and disrupting the life cycle of many species of marine life. With the addition of mercury pollution and the immense quantities of oil dumped into the sea from ships, the dangers of today's technology assume horrifying dimensions.

The benefits of technology cannot be denied; the problem is that man embarked on a path of development without first checking the dangers of his route. We dumped detergents without knowing their impact, we sprayed insecticides without knowing the biological consequences on bird life. Man has caused earthquakes with his atomic weapons, exploded nuclear devices into the atmosphere, released poison gas into the air and dumped some of it into the sea – all without knowing thought of the eventual outcome. Man is adventurous, but can he be wise? Can we continue to put stress on an environment without causing damages which cannot be reversed?

deserts which spread from west China, across Turkestan, Afghanistan, Iran, Iraq, Jordan, Sinai and up to North Africa. In ancient times these latitudes were inhabited by Sumerians, Babylonians, Persians, Macedonians, and Phoenicians – names which are all connected with world power and wealth. The third zone covers Palestine, Syria, Asia Minor, Greece, Italy and Spain.

This epidemic of devastated soil seems to be a contagious one. Attempts at reforestation in Spain, Italy and Greece would certainly have been more successful had the opposite shores of the Mediterranean still been covered with a wide belt of fertile land as once they were. But the terrible desert has already reached the shore of the Mediterranean on a wide front and sends out its drying winds to the European countries.

The ever-blue sky of Italy has not always been as blue. Some 2,000 years ago it was just as grey and cloudy as in northern parts of Europe and the complaints of the old Romans about frost and snow-fall – which seem so strange to those who know Italy today – were probably justified.

While once it took millennia, or at least centuries to deplete fertile land, modern history offers a striking example of how man can start and complete this disastrous chain-reaction in only a few decades. Hardly a century ago the U.S. farmer moved into the Middle West, full of initiative and energy.

At first, the existing forests seemed inexhaustible. They were cut down, houses and bridges were built, the wood was burned in locomotives, on ships and in stoves. Great quantities were felled and burned on the spot to make large areas of ash-fertilized farming land. Later, tractors cleared away those clumps of trees and hedges which had survived.

Water ran off the land too rapidly, soil was eroded, floods occurred and drought appeared between rainy periods. This process was accelerated during the First World War when large areas of what remained of tree-covered prairie were ploughed up for more intensive wheat production.

After the war, part of this land was left idle, but there was no longer any deep-rooting grass or other soil cover to conserve the moisture and stabilize the soil. Storms swept the land from the Gulf of Mexico and Canada unchecked, for there were no forests to break their force. The wind carried away the fertile topsoil leaving only sterile layers and rocks.

The same things happened to former forest areas. Without the protection of the trees, without the firm grip of their roots, without humus, the soil was carried away. In the south, where the frost which usually stabilizes the soil during winter seldom occurs, and where there is seldom snow cover to prevent the damage, soil and wind erosion had the same harmful effect.

Like a network of veins the first small gullies appeared in the soil, gradually deepening to real gorges. The process was repeated a million times all over the country until only naked rock was left in some regions.

Even today North American rivers carry away so much fertile soil that an old Indian once said: "Our country is a new Atlantis; one day it will disappear in the Ocean!"

Erosion is only the first phase of a serious chain-reaction which starts with the regression or disappearance of forests. Sediment deposited in reservoirs, water-courses, fields and cities is an important part of the total damage. This damage seldom comes to public attention because it is often invisible. Sediment increases the total volume and weight of flow in water-courses thus raising the height of flood peaks and their destructive power. In drainage basins and reservoirs, sediment can reduce water capacity in a short time.

The forest also plays an important part in protecting the soil against wind erosion and sand encroachment. Dune stabilization by tree planting is a well-known practice in many parts of the world. It is true that almost any vegetation cover will stabilize loose soil and prevent it from being eroded by wind and rain, but forests are probably more effective because of their height, density, deep-reaching roots and permanency. There are indications that the presence of forests may increase local rainfall, though effects on a regional or continental scale have not been demonstrated.

The denser the forest, the greater will be its power to reduce wind velocity. One authority has proved this protective effect and noted reductions in velocity of over 85 per cent. In Italy, tests have shown that the Cecina forest reduced wind velocity by 56 per cent and a hardwood forest in the same region was responsible for reductions of 89 per cent.

The importance of such protection against wind erosion can hardly be exaggerated. In dry periods and on bare land the particles of certain types of soil become so severed from each other that a strong wind can easily carry them away. The finer particles form clouds and the coarser particles, whipped by the wind, roll and bounce over the surface of the soil. Their movement is halted whenever the wind slackens and they bank up in pits, ditches, canals and sunken roads, or in the neighbourhood of sheltering objects where they may suffocate crops.

This is only one of the perils of strong winds. Drying out of soil, direct damage to delicate products like fruit, and the distortion and stunting of exposed trees can all be traced to this cause.

It is a striking fact that a number of countries have never formulated a forest policy or passed a forest law, in spite of evident symptoms of soil deterioration and in spite of repeated warnings about the results of a further decline.

One of them comes from Professor Flatscher, scientist of the Academy for Soil Cultivation in Vienna. He has estimated that the world's forests produce about 1,600 million cubic metres of timber a year whereas the volume cut annually amounts to between 2,200 and 2,600 million cubic metres. This indicates that the annual fellings are about 50 per cent above the allowable cut.

Any private individual who sanctioned such improvidence would be held responsible for bad management and would certainly be heavily penalized. But mankind as a whole, it seems, can indulge in prodigal waste of this kind without being in conflict with any law.

The total forested area of the world is estimated to be about 10,000 million acres and these forests should be capable of provid-

Air Pollution

"When all is said and done, more will have been said than done."

The full extent of air pollution on the mental and physical health of the city dweller is not yet known, but based on what *is* known, the implications are disturbing.

As anyone who has followed the cause-and-effect relationships of smoking and cancer knows, the exact cancer-causing ingredient of tobacco has not yet been isolated, but large numbers of smokers die of cancer. Similarly, the precise number of fatalities or illnesses caused by air pollution are not known. Air pollution is an environmental stress that, combined with others such as insecticides, mercury pollution, and radiation, continues to take its toll. There is evidence that air pollution contributes to pneumonia, lung cancer, emphysema, tuberculosis, silicosis, asthma, bronchitis, and even the ordinary cold. During major air pollution periods, the elderly and people who suffer from the above-mentioned diseases account for the majority of fatalities.

These incidents are startling, but there are side effects that are not fatal and often go unnoticed. Many people suffer colds, discomforts of the eyes, nose, lungs, and throat from air pollution, but these are not usually reported. Commuters in traffic breathe carbon monoxide, which makes them drowsy. In the city at large, soot and offensive smells contribute to an unpleasant urban environment.

Plants, fish, and animals also are affected, but not always in an obvious way. Crop loss due to spotted or stunted plants is common when air-borne pollution is deposited over farmland. In time, the plants' resistance to cold winters or dryness and its overall hardiness may be impaired by pollution.

Property damage can be traced to the presence of sulphur oxides, which contribute to the corrosion of metal and the hardening or deterioration of rubber, plastic, paper, and other materials. Air-borne dirt means extra wear on rugs, furniture and clothes, as well as extra cost in getting these items cleaned. A further added stress of air pollution can be seen in increased fog over cities, differences in temperature between the city and its surrounding area, as well as increased humidity and cloud cover.

ing reasonably adequate supplies for a population larger than now exists. But the provision of such supplies will entail the treatment of all productive forests as renewable crops, the opening up of forests which are not yet accessible and the cessation of the widespread devastation of forests which still continues.

Of the 4,000 million acres of the earth's original forest area which man has destroyed, 1,000 million might well be replanted especially since much of this land is to be found in places where the population is in greatest need of the products of the forest.

The cost per day of the Second World War was a little over $500 million. The cost of one day of this war would reforest at least 20 million acres, and the cost of 50 days would be sufficient to reclothe the entire 1,000 million devastated acres with proper tree cover.

Of course, no one is so naive as to believe we are on the verge of any such undertaking. But we are in possession of scientific knowledge, industrial skill and technical equipment which could be used to spread the potential benefits of the forest to the uttermost ends of the inhabited earth.

As large a body of water as Lake Erie has already been overwhelmed by pollutants and has, in effect, died. . . . Sewage, industrial wastes, and the runoff from heavily fertilized farmlands have loaded the waters of the lake with so much excess phosphate and nitrate as to jar the biology of the lake permanently out of balance. The fish are all but gone. According to a recent report by a committee of the National Academy of Sciences, within about twenty years city wastes are expected to overwhelm the biology of most of the nation's waterways.

Barry Commoner
The Contemporary Scene

The word ecology first appeared in the English language in 1873. Today, less than a century later, the impact of our race upon the environment has so increased in force that it has changed in essence. When the first cannons were fired, in the early fourteenth century, they affected ecology by sending workers scrambling to the forests and mountains for more potash, sulphur, iron ore, and charcoal, with some resulting erosion and deforestation. Hydrogen bombs are of a different order: a war fought with them might alter the genetics of all life on this planet.

Lynn White, Jr.
The Radical Vision

Earthlings in the space age

Lord Ritchie-Calder

By his own ingenuity, *Homo sapiens*, the Earthling, has shrunk his world to the dimensions of a very small planet. In the arrogance of our conceit, which puts Man and his brain at the very centre of the universe, we have never been quite convinced by the astronomers when they have tried to tell us how insignificant the world is in the immensities of Space. But now the space engineers and the astronauts have reminded us how relatively small our earth is.

In the spirit of new adventure, one may regard the world as a departure platform for fugitives to the moon or a launching pad for escapades to other planets or even beyond our solar system, into other universes. But the Earthlings who cannot so escape must recognize that on its relatively limited surface, 3,000 million people today, 4,000 million in twenty years' time, and 6,000 million or 7,000 million forty years from now, will have to contrive to live and to work together. Or, by the neglect of wisdom or the abuse of human ingenuity, to die together.

An eye, human or electronic, in an artificial satellite in orbit, sees no political frontiers; no iron curtains; and no differentiation of races. It might see H-Bombs going off as the signals of tension; but in general it would see a globe which only three-tenths was land and seven-tenths covered by oceans; mountain ranges reduced to wrinkles; evidence of surviving forests; tawny expanses of hot deserts which cover a fifth of its surface and cold deserts which cover another fifth. It might with difficulty distinguish the pattern of cultivation of arable or cropped lands, which accounts for only one-tenth of the land surface. That is the nature of humanity's family estate for which, at the moment, we are responsible.

The world is not just the relic of a cosmic incident. It provides the living space for the evolutionary process which, we like to think, resulted in Man.

But with a wisdom which we have not demonstrated convincingly so far, we must recognize that that living space and that revolutionary process include other species with which we can coexist or which we can stupidly destroy. Stupidly because our relations with these other species are a condition of our own survival.

A lump of soil no bigger than a football contains a micro-organic population greater than the human population of the world. That micro-organic population includes the germs and fungi which suggest disease or danger but which, in other forms, are indispensable to our existence. In the same way, we think of insects as deserving insecticide and other creatures as deserving pesticide, but in the process we can kill those which are essential to our ultimate needs.

In order to get margarine, we cleared big areas in Africa of brush and tsetse flies which it harboured, but in the process we got rid of the bees which were needed to pollinate other crops.

Similarly, for our short-term, and short-sighted, needs we have destroyed the vegetation cover, preventing the absorption of water by the natural sponge through which it seeps into the underground springs. As a result the scouring rains sluice the soil off the hills, cause floods and eventual erosion.

In the lifetime of the United States, over two hundred and eighty million acres of arable crop and range land have been destroyed – more than ten times the productive acreage of the United Kingdom.

Only slowly – and recently – have we come to recognize that wild animals are not something with which mankind is at war but a part of the balance of life, which is delicately adjusted.

For the first time in history, man has the power of control over the evolution of his species. We share the living space. Into that we have injected, in the past sixteen years, man-made radioactivity. Elements which did not exist in nature have been indiscriminately scattered over the face of the earth, to combine in all living things.

Today there is not a child in the world that does not have radio-strontium in its bones – at least to some degree. The amounts may be insignificant and the possible effects may be emotionally exaggerated and medically in dispute. Much is unproven, much is unknown. But that only emphasizes that men, on faulty evidence or in positive ignorance, are recklessly tampering with the living space on which their present and future depend.

I have, in the past fourteen years, been among the wandering Bedouins in the desert, the Dyaks of Equatorial Borneo, the Eskimo in the Arctic, the peoples of the hinterlands of Latin America and Africa and Asia. In one way or another their lives and their destinies have been consciously touched by scientific and technological achievement.

Many of them have acquired their freedom. But when the intoxicating effects of political independence wear off, there is the morning-after-the-night-before. People are apt to wake up and discover that freedom has been robbed of its meaning; that they are just as hungry, or more hungry; just as poor, or more impover-

Poison Gas: The One that Got Away

In Utah's Tooele County, the U.S. Army maintains a biological warfare centre and proving ground called Dugway. On March 13, 1968, around 6 p.m., an aircraft dropped nerve gas over a test area, to observe the effect. (Nerve gas influences the central nervous system and interferes with normal signals from the brain to the muscles. There is difficulty in breathing, loss of muscular co-ordination, perspiration, convulsions, and death.)

Near the test site is Skull Valley, where ranchers raise sheep, and on that cold March evening, the sheep were grazing on the hillside. On March 14, ranchers reported that the sheep were acting in a strange way, staggering, dropping to the ground, and jerking spasmodically. Some were grazing, others licking the snow that had fallen. As the day wore on, the sheep began to die. Veterinarians summoned to diagnose the malady said that the sheep seemed to have been poisoned. They asked if the Dugway Station had been making tests, but Army officials answered that no tests had been carried out that would cause this difficulty.

A research team moved in and took samples of snow, plant life, and dead animals for analysis. In early April, more animals were acquired by the local ranchers and these also died.

The research tests showed that the sheep had been killed by the nerve gas released by the Army aircraft, and that because of changing weather conditions the gas had drifted farther than planned. Further investigation revealed that the Army had no monitoring program designed to test for gas outside its proving area.

Attack on Hunger: New Seeds for Old

Since World War II the plight of the world's
hungry people has received a great deal of attention. Researchers have brought to bear their
knowledge of agricultural technology and plant
development to help solve this increasing world
problem of feeding the hungry. The success of
their efforts can be seen in higher production
figures: for example, India's wheat crop is up
50% and its food imports have been cut in half
since 1967; Kenya has an export surplus of corn,
while Mexico has surplus wheat, rice, and corn;
the Philippines is self-sufficient in rice, and
Turkey is self-sufficient in wheat.

This increased food production has been made
possible by the development, through biological
engineering, of new varieties of wheat, rice,
and corn. New plants have been developed that
require less fertilizer, yet produce better results.
The old types of grain had stalks that could not
support the heavier heads of grain that developed
when fertilizer was applied. This problem has
been corrected in the new strains, which now
have heavier stalks. Along with the higher-yield
varieties, new strains are being developed that
will resist disease and adjust to a wide variety of
geographic and climatic conditions. Previously
uncultivated areas can now be used to raise
grain and corn for consumption.

Perhaps the most significant development may
be JR-8 "miracle rice", which matures in four
months instead of six and provides a high crop-
yield. The shorter maturing season makes possible
more crops per year, for still greater production.

The yearly mass suicide of Scandinavian lem-
mings, the weird death dance of the March hare,
and similar self-destructive behavior among a
species of rat on some Pacific Islands have
recently been interpreted as direct results of
stress caused by overcrowding. Man may not be
immune to this control factor. Even if technology
permits us to produce unlimited quantities of
food – putting to rest the Malthusian apprehen-
sion that population eventually outstrips food
supply – there remains the certainty that the
supply of terrestrial space, which may be just as
vital a factor in the maintenance of life, is a fixed
quantity on this globe.

William Kloman
Who Am I?

ished; just as sick or more disease-ridden, and just as frustrated in
their seeking for a better way of life.

People in ten underdeveloped countries have been shown what
is scientifically and technically possible. But it is not enough to
show them. To demonstrate what might be done, to people who
have not the means to do it, is just tantalizing. It is just "window-
shopping" – walking along with nothing in your pocket and with
plateglass between you and the things you have been taught to
want.

The peoples of the emerging countries have not the means to go
shopping in the supermarket of science – as Prof. P. M. S. Blackett
has termed it. They cannot even afford the bargain basement.

The object of this kind of assistance is to help people to help
themselves – throwing them a rope with which to haul themselves
out of the morass of poverty. But this is no Indian rope-trick – the
rope has to be tethered to something, and a winch would help to
haul them out more quickly. As it is, the rope is slipping.

After ten years of this new social philosophy by which governments acknowledged that they were responsible, not only for their
own people, but for other, less fortunate peoples as well, the gap
between the prosperity of the highly-advanced countries and of
the slightly-advanced countries and the poverty of the countries
struggling for development has not closed – it has widened. The
rich countries are richer and the poor countries are poorer – despite the thousands of millions which have been spent on aid.

Governments, when the markets skid, cannot "lift themselves by
their own bootstraps" or, if they do, it is by duress. In the meantime their peoples will endure the Misery-Go-Round of Poverty.

Vast surpluses of grain have been stockpiled in various countries.
Canada is a good example. No one should be so foolish as to think
that the distribution of those vast surpluses, even if it were possible, would solve the problem of hunger. Relieving immediate
stresses, yes. By distribution through such agencies as UNICEF,
yes. By turning food into currency, yes. Supplies of food can be
made available to governments to help present needs and the proceeds can be used by a government to help its own agriculture to
increase its yields in future years. That is the only permanent solution – to enable countries and regions to produce their food requirements.

It can be done. We do not need to imagine food artificially produced by photosynthesis. The scientific knowhow already exists.
The knowledge we have got, applied with wisdom, can increase
the yields from existing acreages. By plant-breeding we can extend
the food-growing acreages into what seemed inhospitable regions.

As far as those oceans which cover seven-tenths of our globe are
concerned, we are at the cave-man stage. At sea we hunt our food
and do not husband it. Sea-farming and sea-ranching are perfectly feasible.

For the first time in history, Man, the Earthling, has the power
of veto over continuing evolution. He can exercise that veto by
the nuclear destruction of the race, or, by default in handling the
problems of starvation, prove that Malthus was right.

He can ambitiously reach out to the farther planets, but his species as such must survive on the surface of the earth, subsist from the nine inches of top-soil which feeds, clothes and shelters him or from the seas from which he emerged hundreds of millions of years ago.

All the majesty of his mind can be dethroned by his stomach. Man can feast like Belshazzar and ignore the writing on the wall. He can spend millions a year on the defence of peace and ignore the real content of the peace he is supposed to be defending.

He can split the atom and release the power of matter and use this, his greatest discovery, to poison the goodness of his earth and destroy his species. He can outboast the Ancients, who in the arrogance of their material success built pyramids as the grave-stones of their civilizations, for Modern Man can throw his pyramids into Space and they may orbit eternally around a planet which died of his neglect.

Or he may choose to use his science and his wisdom to co-operate with all his kind in the peaceful enrichment of his Earth and of the people who live on it.

When the time comes for living in a society dependent on scrap for high-grade metal and on common rocks for commercial ore, the affluent society will be over-worked to maintain a standard of living equal to that of a century ago.

Thomas S. Lovering
Resources of Man

Because we wanted to build nuclear bombs and kill mosquitoes, we have burdened our bodies with strontium-90 and DDT, with consequences that no one can now predict. We have been massively intervening in the environment without being aware of many of the harmful consequences of our acts until they have been performed and the effects — which are difficult to understand and sometimes irreversible — are upon us.

Barry Commoner
The Contemporary Scene

Resources for Part 5

Hoopes, N. 1969. *Who Am I?* New York: Dell Publishing Co.

Laskin, R. 1964. *Social Problems, A Canadian Profile*. Toronto: McGraw-Hill Company of Canada Limited.

Martin, J. and Norman, A. R. D. 1970. *The Computerized Society*. Englewood Cliffs, New Jersey: Prentice-Hall, Inc.

Muller, H. J. 1970. *The Children of Frankenstein*. Bloomington: Indiana University Press.

Toffler, A. 1970. *Future Shock*. New York: Random House.

Urick, R. V. 1970. *Alienation*. Englewood Cliffs, New Jersey: Prentice-Hall, Inc.

Part 6

Methods and materials

one   *Research*

Research in the social sciences is a systematic attempt to learn more about man in society, more than one can learn in ordinary day-to-day living. And the key word here is *systematic*. We may use different methods of collecting information with different purposes for collecting it, but we must insist on doing it in a systematic manner.

On occasion, our research will be merely a description of a situation or an event – for example, a riot, or the number of males over forty who voted for Trudeau in the federal elections. But this reporting has two very important characteristics. First, it must be as precise as possible under the circumstances. It is relatively easy to count the number of males and females who responded "yes" or "no" to an item on a questionnaire, but it is quite difficult to be precise when determining what factors contributed to the success of a popular song.

The researcher must be willing to approach his sources of information without bias. There is always the danger that one will reject those pieces of information that do not conform to one's own theory. Also, the researcher must be skeptical of other people's reports of what took place. You need not doubt everything you hear, but you must learn to distinguish reliable from unreliable information.

Second, the researcher must operate from a base of solid ideas; these ideas or concepts are used to form hypotheses. The term "hypothesis" is explained in the next section. Just counting things and describing events are not enough. The researcher must go beyond this to develop explanations, comparisons, interpretations, and relationships with other information on how our society operates.

Although reporting is probably the most common type of research in the social sciences many experiments are also conducted.

In the section that follows, an attempt is made to provide the student with the opportunity to conduct research on his own. Although our approach is relatively basic, the essential ingredients of sound research have been included. It is recommended that the researcher use the survey questionnaire approach as his data collection procedure in his first research attempts. The following selection is built around the use of a specific questionnaire, which has been included, and has been designed to take the students through the development of hypotheses to the analysis and presentation of findings.

Developing hypotheses

We use hypotheses in almost every discussion we have with another person. Statements that include hunches, guesses, and speculations (such as, "I think Montreal will take Toronto tonight in the hockey game"), and even descriptions can all be called hypotheses. A hypothesis, then, is a statement about a relationship that does or will exist between two or more factors, persons, or events. In the case of the hockey game, we are anticipating the result of a competitive relationship – a game – between two hockey teams, and our expectation probably is based on the previous successes of

Researchers on research

It is a commonplace that all research must start from a problem. Research can be successful only if the problem is good; it can be original only if the problem is original. But how can one see a problem, any problem, let alone a good and original problem? For to see a problem is to see something that is hidden. It is to have an intimation of the coherence of hitherto not comprehended particulars.

Michael Polanyi
in Robert A. Nisbet
The Social Bond

. . . all students of human behaviour face a particular difficulty in reporting their findings. We report our findings to our subjects – something a physicist or a botanist does not do. And we regularly find that those who hear our reports claim that a particular finding is obvious even when we doubt it is. That, in fact, is why many sociologists use the device of asking students or the members of an audience to predict in advance a particular finding to reduce the possibility of its being condemned as obvious.

Frank Jones
The Viewpoint of Sociology

each team. In this example, at the end of the game we are able to determine whether the hypothesis was correct. Of course, after the game, the hypothesis has become a fact.

Let us look at another example of a hypothesis: *Boys are taller than girls*. This is simply a general statement of a relationship between one factor – sex – and its two categories, male and female, and a second factor – height – which can be measured in feet, inches, centimetres, and so on. The term "taller" suggests a variation in height between the two sexes. To make this hypothesis testable, we must be a little more specific in defining the factors. For example, we do not mean that eight-year-old boys are taller than twelve-year-old girls or that Vietnamese boys are taller than Masai girls. We should be fairly specific about our categories of boys and girls, if not in our hypothesis, then at least in our own minds. Let us say, then, that we are thinking of Canadian boys and girls sixteen years of age. But there is another very important dimension to relationships of this type. We are not saying that all boys are taller than all girls; rather, we are saying that the average height of boys in this category is greater than the average height of girls in this category.

In the development of most of our hypotheses, we will anticipate a certain fact or finding on the basis of our own observations and our reading. Most hypotheses are designed to investigate issues that we recognize through our own experience. The assumption we make regarding the nature of a particular relationship between two factors typically is arrived at by reviewing our knowledge of these factors. For example, in establishing the above hypothesis, we have drawn heavily on our observations of boys and girls.

Social scientists are often criticized for proving the obvious, and the above example lends support to that hypothesis. But many statements that we assume to be true on the basis of common sense are found to be untrue when tested. Let us examine two examples of hypotheses and two different approaches to testing each of them which anticipate opposite results.

Hypothesis 1: Grade 12 students are more likely to be concerned about their future occupations than are Grade 9 students.

This hypothesis was developed on the assumption that Grade 12 students are closer to a decision about what their life's work will be, and therefore are more likely to be concerned about the factors which relate to that decision than are Grade 9 students. But a counterbalancing argument also could be made – that Grade 12 students have already made career decisions, and therefore are less concerned about this matter than are Grade 9 students who have not done so. Often in testing the hypothesis, we can test the assumptions underlying its development.

Hypothesis 2: Boys are more likely than girls to become involved in student council activities in the school.

As we know, men hold most of the major positions of authority in the community and in the larger society, so we would expect that boys would take on similar responsibilities in the school. This issue, however, may be examined from another perspective. Since girls are more successful students than boys in school, and more successful students are given greater opportunity to participate in student council activities, girls may be over-represented on student councils. In fact, "the greater number of girls than boys in student government and extracurricular activities is a surprising cultural fact. High schools appear to be a girls' world with girls not only more successful in the above-mentioned areas, but, according to other studies, more successful in academic pursuits as well. This active role of the female in the high school society is much different from the role played by the female in our adult, male-dominated society." (William D. Knill, "The Adolescent Society of the High School", *Canadian Society: Sociological Perspectives.*)

Testing hypotheses

After you develop a hypothesis or identify a research question you wish to explore, then you must lay out a research design. The following points should be included:

1) a clear statement of the hypothesis to be tested or the research question to be investigated;
2) a description of the subjects of the study (the individuals who make up the group of people to be studied);
3) a clear indication of the information that will be collected in order to test the hypothesis or provide information on the problem (we will use the words data and information interchangeably);
4) a description of the procedures to be used to collect the data;
5) a tentative indication of the way in which the findings will be presented and analyzed.

A fuller outline of the steps that are normally taken in the lay-out of a research design is presented below. Beside it, printed in blue, is the research design for a sample project.

1) The Hypothesis

Make sure you include each of the factors you are studying in your hypothesis.

Sample Hypothesis

Mothers are more likely than fathers to have the most to say about teenagers helping around the house.

2) The Subjects of the Study*

It is very important that you describe in detail the characteristics of the group of people you have chosen to study. It is equally important that you outline the method by which the subjects were

---

* When you do your research on two or three classes in your school you cannot safely say that your classmates represent all kinds of students in your school. Neither are they likely to be truly representative of students in other schools. Ideally you would like to be able to say that what you have found about your classmates is also true for students throughout your school and for students in other schools. However, you could not say this unless the subjects had been selected in such a way that they were representative of students in other classes or in other schools. While social scientists do have methods for selecting subjects who can be considered representative of large groups of people, these methods are too tedious and complicated for our purposes here. In your research, you may suggest that your findings might be true for other groups of students but you can only be sure that they relate to the subjects you have studied directly.

Subjects

We will need at least thirty boys and thirty girls to make sure that differences will be great enough to take on some importance. This means that we require three Grade 11 classes. The following background information on each subject will be required:

1) sex
2) age
3) mother working (this factor might affect the responses)

Information Required

We need to obtain from the subjects their opinions on which of their parents would have the most to say about their helping around the house.

Then it is necessary to determine the alternative answers the subjects might make. In this case, we can use Father, Mother, Someone else, and Don't know as the alternatives.

Survey Item: Who would have the most say in your family about your helping around the house?

Alternative Answers: a. Mother, b. Father, c. Someone else, d. Don't know.

Data Collection Procedures

Since most of the information to be collected can be obtained directly from the subjects of the study, it is probably most efficient to use a brief questionnaire.

Student Survey No. 1

Please circle the appropriate response.

1. Sex: Male   Female

2. Age: 15 16 17 18 19 or over

3. Does your mother work either full or half-time in a job outside of the home?
   Yes   No

4. Who would have the most say in your family about your helping around the house?
   Mother   Someone else
   Father   Don't know

Data Presentation and Analysis

In order to deal with the hypothesis directly, it was decided to tabulate all of the students' responses to the question, "Who would have the most say in your family about your helping around the house?"

---

selected. Social scientists tend to be concerned about such background factors as the sex of the subjects, their age, the kind of community they came from, their fathers' occupations, the number of children in their family, and so on. If you decide to conduct research on your classmates, you might also consider their grade level, their future plans, and the course they are enrolled in.

3) The Data

After selecting your subjects and determining what further information you need to describe them, you must specify what data are required to test your hypothesis.

4) Data Collection Procedures

There are many ways to collect information, some of which are far more likely to produce accurate information than are others. Certain kinds of information tend to be accurate however obtained, such as a person's age and sex, and the course in which he is enrolled. Others are notoriously inaccurate, such as information that has to be recalled from the past or attitudes toward things and people. Also the researcher must be aware of the tendency for people to give the answers they think the researcher wants to hear rather than the truth. The researcher must ensure that the information he has collected is as accurate as possible. In your research you will probably obtain most of your information through the use of questionnaires and interviews, or by observation. In the design of an interview or questionnaire you should attempt to anticipate the way in which your subjects will respond so that you can handle the information in as efficient a manner as possible. In order to make sure that you are going to get the kinds of answers you expect, you should try out your questionnaire or interview beforehand and then make adjustments if necessary.

5) Data Presentation and Analysis

Many researchers do not anticipate the responses that might arise from their research questions and therefore have considerable difficulty in organizing and presenting their findings. It is to your advantage to anticipate beforehand the tables you will use in presenting your data. If you do, you merely have to fill in the information after it has been collected. Even when you have general questions which might have many answers, you should attempt to determine categories that the answers might fit into. This does not mean that you are restricted to those categories alone in presenting the information, but it makes the process more efficient, and more important, it makes your thinking more ordered.

When you analyze the findings and interpret them to your audience, let your tables do the talking wherever possible. Present them in a simple, straightforward manner and refer directly to them when discussing your interpretation.

Using the questionnaire

Not all research need start with a specific hypothesis. For many types of research it is most effective if the researcher works within a general area of concern. The researcher collects a great deal of information and combines his findings in various ways, and by so doing he may uncover unsuspected relationships. It is often through this approach that major breakthroughs are made in understanding human behaviour. This has been called "ex post facto research" or "research after the fact". This means that you attempt to explain something after you have found that it exists. Of course, to be sure that you have found something of consequence, you should collect the same kind of information from another set of subjects and thereby test the reliability of your findings.

We have designed a questionnaire which you might use to uncover certain relationships. Items have been pulled together from a number of other questionnaires and we have added some of our own. You may use this questionnaire to conduct your own ex post facto research and you may also use it as a model in designing your own questionnaire items. The questionnaire brings together some of the key elements in the research of noted social scientists.

Items 1 to 4 provide background information on the subjects you are planning to study. It is obvious that people of different ages and sexes do not respond in the same way to the various questionnaire items. We have included a father's occupation item because so much of the work done in sociology has related to parents' status and how this affects the way in which children are brought up. Item 4 regarding chronological position in the family is another important social factor affecting a person's attitudes. Items 5, 6, 7, and 8 provide some information on your attitudes and values and your subjects'. The sub-items in Item 9 have been extracted from instruments which were designed to gain some impression of a person's beliefs and emotional feelings. You can combine them in any way that you wish, of course, but they were originally designed to measure such factors as "alienation", "powerlessness", "authoritarianism", "conservatism", and "motivation".

We have also included a questionnaire answer sheet that may be used along with the questionnaire to simplify the handling of the subject's responses. You may use this as a model for your own questionnaire answer sheets.

Table 1
"Who would have the most say in your family about your helping around the house?"

Responses	%
Father	
Mother	
Other	
Uncertain	

It was also decided that it would be useful to present the various sub-groupings of subjects' responses to the question — for example, boys and girls; students aged 17 and over and students aged 16 and under.

Table 2

Responses	% Boys	% Girls
Father		
Mother		
Other		
Uncertain		

Table 3

Responses	17 and over	16 and under
Father		
Mother		
Other		
Uncertain		

The questionnaire

We encourage you to use the following questionnaire, or one modelled after it, in your first attempt at classroom research.

Questionnaire

The following questionnaire is designed to be used as a source of data for students developing research skills. It is important that you respond to it as carefully and honestly as you can so that the student researcher will have the opportunity to work with meaningful information. Please do not sign your name.

Place the number corresponding to your response to a question in the box opposite that question number on the Answer Sheet which follows this questionnaire. For example, in Question 1, if your present age is 17, you will place a number 3 in the box opposite Question 1 on the Answer Sheet.

1. *Age*

1	15 or younger	4	18
2	16	5	19
3	17	6	20 or older

2. *Sex*

1	Male	2	Female

3. *Father's Occupation*

   1   Blue-collar: factory worker, mechanic, truck driver, farmer, etc.
   2   White-collar/Sales/Clerical: book-keeper, sales-clerk, salesman, etc.
   3   White-collar/Professional: doctor, teacher, accountant, lawyer, engineer, executive, business owner, etc.

4. *Are you –*

1	an only child	3	the youngest child
2	the oldest child	4	a middle child?

5. *How much does your father like his work?*

1	A lot	4	A little
2	More than average	5	Dislikes it
3	Less than average	6	Don't know

6. *Who in your family would have the most to say about –*
   (Place a 1 in the box if it is your father, a 2 for your mother, or a 3 for don't know.)

   a   buying a new car
   b   buying a new chesterfield
   c   your helping around the house
   d   your staying out late
   e   where to go on holiday?

7. *Which two of the following do your parents think are most important for you in school?* (Give a 1st and 2nd choice)

   1   that you become creative
   2   that you act responsibly

3   that you obey your teachers
4   that you become popular with other students
5   that you work hard
6   that you participate in athletics
7   that you are considerate to others

8. *Where would you prefer to live if you had to make a choice from the following?*

1   In a large city
2   In the suburbs of a large city
3   In a small town
4   In the country

9. *Please indicate whether you tend to agree or disagree with the following statements. Use 1 if you Agree and 2 if you Disagree. If you really do not feel that you lean one way or the other, please place a 3 in the appropriate box.*

a   It is quite all right for mothers of young children to have a full-time job.

b   If people would do a little less talking and a little more working, we all would be better off.

c   This country is really run by a few people in power and there is very little most of us can do about it.

d   I prefer to do active things rather than sit around and read.

e   Most people really don't know what is good for them.

f   Ambition is the most important factor in determining success in life.

g   Although science is pretty important, there are many things that will never be understood by the human mind.

h   Some people are born with an urge to jump off high places.

i   If I could change, I would be someone different from myself.

j   It is only natural and quite right for a person to think that *his* family is best.

k   Most times if you try to change things too much, you make them worse.

l   While the use of force is usually wrong, it is sometimes necessary to keep people in their place.

m It is pretty hard to know who you can count on.

n   There are times when I feel pretty useless.

o   If I had to choose between happiness and greatness, I would choose happiness.

p   Usually, the tougher the job, the harder I work.

q   If I have a problem I am most likely to talk to my parents about it.

r   Most people really don't care for others.

s   For success, good luck is more important than hard work.

The Answer Sheet

The following answer sheet has been designed to accompany the questionnaire presented above. If the answer sheet is made up on a ditto master (one ditto master for each person who will respond to the questionnaire), then the student researchers will be able to obtain a copy of each of the subjects' responses to the questionnaire. A detailed explanation of how this might be done is presented on page 257.

Questionnaire Answer Sheet

1	☐	9a	☐
2	☐	9b	☐
3	☐	9c	☐
4	☐	9d	☐
5	☐	9e	☐
6a	☐	9f	☐
6b	☐	9g	☐
6c	☐	9h	☐
6d	☐	9i	☐
6e	☐	9j	☐
7(i)	☐	9k	☐
7(ii)	☐	9l	☐
8	☐	9m	☐
		9n	☐
		9o	☐
		9p	☐
		9q	☐
		9r	☐
		9s	☐

Administering the Questionnaire

The questionnaire should be administered to ensure honesty and care in the responses of your subjects. The following factors are important in this regard.

1) The questionnaires should all be administered at the same time. This prevents discussions from taking place among the subjects. In practice, consecutive classes would serve a similar purpose.

2) The subjects should not have the opportunity to talk to other students while answering the questionnaire.

3) The subjects are more likely to respond honestly if they know that they will not be signing their names and that they will be considered as members of larger categories of students.

4) When a question is interpreted, it should be interpreted in the same way for all subjects.

5) The questionnaire should be relatively short, to sustain interest.

Preparing for Data Analysis

If all students in a class conducted their own personal research at the same time, probably the same pool of research subjects would be used over and over again. Your classmates and students in other classes would get pretty tired of answering questionnaires. To avoid this problem, in your first attempts at conducting research, you might be well advised to take advantage of the questionnaire we have provided for you. It has been designed to incorporate numerous possibilities for the investigation of human relationships. Thus, in classroom research, it may be necessary to administer only the one questionnaire. If you decide to devise your own questionnaire, however, you should try to determine what your other classmates' needs are and find out whether it is possible to include all of the items in one questionnaire and administer it to one group of subjects.

Assuming that you use the questionnaire which we have provided, it becomes necessary for you and each of your classmates to obtain a copy of each of the subjects' responses to the questionnaire. This suggests that, if there are thirty students in your class, the subjects will have to answer thirty questionnaires, one each for you and your classmates. Instead of going through this laborious process, you will find it easier if each subject responds to the questionnaire on a ditto master of the Answer Sheet layout. When the subjects have answered the questionnaire on the ditto master, it is a simple matter to run off enough copies so that each student has a copy of every other student's answer sheet. (To be more economical, you might want to share one kit of answer sheets among three or four students.)

Now, assuming that you have a kit of the subjects' answer sheets, how do you go about handling your data? Let us say, for example, that you are looking at the different ways in which boys and girls responded to Question 9 (i): "If I could change, I would be someone different from myself." Our first step is to sort the kit of answer sheets into two piles, one for the boys and one for the girls. To do this, you look at the responses to Question 2 and place those who coded "1" into one pile, and those who coded "2" into another pile. Question 9 (i) has three possible alternative responses – Agree, Disagree, and Uncertain. For the moment, let us assume that none of the subjects was Uncertain in answering this question, so that you need only sort the boys' pile, and similarly the girls' pile, into two more divisions on the basis of their Agree or Disagree responses to the questionnaire item. If a subject has answered question 9 (i) with a figure 1, he means that he agrees with

Table X
Student Responses to the Questionnaire
Item: "If I could change, I would be
someone different from myself."

	Agree	*Disagree*
Boys	20	10
Girls	10	20

Table Y
Student Responses to the Questionnaire
Item: "If I could change, I would be
someone different from myself."

	Agree	*Disagree*
Boys:		
16 and under	10	5
17 and older	10	5
Girls:		
16 and under	5	10
17 and older	5	10

NOTE: If there were responses in the "Uncertain"
category, we would need 12 cells rather
than 8
$(2 \times 2 \times 2 = 8; 2 \times 2 \times 3 = 12)$

the statement; a figure 2 means that he disagrees. You now have four piles of Answer Sheets. If you started with sixty Answer Sheets, of which thirty were from boys and thirty from girls, your table of responses might resemble Table X.

In the example we have used, since the number of boys is the same as the number of girls, it is not necessary to change the numbers into percentages. *However, you must remember that if the numbers of boys and girls were different, you must change the responses into percentages so that the information can be compared.*

If you wish to determine how boys and girls from two different age groups (let us say "16 and under", and "17 and over") responded to this questionnaire item, you must go through three stages of sorting. Again you sort into two piles, for boys and for girls, as above. Second, you have to sort each of the piles for boys and those for girls into two other piles: boys 16 and under, boys 17 and older; girls 16 and under, and girls 17 and older. Third, for each of these four piles you must sort into two more piles based on the responses to the questionnaire item, "If I could change, I would be someone different from myself." (Again we have assumed that no one has answered "Uncertain" to this item.) Now we have eight piles: boys 16 and under who agreed with the item, boys 16 and under who disagreed with the item, and so on. Therefore, we need a table with eight cells. Table Y illustrates how this information might be presented.

Preparing the research report

Research findings must be reported in an accurate and meaningful way. It is the researcher's intepretation of his data that will have the greatest value for others. Below, we have provided a format that you might find useful in the presentation of your findings. There are many alternative ways of presenting the findings of a research report, so you must see this as only one of a number of alternatives. In order to show you how this research format might be used, we have followed through a sample research project.

A) Title: (The title should be brief and convey something of the purpose of the reasearch.) *The Aspirations of Boys and Girls*

B) Problem: (In this section, you should present a brief outline of the thinking that went into the development of your basic hypothesis or research problem. If possible, you should refer to other research on the same topic.) In Canadian society boys and girls are brought up in quite different ways and with quite different values. Boys tend to think of themselves as strong individuals with the responsibility of obtaining meaningful work; and girls tend to see themselves as housewives, linked to men. We may expect, then, that as a measure of success in life, girls are inclined to value happiness in terms of a good relationship with their husbands and families. Since men are more involved in the competitive world of work, and since their success is won in part at the expense of others, they probably value greatness over happiness as a measure of success in life.

Hypothesis: Males are more likely than females to value greatness over happiness as a measure of success in life, and correspondingly, females are more likely than males to value happiness over greatness.

C) Subjects:
The subjects of the study are two groups of students taking classes in Comermere Secondary School, Comermere, Ontario (fictitious name) – thirty-five male students and twenty-five female students. Their ages range from fifteen to eighteen years. Half of the students are bused in to the school from rural areas, and the other half live in the community.

D) Procedures:
A questionnaire was selected as the most appropriate means of obtaining information from the subjects of the study. The questionnaire was designed to obtain information on the sex, age, and subjects' responses to the item, "If I had to choose between happiness and greatness, I would choose happiness." The subjects were provided with three alternative answers to this question – Agree, Disagree, Uncertain. Since there were different numbers of boys and girls, it was necessary to change their responses to percentages.

E) The Findings:
(In this section you should simply present, in a systematic way, the information you have collected. You might also point out obvious trends in one direction or another. Do not interpret or discuss your information until the next section.) It can be clearly seen from Table A that a greater percentage of girls than boys agreed with the statement. Correspondingly, a greater percentage of boys than girls disagreed with the statement. When the data were analyzed in terms of the age of the students, there was no evidence that their age was related to their responses on this item. (Another table could have been included to support this point.)

Table A
Student Responses to the Questionnaire Item: "If I had to choose between happiness and greatness, I would choose happiness."

	Agree %	Disagree %	Uncertain %
Boys	30	65	5
Girls	75	15	10

F) Discussion:
Table A indicates that for the boys and girls in this study, there are real differences in their priorities regarding happiness and greatness. This does not mean that *all* boys and girls have

the same view of life. In fact we can see clearly that some boys and some girls were found in each of the categories. There was, however, a definite trend in the direction anticipated by our hypothesis. From this information, it appears that we can say that the girls have been brought up to value different things from the boys, and in particular, to value happiness in life rather than achievement of greatness. It would be useful to pursue this line of enquiry to determine how the home has encouraged these variations in values.

(You should also include some comment on the design of the study in this section. The above study was particularly limited in that it dealt with only one dimension of boys' and girls' feelings. We cannot even be sure that if we reversed the question item to state, "If I had to choose between greatness and happiness, I would choose greatness," the responses would have been the same.)

Some additional notes

We have emphasized the questionnaire method in this research section. There are, of course, many other methods of obtaining information, and also many different ways of conducting research. However, since you are at an early stage in your growth as a researcher, we recommend that you first develop your skills as a survey researcher. In this regard, you are encouraged to gather information by using questionnaire techniques and conducting interviews, and by collecting information from libraries and other places where data are stored.

If you decide to use interview techniques, you should remember that the interview must be designed with as much attention to detail as is used in designing the questionnaire. You must be quite specific as to the questions you wish to ask and be prepared to probe deeply to get the kind of answer that you can classify. Since it is unlikely that you will be able to obtain enough interviews to be able to present the information in tables, you will have to organize it in a different format. You will probably want to include quotations from some of the people you have interviewed to support the points you have made. Because you are likely to be presenting findings from a comparatively small number of subjects, you must be especially cautious in interpreting what your interviewees have said. To overcome this concern, you might consider using your entire class to conduct interviews. A sample project involving interviewing might be a survey of personnel officials from industry. The purpose might be to determine the characteristics employers look for in their job applicants.

If you go beyond the school in your research activities, you must be careful not to seek information which might be considered private or controversial. While this is also true within the school, it is particularly important for the larger community outside the school. If you antagonize your subjects, you make further research impossible for the groups of students who will follow you. Also, it is a good idea to provide feedback to the subjects from whom you have collected your information. You should remember to thank the participants and, if they wish, supply them with a summary of your findings.

two   Simulation games

Life can be looked at as a game, as a situation in which the things we do become competitive strategies. Often, in order to reach our objectives, we have to compete with others who seek the same scarce rewards. Competing for the attention of a girl or boy, of a teacher or a parent, for a job, for political office, for a business advantage, can all be seen as game situations. Unlike a fight where we attempt to destroy our opponent, in a game our objective is to use superior techniques to win.

It is not surprising that games originated through attempts to simulate war or business competition. The military and the business community have long used games to simulate actual conditions of war and business. They have proven to be very effective in creating life-like situations and forcing accurate decision-making in order to ensure success when a real competition occurs. Some of these games have become so sophisticated that they have had to be computerized in order to include all possible alternatives.

Games have become a part of our culture. We often think in terms of appropriate strategies and the "odds" of winning or losing. And recently, games have become a powerful educational tool, with properly designed games providing meaningful educational experiences. Although the primary objective of an educational game is to educate, a game can make the process of learning quite entertaining. There are three main categories of learning that can take place in games: 1) facts can be learned as a basic requirement for proceeding with the game, 2) learning processes are followed through by simulation, and 3) the costs and benefits, risks and rewards of various strategies of decision-making can be learned. Logical thinking is encouraged and a broad approach to problem-solving is usually taken.

We have included two games in this section. The first of these is a variation of the old "Prisoners' Dilemma" game. In "Prisoners' Dilemma", two suspects have been taken into custody by the police. They are interviewed separately and each one is encouraged to turn in the other in order to get a lighter sentence. Both prisoners know that if neither confesses, the worst than can happen to them is a light sentence for vagrancy. So for each prisoner there are four possible alternatives: turning in the other and receiving no sentence, keeping quiet (along with the other) and receiving a light sentence, or keeping quiet (and getting turned in by the other) and receiving a heavy sentence, or both confessing everything and receiving heavy penalties. The game revolves around these alternatives. In our version of the game, we deal with the natural conflict between parents and teenagers about certain issues.

The second game attempts to simulate problems involved in keeping a large society operating and, at the same time, meeting personal objectives. Both games have been designed to fit into classroom periods of thirty-five minutes and over.

The parent-teenager game

This game attempts to simulate situations that occur in any family. Basically, the focus is on several issues on which parents and teenagers disagree. As the game proceeds, the players become involved in the human relations problems associated with family conflicts.

The Set-up

The class is split up into pairs. In each pair, one person takes on the role of the *Parent*, and one the role of the *Teenager* – a boy or girl, aged 16. It is important that each player assumes his assigned role and argues accordingly. The discussions follow from disagreements over issues that can arise in any home in everyday life. The Parent and Teenager must take opposite stands over the issue in question and put forward their arguments in the form of a two-way conversation. These conversations will prove to be very lively and usually are an educational experience in themselves. However, this simulation has been designed so that scoring can take place to determine *the highest score achieved by a Parent and by a Teenager*.

The Procedure

It is important at this point to establish in your own minds that Parent is not set against Teenager and vice versa, each trying to gain a higher score than the other. It does not benefit either player to gain more points than the other since there will be two winners: the Parent who has scored the most points and the Teenager who has scored the most points.

Write down a list of your five issues for easy reference. Here are some suggestions for issues, but you can use your own ideas:

1) The Parent wishes the Teenager to perform certain household chores. The Teenager does not wish to do these jobs.

2) The Parent does not wish to give the Teenager use of the car on Saturday night. The Teenager wants to use the car.

3) The Parent does not want the Teenager to go out on Saturday night with a certain boy or girl. The Teenager wants to go out with that boy or girl.

4) The Parent wants the Teenager to get a hair-cut (boy), or not to wear make-up (girl). The Teenager does not want to get a hair-cut (boy), or wishes to wear make-up (girl).

5) The Parent has set a curfew of midnight for the Teenager on Friday nights. The Teenager wants it extended to one o'clock.

The Parent and Teenager should discuss each issue until an Agreement is reached. The issues must be discussed fairly and sensibly. An Agreement is reached when one party concedes that the other's argument is stronger. If no Agreement is reached after three to four minutes of discussion, then the Parent can issue an Order to the Teenager. However, it must be very clear that no Agreement has been reached before the Parent can issue an Order.

Materials for the Game

You will need to prepare the following materials for each game.

1) *A negotiation sheet*. Note the result of each issue on this sheet. If an Agreement has been reached, mark down an A followed by

Negotiation Sheet

Issue	Agree or Order
1	A(T) or A(P) or O
2	A(T) or A(P) or O
3	A(T) or A(P) or O
4	A(T) or A(P) or O
5	A(T) or A(P) or O

Actual Behaviour Sheet

Issue	Decision
1	do or do not
2	do or do not
3	do or do not
4	do or do not
5	do or do not

Here are two sample cards – the Parent and Teenager cards for the value 2:

Top side **P**   Other side **2**   Top side **T**   Other side **2**

Briefly, the scoring system is as follows: The Teenager scores by getting his own way

Negotiation Sheet	Actual Behaviour Sheet	Result
A(T)	do	score
A(P)	do not	score minus punishment points
O	do not	score minus punishment points

The Parent scores by getting his own way too

A(P)	do	score
A(P)	do not	no score, assigns punishment points
O	do	scores
O	do not	no score, assigns punishment points

a (T) for Teenager, or a (P) for Parent, depending on who won the argument. If the Parent gave an Order, then mark down an O.

2) *An actual behaviour sheet.* After a settlement has been reached and the negotiation sheet has been made out, the Teenager will decide whether or not he wants to do as he has agreed or been ordered. He should fill out his decision for each issue in secret on the Actual Behaviour sheet. The Parent must not see what the Teenager writes. He must come to a decision for each issue and fill out the whole sheet at this point.

3) *Scoring cards.* Now you will need some scoring cards of the following type. Take ten cards and mark five of them with a P for Parent on one side and the figures 2, 4, 6, 8, and 10 on the alternate sides. Then mark each of the other five cards with a T for Teenager on one side and the same figures on the other side. Make a pile of the five P cards and another of the five T cards. Shuffle the two piles and place them figure-side down. These figures are the scores that can be made by the Parent and Teenager on each of the issues. The cards are shuffled so that it is impossible for either player to know which score he is likely to make on any one issue.

It is obviously advantageous for both players to gain as many points as they can so that each can compete for the position of the player with the best overall score in the two role categories (Parent and Teenager). However, it must be remembered that the two players are not competing against each other for one to gain superiority over the other. The score of one player bears no relationship to the score of the other.

Now let us look at Issue 1 and all of the possibilities for scoring.

If the Teenager has *agreed* to do some work in the home [A(P)], or he has been given an *Order* (O), and has decided *to do* that work on his Actual Behaviour Sheet, then the Parent picks up a card from the P pile and credits himself with the score written on the reverse side of the card. If the Teenager has *agreed* to do some work in the home [A(P)], or he has been given an Order and has decided *not to do* it on his Actual Behaviour Sheet, then the Parent does not pick up a card because the Teenager has not done as the Parent asked. The Teenager picks up a card from the T pile and credits himself with the score because *he has got his own way.* However, he has disobeyed the Parent and so the Parent can assign Punishment points up to the value of 6 (which are subtracted from the Teenager's score). The Parent must decide just how many Punishment points he will give according to how serious he considers the disobedience to be. The decision is entirely up to the Parent. The Parent does not score by penalizing the Teenager and does not benefit by trying to keep the Teenager's score low. If the Teenager has got his own way on an issue, [A(T)], and has obviously done as he wanted to on his Actual Behaviour Sheet, then he scores.

Scoring in the Sample Game

Add up your points or subtract them as you go along.

Issue 1 The Teenager did as he had agreed to do and got his own way. He picks up a card from the T pile and credits himself with the score. Let's say the Teenager scores 2 points. The Parent scores none.

Issue 2 The Teenager did as he had agreed to do but he did not get his own way. The Parent takes a card from the P pile. The Teenager could have disobeyed and then he would have scored, but he would also have suffered Punishment points. The Teenager scores 0 points and the Parent scores 4. The Teenager still has 2 points; the Parent now has 4.

Issue 3 The Teenager did not do as he had agreed to do but he got his own way and so he scores. However, he is awarded Punishment points by the Parent. The Teenager scores 6 minus 4 Punishment points. The Parent does not score. Now, the Teenager has 4 points; the Parent has 4.

Issue 4 The Teenager did as he was ordered to do but he did not get his own way. The Parent takes a card from the P pile. The Teenager does not score but he is not awarded Punishment points either. The Parent scores 2. The Teenager still has 4 points; the Parent has 6.

Issue 5 The Teenager did not do as he was ordered but he got his own way and so he scores. However, he is awarded Punishment points by the Parent. The Teenager scores 8 points minus 3 Punishment points. The Teenager now has 9 points, the Parent has 6.

Therefore, in this sample game, the Teenager has scored 9 points and the Parent has scored 6.

In this game, as in everyday life, the Teenager can benefit by doing as he wishes (he scores if he does this), but the Parent can punish him (by awarding Punishment points). Continual disobedience on the part of the Teenager will prove self-destructive as he runs the risk of being awarded more Punishment points than points he can score by doing as he wishes. The skills of negotiation and persuasiveness can be learned by both parties in the discussions. The game may quickly lead to an airing of problems which arise in the home in the lives of the players.

Final Note

The usual class organization is as follows:
1) Read the game description
3) Play one game
3) Score the results
4) Discuss the results
5) At a rate of three to four minutes of discussion for each issue, it will take one full class period to complete one game. In the next class, the players change roles – the person who played the Parent should now become the Teenager, and vice versa.

A Sample Game

Below are results from a sample game from which the players estimate their scores.

Negotiation Sheet

Issue	Agree or Order
1	A(T)
2	A(P)
3	A(P)
4	O
5	O

Actual Behaviour Sheet

Issue	Decision
1	do
2	do
3	do not
4	do
5	do not

There will be two final overall winners for the class – the person who gained the highest score in one round for his role as Parent, and the person who gained the highest score in one round for his role as Teenager.

Social forces

This simulation has been designed to provide students with the opportunity to interact with each other in situations similar to those operating in a modern, democratic society. It involves the same kinds of balancing of cooperative and competitive activities that are required for the operation of a community system based on the freedom of the individual. This simulation can also be seen as a game, in that it allows individuals and groups to win; but as you will see later, winning can take many forms, depending on the individual objectives of each of the participants.

As a participant you can simply be yourself, but, if you wish, you may also act out other roles. It is necessary for each participant to select his own personal objectives so that he can keep these in mind throughout the course of the simulation.

The game is not structured in the same way as other games you might have played. As you first read through these instructions, you may feel that the game is very confusing, but as you start to play it, you will soon find that you become involved in the action. In many respects, the game operates as life itself does. You will find that you function as a member of a society which can have all of the advantages and disadvantages which we all experience in the world around us.

The game takes place in three or four communities. It is based mainly on the success of two industries located in two of the communities. The ebb and flow of these industries shapes life in the communities. In order to make the game fit into a regular classroom period, it has been necessary to give some of the responsibility of controlling activities in the communities to an outside agent. In the classroom situation, this can be a teacher, but a student or a group of students can do the job just as well. We will call the person who controls the game the *Mediator*. The owners of the two industries are determined by the Mediator at the beginning of the game, but under certain conditions, ownership may change. It is not possible to move freely from community to community – this provides the opportunity for you to appreciate how transportation systems operate, and perhaps more important, the power of communication devices such as newspapers and television.

The Basic Parts of the Game

1) *Three communities* in classes of fewer than twenty students, or *four communities* in classes of more than twenty. If possible, there should be physical divisions between the communities, but since this is not likely to be possible in most classrooms, the four corners of the room can be used. Try to set the game up so

that each community cannot hear what is taking place in the other communities.

2) *Two industries*, the ownership of each to be determined by the Mediator. The owners of the industries will be given a certain amount of money, as well as certain responsibilities.

3) *A television station* should be set up in a community other than the communities in which the two industries are located. It is possible for the television station to be a money-making industry also; therefore, in effect, we have three industries.

4) *Centres for distributing food and housing tickets.* There should be one less than the number of communities. For example, if there are four communities, there should be three distribution centres. These centres will not be seen as industries in the same sense as the two basic industries and the television station. The Mediator will select the persons to operate the Food and Housing Centres. These persons may do as they wish with their food and housing tickets – sell them, withhold them, give them away. At the start of each new session of the game, other individuals will be chosen to run the food and housing centres. In each session, the total number of food and housing tickets available should be two or three less than the total number of participants in the game. This means that, at the end of each classroom session, at least two or three people will not have food and housing tickets. We will explain the implications of this in a later section.

5) *Transportation agencies* are set up in much the same way as the food and housing centres. The Mediator determines the original ownership of the agencies for each session. Therefore, you cannot build a career as an owner of a transportation agency, just as you cannot own a food and housing centre. There should be one less transportation agency than the number of communities. Approximately the same number of transportation tickets should be available for each agency, but the total number of transportation tickets should equal about 50 per cent of the total number of game participants. For example, if there are 24 students, there should be 12 transportation tickets, and if there are 31, there should be 16 tickets.

It is possible for one or two communities to exist independently without cooperating with other communities, in other words, without any of its citizens travelling to other communities. However, in order that all the communities can continue to exist from session to session, there must be some form of cooperation among them.

There is an element of competition built into the simulation since there are not enough food and housing tickets for every person to have one at the end of the session. At the same time, it is necessary for everyone within the society to cooperate with one another in a variety of ways in order that the society and the communities within it can flourish. It is the interplay of the competition for individual success and the cooperation required for the communities to exist that must be balanced.

How Individual Success Is Determined

1) *Each participant must attempt to obtain a food and housing ticket by the end of each classroom session.* If a person does not obtain a food and housing ticket by the end of any two consecutive sessions of the game, he is considered "dead". This means that some organization is required on the part of all the participants to ensure that individuals do not go through two sessions in a row without receiving a food and housing ticket.

2) *Each participant must attempt to obtain a job.* Participants must be paid by industry owners for the jobs they do. If a participant does not obtain a job, he goes on the unemployed list. This can mean that he is unable to obtain a food and housing ticket, and it also affects the overall success of the total society. Job opportunities should become available in the two industries and in the television station. Once a participant obtains a job he does not have to travel to the community where the industry is located.

3) *Each participant should attempt to meet one or perhaps two of the following objectives:*

   a) *Wealth*
   You can accumulate wealth in a number of ways: by investment of your funds in the industries, through growth of the industry if you own one, by offering valuable services to others.

   b) *Power*
   An individual may gain influence over others in a number of ways: he may become the owner of an industry, the leader of a trade union made up of the employees of an industry, an influential member of the television staff.

   c) *Financial security*
   This can mean simply a steady job with a solid company.

   d) *Service to others*
   This can take the form of helping people who are in need, such as those without food and housing tickets, or a job. A person committed to this objective could also try to speak out against injustice to others, and on similar issues.

   e) *Popularity*
   It is possible to become popular in a number of ways. For example, a person could perform for the local television station, be a leader in organizational activities, or just demonstrate those personality characteristics which make people popular.

In summary, a person is successful if he has food and housing and a job at the end of each class session, and if he is progressing toward his personal goals.

How Society's Success Is Determined

It is possible for the total society to be successful, as well as the individuals within it. The industries should grow at a steady rate. An attempt should be made to provide food and housing for all.

If all members of the society have a job, it is possible for them to invest their money in the television station and the industries. The following categories can be used to determine the success of the community in developing in a positive way:

1) *An unemployment rate* of three per cent or less of the total population is considered excellent, an unemployment rate of between three and twelve per cent is considered marginal, and an unemployment rate of more than 12 per cent is considered to be disastrous for the long-term success of the community.

2) *A death rate* (caused by participants not obtaining food and housing tickets in two consecutive sessions of the game) of 0 per cent is considered excellent, a death rate of three per cent is considered marginal, and a death rate of more than three per cent is considered disastrous. You can see that we have put a high value on human life in this system.

3) *A steady growth in the amount of money available* in the total society is desirable, although there is a possibility that this may not take place because of chance factors which are explained later.

How the Game Is Played

1) *Each participant commits himself to at least one of the following five objectives.* It is possible to attempt to meet all of the objectives, but one should be foremost in your mind:

a) Wealth
b) Power
c) Financial security
d) Service to others
e) Popularity

It is not necessary for the participants to write down their objective(s), but if they do, the list is useful as a reminder whenever they are faced with a temptation to change their minds in the course of the game. However, as in life, participants may change their objective(s) at any point in the game.

2) *The Mediator clarifies the money arrangements for the game.* The monetary unit is selected – let us use dollars, but you can use pesos, rubles, francs, or even "fast bucks", or "bits". The Mediator selects the owners of the two industries, the owner of the television station, and the individuals responsible for the food and housing ticket distribution centres and the transportation agencies. The Mediator will act as the bank.

3) *The students are assigned to the three or four communities.* They are told that they cannot carry on conversations from community to community. In order to conduct any activity in another community, participants must travel to that community.

4) *The two major industries are set up.* These industries must be seen as representative of the kinds of industries that we find in Canadian society – an automobile factory, a steel mill, a pulp

and paper mill, a chemical industry. Our industries will not make money selling their products to the participants in the game. Any growth of these industries will result from investment in them by the participants, and by a natural growth process controlled by the Mediator. Both industries have the following characteristics:

a) Ownership is originally placed in the hands of the person chosen by the Mediator.

b) At the outset of the game, the owner receives $150 to use as he wishes.

c) The owner may hire staff. His staff may remove him and replace him with someone else if for any reason they *unanimously* agree to do so.

d) The industry grows when people invest in it. Naturally, a person may invest any amount of money in an industry, but he expects to receive a profit on his investment. The owner must make sure that he has a good chance of making a profit so he cannot give more money back to his investors than he expects to have gained by the natural growth processes. The natural growth of an industry is determined at the end of each game session. The owner is required to toss a coin three times. If "heads" comes up three consecutive times, the industry grows 50 per cent; if there are two "heads" and one "tail", the industry grows 30 per cent; if there are two "tails" and one "head", the industry grows 10 per cent; and if there are three "tails", the industry does not have any growth. Growth is determined by the amount of money the owner had at the beginning of the game session, so that if he started with $150, and tossed two "heads" and one "tail", the natural growth increase would be 30 per cent – $45. This money comes out of the bank, disbursed by the Mediator, and is given to the owner at the start of the next session.

5) *A television station is set up.* The television station has the following characteristics:

a) Original ownership is decided by the Mediator.

b) The station can broadcast in all communities at the same time.

c) The owner receives $75 at the start of the game.

d) The owner can hire staff and the staff may replace him if there is *unanimous* agreement to do so.

e) The station can also grow by investment from participants with money; but because it has a service to sell to the members of the communities, its natural growth is determined by the sales of its services. Of course, the cost of these services will depend on how much they are valued by the communities.

6) *The transportation agencies are set up.* Perhaps it would be useful to think of the communities as island communities and transportation in terms of boat tickets. Therefore, the only way to communicate from community to community is through the television station or by taking a boat trip. (Remember, it is not necessary for a participant to travel to a job in an industry in another community. He can hold a job in another community and still "live" in his home community.) If you have four communities, you set up three transportation agencies. Each transportation agency is given an equal number of tickets (if possible), but the total number of tickets should be approximately one half of the total number of participants. The transportation agencies all have the following characteristics:

a) New agency heads are appointed by the Mediator at the beginning of each game session.

b) The heads of the agencies may do as they wish with the tickets. They may sell, give away, or withhold them, remembering, of course, the importance of a successful society of happy individuals.

c) All unused tickets at the end of each session are returned to the Mediator who selects the new agency head and passes out tickets at the beginning of the next session.

d) One ticket entitles a participant to one trip around all the communities. He cannot revisit a community on the same ticket nor can he go to one community, then back to his home community, and back to another community on a single ticket. At the beginning of each trip he must turn in his travel ticket to the Mediator.

7) *The food and housing centres are set up.* There should be two or three less food and housing tickets than the total number of participants. There will be three centres set up if there are four communities, two if there are three communities. These centres will have the following characteristics:

a) New centre heads are appointed by the Mediator at the beginning of each game session.

b) The heads of the centres may sell, give away, or withhold tickets at their will. It should be remembered, however, that everyone shares the responsibility for keeping the society going.

c) At the end of the session, all unused tickets will be returned to the Mediator.

d) If a participant does not obtain a food and housing ticket at least once by the end of two sessions, he is "dead".

Note: The Mediator can make adjustments in the number of transportation and food and housing tickets he assigns, in order to vary the game. These changes have interesting implications for the way in which the game is played that are worthwhile exploring in second or third tries at the game.

The Game Begins

Each participant should remember the following basic features:

1) There is no communication possible from community to community except by use of the transportation tickets or through the television station. Remember, although the television station can talk to you, you cannot talk back to it. If you need to transmit a message via the television station, you must go to the community which has the station to conduct your business or deal with a travelling agent for the station.

2) One transportation ticket allows the participant one round trip through each of the other communities. During the trip, he cannot go back and forth between the other communities.

3) Each participant must "live" in his own community through the course of the game. Using a travel ticket, he may visit other communities but he must always come back to his home community.

4) To be successful as an individual, the participant must have a job at the end of each session, and a food and housing ticket at the end of one of two sessions.

When the Game Starts?

As we have noted before, this game is unstructured, and to many people it may appear to be confused and without direction. But, if you see the purpose as that of developing a society in which to live and fulfill oneself, then you can start to shape such a society by your activities. In each community you will probably hear opening comments and questions as "What's going on here?" or "Do you know what we are supposed to do?" But shortly, the nature of the questions will change, and you will hear "Does anyone here own an industry?" or "Do we have a transportation agency?" Then the game is under way.

Usually, the individual's main concern during the first session is to get a food and housing ticket before the session is completed. Except for this activity, a large segment of the first session probably will appear disorganized. In succeeding sessions, strategies are usually developed for obtaining food and housing tickets, and then the participants start to think of other things such as gaining power, collecting wealth, or starting organizations of various kinds. This is very similar to what takes place in our own society after people are assured of a steady job, food, and housing. The game can last for any number of sessions, of course, but it appears to be most effective over approximately six class periods. The game works most effectively when students take a portion of one class session to read the instructions, and then start the game the following day. For variety, the number of food and housing tickets available can be reduced and the number of transportation tickets increased. This makes the system more competitive, but allows for more movement among the communities.

Set-up for a class of twenty-eight students

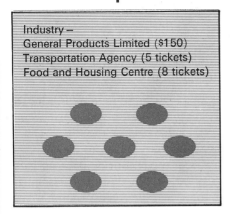

Industry —
General Products Limited ($150)
Transportation Agency (5 tickets)
Food and Housing Centre (8 tickets)

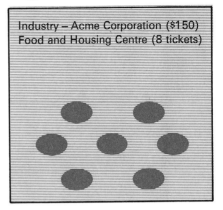

Industry — Acme Corporation ($150)
Food and Housing Centre (8 tickets)

Bank
Mediator

Television station ($75)
Transportation Agency (5 tickets)
Food and Housing Centre (9 tickets)

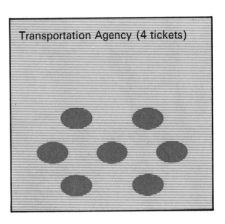

Transportation Agency (4 tickets)

Tickets and money required for set-up

Food
and
Housing
ticket

25 required

$1

60 required

$5

30 required

Transportation
ticket

14 required

$10

20 required

$20

20 required

On page 273, we have provided a description of how the classroom might be set up for the game, along with samples of the various tickets that are required for the game.

A Final Note

Let us look at the kinds of questions that might arise during the course of the game and the implications of these questions.

Question. What if a person spends more time in another community while on a travel ticket away from his home community, perhaps to build up his own wealth?

Answer. Naturally it is possible for a person to do this as long as he does not violate the rules of travel. But he must go back to his home community for the start of each classroom session. If he has behaved in a way that the remainder of his community feel was not fair to the community, they will probably find some way of disciplining him.

Question. But what does the television station broadcast?

Answer. Once it is known that the television station has services to offer, it is likely that the major industries will require its services to encourage investments and to offer job opportunities. Individuals also can use the television station to broadcast pleas of help if necessary for their communities.

Question. What if someone steals?

Answer. If someone steals, it is likely to be at the expense of someone else. In order to achieve any stability in a community, it will probably be necessary to discourage this behaviour in some way. In some societies, people throw rocks at thieves; in others, the people make rules which are enforced by policemen. It is up to the individuals in the communities to deal with wrongdoers.

In this simulated society, every one of you is free to use his imagination to create a life for himself. Keep in mind that as an individual you have to try to be successful in terms of one or more of the objectives you have set for yourself, and that as a member of a community and of a larger society, you have a responsibility to be instrumental in the creation of a happy and successful society.

three   # The case study

The following six case studies have been designed to illustrate the influence of certain social factors on the behaviour of individuals. Although they are hypothetical situations, they could just as easily have been drawn from the pages of our daily newspapers. These case studies provide an opportunity for students to focus on social issues found in our society. The impact of such social phenomena as alienation, stereotyping, and social class are widespread in our society, and have implications for all of us. If solutions to societal problems are to be found, we need to understand the nature and origin of the problems. We are not suggesting that there are simple solutions to these social problems, but only that they require greater understanding than we have given them in the past.

It is hoped that you, the reader, will attempt

1) to analyze in detail the circumstances that are described, filling in missing information where it is necessary to complete the problem;

2) to determine the conditions that caused the events;

3) to offer solutions, where possible, by utilizing the insights and knowledge you have derived from your own experiences and from your reading.

Case study 1

Judy

Theme : alienation

Last year, the whole issue of Judy's life style came to a head when she announced that she was leaving home, leaving school, and leaving the city for a place where she could think. Her family was shaken, particularly her father who had been very close to her when she was a little girl. They promised to support her in anything she wanted to do, and that her return would not only be welcomed but prayed for.

The remainder of her family still lives at home and consists of her mother, her father who is a business executive, a brother at university, and a sister in Grade 11. The family is closely knit and, to all appearances, is an ideal middle-class family where the children have been loved, well cared for, and encouraged in their activities. Judy's father has worked hard in his business and prosperity has resulted. The family house is located in a good suburb overlooking the city. It is well furnished and equipped with all the modern electrical appliances. Judy says, "You could rent the whole family out to an advertising agency, they are right out of the middle-class 'good life'. But who wants to live in a magazine ad?"

Judy was a good student, almost a model child: bright, pretty, polite, hard-working, and sociable. She did well in elementary school, and was accelerated. She entered high school at twelve years old. Judy recalls that Grade 9 was "terrible". She was the youngest in her class and experienced initial difficulty in making new friends and fitting in. By Grade 10, Judy was "well adjusted" in high school and doing well in all her subjects.

In her last year at school, she began to change. Her family reports, "She was more and more interested in ideas, and was reading philosophy." About this time Judy became active in what her brother calls "causes". She picketed against the treatment of Canadian Indians, worked for an underground newspaper, and joined a number of (to quote her father) "radical clubs". Her mother became very concerned about Judy's lack of interest in her appearance and about her friends. A family crisis was reached when Judy was arrested during a disturbance in front of the Welfare Department office. Judy recalls being arrested and taken to jail as "the most terrible thing that ever happened". Her father says, "Judy became very quiet and inward-looking after that experience. She broke all association with her causes, and spent a great deal of time reading." Her brother reports, "Judy was supported by all of us. No one complained about her arrest or behaviour, but relations were sure strained."

Judy now lives in a house with fourteen other people of her own age. She has her own room, shares the household duties, and works part-time with an underground newspaper. In her spare time she reads and does some painting, an activity in which she shows considerable talent. When asked about her lack of involvement in society, she gave this explanation: "When I was at home, I joined in, and worked, and cared about what I was doing, and got nowhere. Despite all that effort, my impact was zero. I love ideas, I like to paint, to walk, to be close to nature, and to think my own thoughts. Life is a rat-race, with people trying to force you to do things you don't want to do. Someone is always trying to own you or control you. I just don't like it and I don't buy the materialistic bit. So here I am, doing what I like, running my own life. I can live in this society, but I don't have to be part of it."

Case study 2
Bill
Theme : criminal behaviour and social class

Bill was very popular, a good college student, interested in campus affairs, and a member of several clubs in which he held leadership positions. Bill's father was a successful manufacturer in a small city about forty miles from the city where the university was located.

On the evening before Hallowe'en, Bill and two of his friends had gone downtown after doing their school work. Bill and his friends, Fred and John, spent from 9:00 P.M. to 11.35 P.M. at a movie and were on their way home when they saw a city bus, empty at the curb, with the engine running. They saw the driver inside a variety store buying some cigarettes. On a spur-of-the-moment impulse, Fred dared Bill to drive off in the bus. Without much thought, Bill laughingly said, "O.K., watch me."

The bus pulled away with Bill at the wheel just as the driver came out of the store, shouting that his bus was being stolen. Fred and John took off, not wanting to become involved in what might follow.

The driver went back into the store, called the police and reported the theft, and then called his bus company. The police notified all prowl cars of the theft and of the direction in which the bus was travelling. Bill was stopped, arrested on a theft charge, and taken to the police station.

This was a new experience for him, but he remembered the television shows in which the arrested man always calls his lawyer. Bill called his father who called the family lawyer. Both men arrived at the police station within 90 minutes of the time Bill called.

The lawyer talked to the arresting officer and the sergeant at the station. He argued that Bill was a university student and, while it was quite a prank, he had meant no harm. Bill's father vouched for his son's good character and pleaded that Bill be charged with a minor demeanour, such as public mischief. The lawyer called the Crown attorney to explain the situation, and the police sergeant talked to the Crown attorney as well. A few minutes later, Bill was on his way back home, charged with public mischief.

Five weeks later, Bill, his parents, and his lawyer appeared before a magistrate. Bill pleaded guilty to the public mischief charge. The magistrate lectured him severely, pointing out that the theft of the bus was silly, and could have ended in tragedy with an inexperienced driver at the wheel of such a large vehicle. Bill apologized, saying that he agreed it was silly and that he would never be so stupid again. The magistrate put Bill on probation for a year under his father's supervision. The case was closed.

Case study 3
Gary and Jim
Theme: criminal behaviour and social class

Gary (sixteen) and his friend Jim (seventeen) were standing at a busy downtown corner near the low-rental housing project where they lived. Both boys were on a year's probation for vandalism, having broken 120 windows in their school six months earlier. Both boys attended the same school, where they were studying auto mechanics.

A late-model, expensive car was sitting in front of a drug store; the owner was inside talking to the proprietor of the store. Jim said, "Let's go for a ride" and Gary replied, "Okay. I'll drive." With that, they walked up to the car, jumped in, and drove away at a high speed. The owner saw the incident, but realizing that there was no time to stop them, he immediately called the police, giving a full description and the licence number of the car, as well as a description of Gary, whose bright red jacket made him more noticeable.

An officer in a police cruiser spotted the car travelling well above the speed limit, recognized the licence number, and noted the red jacket worn by the driver. The police car chased the stolen car for three blocks, finally forcing it into the curb. Both boys were arrested and taken to the local station, where they were charged with car theft and reckless driving. They were taken immediately to the lock-up downtown to spend the night. Gary and Jim made no phone call; they were not advised that they could, nor did they request the privilege.

After a night in jail, they came before a magistrate who remanded them for trial, and asked that a pre-trial report be prepared. The boys were released without bail, despite the Crown attorney's objections. They were assigned a lawyer from Legal Aid, and the trial was scheduled for six weeks later.

In conversation with Gary's mother and Jim's parents, the lawyer was not optimistic, since the boys were already on probation. He advised them to plead guilty, and told them that he would argue the case on the basis of the environment in which the boys lived.

At the trial, the Legal Aid lawyer argued that the unstable, underprivileged environment was as much to blame for the crime as anything else. Gary's mother and Jim's parents said that they were good boys, but needed more supervision. Jim's father worked nights and his mother worked days, so that his home life lacked conventional stability. Gary's mother, a widow, worked long hours at a nearby factory, making close supervision of her son impossible. The social worker reported that home conditions, including cleanliness and nutrition, were good in both cases, but that the boys, while well cared for physically, were not cared for emotionally. The judge said that he understood all the problems that might have contributed to the theft, but felt that the reckless driving demonstrated the irresponsibility of the two boys, reinforced by the fact that they were both already on probation. Both boys were sentenced to six months in reformatory where, the judge said, "They will learn to behave themselves."

Case study 4
The Smiths
Theme : poverty and social class

Mrs. Smith is thirty-five years old and the mother of four children: three girls, ranging in age from six to ten, and a boy fourteen. Her husband was killed in a construction accident three years ago.

After her husband's death she found a job as a waitress in a downtown restaurant. Her income is such that she needs low-rental housing accommodation to make ends meet. Low-rental accommodation in the downtown area is scarce, and for a year the family lived in crowded quarters, at a rent that Mrs. Smith could barely afford; but she worked hard and managed.

This spring she was offered low-rental accommodation in a new housing project in the suburbs. This project is an experimental one, where subsidized rental accommodation is mixed with housing that is purchased by middle-class people whose incomes range between $10,000 and $20,000 per year. The surrounding community is a suburban, single-dwelling area, which has been established for about fifteen years. Mrs. Smith felt that life in the project would be good for her children, and agreed to move.

In the housing project there is a new, open-plan elementary school and a secondary school that offers a wide range of programs. Three of her children attend the elementary school, and the oldest boy goes to the secondary school. The children like their schools; they find that the teachers are friendly and interested, and that good programs are available.

Mrs. Smith found that without a car it became impossible for her to work downtown and still care for her children. Since a car was out of the question, and no work was available in the area, she applied for and was given public welfare. At this point, unhappiness began for the children. The eight-year-old reported, "The other kids won't have anything to do with us outside school." The six-year-old came home crying that the other children said she was on relief, and that she was poor.

Home-owners in the area claim that there has been a rise in vandalism since the housing project was built. Others say that general thievery has increased, and that many children report their toys have been stolen by the "project kids". Some owners claim there should have been more careful selection of tenants. Others report a dislike of people they describe as "lazy", "dishonest", and "a drain on the overburdened taxpayer".

Mrs. Smith has become very disillusioned with her present housing. She reports feeling depressed over "the whole mess".

Case study 5
George
Theme : family conflict

George had been a good student and a happy, carefree teenager. His mother and father had moved to a medium-sized city of 200,000 people from a small town of 8,000. George had enjoyed life in the small town; the high school he attended had an enrollment of 500 students when George was in Grade 10. He was class representative on the student council and co-captain of the football team. While he did not have a steady girl-friend, he went out with several girls. He was well liked by almost everybody.

George liked to go hunting in the fall with his dad. Although this meant that he missed a week of school, he was able to work hard and catch up. He liked to go to the Sunday night meeting of the church young people's group, of which he was vice-president. He had been praised highly by the whole town for his work in organizing a children's fair to raise money for the United Appeal. The mayor had said to his father, "That boy of yours will go a long way, mark my words."

George's father was promoted to plant superintendent, necessitating a move to a new city. His mother was very happy; it meant a new house and some new furniture. "The whole world looked pretty good," says his father.

George enrolled in a new school with 2,000 students. He told his mother that he liked his home-room teacher very much.

But as time went on, George talked less and less about school. He said he had no homework in his new courses. After three months at the school, George's mother reported that he began to dress "differently". His father observed, "He fell in with a bad bunch down at the plaza, and outside of the time he spends with that bunch, all he does is eat and sleep." His mother tried to encourage him to get some nice friends, "like those in Centreville".

George has another view. "Those kids in Centreville are dull. They're irrelevant, just like the school. They don't know where it's at. I know what's good for me. My life doesn't include doing a lot of dull things at school. I have some new friends and we have a good time, you know. The rest of that jazz about school, and hard work, and getting somewhere, is phoney. My old man works all the time and I never see him. The only thing my mother is concerned about is her new Indian broadloom rug. I swear that rug is more valuable than I am. I'm just not buying this nonsense. I have my own life to lead and I'm going to lead it. The school has the same line as my parents, they're both reading from the same script. The school is for marionettes, not for me. I'm not about to listen to those teachers who don't know as much about real life as I do. My life is mine and I'll do what I want."

Shortly after this interview, George dropped out of school against the advice of his parents and the school guidance service.

Case study 6

Andy

Theme : alienation

Andy's Grade 3 teacher described him this way: "Andy is a quiet boy, he does not take part in recess activities with other children. He has few friends and does not appear to be interested in school. He loves to draw and shows real talent in this activity." A Grade 8 teacher wrote this comment: "Andy has missed a great deal of school this year. His truancy has been a source of great concern. Unless he begins to settle down, his chances of success in school are limited." The next year an attendance officer reported: "Andy has no interest in high school except in his art class. He skips the rest. His parents have been contacted but they seem indifferent. His father said during the last interview that the sooner Andy gets a job, the better. Andy's mother says she has her hands full with the five younger children, and that Andy will have to make out the best way he can."

Shortly after this report was filed, Andy left school to take a job driving a pick-up truck for a wholesale car parts firm. After six months he quit, following a disagreement with the parts manager. He also had had two accidents with the truck during that time. His next job was in the railway freight yards, unloading express cars.

This job lasted for two and a half years. Andy left after a disagreement with the foreman, who freely admitted he disliked "that kid". He held and either left or lost a series of jobs over the next two years, finally being employed in the shipping department of a large store. "The money is good but the work is awful," Andy reports. "I have to keep it to feed my wife and little daughter."

He left home shortly after he dropped out of school, and got married six months later, at the age of seventeen, to Gail, aged sixteen. They have had only one child, Mary. Andy has often said that he feels trapped by "the old lady". Now, at twenty-two, Andy has a job he dislikes, a family situation he doesn't want any more, and crowded living conditions – three rooms in a downtown house. Gail claims that Andy fights with her over money, but that she is doing her best to manage on his wages. Andy claims that Gail is constantly nagging him.

Andy lives for the weekends, when he can ride his motorcycle with his buddies. In the summer he goes on extended trips. In the winter he spends his weekend time at the motorcycle clubhouse in the country. The clubhouse is in fact an old abandoned house, rented to the club by a man who owns the land but lives in the city. With his club "brothers", Andy feels he has a place. "These guys are my friends. They stand by you if you're in a beef. They'll protect you. It's all for one and one for all."

All club members wear the same "uniform" – motorcycle jack boots, leather jackets with the club insignia, and crash helmets as required by law. Club members obey the club rules unquestionably. These require that a man aid his friends, protect those in trouble, keep his mouth shut (particularly to the police), and prove that club members are "real men" – which is usually demonstrated through fighting, drinking, and skill in handling motorcycles. The club despises "the fuzz", "hippies", "square johns", certain minority groups, most people in society who have an authority role, and "weaklings".

Gail expresses her feelings this way: "I don't mind if Andy goes out with his friends, but I wish he would spend some time with Mary and me." To Andy, the club is "part of my family".

Case study 7

Tenants vs. owners

Theme : organization for action

Jane and Murray returned home from work at 5:45 one Thursday evening. They lived in a high-rise building in a large city. As they entered the building, they discussed dinner and their first wedding anniversary party, which was to be held the next Saturday. The elevator took them to the ninth floor and Murray reached into his pocket for the key. Both Jane and Murray were surprised to find that the key would not fit. Murray tried the door several times with no result. As they were standing at the door, the superintendent of the building arrived. Murray asked him to help open the door since the lock did not seem to work.

The building superintendent said, "Your key won't fit that lock. You've been evicted by order of the owners unless you pay your back rent. You're a trouble maker and we're fed-up with your nonsense."

Murray said he would kick down the door. The superintendent said he would call the police.

At about this time, Alice, a friend from the next apartment, arrived home laden with groceries. Jane explained the situation to Alice, who suggested that Murray and Jane come into her apartment until the trouble was settled. Alice's husband, Tom, arrived home a few minutes later. Tom worked in an advertising agency near Murray's graphic arts studio, and both men were active in a tenant association that had recently been formed in the building.

Both couples discussed their next move, and decided that a meeting of the tenants should be held to gain support to fight the owners. Alice phoned the executive committee members to discuss their strategy.

The meeting was called to order with ten people present, along with Alice and Jane who were not on the executive. Suggestions were presented, summarized as follows:

1) To call the police and charge the owners with theft.

2) To sue the owners, charging assault, since the superintendent had attempted to restrain Murray.

3) To contact the mayor and city council.

4) To call the newspapers and give them the story.

5) To contact the owners (this had been impossible up to this point).

6) To call for a rent boycott by all 500 tenants.

Discussion continued through the evening. The tenant association had relatively few members, only 70 to date, and their case was not well known by the other occupants. Alice, generally a shy girl, stated, "Let's not let these owners push us around. We need publicity and support from the other tenants and we need to hit the owners where it hurts most – in their pocket books." Alice was somewhat embarrassed by the round of applause she was given.

Several steps were then quickly agreed on. The first was to call the two big daily newspapers on the following day, and then to make an announcement of a proposed tenants' meeting for the coming Saturday. They also decided to draw up a letter listing the grievances of the tenants against the management. There had been many reports of people who were unable to get their security deposits back because of alleged damage to their apartments. Other grievances centred around periodic inspections of apartments by the owners without prior notice to the tenants, the difficulty in contacting the owners, and the fact that there was no guest parking area.

Friday was a busy day. There were interviews with reporters, calls were made and meetings held with lawyers, city housing officials, local politicians, and as many tenants as possible. The executive committee of the tenants' association was unable to contact the owners of the building. Jane and Murray were forced to stay with Alice and Tom.

On Saturday a large group of tenants attended the first general meeting held since the problem had arisen. Murray explained the situation. The tenants were annoyed and exhibited a great deal of support for Murray's case. It was agreed that 270 tenants would withhold their rent until the tenants' grievances were listened to and some positive actions in their favour were taken.

On Saturday evening a representative of the company that owned the building arrived at Tom's apartment to talk to Murray, who was at this point the president of the tenants' association. The executive committee of the association was called in to participate in the discussion. The representative bemoaned the fact that many tenants vacate their apartments without paying their rent, and that others wreck the property. He told of an incident where kitchen cabinets had been torn apart, another where the electrical fixtures had been stolen, and another where the departing tenant broke the sliding glass door to the balcony. He went on to describe how the elevators were frequently defaced, how bathrooms have been damaged, and how barbecues had been used inside apartments. Each side of the argument presented its case, and negotiations continued until 3 A.M. Finally, an agreement was made whereby Murray would be allowed back into his apartment and that he would pay the rent he owed. The tenants agreed to call off their boycott. In return, the owners would modify the currently held leases on the apartments to suit the requests of the tenants, and they would allow a committee of tenants to decide whether or not a security deposit should be withheld in the event of damage to an apartment. The tenants themselves agreed to try to keep a check on willful damage to elevators, and on the defacing or destruction of property. Further, the superintendent of the building was appointed as a liaison officer between the owners and the tenants, and it was agreed that in the future, all grievances of the tenants would be given a hearing by the owners.

Subject index

Aborigine: infanticide, 83n; skin color, 26

Achievement, 212n; social class of children and, 39n

Acta Divina, 61n

Adaptation: body build and, 29–31; environment and, 35; hair and, 28–29; skin color and, 25–28

Ad men: creativity and, 123n; culture of, 123n–124n

Adolescence: in a changing world, 217–222; definition of, 217

Adolescents: culture of, 218; dress of, 189n; hostility and, 101; school and, 140n. *See also* Youth

Advertisements, 76n, 156n; ad men and, 124n; of Beatles, 90n; Code of Canadian Advertising, 77n; in *Mad* magazine, 95; propaganda and, 75n; social class and, 148; techniques of, 159n

Advertisements in Quebec: during French Canadian revolution, 82–89; of Kébec beer, 87; nationalism of, 86; nature of, 83

Africa, 232n

Aggression, 20–24; of Arapesh and Mundugamor, 83n; in boys, 23n; control of, 22; *Mad* magazine and, 101; major cause of, 22

Air pollution, 241n; disasters from, 238n; effects of, 241n; poison gas, 243n

Aleuts, territory and, 24

Alienation, 217, 222, 223, 224n; case study of, 275–276, 280–281; definition of, 217; mass media and, 65n; of prisoners, 201n, 203–204

Americans: characteristics of, 153; cultural traits of, 84n; education and, 196n; youth revolution, 224–225

Andaman Islanders, 79n

Anger, physiological origin, 21

Animals: adaptive, 11–19; extinction of, 13; human, 11–14; language of, 48n, 50

Anthropology: culture and, 33; definition of, 5n

Anxiety, panic and, 174n

Apes, 10; tools of, 18

Arapesh: aggression and, 83n; cultural traits of, 84n; marriage and, 116n

Army, as a total institution, 204n, 205n

Asia, 232n

Assembly line, alienation on, 222n

Attitudes, work and, 85n

Australopithicus, 10

Authority: in organizations, 211n; of sea captains, 202n

Authority figures: as a source of truth, 2; TV portrayal of, 68

Automation, 115n; jobs and, 110, 226n; in modern society, 226n

Aztec language, 48

Baboons, territory and, 23

Balinese customs, 89n

Bar Mitzvah, 116

Beatlemania, 90–94. *See also* Beatles

Beatles, 90–94; in advertisements, 90n; enthusiasts of, 92–93; group identity and, 94; group solidarity and, 91; male image of, 94; resisters of, 93–94

Behavior: aggressive, 20–24; culture and, 36, 44n; in disasters, 173n, 175n; of hippies, 130n; language and, 55; magazine's influence on, 100n; manipulating, 69–77; panic, 174n; of the sexes, 109; spending, 146–151

Beliefs, 39; in boxing world, 119, 121–123; in prison, 203–204

Body build, 29–31; adaptation and, 29; differences in, 30; geographical distribution of, 30; shape and size of, 29–30

Bomb: nuclear, 234n; survivors of a, 235n. *See also* Hydrogen bomb

Boxers: beliefs of, 119, 121–123; code of, 122; culture of, 119–127; effects of boxing on, 126–127; image of, 122; kinds of, 123; social structure of, 119, 124–126; superstitions of, 122–123

Boys: aggressive behavior and, 23; corner, 164–169; world of, 109–113

Brainwashing: Chinese program of, 72; criminal confessions and, 70n; fear and, 71; Korean War, 69n, 69–77; prisoners' group structure in, 72; social isolation and, 73

Buddhism, Zen, 220

Business organizations, 209–214

Buying patterns, 156–160

Cabbagetown: clothes and, 137; Don Mills and, 136–139

Canada: education in, 187–198, 196n;

families of 1864 in, 183n; youth revolution in, 224–225. *See also* French Canada

Capitalism, 89n

Car: models and stereotypes, 157n; pollution, 240n

Carbon dioxide, 237n; effects of, 236n

Careers, marriage and, 118

Case studies, 275–283; on alienation, 275–276, 280–281; on criminal behavior, 276–278; on family conflict, 279–280; on organization for action, 281–283; on poverty, 278–279; on social class, 276–278, 278–279

Castes, rank and, 38

Ceremony: initiation, of sailors, 206–207n; marriage, 117

Change: adolescence and, 217–222; of roles, 108, 111, 116–118; in schools, 187–198; social, 119; women and, 113n

Children: advertising and, 159n; families and, 181–184, 185, 185n; fathers and, 128; first born, 181n; housewives and, 128; prejudice and, 153n, 155n; punishment and, 181n; rearing of, 139n, 181n

Chinese, 155n; characteristics, 153

Civilizations, zones of dominant, 239–240

Class differences, 38

Class, social. *See* Social class

Class system, 146

Clearview High School, 188–198

Climate, 236n

Cliques, 165n

Clothes: adolescents and, 189n; in Cabbagetown and Don Mills, 137; men and, 93n; skin color and, 27; social class and, 102n; as symbols of rejection, 220

Code of Canadian Advertising, 77n

Collaboration, among prisoners of war, 75

College, social class and, 139n

Colors: communication and, 56n; cool and warm, 56n

Comedies, situation, 65–68

Committees, advantages and disadvantages of, 168n–169n

Common sense, as a source of truth, 3

Communication, 50–58; animal and human, 48n; barricade approach, 79n; case study of, 61–64; color and,